Publications of the Wertheim Committee

Published by Harvard University Press

Wertheim Lectures on Industrial Relations, 1929

O'CONNOR Psychometrics, 1934

BROWN Union Policies in the Leather Industry, 1947

GALENSON Labor in Norway, 1949

DE SCHWEINTZ Labor and Management in a Common Enterprise, 1949

DUNLOP AND HILL The Wage Adjustment Board: Wartime Stabilization in the Building and Construction Industry, 1950

GALENSON The Danish System of Labor Relations: A Study in Industrial Peace, 1952

FISHER The Harvest Labor Market in California, 1953

PURCELL The Worker Speaks His Mind on Company and Union, 1953

WHITE The New England Fishing Industry, 1954

LORWIN The French Labor Movement, 1954

TAFT The Structure and Government of Unions, 1954

BALDWIN Beyond Nationalization: The Labor Problems of British Coal, 1955

WALKER Industrial Relations in Australia, 1956

MYERS Labor Problems in the Industrialization of India, 1958

SPIRO The Politics of German Codetermination, 1958

LEISERSON Wages and Economic Control in Norway, 1945–1957, 1959

PEN The Wage Rate under Collective Bargaining, 1959

STIEBER The Steel Industry Wage Structure, 1959

PURCELL Blue Collar Man: Patterns of Dual Allegiance in Industry, 1960

KNOELLINGER Labor in Finland, 1960

SLICHTER Potentials of the American Economy: Selected Essays, edited by John T. Dunlop, 1961

CHRISTENSON Economic Redevelopment in Bituminous Coal, 1962

HOROWITZ The Italian Labor Movement, 1963

STURMTHAL Workers Councils: A Study of Workplace Organization on Both Sides of the Iron Curtain, 1964

JENSEN Hiring of Dock Workers and Employment Practices in the Ports of New York, Liverpool, London, Rotterdam, and Marseilles, 1964

Studies in Labor-Management History

ULMAN   The Rise of the National Trade Union: The Development and Significance of Its Structure, Governing Institutions, and Economic Policies, 1955

GOLDBERG   The Maritime Story: A Study in Labor-Management Relations, 1957, 1958

GALENSON   The CIO Challenge to the AFL: A History of the American Labor Movement, 1935–1941, 1960

HOROWITZ   The New York Hotel Industry: A Labor Relations Study, 1960

PERLMAN   The Machinists: A New Study in Trade Unionism, 1961

MUNSON   Labor Relations in the Lithographic Industry, 1953

MANGUM   The Operating Engineers: The Economic History of a Trade Union, 1964

BRODY   The Butcher Workmen: A Study of Unionization, 1964

Published by McGraw-Hill Book Company

ALEXANDER   Labor Relations in Argentina, Brazil, and Chile, 1962

STEVENS   Strategy and Collective Bargaining Negotiation, 1963

DUNLOP AND DIATCHENKO   Labor Productivity, 1964

Conference on

Labor Productivity,

Cadenabbia, Italy, 1961.

JOHN T. DUNLOP

Professor of Economics
Harvard University

VASILII P. DIATCHENKO

Professor and Vice-Chairman of the
Presidium of the Association of
Soviet Economic Scientific Institutions

McGRAW-HILL BOOK COMPANY

New York   San Francisco   Toronto   London

LABOR PRODUCTIVITY

Introduction

The Conference on Labor Productivity, held at Cadenabbia, Lake Como, Italy, August 31 to September 8, 1961, brought together approximately 40 economists, equally divided between Western and Eastern countries to discuss in scientific terms various aspects of labor productivity. The conference was held under the auspices of the International Economic Association, and the planning and the arrangements were made by a Program Committee appointed by the association.

Labor productivity is of very considerable interest to economists from the Soviet Union and Eastern European countries not only on theoretical grounds but also because of its role in specific planning activities. The topic is no less significant to economists in the United States and Western Europe for economic policies. The meaning and measurement of productivity, within a country and among countries, present a wide variety of methodological and statistical problems of great concern to both groups of economists. Labor productivity has very considerable implications for wage setting both at the plant level and for the economy. There are a wide range of factors, technical and organizational, which influence labor productivity. The topic thus proved to be ideal for an exchange of ideas and for discovering common ground and identifying differences in concepts and views.

The Villa Carlotta and its beautiful grounds stimulated the dispassionate exchange of ideas. The simultaneous translation materially facilitated free discussion in the conference, and there was very considerable opportunity for fruitful informal conversations.

A report on the work of the conference was prepared by the Program Committee and is reproduced immediately following this Introduction. It presents both areas of agreement and problems which were found to need more extended discussion and further exploration or statistical information. At the request of the Program Committee, Professor Abram Bergson, of Harvard University, prepared a glossary of terms to facilitate the understanding of the papers. One of the benefits of the conference discussions was to teach us all something of the concepts and ideas used by the other and the problem involved in translating one set of concepts into another.

The International Economic Association acknowledges the financial assistance of the Ford Foundation in meeting the expenses of the conference during its sessions. In the publication of the English edition, financial assistance is gratefully acknowledged to the Meyer Kestnbaum Memorial Fund.

The Program Committee met in Vienna at the August-September 1962 meetings of the International Economic Association and planned a further conference, held in December 1963 in Geneva, on the topic of Unemployment and Underemployment in the Developing Countries, sponsored by the International Institute for Labour Studies.

The members of the Program Committee are as follows:

Professor V. P. Diatchenko
Professor G. A. Prudensky } Soviet Union

Professor B. Minc
Professor M. Pohorille } Poland

Professor A. Nove } England

Professor W. Galenson
Professor John T. Dunlop, *chairman* } U.S.A.

Mr. B. Zoeteweij was an observer from the ILO, and Mr. V. Kondratiev was a representative from the Association of Soviet Economic Scientific Institutions.

The Program Committee agreed that Professor Dunlop would be responsible for the English edition, and Professor Diatchenko would be responsible for a subsequent edition in Russian.

Report to the Conference on Labor Productivity

Prepared by the Program Committee

The Conference on Labor Productivity under the auspices of the International Economic Association met at Cadenabbia, Lake Como, Italy, from August 31 to September 9, 1961. The conference participants were twenty economists from Western countries and seventeen from Eastern countries. Thirty-two papers were prepared for the conference. These papers were discussed during ten sessions with the assistance of simultaneous translation in English and Russian. There was also considerable informal discussion among the participants outside the sessions.

The conference papers were discussed under four general headings:

> Concepts and Measurement of Productivity
> International Comparisons of Productivity
> Wages and Productivity
> Technical, Managerial and Organizational Factors
> Affecting Productivity

I

The participants found the discussion very useful in that it permitted the experts of different countries better to understand the various points of view on the subject discussed.

Despite the existence of differences of views, the participants considered it possible to make the following methodological points:

1. Labor productivity represents a complex economic concept, expressing the degree to which labor is utilized effectively. This necessitates the need to study the utilization of the various elements affecting production, including technology, equipment and machinery, the quality of management and its organization, the skill and education of the work force, the use of high-level manpower, and the methods of wage payment. The discussion re-

flected that there are a number of different concepts and measures of productivity entailing different definitions of labor inputs and definitions of output. Moreover, measures differ according to whether the interest is an enterprise, an industry, or any economy as a whole.

2. The necessity for a well-rounded study of labor productivity requires the use not of one single measure or index, but of a whole system of mutually supporting measures of levels and changes in labor productivity. The use of different indexes is important in each country at the enterprise level, for branches of industry, for industry as a whole, and in international comparisons. These indexes should include measurement in physical output and money terms, calculated for different groups of employees and different periods of working time. For analysis of labor productivity at various stages of production it is useful to measure labor inputs per unit of output.

3. In international comparisons, it is desirable, for the purpose of arriving at objective conclusions:

(a) not to confine the comparison to isolated and partial measurements, but to make the comparisons on the basis of an entire system of measurements. In particular, in addition to comparing productivity in physical terms, it is desirable to compare output in terms of gross or net output per employed person (per annum, per day, per hour) as well as comparing indexes of utilization of energy and electric power.

(b) in utilizing figures in money terms, output of the countries being compared should be expressed in the prices of both countries.

(c) there should be taken into account the qualitative aspects of the comparisons. This includes not only qualitative differences in the commodities produced, but also qualitative differences in the composition of the labor force.

(d) for more effective analysis of labor productivity, it is useful to study more deeply the factors which affect it, in particular technical progress, including mechanization and automation, the organization of labor and production, and the training of productive personnel.

4. In comparing growth rates of productivity of labor with the trend of wages, it is desirable to take into account not only money wages, but also real wages or real incomes, with due attention to price changes for goods and services, taxation, and payments and services provided to the workers from the state budget or by enterprises.

5. In considering the growth of productivity of an economy as a whole over a period of time, it is necessary to combine the changes in productivity in the various segments of an economy by means of appropriate weights. The

discussion reflected that both weights of a base year and a current year provide significant measures of productivity for international comparisons.

6. The papers and discussion indicated that interindustry wage rate differentials, the experience with incentive methods of pay and the concern with increasing technical and managerial manpower among countries showed a number of resemblances, taking into account, however, differences arising out of variations in social systems.

7. Notwithstanding recent improvements in labor productivity statistics, it was suggested by the discussion that it would be useful to scholars in all countries if more statistical information with accompanying detailed explanations of the statistical procedures and methods employed were to be made available, and at more frequent intervals, in all countries.

II

There were a number of topics on which the discussion indicated the need for more extensive discussion and further exploration of statistical information.

A. Concepts and Measurement.
  (a) The measurement of output and national income.
  (b) The special problems involved in the measurement of service type activities.
  (c) The index number problem.
  (d) The meaning of employment and turnover of the labor force.
B. The relation of working hours to productivity.
C. The role of decentralization and centralization.
D. The influence of international specialization on productivity.
E. The experience with incentives for both workers and management personnel.
F. The statistical methods of measuring the specific contribution of particular factors in the growth of productivity.
G. The role of scientific research and invention in increasing productivity.
H. The special problems involved in raising the productivity of labor in the underdeveloped nations is a particularly important subject for future consideration.

Conference on Labor Productivity

Participants

Aganbegyan, A. G., USSR Moscow University
Bakke, E. Wight, USA Professor, Department of Economics, Yale University
Baklanov, G. I., USSR Moscow Institute of Economics and Statistics
Batty, Josif, RUMANIA State Planning Committee, Rumanian Peoples Republic
Behrens, Friedrich, GERMAN DEMOCRATIC REPUBLIC Professor, German Academy of Sciences, Berlin
Bergson, Abram, USA Professor, Harvard University
Brandini, Pietro Merli, ITALY Italian Confederation of (Free) Trade Unions, Rome
Cěrvinka, Antonín, CZECHOSLOVAKIA Czechoslovak Academy of Sciences, Prague
Chamberlain, Neil, USA Professor, Yale University
Cukor, Gyorgy, HUNGARY Hungarian Academy of Sciences, Budapest
Dean, Joel, USA Professor, Columbia University
Dunlop, John T., USA Professor, Harvard University
Diatchenko, V. P., USSR Association of Soviet Economic Scientific Institutions
Fabricant, Solomon, USA Professor, New York University
Fenninger, Laurence, Jr., USA Bethlehem Steel Company
Fuchs, Victor, USA Observer for Ford Foundation
Galenson, Walter, USA Professor, University of California
Greenberg, Leon, USA U. S. Department of Labor, Washington
Harbison, Frederick, USA Professor, Princeton University
Kapustin, E. I., USSR Research Labor Institute, Moscow
Kerr, Clark, USA President, University of California

Knowles, K. G. J. C., ENGLAND   Oxford University, England

Kondratyev, V., USSR   Association of Soviet Economic Institutions

Kutta, Frantisek, CZECHOSLOVAKIA   Czechoslovak Academy of Sciences, Prague

Maddison, Angus, FRANCE   Organization for Economic Co-operation and Development, Paris

Minc, Bronislaw, POLAND   Institute of Economics, Polish Academy of Sciences, Warsaw

Morecka, Zofia, POLAND   Professor of Political Economy, University of Warsaw

Myers, Charles A., USA   Industrial Relations Section, Mass. Institute of Technology

Nove, Alexander, ENGLAND   London School of Economics

Pohorille, Maksimillian, POLAND   Prof., Central School of Planning and Statistics, Warsaw

Prudensky, G. A., USSR   Academy of Sciences of the USSR, Novosibirsk

Rachmuth, Iohn, RUMANIA   Economical Research Institute

Richter, Gerhard, GERMAN DEMOCRATIC REPUBLIC   Professor, Karl Marx University, Leipzig

Román, Zoltán, HUNGARY   Dr., Hungarian Central Statistical Office, Budapest

Ruist, Erik, SWEDEN   Jernkontoret, Stockholm

Schroeder, Gertrude, USA   U. S. Bureau of the Census

Sellier, François, FRANCE   Université d'Aix-Marseille

Silberston, Aubrey, ENGLAND   Professor, Cambridge University, England

Tlusty, Zdenek, CZECHOSLOVAKIA   Czechoslovak Academy of Sciences, Prague

Tolkachyov, A. S., USSR   Research Economic Institute, Moscow

Zoeteweij, H., SWITZERLAND   Observer for the ILO

Glossary

The papers contributed by Soviet and East European authors use a number of terms which may be unfamiliar to many Western readers. For their convenience, brief explanations are provided for the more important of these terms. In order to help identify the terms in question, reference is made in this glossary to the Russian language original. Where the term reflects statistical practice, reference is made especially to the usage in the USSR, although it is believed that the meaning in East European countries is essentially the same.

Living labor (*zhivoi trud*); *embodied labor* (*oveshchestvlennii trud*). The terms refer to a distinction derived from Marx between the labor of workers currently engaged in productive activity and the labor of workers previously engaged in productive activity and now embodied in commodities that are currently available. Among the latter, of particular interest are means of production of all sorts used by the currently engaged workers. If reference is made to the amount of embodied labor currently used up, the two categories correspond essentially to the "direct" and "indirect" labor distinguished in contemporary Western input-output analysis.

Workers (*rabochie*); *employed personnel* (*rabotniki*). Almost inevitably usage of such categories is not always precise, but in Soviet statistical practice workers (*rabochie*) are ordinarily understood to represent employees of a rank below that of foremen; in other words, they are essentially the counterpart of "wage earners" in the United States statistics. However, the category workers is usually, although not always, understood not to include apprentices (*ucheniki*) and janitorial and other service personnel (*mladshii obsluzhivaiushchii personal*), which are treated as separate categories. Employed personnel (*rabotniki*) usually is understood more generally to refer to employees of any sort, including not only workers but other categories that are distinguished, particularly "engineering-technical personnel" (*inzhenerno-teknicheskie rabotniki*) and various sorts of "office workers" (*sluzhashchie*).

National income. As understood by economists in Soviet-type economies, this term is most nearly the counterpart of "net national product"; that is, reference is to the final output of a given period valued at market prices less an allowance for depreciation on fixed capital. However, in contrast to Western usage, national income in Soviet-type economies does not include all goods currently produced. Under the influence of a Marxian distinction between productive and unproductive activity, economists in Soviet-type economies limit national income more or less to material products and for the most part omit services from this category. Thus, they omit not only personal services, such as those of teachers, medical personnel, and domestics, but other categories such as those including government and military personnel. While trade is included, apparently at one time or another certain related categories, such as passenger transportation, have been omitted.

Gross output (valovaia produktsiia) and *marketable output (tovarnaia produktsiia).* For any one enterprise, "gross output" is the volume of goods currently produced, including, in addition to finished products, sales of unfinished goods. In varying degrees in different industries, increments to inventories of work in process are also included; on the other hand, in some cases gross output includes the entire output of intermediate products which are subject to further processing in the enterprise in question. In addition to its main semi-finished and finished products, the gross output of the enterprise includes special types of output, such as work of an industrial character performed to order for other enterprises. Finished goods and services (power, water, and so forth) produced not for the market but for use in construction and other secondary activities of the enterprise are believed also to be covered in gross output. For any one factory "marketable" (sometimes designated instead as "commodity") output corresponds to gross output except that generally it omits work-in-progress other than that actually transferred. For industry as a whole, corresponding "gross" and "marketable" output may be calculated in different ways, but most often use is made of the "factory method" where the procedure is simply to sum without any allowance for "double-counting" the outputs, gross or marketable as the case may be, of all enterprises.

Group A and Group B. In Soviet usage, industrial enterprises are considered as "Group A" if they produce goods intended for further productive use, while all enterprises producing products intended for industrial and household consumption are classified as "Group B." Where an enterprise produces goods of both types, its classification usually is determined according to the kind of product that is predominant. Where enterprises produce consumer goods that are intended for further processing, such enterprises are classified as Group A.

Contents

PART III—WAGES AND PRODUCTIVITY

PART IV—TECHNICAL, MANAGERIAL AND ORGANIZATIONAL FACTORS AFFECTING PRODUCTIVITY

CONTENTS

Tables

Figures

PART I

*Concepts and Measurement
of Productivity*

CHAPTER 1

Labor Productivity: Concept, Factors, and Growth Reserves

G. A. PRUDENSKY

Academy of Sciences of the USSR

Soviet economists universally recognize the principle that labor productivity is an important index of the economic development of every society, and they realize, too, that its growth is in the nature of a general law which manifests itself in a special way in each socio-economic structure.

The deliberate application of the law of constant growth of labor productivity in the USSR ensures a high rate of development in industrial output. It has made it possible within a brief period to put an end to the country's centuries-old backwardness and to raise steadily the working people's living standard.

During the USSR's first five-year plan, increases in labor productivity accounted for 51 per cent of total increase in industrial output; during the second five-year plan, 79 per cent; in the war years and during the fourth five-year plan, 69 per cent; and under the fourth five-year plan, 68 per cent. With the seven-year plan of economic development, covering the years 1959 through 1965, increases in labor productivity will account for three quarters of the total increase in output.[1]

Now that the USSR has entered the phase of extensive communist construction, labor productivity is especially important. We are not interested

1. *SSSR v tsifrakh v 1960 g* (Moscow, 1961), p. 92.

simply because labor productivity in industry will rise approximately 4 to 4.5 times its present rate in the next twenty years. We are interested because such a rise will make it possible to ensure the Soviet people of the highest standard of living in the world. Within two decades the national income will increase fivefold, and, on the average, the real income of wage and salaried workers will go up three to three and a half times per worker.

Labor Productivity Indexes

The labor productivity index is composite. In the final analysis, it reflects the realization of many other economic objectives (reduction in the cost of production, advantageous location of industry, degree of specialization, effectiveness of capital investment, use of basic funds, and so on). This accounts for the great importance we attach to the problem of increased labor productivity in the development of the national economy as a whole, in each branch of industry, in each economic region, and in individual industrial enterprises.

The great social significance of this problem has given rise in the Soviet economy and in economic science to an almost social approach to its analysis, to an examination not only of particular examples of labor productivity but also of over-all social productivity.

In the Soviet Union this has not only attracted the attention of state planning and scientific institutions, but of the public, the trade unions, production conferences, scientific societies, and so on.

Active participation in labor productivity investigations by enterprise directors and a large number of foremost workers has made it possible to pinpoint additional sources for increased labor productivity.

The problems of labor productivity are the subject of many scientific conferences; among them was the conference on methods of studying and measuring labor productivity held in Moscow in 1956. A direct result of these conferences and of the regular discussions of labor productivity problems in the press was the revision by the state planning bodies of the earlier methods of gauging productivity. To illustrate, since 1959 labor productivity has been calculated in the USSR per head of industrial personnel, and not merely per worker.

Of late, in connection with the compilation of the seven-year plan of national-economic development and the estimates for the establishment of the material and technical foundations of communism, still greater attention has been given to increased labor productivity. An illustration is the work done in analyzing reserves of increased labor productivity, a task in which some 100 branch-industry institutes took part. More than 500 enterprises were directly investigated, and close to 3000 by means of questionnaires.

The investigation revealed that it was quite possible to better the seven-year plan goals for increased labor productivity, a study showing that in industry, in particular, labor productivity could rise in the 1959–1965 period roughly 60 per cent against the 45 to 50 per cent envisaged by the plan. Overfulfillment of this plan could mean a boost in industrial output of approximately 30,000 million rubles.[2]

Soviet economists apply the term "labor productivity" only to the labor of a worker who takes part in social production. This by no means excludes from economic analysis the investigation of savings in materials, of efficient utilization of basic funds, or of production capacities, and so forth. Moreover, many of these questions have to be studied as conditions and factors influencing labor productivity.

Labor productivity is measured by the input of labor time necessary for turning out a unit of output, and the increase in labor productivity is expressed in the reduction of this input.

The general socialist law of economy (economizing) of labor time operates in two ways: 1) by lowering the input of living labor and 2) by lowering the input of embodied labor.

From the social angle a real increase in labor productivity can be attained only by reducing the total labor input, both past (embodied) and living.

In regard to labor productivity at the individual enterprise, its increase is determined by the reduction in living labor. Although in social labor productivity, reduction in labor time includes aggregate labor, living as well as embodied, this does not by any means minimize the special role played by living labor. At every given stage of the production process, it is precisely living labor that brings into play the use values created in the preceding stages of production. Living labor creates the product, and living labor is the reason for increased labor productivity. Human labor alone creates material values and spiritual values. Emphasis, therefore, should be placed on a thorough study of the rationality of input of living labor and on an analysis of labor time according to its structure.

It seems to us that the relation of labor time to the analysis of labor pro-

2. *Rezervy rosta proizvoditelnosti truda v promyshlennosti SSSR*, M. D. Gorshunov and A. I. Zalkind, eds. (Moscow, 1961), p. 14.

ductivity is as follows: The total labor time at the disposal of production in the course of a specific period (day, month, or year) characterizes the labor-time fund, measured in man-hours. The labor-time fund can be broken down into two parts: (*a*) time spent in productive labor, and (*b*) breaks in work time—time lost because of something amiss at the plant or because of other non-productive labor expenditures.

Productive labor time is part of the total amount of labor time during which a worker performs a technological operation, and it is incorporated in the labor consumed in manufacturing the article. To get the total labor picture, we must take into account the labor input of the auxiliary workers, service and managerial staffs, as well as the principal workers.

The productive-labor time revealed by the total amount of labor consumed in a given industry (plant) can be broken down, first of all, by stages in the technological process, and by individual operations within each stage. Operational time, in turn, is divided into basic technological time and auxiliary time (the time required to service the workbench and the time needed for preliminary and final work—elements well known to us from the theory and practice of rate setting).

The study of labor time has considerably broadened our ideas of labor productivity, enabling us more concretely and objectively to estimate the effect of individual factors. This study gives us a basis by which we can comprehensively estimate the existing level of productivity and analyze the possibilities of its future growth for individual enterprises and each branch of industry.

An important methodological question involved in the study of labor productivity, which is also important in every other sphere of economic analysis, is the employment of a system of indexes. Only in this way, and not by means of a single universal index, can so complicated a process as the movement of labor productivity be characterized in all its facets.

It is necessary that development of future scientific research follow this methodology. Of course, each sector of production will have a system of indexes specifically applicable to it and conforming to the purposes of the analysis.

It is advisable for individual countries, and particularly for international comparison, that the system of indexes show not only the level of labor productivity but also its rate of increase.

A characterization (description) of the utilization of labor should also be an important element in every system of indexes. In analyzing social labor productivity (particularly in international comparisons), it is necessary to study the employment record of the able-bodied work group and the indexes giving a total picture of unemployment.

Whatever system of indexes is used in studying labor productivity, it must not be forgotten that the fundamental issue is man and his particular labor.

Factors Influencing Labor Productivity

The growth of labor productivity and economizing labor time result from many complex factors. Practical experience in conducting research (in definite branches of industry), whether in the study of the existing level of labor productivity or in determining its potential, has made it possible to specify the following principal factors:

(1) Introduction of new machinery and progressive technology based on the achievements of contemporary science.
(2) Specialization, cooperation, and combined production.
(3) Rational organization of work and production.
(4) Improvement of workers' skills.
(5) Improvement of industrial organization and management techniques.
(6) Changes in industry structure.

For long-range calculations these factors can all be combined into two enlarged groups:

(A) The introduction of new machinery and progressive technology.
(B) The improvement in the organization of work and production.

A greater breakdown of the factors by which labor productivity is calculated may be necessary because of the individual features of particular branches of industry.

An analysis of industry's potential in the current seven-year period has shown that new machinery and technology are decisive factors in increasing labor productivity. They account for more than half the total increase in industry, for 63.9 per cent in oil and gas, 64.5 per cent in lumber, 70.9 per cent in chemicals, and 78.3 per cent in building materials—the higher percentages in the latter industries the result of the addition of new equipment during the current plan period.

The most important condition for higher labor productivity is improvement in workers' skills. The USSR Census of 1959 shows that while in 1939 the country had 83 persons with a secondary or higher education per 1000 of population, in 1959 the number was 281; for 1000 persons employed chiefly at manual labor the figures were 43 and 316 respectively.

Also testifying to the steady rise in the skill of those engaged in social production are the following figures: nearly 9.6 times as many specialists were working in 1959 as there were in 1913—the higher-education group being up 5.4 times and the specialized secondary-education group being 20 times over the former figure. By 1959 the number of scientific workers for every 100,000 wage and salaried workers had increased roughly sevenfold as compared with 1914.

It is important to note that the factors which ordinarily gauge the degree of their influence on labor productivity indicate the development of the productive forces of society. In a socialist economy, however, there are a series of conditions specific to socialism that exercise a tremendous influence on labor productivity. These are, first of all, the planned organization of production on a nation-wide scale and, second, the personal interest the people have in the development and perfection of production.

Development of social production under a single national-economic plan makes it possible to ensure the balanced distribution and use of labor resources and input of labor time on a society-wide scale, precluding the possibility of unemployment.

Planned organization of production on a nation-wide basis permits the fullest use of the rapidly expanding production capacities and the available material resources.

Influencing the rise of labor productivity are the creativity and initiative of the masses demonstrated by the unending attempts to excel and by the constantly growing activity of innovators and inventors.

In addition to material incentives offered by work in socialist enterprises, moral stimuli also play an important part. This is particularly evident today in the highest form of emulation—the movement of collectives and the advanced workers of communist labor. More than 12 million working people took part in this movement in the USSR in 1961.

While the factors relating to industrial activity are many and varied, their operation is interdependent—an important fact to be taken into account in this analysis.

Reserves for Increasing Labor Productivity

One growing aspect in the study of labor productivity in planned socialist production is an analysis of its reserves—the over-all consideration of the possibilities of further raising labor productivity by taking into account all reasons for its increase.

This trend is on the upswing because it is well understood that the comprehensive use of internal production potentials is an important factor in the increase in the rate of expanded socialist reproduction.

At the same time, other methods of studying the growth of labor productivity reserves are also being developed. One method is to analyze them by the input of labor time. In this analysis we find the decrease in labor time showing up in the following forms: (*a*) decrease in labor time consumed in making the product, and (*b*) rational and full use of the labor-time fund during the allotted period by the work schedule (day, month or year) with elimination of all losses and non-productive uses of labor time.

Thus, increased labor productivity reserves can be reduced to two main groups: the lower labor-consumption reserves (*RL*), and the labor time fund reserves (*RF*).

Possibilities for decreasing labor consumption depend chiefly on the introduction of new machinery and improvement of technology. The most important factor in the second form of reserves is improvement in organizing work and production. The sum of the two main reserves determines the total value of increased labor productivity reserves for a given industry, that is, $R = RL + RF$.

In analyzing reserves, it is necessary to realize that each of the two values can be measured independently. The first value (the lower labor-consumption reserves) is determined by its ratio to output, and the second (the labor time funds reserves) is determined in relation to the labor time budget. The commensuration of the two values can be properly examined only in the balance sheet of input of labor time of a given working force.

A balance sheet of labor time inputs can be made up for a month, a quarter, a year, or for a longer period, and it can be compiled for every category of worker, shop, plant, or branch of industry. It may be a summary of conditions of production that have developed or the time input, or it may be in the nature of a plan, taking into account the magnitude of the reserves and their use for developing production.

Further improvement of the balance sheet method in studying labor time is important in improving production analyses.

The earlier classification of the types of reserves by expenditure of labor time does not rule out the use of the reserves and their other groupings in analyses. Thus, depending on the sources of the different reserves according to sectors of the social production structure, they can be subdivided as follows: (1) general reserves of the national economy; (2) intra- or interindustry reserves; (3) intrabranch of industry or interplant reserves; (4) intraplant and intrashop reserves.

In actual analyses, higher labor productivity reserves may be examined also from another angle—their use with respect to time. The reserves are subdivided into current (those that can be realized in an immediate planned period—a month, a quarter, or a year), and long-range. The latter are, as a rule, conditioned on radical improvements in production, the introduction of brand-new technologies and up-to-date machinery.

Reserves have to be studied comprehensively. They have to be analyzed from every angle. It is proper to speak of the degree of completeness, which will be the greater the more comprehensively the growth of labor productivity reserves have been explored. Important in this respect is a system of indexes by which we can arrive at the truest picture not only of the level and dynamics of labor productivity but also of its growth reserves.

One variety of such a system of indexes is revealed by the following three interdependent groups: (a) output per unit of labor time; (b) rated and actual inputs of labor time per unit of output (labor consumption); (c) use of the labor-time fund within the limits of its balance sheet.

A system of indexes in economic analysis is not a special feature in the study of reserves. A system of indexes should be used in every type of economic research, because only a system and not an individual index can fully characterize the complex economic phenomena of industry and the economy. This applies wholly to the study of the profitableness of production, the effectiveness of capital investments, estimates of the economic effects of machinery being designed, and to other matters that are the subject of economic research.

We have touched upon a number of methodological questions relating to the problem of labor productivity, based on the experience of economic research in the USSR. In further studying this problem, the following questions would appear to require special attention:

(1) The measurement and planning of labor productivity, using mathematical calculation.

(2) Labor productivity and the shorter workday.

(3) Economic aspects of labor productivity and the influence of science.

(4) Ways of further improving the organization of work and production.

(5) Over-all analysis of reserves and growth factors of labor productivity.

(6) Improvement of methods of comparing labor productivity internationally.

We are certain that our efforts, coupled with the creative work of scientists and economic societies in other countries, will lead to more comprehensive knowledge on the question of labor productivity, which will undoubtedly contribute to social progress.

CHAPTER 2

Meaning and Measurement of Productivity

SOLOMON FABRICANT
New York University

Everybody knows what productivity signifies generally. When productivity is reported to be higher here than there, or now than before, those here or now are pleased. They see in the report signs of superior economic welfare, or at least of a basis for greater economic welfare. For productivity is the power to produce economic goods and services.

But this, in turn, means so many things that even when modified by adjectives the term, productivity, is rather broad. Different measurements with the same name are possible, and a variety of figures are in fact published.

It is well, therefore, for all who discuss productivity to make as clear as possible what it is they are talking about and what the measurements measure. The need is especially great when economists from different parts of the world join in the discussion.

To assist in this preliminary, I shall illustrate the wide variety of concepts and measurements, ask why the differences among them arise, and then comment on some questions of measurement.

The discussion will not be confined to labor productivity alone, even though we are assembled in a Conference on Labor Productivity. To understand the meaning, limitations, and uses of a particular class of productivity measurements, it is necessary to consider how it differs from other classes.

Nor will the discussion be directed toward reaching the best concept and measurement. There is none best for all purposes or under all circumstances.

The Variety of Productivity Concepts

Economists sometimes compare the current output of an economy, industry, factory, worker, or machine, with the theoretically possible output —that is, the output that would be produced under certain assumptions (often merely implied) of change in the determinants of output. In most discussions of productivity, however, the comparison is not of current output with theoretically possible output, but of current output with current input of resources. Of the several senses of "power to produce," then, it is to the comparison of output with input—particularly, the ratio of the one to the other—that the term, productivity, is ordinarily attached.

The ratio of output to input in a particular time or place is further compared with the corresponding ratio of another time or place. The comparison is usually put in relative form—output per worker, for example, at time 1 or in country 1 is divided by output per worker at time O or in country O (and the ratio almost always multiplied by 100), to yield an index of labor productivity on the base O.[1]

It is this relative of output-input ratios that we consider here.

Productivity in the sense of output compared with input relates, as the discussion at the first meeting of the U.S. Conference on Productivity brought out,

to a whole family of concepts rather than to any specific member of that family. Almost any comparison of output with input is covered by it. Output may be defined in various ways, however, and input may be measured by one factor or another or by several factors in combination. Further, productivity may be the relation between output and the input of one factor, all other input factors being kept constant, as in an experiment under controlled conditions; or it may be the relation between output and the input of one factor, with changes occurring in all other factors. Still further, productivity may be the relation between the total output and input of a period, or it may be the relation between the increment in output associated with the addition of one unit of a given factor of production; that is, it may be "average" or "marginal." Thus,

1. Of course, the two ratios may also be compared by subtracting one from the other. This alternative conveys somewhat different information.

economists writing on the "theory of marginal productivity" use the term quite differently from statisticians who compute indexes of productivity.[2]

The discussion that follows will not attempt to cover all these productivity concepts. It will be limited to average productivity, the ratio of a period's output to the corresponding input of one or more specified factors of production, with other inputs not assumed to be constant.

A Sample of Productivity Measurements

The participants in the 1946 conference recognized that measurements as well as concepts will differ:

Stemming from the acceptance that there is a whole group of productivity concepts was the realization that a variety of measures is possible. Measures may be made of output per unit of capital equipment or per unit of labor; of output per man or per man-hour; of physical output per man-hour or value output per man-hour; of "net" physical output per man-hour or "gross" physical output per man-hour; and so on.

Also, the numerator or the denominator of the productivity ratio may be calculated on the basis of one rather than another set of statistical data.

To illustrate further this variety of measures of productivity change, and to indicate how some of them differ quantitatively, Table 1 is reproduced from a publication of the National Bureau of Economic Research. Although the table is limited to "average productivity" indexes of one country and one period, and some available measurements are omitted, a considerable variety and quantitative range is revealed.

Some of the differences arise because output is defined in more than one way. On the first line of the body of the table, for example, the output in the productivity ratio is measured gross of depreciation and other items of capital consumption; and on the second line the output is measured net of capital consumption. In the third column of figures, military outlays are treated as "final goods" (the "national security" version of output); in the fourth column, military outlays are treated as "intermediate goods" (the "peacetime" version of output); and in the fifth column, in which use is made of the Department of Commerce definition of national product, military outlays are treated very much, but not quite the same, as in the

2. U.S. Department of Labor, Bureau of Labor Statistics, "Summary of Proceedings of Conference on Productivity, October 28–29, 1946," *Bulletin No. 913* (Washington, 1947), pp. 2–3.

Table 1. Broad measures of the long-term rate of increase in productivity in the United States.
(Average annual percentage rates of change, 1889-1953)

Output	Aggregate of industries for which individual productivity indexes are available	Entire economy, including government			
		Entire private domestic economy	"National security" version of output	"Peace-time" version of output	Dept. of Commerce version of output
Gross physical output per unweighted man-hour	2.3	2.3	2.2	2.0	2.2
Net physical output per unweighted man-hour	—	2.3	2.2	2.0	2.2
Gross physical output per weighted man-hour	1.9	2.0	1.8	1.6	1.8
Net physical output per weighted man-hour	—	2.0	1.8	1.6	1.8
Gross physical output per unweighted unit of tangible capital	1.0	1.2	1.0	0.9	1.0
Net physical output per unweighted unit of tangible capital	—	1.2	1.0	0.9	1.1
Gross physical output per weighted unit of tangible capital	1.0	1.0	0.8	0.7	0.8
Net physical output per weighted unit of tangible capital	—	1.1	0.9	0.7	0.9
Gross physical output per weighted unit of labor and tangible capital combined	1.7	1.7	1.5	1.4	1.5
Net physical output per weighted unit of labor and tangible capital combined	—	1.7	1.6	1.4	1.6

Source: John W. Kendrick, Productivity Trends in the United States (Princeton, 1961). The underlying indexes are subject to some revision. Use was made by Kendrick of estimates developed in other National Bureau studies by Kuznets, Goldsmith, Blank, Tostlebe, Ulmer, Creamer, Borenstein, and Barger, among others, as well as of data published by the Departments of Commerce and of Labor.

Gross output differs from net output by the amount of depreciation and other items of capital consumption, in the case of the national indexes; and also by the amount of materials, fuel, and supplies consumed, in the case of the industries covered in the first column of figures (except agriculture).

Industries for which individual productivity indexes are available for 1889-1953 include farming, mining, manufacturing, transportation, and communications and public utilities.

The three sets of indexes for the entire economy differ mainly in the treatment of defense outlays in the calculation of national product and of inputs. The "national security" and "peace-time" versions of national product are based largely on concepts developed by Kuznets; the Department of Commerce version is that currently published by its office of Business Economics.

[Reproduced from Occasional Paper 63, National Bureau of Economic Research (Princeton, 1959), p. 5.]

third column. Other differences reflect differences in the scope of input. In some of the indexes, for example, labor input is unweighted, while in others it is weighted, that is, a man-hour of skilled work is counted as more than a man-hour of unskilled work. Further, the measurements differ between the first two columns of figures in the table because of differences in coverage and in the statistical data used.

It should be added that the average rate of growth obtained depends also on the technical method (for example, least-squares or compound-interest) used to derive the average rate, for productivity change does not proceed smoothly from year to year.

Reasons for the Variety of Concepts and Measurements

Concepts and measurements of productivity vary for several reasons.

First, purposes differ. Different productivity concepts are, or should be, adapted to different purposes.

Second, even when purposes are identical, values will differ among and within social systems. While productivity is simply the ratio of output to input, neither output not input is a simple physical quantity independent of what men consider valuable.

Third, economies in various parts of the world differ in organization and in the character of their outputs and inputs, as well as in their value systems. So does the same economy at different times, because productivity change is accompanied by alteration in organization, output, and input. These differences and changes raise serious problems of definition and measurement of output and input to which different solutions are offered.

Fourth, a major use of productivity concepts and measurements is in the analysis of economic growth. But forms of analysis, and theoretical preconceptions as well, differ among investigators. These, too, make for differences in the definition and measurement of productivity.

Finally, apart from other reasons, productivity measurements differ simply because statistical information is inadequate, and the ways of overcoming the inadequacies are more or less arbitrary.

A Variety of Purposes

One major purpose of productivity indexes is to get at the reasons for progress in production; another, to provide a criterion for the distribution of income; a third, to measure progress in production.

Suppose the purpose is analytical. Change in output may, for example, be viewed as the result of change in two factors—the quantity of resources and productivity in the sense of efficiency in the use of resources, and an effort made to measure the separate contributions of the two factors. In that case, the appropriate productivity measure is change in output per unit of total input. Output per unit of any particular kind of input, such as labor or tangible capital, will reflect not only the contribution of efficiency to output but also substitution between the particular input and other inputs.

The discussion here is focused on national productivity. Total input is defined to include the services of labor and capital, and output is defined net of materials consumed. The same concepts may be used when interest lies in the productivity of a sector of the economy. However, there is some point in defining the input of the sector to include the materials consumed by it, as well as the services of labor and capital consumed, and correspondingly to define the sector's output gross of materials consumed. Each set of definitions has its advantages: the former, because it lends itself to simple aggregation of sectoral inputs or outputs to get the input or output of the economy as a whole; the latter, because it is more appropriate if comparison is to be made between change in productivity and, for example, change in the selling price of the sector's product.

Sometimes, of course, output per man-hour is deliberately used as a measure of productivity in lieu of and as an approximation to output per unit of total input, because the latter is not available or cannot be calculated within a reasonable margin of error. This is perfectly legitimate, but a question then arises about the degree of approximation and the direction of bias. Even so-called indexes of output per unit of total input are approximations when (as is usual) they are really indexes of output per unit of labor and reproducible tangible capital alone, for total input must include also the services of land and of intangible capital.

Frequently, what is wanted is a criterion for judging whether change in hourly wages is, or tends to be, inflationary. For such a purpose, the criterion commonly used is an index of productivity defined by real national output per man-hour. In effect, a given change in money wages is viewed as inflationary only if it exceeds the amount "permitted" by rise in national efficiency and increase in scarcity of labor. More specifically, the criterion, output per man-hour, is a particular combination (the mathematical product) of (1) output per unit of total input (the measure of efficiency) and (2) total input relative to labor input (the measure of labor scarcity). This particular combination of efficiency and scarcity is an appropriate criterion in a competitive market on certain assumptions concerning the shape of the production function and its relation to technological change.

To measure progress in production, the third purpose, total output today may be compared with total output yesterday. In this case, the productivity index is simply the output index, and the progress that is being measured reflects change in both resources and efficiency. Sometimes progress in production is measured by a productivity index that relates to change in output per capita or per equivalent-adult or other population unit. While it is more customary to think of productivity as the ratio of output to input, the term is sometimes applied to these measures of output or output per population unit, and it is therefore necessary to be wary.

Differences in Values

How productivity is defined depends not only on the use to be made of the productivity measurement, but also on national goals and individual tastes—that is, on what is considered to be output and input.

Some differences in values will be reflected (along with differences in resource availability and other factors) in differences between relative prices in the two places or periods compared. The differences will materialize as the discrepancy between the Laspeyres and Paasche indexes. There will therefore always be at least two measures of any change or difference in productivity. The number will be more than two, when comparisons between points in time or space are also made circuitously via other points.

But differences in values may be broader than the differences between Laspeyres and Paasche indexes. One may refuse to accept the judgment of the market of either period or place, as it is expressed in price or cost per conventional unit. The answers to the questions—what to include in output, what units to use in measuring each type of output, and what weights to apply to each type of output to get an aggregate—will then be answered on other grounds. Thus, those who dislike fins on passenger automobiles, and refuse to accept the judgment of purchasers and sellers, would count an automobile decorated with fins as no more than one not so decorated. The question is especially important when prices (and costs) are significantly influenced by imperfections of competition or by governmental decisions. But there is no accepted solution, when market prices and costs are rejected, to the problem of finding something to substitute for them. What is finally done will vary, and comparisons of productivity levels between different times and places may therefore depend significantly on who makes the comparison.

It is true that most calculations follow fairly conventional lines. Only when it is asked what the conventional figures "really mean," is the use of market prices or costs questioned. It is a question that economists from different economic and cultural backgrounds must ask when they face one another.

Difficulties in Comparing Different National Economies

Even when purposes and values are given, there will be differences among productivity concepts and measurements.

The national economies (or other economic units) for which we wish to calculate productivity indexes differ among themselves not only in their power to produce but also in how they produce, what they produce, and with what they produce. These differences in organization, output, and input make productivity comparisons difficult. To compare productivities we must somehow compare situations that are substantially incomparable. The difficulties cannot be escaped; they must be met. How they are met in the practical task of measurement is often a matter of compromise involving arbitrary or at best conventional decisions.

Differences among economies at different times and places are many. Let me merely mention that advance in productivity brings with it, and also results from, the development of new products, materials, machines, and skills, and the obsolescence or disappearance of old. Output and input indexes alike are affected by the way these changes are dealt with.

Advance in productivity also brings, and results from, change in economic organization. Workers shift from farming to manufacturing, and from manufacturing to the service trades. Families move from rural to urban, and from urban to suburban communities. Production is transferred from household to factory and back from factory to household. Children are relieved of farm chores and kept in school longer. Government takes on new functions; private philanthropy changes in scope and importance; the relative importance and composition and terms of foreign trade and investment are altered. As a result of these and other developments, conventional definitions of output and input often break down, and even uniform systems of accounts distort the facts with which we are concerned.

Alternative Forms of Analysis

A major use of productivity concepts and measurements is to learn something of the process by which production is raised. But there is not yet, if there ever will be, agreement on the best form of analysis, that is, on the best path to knowledge of the factors affecting power to produce. In the end, perhaps, it will not matter much which choice is made in the form of the analysis. In the meantime, however, it is well to be clear that these vary, and therefore that definitions and measurements of productivity differ.

Thus, output may be viewed as dependent on resources and on productivity. Resources may then be defined as labor and tangible capital; productivity measured by output per dose of labor and tangible capital combined; and the problem of explaining change in productivity so measured left, for a second and usually qualitative stage of analysis, to such factors as intangible capital, economic organization, size of the economy, and other factors. Or, broadening the concept of resources and correspondingly altering the concept of productivity, resources may be defined as labor, tangible capital, and intangible capital; productivity measured by output per unit of labor and total capital combined; and productivity left to be explained by the residual factors. Or the concept of resources may be narrowed to cover only labor time spent at work; productivity, defined as output per man-hour; and all kinds of capital, tangible and intangible, grouped among the factors explaining productivity. Even more narrowly, hours per worker may be counted as a productivity factor, and productivity itself defined as output per worker.[3]

Historically, the choice among these forms of analysis has been influenced largely by the availability of data. As information on hours, then tangible capital, and most recently intangible capital, have become available, the definitions of resources and of productivity have been altered. This is a natural development, for in empirical work the form of analysis has to be adapted to the information at hand.

3. The broader the definition of resources, and correspondingly, the narrower the definition of productivity, the smaller, also, will be what has been called the "inter-industry component" of change in productivity. See Simon Kuznets, *Income and Wealth of the United States, Trends and Structure,* Income and Wealth Series II, International Association for Research in Income and Wealth (Cambridge, 1952), pp. 123–31. For example, if inter-industry differences in value of output per man-hour are entirely due to corresponding differences in capital per man-hour, the inter-industry component will be zero for change in total productivity but not for change in labor productivity. In effect, the total productivity index identifies some or all of the factors back of the inter-industry component.

But the choice—and the data needed to implement it—has been influenced also by the knowledge and the hypotheses of the investigator. When it is realized, for example, that level of education influences output, and that education is in part or whole a form of investment, there will be more interest in counting education among resources and defining productivity as output per unit of resources that include capital invested in the skills and knowledge of human beings. And efforts will be made to measure productivity so defined.

Inadequacies of Information

Even when there is agreement on everything else, indexes will differ simply because information on output or input is inconsistent, and because there are differences of opinion on how to pass from a given sample to the population.

Thus, the U.S. Bureau of Labor Statistics publishes two indexes of national output per man-hour, one using man-hour data obtained from a sample of families, and the other, man-hour data obtained from a sample of employers. Again, some index makers have adjusted for change in the coverage of production statistics by assuming that the prices of the covered items have paralleled the prices of the uncovered items, while some statisticians have entirely ignored the problem. Difficulties in measuring the output (and input) of governmental agencies have been resolved either by excluding government entirely and concentrating on the private sector, as in one section of Table 1; or, as in another section, by treating as eligible for the measurement of government output and input kinds of data that others would not accept for the purpose. Conventional accounting measurements of capital have been used "as is" by some; others have made all kinds of adjustments.

Much more could be said about the sources of differences in productivity concepts and measurements. But I will turn to certain of the problems that arise in the measurement of output and input, and thus of productivity, because so many of the measurements available are in some degree conventional in character. The conventions may be appropriate enough for industrialized economies at certain stages of development. But they are less suitable, and sometimes much less suitable, for economies at other stages of development, when economic organization, output, and input are different.

Measurement of Labor Output

The point of view is that of measuring the productivity, in the sense of efficiency in the use of resources, of a market economy—though some of the questions apply also, I suspect, to socialist economies. Market valuations are accepted, but accounting and statistical conventions are questioned. Indeed, the problem is what to substitute for the conventionally calculated data. I offer suggestions mainly to stimulate discussion.

Reference has already been made to the kinds of changes and contemporary differences in organization, output, and input that are involved. Specifically, questions arise about the effect on the measure of output, and thus on the measure of productivity, of the treatment of the following:

(1) *Capital consumption.* It would be better, as a rule, to measure output in terms of net rather than gross national or domestic product. The rather general hesitation or inability to do so is an indication of the difficulties of determining the depreciation, obsolescence, depletion, and other items that constitute capital consumption, and of doing so on a comparable basis. But use of the gross national or gross domestic product figures currently available does not get around the problem entirely. Net product and gross product differ by an amount and proportion that depend on past and current rates of change in gross capital formation and on past and current rates of depreciation and obsolescence. Gross product does not parallel net product, as Kuznets has shown for the United States.

Further, inconsistencies in the treatment of maintenance charges, that is, in the definition of gross capital formation, lead to incomparabilities among the gross product series. So also do differences in the application of the inventory revaluation adjustment, and even in the inclusion of inventory investment in gross product.

(2) *Household production.* The shift from domestic to commercial production—of food, fuel, shelter, clothing, recreation, housing construction and maintenance, health care, education, and still other items of consumption and investment—that occurs during industrialization has been well recognized, though not much is yet known of its quantitative importance. It is less widely accepted that in recent decades a reverse shift has occurred in countries like the United States. The shift has been associated with the increase in the stock of family-owned and family-operated consumer durables such as automobiles, washing machines, television sets, and freezers, with the greater importance of owner-occupied housing, and with shortened

hours of work in industry. Relatively more production now goes on in the household in the form of "do it yourself" work and in the operation of domestic equipment. Because conventional definitions of output do not include housewives' services, the spare-time work of men, or the services of household equipment, incomparabilities result when the productivity of economies at different stages of development are compared. The efforts made to overcome the difficulties are often incomplete and inconsistent.

A similar incomparability arises from the conventional treatment of education. Economists generally recognize that among the costs of education are incomes foregone by students and the imputed rental value of school buildings and equipment, as well as outlays on teachers' salaries and the like. However, the former costs—or more accurately, the production associated with them—are not generally counted as output, in determining the national product. This omission distorts the level and trend of production, and to a greater degree at some times and places than at others.

(3) *Quality change.* Some quality improvement (or worsening) is taken into account, in the calculation of national product, to the extent that a unit of high-price goods and services is counted as more than a unit of low-price goods and services. But it is likely that most quality change—in food, clothing, health services, and distributive services, as well as in many other commodities—is not covered by the available figures.

The difficulties standing in the way of taking full account of quality change are serious. Quality has many dimensions. The quality of an automobile tire, for example, is determined by its durability, resistance to blowouts, riding characteristics, maintenance costs, and appearance, among other things. But the quality of a commodity depends not only on its own characteristics but also on the environment within which it is used. The durability of a tire is determined by what is put into it and how it is constructed; it is determined also by the character of the road and the vehicle and the care the tire receives, and these also vary. Indeed, a "high-grade" tire in one environment may be a "low-grade" tire in another.

Related sources of bias may be worth mentioning. One is the failure to take into account the variety of goods and services at the disposal of consumers. Another is the practice of counting as output such items as hospital time rather than diseases successfully prevented. It is hazardous to assume that the bias that results from these and other inadequacies in the determination of quality change is uniform in time and space and therefore does not affect productivity comparisons.

Measurement of Labor Input

The omission of the labors of housewives and students understates inputs as well as outputs, and not necessarily in the same proportion.

Also of interest in the measurement of labor input is the cumulative effect of education, formal and informal, on the quality of the labor force. The "stock" of intangible capital invested in human beings is treated as a factor affecting labor productivity, when the latter is measured by output per unweighted man-hour of work done. Alternatively, educational capital gets into the denominator of the labor-productivity ratio when different classes of man-hours are weighted by hourly earnings. A few such indexes have been calculated—one is given in Table 1—and it is clear that over a period of sixty years or so, the inclusion makes a substantial difference. However, these indexes are as yet very crude, since they are based on just a few categories of labor and do not take account of general improvements in the quality of labor.

Industrialization affects labor input also by bringing shorter hours of work and making work less laborious. Shorter hours usually enter the calculations of productivity, now that data on hours are generally available. The lighter burden of work is passed over, however, as are many of the other benefits of economic progress, such as better working conditions and lower accident rates. Ignored, too, is the disadvantage of longer travel time between home and place of work that may be forced by urbanization and suburbanization. This, like other items, may be minor in itself, but it should serve to remind us of the many costs of economic growth—for example, pollution of the atmosphere—that are left out of the calculations.

Measurement of Capital Input

At one time it was believed sufficient to measure change in capital input by change in the depreciation and other capital consumption charges obtained from accounting records. A later variation of this procedure involved the use of an input-output table to translate the capital consumption charges into labor-input equivalents. Both procedures are deficient, however. It is the value of the services of capital that constitutes capital input. This value includes more than capital consumption, and is not necessarily related to capital consumption in any close way. Currently, therefore, the usual index of capital input is calculated by recourse to net capital assets, roughly adjusted for changes in reproduction costs. These net assets presumably bear a closer relation to the value of the services rendered by capital.

Occasionally, however, it is proposed that the measure of capital input be based on gross capital assets, before deducting accrued depreciation and similar charges. This seems in part to be an effort to get around the conventional accounting practice of straight-line depreciation, which economists have always found unpalatable on theoretical grounds. A more explicit solution of the problem, if information could be obtained, would be to use as the index of capital input a direct estimate of the gross rental value (less current expenses) of capital goods, adjusted for price changes. This index would be similar to, but not identical with, the index of real gross capital assets.

A better theoretical solution might be to substitute for the straight-line depreciation formula a compound-interest formula.[4] Corresponding changes would be made in the calculation of net capital assets and of net product and thus of both numerator and denominator of the productivity ratio. Difficulties would be encountered in deciding on the appropriate interest rates, but this problem is inherent in the measurement of capital input and it is better to be aware of it.

Conclusions

(1) To lessen confusion, it would be better to avoid broad terms like "productivity" or even "labor productivity," and whenever it is not too inconvenient, to use more specific terms like "physical output per man-hour." But even the more specific terms should be supplemented by explicit definitions and the indexes accompanied by notes on sources and methods of derivation.

(2) Because concepts and measurements should be suited, as far as possible, to specific purposes, it is desirable to be clear on the purposes, to ask whether the available indexes are the best for the purposes, and to determine how far the indexes fall short of what is needed.

(3) Even for specific purposes, several different productivity indexes are better than one, when they provide somewhat different views of the phenomena under study. Even if the concept is the same, indexes derived from

4. The appropriate formula is identical with that used in amortizing bonds bought at higher than par value. Under this formula the depreciation charge would rise from a level initially lower than the straight-line depreciation charge to one eventually higher.

different sources are useful. They may confirm one another, or by their differences suggest the margin of uncertainty surrounding the facts.

(4) In an era when much attention is being paid to the (frequently) small differences in rates of growth that tell whether growth is accelerating or retarding or is more or less rapid than in other countries, a burden is placed on available measurements that is sometimes more than can be borne by them. We should put no more confidence in small—or big—differences than they deserve; and to make them deserve more confidence, we should try to improve concepts and measurements.

(5) On the other hand, it is easy to draw up long lists of qualifications that seem significant on *a priori* grounds but are in fact insignificant, and I have undoubtedly fallen into this error. The only way to avoid being inhibited by unimportant qualifications is to learn more about their quantitative importance. Sometimes even a few facts or some hypothetical calculations may suffice to reassure us. However, it should be kept in mind also that a qualification or limitation that is unimportant in one set of circumstances may sometimes be quite important in another.

(6) A major use of productivity indexes is to learn something about the nature and strength of some of the factors affecting growth of output. The construction of these indexes involves decisions about the classification of factors according to their causes, and assumptions regarding the allocation of responsibility for change in output among the groups of factors. There is always a danger that these decisions and assumptions will mislead the user of the results if he fails to understand and keep in mind their basis in theory, convention, and the availability of data.

(7) As knowledge of the process of economic change develops, some of the arbitrary decisions that now account for differences among productivity concepts and measurements may become unnecessary, and a fuller measure of agreement on what is appropriate reached. But for a long time to come we must be prepared to encounter these differences.

(8) More important than deciding how to classify factors between the two categories of resources and productivity is to know what each factor is, how important it is, and how it is related to the others. One definition and measure of productivity may provide a more useful summary and more helpful starting point than another. But none will by itself tell all we need to know about the process and causes of growth.

CHAPTER 3

Problems in the Measuring and Analysis of Labor Productivity

Bronislaw Minc

Polish Academy of Sciences

In Poland and in other socialist countries the measuring and the analysis of labor productivity in particular enterprises, in industries, and in the whole national economy are of great significance because they constitute a basis for rational economic decisions. This is the reason for using a proper concept of labor productivity, in determining yardsticks for measuring it, and in applying appropriate methods of analysis. In this study an attempt will be made to define basic concepts related to labor productivity, to discuss measurements, and to present a new, analytical method for its measurement.

The Concept of Labor Productivity

Labor productivity is the sum of use values produced (products or material services) per worker employed in material production. Labor productivity is always calculated with reference to some unit of time (hour, day, month, or year).

It comprises the whole result of labor within a unit of time determined jointly by factors dependent on and independent of the worker. Thus, it also depends upon the degree of intensity of his work.

Labor productivity is contingent, first of all, on the productive power of labor, that is, the ability of labor to produce use values which can be considered normal at a given state of technique and organization.

Labor's productive power is influenced by objective factors independent of individual workers, and particularly by

(1) the degree of mechanization and automation of labor;
(2) the level of the organization of work, and especially of cooperation and specialization;
(3) natural resources used in production—the fertility of soil, the richness of deposits, and so forth.

Labor productivity depends not only on the productive power of labor determined by objective factors, but also on how these factors actually develop or how they are in fact used. It is also contingent on subjective factors relating to the worker himself.

Thus labor productivity depends upon the deviation of the actual vector of objective factors from the vector considered normal (the influence of poor crops, or crops better than average, on labor productivity in agriculture, for example.)

The subjective factors influencing labor productivity are

(1) the skill or qualifications of the worker;
(2) the intensity of his effort in the process of labor, or the intensity of work;
(3) the innate ability of the worker, that is his physical and mental energy.

The productive power of labor constitutes a basis for the actual level of labor productivity. This shows up particularly clearly in that designs of productive establishments are based on a certain level of labor's productive power and not on labor productivity (which depends on the actual conditions during the workday and may be less than the productive power of labor). Sometimes, in consequence of poor organization, with related breaks in production affecting both workers and equipment, labor productivity is lower than labor's productive power (which is determined by the productive capacity of the establishment).

The concept of labor productivity should be distinguished from the concept of the effectiveness of production (that is, the ratio of the amount of use values produced to the total amount of labor used—"living" labor and "stored up" labor). When labor productivity is measured by the formula $P : t_1$ (where P is the amount of product [use values] and t_1 is the amount of "living" labor), then the effectiveness of production is measured by the formula $P : (t_1 + t_2)$; t_2 being the amount of "stored up" labor.

In practice, because of the difficulties involved in calculating the amount of "stored up" labor outlays, the index of the effectiveness of social labor outlays in a contemporary socialist economy is replaced by a somewhat similar index of production costs. The latter are composed of the cost of used up means of production (the cost of materials, depreciation, and wages).

When we replace t_2, that is, the outlays of "stored up" labor by the cost of these outlays—the cost of used up means of production (the cost of materials and depreciation)—and t_1, that is, the outlays of "living" labor, by wages, then the sum is cost of production.

An analysis of labor productivity should be combined with an analysis of the effectiveness of production (which in practice means an analysis of production costs) in order to determine whether an increase in labor productivity has not been achieved by an excessive increase in "stored up" labor outlays and to what extent the productivity increase has contributed to the lowering of the costs of production.

From the point of view of the whole national economy, labor productivity is a ratio of national income as the sum of use values, to "living" labor outlays. The effectiveness of production is a ratio of this income to the outlays on "living" and "stored up" labor.

Measures of Production

The main problem in measuring productivity is *the problem of choosing a measure of the quantitative results of production.* It may be

(1) a physical unit (tons, meters, units of a product)
(2) a standard unit
(3) total production expressed in comparable prices
(4) commodity production, that is, production earmarked for sale by the enterprise, at comparable prices
(5) net production at comparable prices
(6) production expressed in terms of working time
(7) production expressed in terms of constant wages

The number of yardsticks that can be used for measuring labor productivity is substantial especially if the possibility of using measures of both variable and constant composition is considered.

The choice of a measure depends upon the nature of economic analysis and upon its subject (whether it is an enterprise, and if so, of what type, or an industry, a region, or the whole national economy).

In many cases the application of only one measure is insufficient, and two, three, or more measures have to be selected to throw light on the problem from different angles so that a comprehensive analysis of the dynamics of labor productivity can be made on that basis. There is no doubt that by using several measures and by a comparable analysis the dynamics of labor productivity can be better determined.

Total and Net Production Indexes

The total production index and the commodity production index are general statistical and economic indexes, and they do not always adequately reflect a real growth in production and labor productivity. This is because differences between total production indexes (or commodity production indexes) at two periods of time compared may be caused by (1) real growth (or a decrease in production), or (2) changes in the structure of production, including changes in material-absorption and the degree of cooperation in production. Changes in the structure of production in particular industries may cancel out for the whole economy within certain periods, and then the total production index (or the commodity production index) may show the actual growth in production and in labor productivity. However, since changes in the structure of production of the enterprise in a contemporary economy are not an exception but a rule, it is not correct to consider the total production index or the commodity production index as adequately measuring its actual dynamics of production or productivity of labor.[1]

1. Characteristic opinions of Soviet economists are worth quoting here. A. Tolkaczew writes that "for a proper appraisal of the operations of the enterprise it is necessary to work out methods of measuring production with regard to value and the productivity of labor, methods more progressive than the method of total production" (*Planowoje Chaziajstwo*, 1960, no. 12, p. 14). W. Pereslegin writes: "Many economists, and among them also the employees of the planning authorities, have often indicated that the total production index does not reflect the real size of production of the enterprise" (*ibid.*, p.19). Many similar utterances criticizing the use of total production index for measuring the growth of production and of labor productivity can be found in economic literature in the Soviet Union and in people's democracies.

The indexes of net production, or gross production, or the kind of net production index that the commodity production index becomes after deductions for materials and depreciation, or materials only, may under certain circumstances reflect the dynamics of actual production more correctly than the total production index. It should be remembered, however, that when the net production index is used, the picture may be distorted by changes in the product structure consisting in changes in the percentage of material and labor-consuming goods and also in changes in the percentage of goods with different ratios of profits to wages. The latter also affect total production, but their influence is much stronger on net production than on total production since the ratio of profit to net production is greater than the ratio of profit to total production.

The disadvantages of using different types of net production indexes for measuring growth in production and in labor productivity in certain enterprises are related to the fact that the volume of net production in certain enterprises may differ considerably from the contribution of these enterprises to national income. For instance, an enterprise may produce goods on which the margin of profit is small, and therefore its net production may be low, but it may contribute considerably to an increase in profits and net production in other enterprises which buy its products.

In consequence it can be stated that national income, as the sum of the net production of the enterprises, adequately reflects an increase in production in the whole national economy. However, the net production of particular enterprises does not always reflect the actual growth of production of these enterprises.

In a socialist economy, indexes determining the growth of production are important not only from a statistical point of view, but also because they affect the choice of goods to be produced. The application of the total production index (or the commodity production index) to measuring production growth may induce the enterprise to produce more material-consuming goods. And, on the other hand, the use of the net production index for measuring production growth may induce the enterprise to produce more labor-consuming goods, thus constituting an incentive limiting the development of cooperation among enterprises and limiting technical progress. The use of the net production index may also induce the enterprise to produce goods in which the ratio of profit to wages is high.

Therefore, neither total production, commodity production, nor net production, or its varieties can be used as the only measures of production

growth in a socialist economy, although they undoubtedly have to be calculated for statistical and planning purposes as well as for economic analysis.

A New Index of Productivity Growth

It is impossible to construct a perfect index of production growth under
the complex conditions of modern industrial production. It is only possible
to construct an index which—in addition to the total production index, the
commodity production index, and the net production index—would enable us
to analyze better, although only approximately, the actual growth of production. In a socialist economy, such an index should eliminate effectively
the influence of choosing the most "convenient" range of products for the
enterprise from the point of view of production statistics and should take
into account savings (or the lack of them) in the consumption of materials.

The new index of production growth should be based on total production calculated by "the enterprise method," since only production calculated
in this way comprises the whole range of production. However, the new
index cannot be based exclusively on net production or on weighted production increases in particular goods, since these measures omit a certain part
of production. Production growth indexes in capitalist countries, based on
weighted production increases of particular goods, are imperfect and often
misleading because they are based only on certain goods whose weights in
total production change, and they do not include other goods, especially
the new ones.

The new index of productive growth should be based on total production, providing an additional factor is introduced which would allow for
changes in material-absorption in the period under consideration as compared with the starting period.

The new index of production growth which I propose to call *the stabilized-
material-absorption index* is expressed by the following formula:

$$Y = \frac{P_{c_1} + (P_{g_1} \cdot M_0)}{P_{g_0}}$$

P_{c_1} = net production during the given period; P_{g_1} and P_{g_0} = total production during the given period and the base period; M_0 = the share of
materials in total production during the base period.

The above formula relates corrected total production during the given
period to total production during the base period. Corrected total production comprises net production during the given period and the materials

required for total production during this period if the degree of material-absorption (the share of materials in total production) were constant, that is, remained the same as in the base period.

The stabilized material-absorption index of production growth may also be presented by a transformed formula. Net production during the given period equals total production in this period minus materials used up in this period.

$$P_{c_1} = P_{g_1} - (P_{g_1} \cdot M_1)$$

$M_1 =$ the share of materials in total production during the given period.

Thus the stabilized material-absorption index of production growth will assume the following form:

$$Y = \frac{P_{g_1}[1 - (M_1 - M_0)]}{P_{g_0}}$$

This index may also be presented in the following form:

$$Y = \frac{\Sigma q_1 P_0}{\Sigma q_0 P_0} [1 - (M_1 - M_0)]$$

$P_0 =$ comparable prices.

If the degree of material-absorption (the share of materials in total production) is greater than it was during the base period, then the correction of total production during the given period consists in *reducing it* appropriately. And, on the other hand, if the degree of material-absorption is smaller than it was during the base period, the correction of total production during the given period consists in *increasing it* accordingly.

Suppose that the degree of material-absorption of total production during the base period amounted to 0.40, and during the given period it increased to 0.45. An increase in the degree of material-absorption may be caused either by an increase in the percentage of goods which are characterized by a high degree of material-absorption, or by increased unit costs of materials, or by both these factors. When the stabilized material-absorption index of production growth is used, total production during the period studied should be reduced in the above example by 5 per cent.

The increase in production calculated by the new index will be smaller than the increase calculated on the basis of the total production index but a little higher than the increase based on the net production index. This can be explained by the fact that the processing of *a greater amount* of materials by the enterprise should enter into the picture.

Let us suppose that during the period studied the material-absorption of total production has decreased from 0.40 to 0.35. A decrease in material-absorption may be caused either by a decrease in the percentage of products with a high degree of material-absorption or by a decrease in the amount of materials used up per unit of product (a decrease in unit material costs) or by both these factors together.

When the stabilized material-absorption index of production growth is used, total production in the above example should be increased by 5 per cent. The increase in production calculated by using the new index will be greater than the increase calculated on the basis of the total production index but smaller than that based on net production. This is explained by the fact that *a smaller* amount of materials processed by the enterprise should be taken into consideration.

A New Index of Labor Productivity

The new index of production growth can serve as a basis for a new index of labor productivity, which is expressed by the following formula:

$$Y = \frac{\Sigma \, q_1 P_0 [1 - (M_1 - M_0)]}{\Sigma \, T_1} \frac{\Sigma \, q_0 P_0}{\Sigma \, T_0}$$

T_0 and $T_1 =$ labor outlays during the base period and the given period.

As we know, none of the indexes now in use adequately presents the actual growth of labor productivity. This is because these indexes incorrectly reflect increases in production. A labor productivity index proposed by S. Strumilin and based on the "constant index" principle is designed to eliminate the influence of structural changes in production on the dynamics of labor productivity, but it has certain drawbacks. The problem of taking into consideration new products cannot be solved by his index, and it is necessary to show the number of products and the number of workers employed in producing them; this complicates not only the index itself but also its preparation. These drawbacks of the Strumilin index show why it has not been widely adopted. The method I propose goes basically in the same direction as the Strumilin index but takes into consideration new products as well as savings in raw materials.

The proposed method of analyzing production and labor productivity may also be used for comparisons of the level and growth of production and labor productivity in different enterprises and industries. In this case the average degree of material-absorption or the degree of material-absorption of a certain enterprise or industry should be accepted as a base.

The stabilized material-absorption indexes of production growth or of labor productivity are tools of analysis and approximations only and cannot adequately express this growth under all circumstances. It would be advisable to compare the results obtained with these indexes with those obtained with the total and net production indexes and other indexes. The differences between indexes should be a subject of statistical research and economic analysis.

CHAPTER 4

Measurement of Labor Productivity in Soviet Industry

G. I. Baklanov

Moscow Institute of Economics and Statistics

Statistical study of labor productivity is one of the most important sections of industrial statistics in the Soviet Union. It covers: measuring the level and dynamics of labor productivity and plan fulfillment, and determining and measuring the influence of various factors on labor productivity dynamics and plan fulfillment.

In peaceful economic competition with the most advanced capitalist countries our country will soon be foremost as the rates of development and the level of labor productivity grow in all branches of our national economy, especially the key industry branches.

In this study, we are only interested in unbiased data, since only unbiased data can help us reach our goal.

Industrial statistics in the Soviet Union use a system of indexes which make possible an extensive study of labor productivity. Most of these indexes are calculated on the basis of exhaustive information about the output produced and labor expended; the basic figures needed for calculating the labor productivity indexes are presented by industrial enterprises to statistical agencies in their reports on standard forms and on established dates.

Since the level of labor productivity is expressed by the ratio of output and the quantity of labor expended, it is necessary to establish, first of all,

how the volume of output is to be expressed, second, what group of workers should be counted in determining the level and dynamics of labor
productivity, and, third, in what unit of working time labor productivity
should be calculated.

The industrial statistics in the Soviet Union concerned with labor productivity deal with various groups of working people. There are, for example, workers directly engaged in the extractive industry or its processing in
the manufacturing industry—weavers, spinners, and so on—that is, a definite group of the main production workers. Average output per worker is
established for each such group. But the results of the labor of the principal
workers largely depend on the condition of equipment, the supply of materials, the cleanliness of the working premises, and so forth—in other words,
on the functions performed by auxiliary workers. In view of this, in a
shop and an industrial establishment as a whole, the labor productivity of
all workers is measured. Up to 1958 inclusively, the basic index of labor
productivity in an enterprise, a branch of industry, and industry as a whole
was the index of average output per one listed worker (including the principal and auxiliary workers). But it is possible and necessary to measure the
labor productivity of all persons employed in the main activity of industrial
enterprises since the process of industrial production is inconceivable without the participation of engineers and technicians, bookkeepers, clerks, service personnel, and other categories. As mechanization and automation develop, the distinction between the labor of workers and the labor of engineers and technicians is being increasingly diminished. On the other hand,
measurement of the labor productivity of all persons engaged in the basic
activity of an enterprise gives a fuller evaluation of the social productivity
of labor. Proceeding from these considerations, since 1959 our state plans and
statistical reports give an index of average output per employed person or,
more accurately, per employee of the industrial production personnel. This
includes all people working in the production shops, managerial personnel,
and people engaged in the warehouses and other services related to the main
activity of the enterprise. This listing does not include people engaged in
non-industrial services of the enterprise (clubs, housing facilities, kinder-
gartens, nurseries, and so on).

It is also necessary to mention the procedure used in determining the
number of employees to be counted in measuring labor productivity. Our
statistics do not take the number of employees on a selected date, but the
average number listed, or, as it is called, the average daily listed number.
(The listed number includes all regular, seasonal, and temporary employees

of an enterprise, those who reported for work on the given day, and those absent.) One system of calculating this index is used at all enterprises. For example, the index for the month is obtained by adding all the daily lists (including nonworking days, for which the list of the previous working day is taken) and dividing this sum by the number of calendar days.

For a month, such a system gives the full number of listed man-months; for a quarter, the full number of the listed man-quarters, and so on. This makes it possible to sum up the average listed number of employees at all enterprises because it eliminates double-counting.

Because our enterprises keep a systematic account of the time of the workers in man-days and man-hours, state statistical agencies are able to determine, in addition to the magnitude of the average monthly (quarterly, annual) output of workers, the magnitude of their average daily and hourly outputs. In the first case, the volume of output is divided by the number of man-days worked and, in the second case, by the number of man-hours worked.

Each of these indexes has its own economic significance. By calculating the average daily output for two periods we are able to establish how labor productivity has changed during the time of actual work. A comparison of the average daily output indexes for the two periods will reflect, moreover, the influence of the changed length of the working day; lastly, a comparison of the indexes of average monthly output for two months (or the average annual output for two years) will also reflect the influence of the change in the duration of the working month (or year). The longer the unit of working time taken, the more factors influence the level and dynamics of labor productivity.

On the basis of reports of enterprises, our industrial statistics are able to construct the system of interconnected indexes of labor productivity calculated for various categories of workers and various units of working time shown in Table 2.

The main index in our statistics is the average output per employee,

Table 2. System of interconnected indexes of Soviet labor productivity.

Average hourly output per worker	Average daily output per worker	Average monthly (annual) output per listed worker	Average monthly (annual) output per employed person
Average length of the working day (in hours)	Average number of days worked per month (year)	Share of workers in the total listed industrial personnel	

and the change in the average daily output per worker is the factor that determines the dynamics of this index.

The parallel study of the dynamics of average monthly output per listed employee and the average hourly output per worker has become particularly significant since all industrial workers and other employees have switched to a seven-hour working day, and underground workers in the key trades of the coal and mining industries to a six-hour day. This changeover was completed in 1960. Reduction of the working day was not supposed to, and actually did not, bring about a decline in the average monthly (annual) output per employee. This was achieved by a combination of factors (greater mechanization, better use of equipment, more rational placement of labor, and so on) directed toward raising average hourly output.

Average annual output per employed person in Soviet industry (1958 = 100) was 107 in 1959 and 113 in 1960.

In considering the index of labor productivity as an expression of the volume of output, three methods which determine three corresponding systems of measuring labor productivity are singled out: (1) measurement in physical terms, (2) measurement in terms of value, and (3) measurement in terms of labor expenditure. In our statistics, (2)—the value (or money) method—is the main one. Here are the advantages of the value method over the other two:

(*a*) It is possible to obtain general indexes of the volume of output and, hence, of labor productivity in the manufacture of the most diverse categories of goods, including both finished products and unfinished products (semi-manufactures and so-called incomplete production), and it also includes jobs of an industrial nature which do not result in new products (repair jobs, painting, tempering, drying, and so forth).

(*b*) It reveals not only the quantity of the goods produced, but also their quality, since in the evaluation of output a unit of goods of higher quality adds a greater magnitude to the total value than a unit of the same goods of lower quality.

(*c*) It makes it possible to obtain indexes of the volume of output and, hence, of labor productivity for all levels, beginning with the enterprise and ending with industry as a whole. This cannot be done by method 1; to do it by method 3 would require a radical reconstruction of the entire system of accounting and statistical reports.

Of the general system of value indexes used in our industrial statistics (gross turnover, gross output, commodity output, and net output), the most suitable index is gross output, inasmuch as the gross turnover of an enterprise contains elements of double-counting within the bounds of the enterprise; commodity output is not directly connected with the expenditure of labor in the reported period; while net output in some enterprises, in view of the specific features of price formation, is not counted at all.

For any group of enterprises (branches of industry, economic councils, industries of a union republic, industry as a whole in the USSR) the level of average gross output per employed person is established by adding the gross output of all enterprises in the given group, adding the average listed number of employees of the same enterprises, and dividing the first sum by the second. The level of labor productivity thus obtained is not of absolute but of relative significance. A comparison of the actual level for the reported period with the planned level makes it possible to judge the plan fulfillment for labor productivity. A comparison of the actual level with a similar level of any other period, taken as a base, expresses the dynamics of labor productivity.

The indexes of the dynamics of labor productivity (average gross output) in Soviet industry compared with 1940 (1940 = 100), calculated per employed person, were: 281 in 1959, and 295 in 1960; calculated per worker, 256 in 1959, and 269 in 1960. The higher growth rate of labor productivity per employed person is explained by the fact that during these years the proportion of workers in the total number of listed employees increased.

The general industrial index of labor productivity is not obtained by weighing branch indexes or other indexes, but rather by comparing directly the levels of average output; the data of both gross output and the number of employed persons cover all industrial enterprises and are based on the materials of the direct and complete accounting of the output and the employed personnel.

It should be noted that the possibility of dynamic comparisons of labor productivity levels is ensured in our statistics by the use of invariable (comparable) prices for calculating the gross output index. It goes without saying that these prices can be invariable only for a certain period, after which they have to be replaced by others, more correctly reflecting the correlation of separate categories of goods in the new conditions. Our industrial statistics have used the following as comparable prices: prices in 1912, prior to 1928/1929, between 1928/1929 and 1950, the prices of 1926/1927; between 1950 and 1956; the prices of January 1, 1952; since 1956 the wholesale prices of enterprises as of July 1, 1955. A study of the dynamics of the volume of output and the dynamics of labor productivity for a long period is done by joining the index number series arrived at on the basis of the various prices used as invariable prices.

The gross output of an industrial enterprise includes (in money terms):

(a) the finished articles produced during the given period, except those consumed at the enterprise itself for production purposes;

(b) semi-manufactures produced at the enterprise and delivered to other consumers;

(c) jobs of an industrial nature performed on orders outside the enterprise;

(d) changes in the stocks of semi-manufactures produced at the enterprise;

(e) changes in the stocks of tools, dies, and fixtures produced at the enterprise;

(f) change in the stocks of unfinished output.

For enterprises in some branches of industry our statistics allow some deviations from the generally accepted methods of calculating gross output and, hence, the level of labor productivity. For example, in sugar refineries, gross output includes the value of all the granulated sugar produced, as well as that processed into lump sugar; in enterprises of the fish industry, the value of fish is its own catch processed into fish products, and so forth. But it should be remembered that such deviations have occurred for a number of years, in view of which the relative indexes of the dynamics of output and labor productivity do not present a distorted picture. The overwhelming majority of our industrial enterprises (except engineering works, structural steel plants, and repair plants) do not include in gross output the difference between the value of the stocks of unfinished output at the end and the beginning of the period, which hardly exerts influence on the indexes of the dynamics of output and labor productivity.

The practice of calculating the dynamics of labor productivity, over the years, according to the single method described above, gives Soviet statisticians grounds for reasoning that this methodology gives a correct idea of the dynamics of labor productivity in industry. At the same time, our theoreticians and practical workers are striving for further improvement of the methodology of calculating the indexes of labor productivity with the aid of a money measure, specifically for enterprises in certain branches of industry.

In a number of branches of the manufacturing industry the value of raw materials comprises a big share of the total value of the output; moreover, the share of the value of raw materials varies considerably in the prices of different finished goods. When the assortment of output changes sharply, the magnitude of gross output per person may fluctuate greatly up or down, which will not always conform to the change in the labor productivity of the personnel. In view of this, our statistics have introduced a magnitude of the standard value of processing to characterize the plan fulfillment for labor productivity; this magnitude is the sum calculated on the basis of average standard outlays for the processing of the given item. Such calculations are already applied in the clothing and painting industries and will be introduced in other branches of industry as well. But besides this index of labor productivity, the average output per person employed is the single index for separate enterprises and for industry as a whole.

The absolute level of labor productivity cannot be expressed by the value method. This can be done only by the physical method, that is, measuring output in physical units (pieces, tons, meters, and so on). Our industrial statistics use the physical and conditional-physical method of measuring labor productivity in separate categories of production and in branches of industry (primarily extractive) with one kind of product.

For example, in the iron and steel industry, the indexes of output of rolled stock (without pipes and forgings from ingots) are calculated in tons per worker in the rolling mills; output of open-hearth steel is calculated in tons per worker in the open-hearth furnace departments; output of pig iron (in terms of merchant iron) is calculated in tons per worker in the blast furnace departments. The textile industry calculates output per man-hour in spinning (quantity of yarn in kilograms multiplied by the number of skeins —the thicker the yarn, the smaller the number) and in weaving (gray fabric figured in number of weft threads). In coal mining the average monthly output in tons per listed worker is figured for the industry as a whole and separately for open-cut mines and collieries. Other such examples of calculations in physical terms could be cited.

It should be noted that in our statistics the physical method supplements the value method but does not replace it. In most cases indexes of average output in physical terms are calculated per worker and not per person employed. Giving a very graphic index of the level of labor productivity, the physical method is limited in its application. First of all, it is limited by the bounds of production of goods of one kind with a comparatively brief production cycle. Specifically, it is impossible to express in physical terms the labor productivity of all workers in an engineering plant, even one producing machines of a single type. But even in a textile mill where the production cycle is much shorter, it is advisable to calculate the labor productivity in physical terms not of all workers taken together but of workers in separate categories of production (shops); otherwise, all conditions being equal, the output level of fabrics per worker in a spinning and weaving mill will always be underestimated as compared with the output level of fabrics in a weaving mill alone. Lastly, the use of the physical method usually boils down to expressing the quantity of output per unit of working time, regardless of quality.

The above comments do not negate the significance of the physical method of measuring labor productivity, which in our experience is used not only in certain categories of production, but also at separate production sections where it is often the only method.

Mention must be made of the indexes of labor expenditure per unit of output used in our statistics. While the level of labor productivity expressed in physical terms is the ratio of the number of units of output to the quantity of working time expended, the level of labor expended per unit of output represents an inverse magnitude—the ratio of the quantity of working time expended (usually figured in man-hours or in man-days) to the number of units of output. Many economists in industrial enterprises and the staff of a number of research institutes are giving this problem much attention.

Compared with any other method of measuring labor productivity, the method of expressing it through the actual labor expended per unit of output has the advantage of making it possible to analyze labor productivity at separate stages in the production of the given item. If the level of labor productivity is expressed by the quantity (or value) of output per worker (for one man-day or man-hour worked) it will not be possible to establish what part of this item was created by labor at the first, second, and third stages of manufacture, and so on. But by determining the total quantity of working time spent for the manufacture of a unit of output, we can establish what part of this time was expended at the various stages of manufacture.

Measurement of the labor expended per unit of output broadens the bounds of applying this method in comparison with the physical method. In this case it becomes fully possible to study labor productivity in the manufacture of an item which passes consecutive stages of production and has not only a short, but also a long, production cycle. Moreover, it is the existence of a number of stages in production that makes the use of this method especially valuable for analysis.

The Council for the Study of the Productive Forces (Academy of Sciences of the USSR), for example, has studied labor expenditure by stages and types of jobs in the timber industry of the Novosibirsk region, and the results were published in 1960 in a collection of articles edited by academician V. S. Nemchinov, "Labor Productivity in the Timber Industry."

A comparison of indexes of the actual expenditure of labor per unit of output for characterizing the dynamics of labor productivity is used in our industrial statistics for separate sections of production and the manufacture of diverse goods. The volume of output produced in the reported period is used, and, since the level of labor expenditure per unit of output is an inverse magnitude of the level of labor productivity, the index of labor productivity is calculated according to this formula:

$$\frac{\Sigma \, q_1 t_0}{\Sigma \, q_1 t_1}$$

in which q_1 is the quantity of output in the period under review and t_0 and t_1 are the expenditures of working time per unit of output in the base period and the reported period respectively. The difference between the numerator and denominator of the fraction expresses the quantity of labor saved owing to a rise in its productivity. The positive feature of such an index is that in calculating it the actual volume of output and actual labor expenditure are used—that is, no additional commensurates of output are employed.

Lastly, in manufacturing diverse goods and in the absence of prices for the output of some shops (for example, in machine shops of engineering plants) and in separate production sections, the dynamics of labor productivity is calculated by relating the number of various items to the labor expenditure stipulated by the norm for the manufacture of a unit of output:

$$\frac{\Sigma \, q_1 t_n}{\Sigma \, T_1} : \frac{\Sigma \, q_0 t_n}{\Sigma \, T_0}$$

Here q_1 and q_0 are the quantity of output in the reported and base periods, t_n is the labor expenditure per unit of output according to the established norm, while $\Sigma \, T_1$ and $\Sigma \, T_0$ are the total quantities of expended working time (or the average number of listed workers) correspondingly in the reported and base periods.

CHAPTER 5

Productivity Measurement for Economic Analysis

LEON GREENBERG

U.S. Department of Labor

This paper describes the current productivity measurement program of the U.S. Department of Labor's Bureau of Labor Statistics, presents information on recent productivity trends in the United States, and discusses several technical aspects of measurement problems. Each of these topics could be the subject of a separate paper, and obviously they can only be highlighted in this kind of review. However, some subjects are given more attention than others which have already been extensively covered in publications.

Our measurement program is primarily designed for economic analysis. The results of our work are used in connection with studies of economic growth, and evaluation of the progress of industry which stems from the combined effects of technological progress, increased capital per worker, and improved skills of management and workers. These broad objectives include the use of productivity measurement in connection with studies of employment and unemployment, the relationship of productivity, wages, and prices, the relationship of productivity to real earnings and standard of living, projections of Gross National Product, and others.

Basic Program

The current program of the Bureau of Labor Statistics includes the measurement of trends in output per man-hour for the economy, major sectors, and industries. Two concepts of output are used in these measures, both of which are well known to students of productivity measurement. One is the concept of Gross National Product. The other is physical output, based on the use of physical quantity data combined with a suitable system of weights.

Economy and sector measures. Our program of measures for the economy was begun a relatively short time ago. We published indexes of this type for the first time in 1958, and our first major publication in this area describing trends, methods, and sources of data, was issued in 1959.[1]

These measures include indexes of output per man-hour for the total private economy, agriculture, and nonagriculture beginning in 1909, and for manufacturing and nonmanufacturing beginning in 1947. Government is excluded for the usual reason, that the regularly published constant dollar estimates of the output of the government sector are based on wages and salaries and are inadequate for purposes of productivity measurement.[2]

The output components of the measures for the private economy, agriculture and nonagriculture are based on estimates of Gross National Product, in constant dollars, published regularly by the U.S. Department of Commerce.

Two labor input measures are used. One is based on payroll data collected from establishments. The other is based on information collected from individuals in a sample labor force survey of households. The establishment data refer, in concept, to total hours paid for. The labor force data refer to hours worked, that is, they exclude those hours on paid vacation, holidays, and sick leave. We would prefer, for most purposes of productivity analysis, to use the hours-worked estimates, but they are not available in any industry sector detail. Moreover, actual differences between the two measures are due to sampling, reporting, and other statistical errors, as well as to concept.

Constant dollar values of Gross National Product are obtained by deflat-

---

1. U.S. Department of Labor, *Trends in Output per Man-Hour in the Private Economy, 1909–1958,* BLS Bulletin No. 1249 (Washington, December 1959).
2. However, certain government enterprises whose activities involve the sale of a product or service are included with the private sector (for example, the postal service, Tennessee Valley Authority).

ing the components of current value GNP. The deflation is carried out in considerable detail for final demand categories of goods and services, although in many cases imputations and other types of estimates have to be used because of lack of appropriate price indexes.

Estimates of the trend of GNP originating in manufacturing are derived by the BLS, using the double deflation method. Dollar value of output and dollar value of materials and fuel input are deflated separately for more than 300 individual industries and industry groups. The resultant constant dollar values of inputs are subtracted from the constant dollar value of output, yielding a measure of constant dollar value added. These industry estimates are summed to arrive at a total for manufacturing. This measure is not exactly equivalent to GNP originating but is considered adequate for measuring trend, and benchmark adjustments are made (1954, for example) to levels indicated by data from National Income Accounts.

The estimate for nonmanufacturing is obtained as a residual by subtracting the derived manufacturing estimate from the nonagricultural totals of GNP.

Eventually, we hope to develop and publish estimates for other major sectors and industry groups, consistent with the major framework of Gross National Product. The Department of Commerce is working on estimates of GNP originating in various sectors, and when that work is completed we will use as much of it as we can. But this also depends on the availability of adequate data on labor input.

Meanwhile, some experimental work along these lines has been done by two of my colleagues in the BLS.[3] They derived estimates of real product for sectors of the economy using various kinds of available data. Most of these data were not in the form of the desired concept and had to be converted to estimates of GNP originating in the respective sector. Their indexes for the individual sectors were summed (using appropriate weights) to a GNP total and turned out to be quite close to the regularly published GNP series.

Industry estimates. The BLS methods of computing indexes of output per man-hour have been described rather extensively in various publications, and it is not necessary here to repeat the detailed procedure.[4] Suffice

3. Jack Alterman and Eva E. Jacobs, "Estimates of Real Product in the United States—By Industrial Sector, 1947–55," in *Output, Input and Productivity Measurement* (Princeton, 1961).
4. U.S. Department of Labor, *Trends in Output per Man-Hour and Man-Hours per Unit of Output—Manufacturing, 1939–53*, BLS Report No. 100 (Washington, 1955);

it to say that we use data on physical units of output, combined with unit man-hour weights when they are available or can be obtained. Frequently, they are not obtainable, and substitute weights are used—unit labor costs, unit value added or unit value.

In theory the use of different kinds of weights, for example, unit man-hours, or unit value, could yield substantially different indexes of output per man-hour, particularly in those cases in which unit values are established arbitrarily or to meet specific market conditions. It has been difficult to test this empirically because the various types of weights are usually not available industry-by-industry. However, we have made comparisons of weighted and unweighted indexes for a few industries and find that the results are not very far apart. Of course, this may not hold in all types of industries. We have also found that use of 1947 or 1954 product weights makes very little difference in many manufacturing industries, but substantial differences in a few industries suggest that the particular weighting scheme used may have a much greater effect in industries with a rapidly changing composite of goods or form of technology. It should also be noted that findings with regard to trends in one country may not be at all applicable to international comparisons of trends or levels of output per man-hour, where the composites of output and the weights for products (final or intermediate) between countries may be at considerable variance.

We have published indexes for 22 industries in mining, transportation, and manufacturing. Work is currently under way on about 10 more, and we hope to expand this list over the next few years.

In the past, the BLS indexes of output per man-hour for individual industries have been based on the man-hours of production and related workers. Since the war, however, because of the advanced stage of technology in U.S. industry, the so-called nonproduction workers (administrative, technical, clerical, and so forth) have increased as a proportion of total employment. In some industries this change has been quite marked. Consequently, we are now trying to develop indexes of output per man-hour of all employees to supplement those based on production worker man-hours only.

Man-Hours per Unit of Output in the Basic Steel Industry, 1939–55, BLS Bulletin No. 1200 (Washington, Sept. 1956); *Measurement of Productivity, Organization for European Economic Cooperation* (Paris, October 1952); *Methods of Labor Productivity Statistics* (Geneva, 1951).

Results of Measurement

Postwar trends. Output per man-hour in the private sector of the U.S. economy for the period 1947–60 rose at an average annual rate of 3.1 or 3.4 per cent, the lower figure being based on establishment man-hour data and the higher on labor force man-hour data.

The increase for major component sectors varied considerably. Probably the outstanding feature of the postwar increase was the striking performance of agriculture, where the average annual rate was about 6 per cent, with fewer and fewer farm workers required for expanding farm production. On the other hand, nonagricultural industries showed an average gain of 2.5 per cent based on establishment data and 2.8 per cent based on labor force data. Estimates for the manufacturing and total nonmanufacturing sectors for the period 1947–57 (the latest data) show increases of 2.9 and 2.3 per cent, respectively, based on BLS establishment man-hour data.

A shift of manpower resources from the agricultural to the nonagricultural sectors also contributed to the over-all rate of increase. If the effect of this man-hour shift from agriculture to nonagriculture is excluded the average annual rate of increase is reduced from 3.4 to 3.0 per cent. Shifts within nonagriculture (among 2-digit industry groups) worked in the opposite direction, but to a lesser degree.

It was also found that the year-to-year changes in the private economy varied considerably, ranging from practically zero to nearly 8 per cent; the gains were above average during periods of economic expansion and below average during periods of stable or declining economic activity. For example, during the recession years of 1954 and 1958, the increases in productivity were relatively small, whereas in the recovery phases of the business cycle in 1950, 1955, and more recently in 1959, the gains in output per man-hour have been better than average.

As might be expected, there has been wide variation in the trends in output per man-hour for individual industries.[5] For example, output per production worker man-hour has nearly tripled since 1947 in the synthetic fibers industry, doubled in both the anthracite and bituminous coal mining industries, increased by about 50 per cent (more or less) in the confection-

---

5. These are based on physical quantity data and on production worker man-hours and are not conceptually consistent with measures for the private economy and major sectors.

ery, canning, preserving and freezing, paper and pulp, and basic steel industries but gained very little in the coke, and glass containers industries.

Long-term trends. With this summary of the trends in output per man-hour for the postwar period as background, we can turn to the question of how the rate of increase in the postwar period compared with the increase for the long-run period since 1909, the first year for which adequate data are available.

Our estimates indicate that the rate of increase in output per man-hour between 1909 and 1960 was about 2.4 per cent, substantially lower than the postwar rate of increase.

Further investigation indicates that the long-run rate of increase was not evenly distributed over time. There were periods such as the decades starting in 1917 and 1933, and the postwar period, which showed substantially higher rates of increase than the long-term average. In this sense, the experience of the postwar period was not unique.

One way of analyzing the long-term trend is to try to fit a second degree curve to the data to see if there is any mathematical evidence of a change in the rate of increase in output per man-hour. This was done, and we found an acceleration in the rate of increase. Further analysis indicated that the acceleration resulted primarily from the spectacular performance of the agricultural sector of the economy, which averaged 2.2 per cent over the long run, but rose moderately in the earlier years, changed direction in the 1930's and again in the 1940's, and rose very rapidly through the postwar period, as already mentioned.

Output per man-hour in the nonagricultural sector increased at an average annual rate of about 2.1 per cent over the whole period 1909–60. However, the pattern of change was not the same as in agriculture. The gains in nonagriculture were quite small for the first decade, 1909–19, and averaged about 2.3 per cent for the period 1919–60, compared with the postwar average of 2.5–2.8 per cent.

The Effect of Inter-Industry Shifts

Some reference has already been made to the effect of inter-industry shifts on past trends in output per man-hour. In this connection, it is interesting to note that the long-term average increase of 2.4 per cent in the total private economy is higher than the 2.2 and 2.1 per cent gain in the components agriculture and nonagriculture. If the effect of the manpower shift from relatively low-productivity agriculture to relatively high-productivity nonagriculture is removed, the increase for the total private economy is also 2.1 per cent.[6]

Thus far, shifts of manpower resources from agriculture and among industry groups seem to have contributed to the rise in output per man-hour in the United States economy during the postwar period, as well as for the long run. To what degree and for how long this positive effect will continue is not certain. It is not anticipated that the positive effect will be reversed during the next decade, although it may be moderated.

In economies which are undergoing rapid change in various parts of the world, inter-industry shifts may have a very great effect on rates of productivity change for the economy or for major sectors. The shifts for example from agriculture to nonagriculture, from cottage industries to large-scale industries, would undoubtedly contribute substantially to the over-all level and rate of increase of productivity. The question of the effect of shifts is, therefore, important and deserves some attention.

The preceding discussion of the effect of inter-industry shifts has been in terms of the shift of manpower from one sector to another, and this is appropriate to those concerned with labor force analysis and manpower allocation. However, changes in the structure of the economy are frequently discussed in the context of change in the structure of demand, that is, in terms of shifts in relative output of industries. In fact, in analyzing the relationship of productivity and changes in structure of the economy to economic growth it may be quite useful to examine the influence of both kinds of shifts, that is, shifts in demand and shifts in employment.

In trying to measure the effect of these shifts, a simple technique is to combine the output per man-hour indexes for the individual sectors with constant output or man-hour weights. Since the relative proportions of the sectors are held constant, the resultant productivity measure is one which is not affected by shifts.

But "constancy" can also take several forms. Output or man-hours can be held constant as of a base year, a current year, or an average period of years. This is the familiar Laspeyres-Paasche index number problem. Thus, it is possible to have at least four types of measures of productivity which are not affected by shift: output proportions constant or man-hour proportions constant, and each in terms of base year or current year proportions.

We have made such computations for the agriculture-nonagriculture shift for the period 1947–60. There is an important difference depending on

6. This is not intended to detract from the over-all gain. The shift effect is also a reflection of technological progress.

whether output or man-hours are held constant. If output is held constant, there is only a slight effect—the 1947–60 average rate of 3.4 per cent is reduced to 3.2 per cent. Holding the man-hours constant, however, reduces the average annual change from 3.4 to about 3.0 per cent, as mentioned earlier. The choice of base year (1947) or current year (1960) proportions made practically no difference—at most 0.1 of a percentage point.

These calculations indicate that the shift in manpower was much more important, in its effect on productivity, than the shift in relative output. They do not imply that there was no change in relative output.

There are actually three components of the over-all change in output per man-hour: (1) Change in productivity of the component sectors. (2) Shift in relative importance of the sectors (measured by output or by man-hours). The shift effect can be measured directly, by holding the sector levels of output per man-hour constant and applying them as weights to the sector changes in output or man-hours. This technique yields an estimate of shift effect which when added to the net figure obtained in 1 does not equal the total productivity change. (3) The difference is the interaction between change in productivity of the sectors and change in relative importance of the sectors.[7]

There are different opinions on how to handle this residual—allocate it to each of the other components on a weighted or 50–50 basis, allocate it completely to the shift effect, or retain it as a separate statistic.

Another technique for removing the effect of shifts is to work directly with the real product per man-hour ratio. In this event, the denominator, man-hours, is broken down by industry and recombined with value added weights. If base-year value-added weights are used, the result is equivalent to combining industry productivity measures with current year man-hour weights, and vice versa. This technique is useful where annual productivity estimates for the industry components are not available.

Problems of Measurement and Application

The deficiencies in data required for productivity measurement are not unique to the United States. Most countries have similar statistical problems

7. Karl Borch, "Causes of Increase in National Productivity," in *Productivity Measurement Review*, no. 7, November 1956. European Productivity Agency; Technical Appendix to article by Harlow D. Osborne and Joseph Epstein, "Corporate Profits Since World War II," in *Survey of Current Business* (Washington, January 1956); Irving H. Siegel, *Concepts and Measurement of Production and Productivity* (Washington, 1952).

in the development of production and productivity estimates, although the degrees of difficulty may vary. This subject has been covered extensively in existing literature,[8] but it may be advisable to restate briefly some of the more important problems.

Problems of measurement.

(1) Output and man-hour data are sometimes inadequate or provide only partial coverage for some industries or categories. In some cases, price data needed for deflating the value of output are inadequate because of lack of coverage or the absence of weights appropriate to the requirements of the deflation procedure.

(2) Existing data and techniques do not provide for a full accounting of the continuing changes in the quality of goods and services produced. To a limited extent, identifiable changes in product specifications are taken into account in the price and output indexes. In other instances, quality change is so intangible that it cannot be measured with existent techniques.

(3) There may be problems of consistency and comparability between the data used to estimate output and those used to estimate labor input. These tend to occur most often at finer levels of industry detail, but are minimized at higher levels of aggregation.

(4) For many activities, for example, services, finance, research, and nonprofit institutions that do not have directly measured products, indirect and rough techniques of estimation have to be used which yield measures that are conceptually obscure. In general, the methods used to estimate output in these areas tend to understate gains in production and output per man-hour.

(5) Changes in plant or industry integration may affect statistics of output and labor input in different ways and thus distort the estimates of productivity change.

(6) Limited data are available on the man-hours of supervisory, administrative, research, and other "nonproduction" workers.

(7) Although the subject of this paper (and of the conference) is labor productivity, I should like to say a few words about the problems of measurement of capital productivity. Conceptually, there is the question of whether capital stock or capital used should be used for the denominator. Statistically there are problems of valuation; deflation life expectancy tables are frequently old and out of date; book values may be affected by variabil-

8. Leon Greenberg, "Data Available for the Measurement of Output per Man-Hour," in *Output, Input and Productivity Measurement* (Princeton, 1961). See also publications listed in footnote 4.

ity in accounting practices and changes in tax laws; price data for deflation are often inadequate or unavailable.

A leading expert in the field summarizes the problems of capital measurement in this way: "there is hardly a subject in which the gap between what we ought to know and what we do know is so serious, considering the importance of the missing data for economic theory and public policy, as in the field of investment and capital stock." [9]

Application of productivity data. In view of the deficiencies and limitations in some of the basic data needed for productivity measurement, it is appropriate to ask, "How important are they?" Unquestionably, in some cases the output and input data are so poor that measures of productivity may be quite meaningless. But at other times, despite the data deficiencies, it may be possible to derive reasonably adequate indicators of productivity change. For example, we have found in a few cases that a carefully weighted index shows a trend which differs from an unweighted index by only a few percentage points (by less than 5 per cent when measured over a period of several years). I have already indicated that in many industries in manufacturing (based on unpublished estimates) the use of 1947 or 1954 weights makes little or no difference in trend (but a substantial difference in some). The possible extent of changes in industry integration can be tested—although not proved—by examining ratios of material costs to value of output, in current and constant dollars.

The need for precision in a productivity index depends partly on its purpose. Definitions, weighting, coverage, adequacy of price deflators, and so forth, may be extremely important in international comparisons because of wide variation in structure of industries, changes in product mix, price trends and other factors. Similarly, within an economy, attention must be given to the possibility of rapid changes and the extent to which they are captured by existing statistical data. If productivity measures are to be used in connection with wage and price analysis, a higher degree of precision may be required than for other broader types of analysis. In addition, consistency of concept and formulation between various kinds of measures should also be observed.

For some types of economic analysis, it seems to me that cruder measures of productivity may be acceptable. If one industry is estimated to have a productivity gain of 10 points and another industry a gain of 100 points,

9. Raymond Goldsmith, "Capital Investment and Capacity—Discussion" in *The American Economic Review,* Papers and Proceedings of the 70th Annual Meeting of the American Economic Association, December 1957.

does it matter for broad comparisons that both estimates may be in error by 20 per cent? One industry has clearly had a much higher gain than the other. In other words, it may be useful for analysis merely to group the industries by high, low, or average productivity change. For example, if one is interested in determining whether there is a general relationship, among industries, between productivity change and employment change, a high degree of precision may not be essential. Frequently, the data may be good enough to determine whether a high or low relationship exists.

In short, decisions as to the usefulness of productivity indexes should be based not only on their statistical limitations but also on their purpose. In any case, when indexes or rougher indicators are published they should be carefully labeled and accompanied by a statement which provides the user with knowledge of their limitations.

Other Programs

The Bureau of Labor Statistics also engages in other measurement programs which may be of interest not only because of their substantive content but also because of their technical features. One which I should like to mention is concerned with individual worker performance; the other deals with labor requirements in construction.

The U.S. Department of Labor has been concerned with employment problems of older workers and has devoted great efforts to improve their employment opportunities. As part of this effort we conducted several studies to measure the relative work performance of older and younger workers under actual job conditions.[10] Data were obtained for individual workers from plant records on output and hours worked.

In this study it was important that the age factor be isolated from the many other factors which might affect performance on the job. We could not combine the absolute performance figures (output per man-hour) of individual workers because they would be affected by many factors other than age. So workers were classified into groups by plant where employed, sex, specific occupation, and length of experience. It was only after this careful grouping that the workers were divided into six age classes. The

10. U.S. Department of Labor, *Job Performance and Age,* Bulletin No. 1203 (Washington, 1956); *Comparative Job Performance and Age (manufacturing plants),* Bulletin No. 1223, 1957; *Comparative Job Performance and Age, Office Workers,* Bulletin No. 1273, 1960. Also summarized in *Monthly Labor Review* issues of December 1956, December 1957, and January 1960.

performance of each worker (output per man-hour) was then related to the average performance of the age class thirty-five to forty-four in each group. These ratios or indexes were then combined to obtain averages for larger groupings, using a complex weighting system based on number of workers in each age group and in each occupation.

The studies showed that, in general, the average performance did not vary greatly between age groups. They also showed great variability in individual worker performance and, in this respect, emphasized the importance of evaluating an employee's worth on the basis of his individual qualifications.

The other program is concerned with labor requirements in various types of construction such as schools, highways, public buildings, and housing. The program covers both the on-site labor requirements and the total labor required to produce the various construction materials used in construction. We obtain on-site labor requirements and materials used directly from contractors' records. The materials list is converted into labor required at the last manufacturing stage, and then carried back to labor required in other parts of the economy for processing, distribution, and extraction. For this last phase, we use the input-output matrix developed by the BLS.

This represents one of the uses made of the BLS input-output matrix as part of our work in productivity measurement and analysis. The input-output matrix is also used as the basic weighting structure in developing the price indexes for deflating current values of outputs and inputs in deriving the net output measure for manufacturing.

The input-output matrix is also used in analyzing the impact of foreign trade on domestic employment, covering direct and indirect employment.

The current work of the Department of Commerce, Office of Business Economics, on a new input-output matrix for the United States will provide the basis for introducing more current input-output relationships in our own analytical work.

CHAPTER 6

The Concept of Social Productivity
of Labor and Elementary Methods
# of Measuring It

ZDENEK TLUSTY

Czechoslovak Academy of Sciences

Among the problems discussed in socialist countries in recent years, the most significant is the methodology of measuring so-called social labor productivity. This should cover not only changes in the consumption of live labor in the making of a product in a given sector of production but should also show the changes in the consumption of embodied labor.

Most of the methods used currently are based on the quantitative expression of labor productivity as a relation of Q/T, (1), where Q is the quantity of use values of the gross product, and T is the quantity of live labor expended in the production of Q in the sector of production under examination. Some economists and statisticians have objected to this method, stating that it does not express the actual increase in labor productivity, because it does not measure changes in the consumption of embodied labor. They propose a change of methodology. We knew for instance the proposals of academician S. G. Strumilin and others, who suggest measuring the change in labor productivity according to the following relationship:[1]

$$\frac{Q_1}{T_{v_1} + T_{c_1}} : \frac{Q_0}{T_{v_0} + T_{c_0}} \qquad (2)$$

1. The symbol o and 1 mark the base (o) and given (1) periods.

where the denominator shows not only live labor T_v, but also total labor including the embodied labor T_c.

This has brought about a number of objections. Many critics pointed out that embodied labor, from the economic point of view, is nonproductive labor. It creates neither labor value nor use value and therefore should not be included in relation (2). This general criticism is one-sided and therefore not accurate.

Relation (2) doubtlessly has an economic significance, but it cannot be applied in measuring changes in the productivity of the labor exerted in a specific sector of production. Measuring labor productivity in an individual sector (in steel mills, ore mines, the machine industry, and so forth) always applies to the effectiveness of the actual work (the producing of steel, the mining of iron ore, and the like). However, relation (2) also measures the effectiveness of labor used in those branches of production supplying materials as well as the effectiveness of embodied labor T_c used in the production of output Q. This simple fact shows that relation (2) shows the effectiveness and labor productivity, but that it is the effectiveness of labor exerted on the product—in our case steel, ore, machinery, and so forth—in all the involved sectors of social production. It follows that relation (2) has a different economic meaning for the single participating sectors of social production on the one hand and for the general production process where it is most applicable on the other.

Similarly, we can deal with the suggestions to measure the changes in social labor productivity on the basis of changes in the labor value of a product, or rather its aspects—on the basis of changes in costs of production or current prices, for example. In this instance there are further shortcomings resulting from the disparity between forms of labor value and real social labor time.

Neither relation (1) nor relation (2) thus meets the requirements of measuring social labor productivity in the individual stages of social production. On the other hand, it is indisputable that both these forms characterize certain aspects of labor productivity and show its changes. This is in keeping with the need to create a system of basic quantitative expressions of labor productivity. The question of a proper measure cannot be considered as a problem of constructing a single universal index, but of setting up a fundamental system of indexes, and of determining their economic nature and interdependence. The basic system of indexes then has to be made concrete according to specific conditions of the various levels and sectors of social production and in accord with practical requirements and the possibilities of quantification.

We shall therefore concentrate on two fundamental questions:

1. Substantiating the basic quantitative expressions of labor productivity.
2. Defining the indexes of social labor productivity from the point of view of the various stages of social production.

Productivity of Labor, Factors Affecting Its Growth, Possibilities of Its Quantitative Expression

The definition of labor productivity is closely linked to the idea of productive labor as a socially useful activity of man, characterized by the creation of material use values—including transformation, necessary storage, and transportation. In this paper we analyze labor productivity as the quantitative side of productive work. We therefore define it as the effective and fruitful result of productive labor, and we measure it by its product.

Economic statistics usually use the index $Q/T = v$, referred to earlier, to express the characteristics of labor productivity. Of similar significance is the inverse of labor productivity, $T/Q = t$, that is, the product's laboriousness,[2] specifying for a given sector over a given period the number of units of work time necessary for its production.

For measuring changes in labor productivity and its dynamics, a simple comparative calculation of the absolute level of productivity v_1/v_0 or of labor input t_0/t_1 might seem to be satisfactory. Most of the currently used methods are based on this premise. In a more detailed analysis, we find that these methods leave out some important considerations.

We first examine how labor productivity increases in individual sectors of production.

The production process, generally speaking, is the active combination of human labor and the means of work by which human labor transforms the work objects into use value.[3] The entire history of the development of social

2. "Laboriousness" might have been translated as "labor input" (Editor's note).
3. Three terms should be explained for Western readers. "Objects of work," *predmety truda,* refer to original materials in their natural form which are to be transformed in the production process. "Means of work," *sredstva truda,* refer to those material things which are used for transforming the objects of work (machines, factory buildings, and so forth). Finally, "means of production," *sredstva proizuodstva,* includes both the "means of work" and the "objects of work" (Editor's note).

production shows how human labor equips itself with a continually increasing quantity of improved means of work. Therefore, a unit of human labor brings into motion not only these improved means of work but also a greater number of objects of work—raw materials, other materials, power, and so forth. Thus, the quantity of the means of production continually increases.

Using only a rough model for a schematic illustration, we can express the result of the productive effects of human labor on the object of work with the help of means of work—the gross volume of production (Q) by the equation

$$Q = 1/m \cdot K \cdot T. \tag{3}$$

where $m = M/Q$ is the quantity of the means of work (M) used for the production of one production unit

$K = M/T$ is the degree to which live labor is equipped with means of work (M), T being the amount of live labor.

As shown in relation (3), total production depends upon the following factors: The amount of live labor T; the ratio K, which may be considered an indirect indicator of the potential level of labor productivity; and finally the amount of work means used for a unit of output, m, indicating the degree of effectiveness in the use of technological development.

For measuring labor productivity, another dependence should be noted which is obvious in relation (3). With the same amount of live labor (T) expended in production, the volume of production increases, and thus the productivity of live labor increases under the following conditions:

(a) A unit of live labor uses the same quantity of work means ($K_1 = K_0$) which are more effective ($m_1 < m_0$);

(b) A unit of live labor puts into operation a greater number of work means ($K_1 > K_0$) of the same effectivity ($m_1 = m_0$);

(c) A combination of (a) and (b) takes places; or even a drop in ratio K or in the effectiveness of work means—, but resulting in a net positive effect.

In relation to the technological development—as it affects the means of work—the dependence of labor productivity on the above factors is expressed by the relation:[4]

4. The level of labor productivity naturally does not only depend upon the potential conditions which are offered by technical development. An important role is played by the full exploitation of technical development which, to a great extent, depends

$$v = \mathrm{I}/m \cdot \mathrm{K} \tag{4}$$

A number of more or less measured partial factors, not excluded but only included by implication in formula (4) also influence the level of labor productivity and its changes. These are factors which function in the sphere of manpower, work objects, organization of the work process on the level of the enterprise as well as on a larger, social scale, and in the sphere of natural conditions.

Nevertheless, ratio (4) reflects the most important factor in the long-run increase of labor productivity: the better equipping of human labor with a growing amount of more effective means of work.

From the social point of view, this means that in some sectors of production as compared to others, a greater or lesser amount of work is expended on the factors which increase labor productivity. The saving of live labor attained in the various production sectors by increasing labor productivity does not represent, from the social point of view, an absolute saving in work time. The saving can be higher or lower, depending on the changes in the amount of embodied labor used in the production of a given product.

The foregoing conclusions are also confirmed by data obtained from Czechoslovak industry. The high rate of increase of labor productivity in our industry during the first five-year plan—an annual average of 11.5 per cent per workman—was achieved mainly by a more complete exploitation of the existing technique, particularly by the full use of reserves resulting from the socialization of industry, by the utilization and concentration of capacities, by the elimination of unproductive small-scale production, by strengthening the work morale which was badly affected by the war, by starting socialist emulation, and so forth.

In 1953–57 the amount of short-term, easily used reserves dropped, and the annual rate of the increase in labor productivity decreased to 5.7 per cent per workman. This was caused by the lack of new equipment and the lack of more perfected means of work. The increase in the amount of necessary equipment, works means, and electrical power, achieved in the following years, as well as the draft proposal of the third five-year plan prove that improved equipment and power represent a source for the growth of

---

on the social relations in production. These relations stimulate, and as is known, call forward or hinder technological development. In this connection the influence of the rate of the industrial production increase manifests itself here, because it provides for the constant, rapid and mass-scale equipment of production by the most perfect technical equipment. This again has its effect on the high rate of the increase of production.

productivity, and this can[5] rapidly increase under our conditions. This is illustrated by Table 3.

The increase in labor productivity in industry, secured by the growing

Table 3. Growth of labor productivity in Czechoslovak industry under three 5-year plans.

Means	1948–1952 (%)	Yearly[a] average	1952–1957 (%)	Yearly average	1960–1965 (%)	Yearly average
Labor productivity of workers (v)	154.4	13.60	131.8	6.35	140.7	8.14
Equipment of workers						
with basic funds (K)	101.3	0.33	117.4	3.48	134.6	6.92
machine funds	109.8	2.45	125.8	5.16	144.4	8.88
electrical power	117.2	4.30	135.3	7.06	143.2	8.64
Ratio of increase in equipment of workers to the increase in productivity of labor (m)						
in total basic funds	65.6	−8.60	89.1	−2.18	95.7	−0.86
machine funds	71.1	−7.23	95.4	−0.92	102.6	0.52
electrical power	75.9	−6.03	102.6	0.52	101.8	0.36

a. Yearly average is the arithmetic average.

amount of work means (K) and electric power, was caused and causes changes in material labor, shown by the means of work per unit of industrial production. The indexes of labor productivity construed on the basis of relation (1) do not reflect these changes in the social consumption of labor and their effects on this most important factor in the increase of the social labor productivity in industry.

This not only concerns the effectiveness and the changes in the consumption of work means, but, at the present time, a very active role is also being played by the work objects in production. This is due mostly to the chemical industry which today supplies raw materials and other materials, the quality of which usually exceeds the original "classic" materials. This makes it possible to decrease the laboriousness of processing and the use of less costly means of work. In addition, artificial materials usually require less social labor than the classic materials which are replaced. Here, too, technical development manifests itself as a significant factor for increasing labor productivity. But these changes in the consumption of social work time are also not reflected in relation (1).

5. Data from M. Pick, "The preconditions for the increase of the productivity of labor and the cutting down of the work time," *Prace,* vol. 112, p. 18.

Since an increase in labor productivity brings about changes in both the consumption of live labor and of embodied labor per product in individual production sectors, corresponding types of indexes must be found. Indexes of type (1) cannot be blamed for not reflecting this aspect of labor productivity. Neither can the indexes of type (2) be blamed if they cannot be used for measurement in individual production sectors, as long as they can express the changes in the total consumption of social labor time expended per product in the entire production process.

If we project the foregoing considerations into the methodology of measuring labor productivity, we can construct three basic types of indexes:

(a) indexes of the productivity of live labor, showing only the changes in the consumption of live labor expended on the product in the examined stage of social production;

(b) indexes of the social productivity of labor, showing the changes in the consumption of live and embodied labor, used on the product in the examined stage of social production;

(c) an index of the productivity of the total labor, which also acts as an index of social labor productivity, expressing the changes in the consumption of live and embodied labor used on the product during the entire process in all stages of social production.

Let us now look briefly at the most important characteristics of these indexes.

Measuring the productivity of live labor. Methods of measuring the productivity of live labor are based on the relation (1), that is, changes in the amount of gross product Q per unit of live labor T, or the inverse of relation (2), the number of units of live labor necessary for the gross product on the production level over the examined period. Not considering certain practical problems, notably difficulties in calculation, this method is very straightforward for a homogeneous output. However, a whole series of technical and theoretical problems arise in measuring the average productivity of live labor for the heterogeneous output of a group of production sectors.

Theoretically, the best method for measuring real changes in the expenditure of live labor in the total output of those sectors under investigation is that in which aggregation is made in terms of the average laboriousness of the various types of products. Proceeding from the laboriousness in the base period (t_0), our index for productivity of live labor is

$$\frac{\Sigma\, Q_1 t_0}{\Sigma\, Q_0 t_0} : \frac{\Sigma\, T_1}{\Sigma\, T_0} = \frac{\Sigma\, Q_1 t_0}{\Sigma\, Q_1 t_1} \qquad Qt = T \qquad (5)$$

The index on the right side of the equation expresses the volume of live labor expended in the individual production sectors with heterogeneous production. In using laboriousness coefficients for the production of the base period (t_0), we get the volume of live labor expended on the volume and structure of a heterogeneous production of the current period (Q_1) in the base and given periods. (In using coefficients of laboriousness of the current period t_1 we would commensurate the work time expended on the structure and volume of production over the base period Q_0.)

In practice, we do not have such a detailed record of the work time expended, therefore, we have to use substitute coefficients. In the majority of cases we use prices

$$\frac{\Sigma Q_1 p}{\Sigma Q_0 p} : \frac{\Sigma T_1}{\Sigma T_0} \tag{6}$$

Theoretically it can be proven that the use of prices as a measure of heterogeneous production is substantiated in measuring labor productivity under certain conditions. If we use constant and unchanging prices for the same types of products (as is the general practice in socialist countries), in ideal cases we reach the same results as would be the case with the above laboriousness index, if: (*a*) there is an unchanging structure of the heterogeneous production—as, for example, a single rate of growth for the various types of production; (*b*) the price relationships of the individual types of products correspond to the relationships of the labor inputs of these products ($t = k \cdot p$; $p = $ price, $k = $ constant proportion).

Although the second instance is economically unreal, the first gives us sufficient bases for conforming results of measurements founded on the laboriousness of production or on the prices of production.

On the above basis, we can conclude that a distortion of the dynamics of the productivity of live labor using price measurements is dependent upon the variability of the relationship of laboriousness and prices of individual products, and upon the variability of the increase in the production of individual products.[6]

6. If the necessary data are available, the degree of distortion can be figured out on the basis of the relation

$$I_t : I_p = 1 + r_{i_q} \cdot t_0/p \cdot V_{i_q} \cdot V_{t_0/p}$$

where I_t is the index of the productivity of labor, where the coefficient of summing-up a heterogeneous production is the laboriousness,

I_p is the index of the productivity of labor, where the coefficient of summing-up a heterogeneous production is the price,

$r_{i_q} \cdot t_0/p$ is the coefficient of correlation,

But calculations as well as practical application show that a considerable distortion usually takes place only in extreme cases under very unfavorable combinations of conditions (*a*) and (*b*). In addition to this, in larger computations it can be expected that the deviations will compensate each other to a certain extent. The variability of the rate of increase in production, particularly for aggregated production sectors, is not very considerable.

Therefore, the use of price indicators of production for measuring the productivity of live labor on a large national economy scale is substantiated. Price indicators of production can, in many cases, also be used on a lower level. In those cases, where the measuring would be distorted—a greater disturbance of conditions (*a*) and (*b*)—it is necessary to select a more suitable type of coefficient for the heterogeneous production. But even for ratios other than those expressed in prices, the above-mentioned relationships apply. For these reasons socialist countries dedicate such great attention to the working out of differentiated methods of measuring labor productivity in accordance with the specific conditions existing in the production sectors being measured.

The problems involved in using fixed price values for measuring labor productivity is further complicated by the fact that these production indicators are valued in prices of a varying specific structure. It is not a simple evaluation of products by prices. These problems have to be analyzed separately. In our paper, we can only point out this necessity.

Measuring the social productivity of labor at a stage of production. The methodology of measuring social labor productivity, which expresses changes in the expenditure of live and embodied labor expended on the product at a given level of production, can be deduced from the basic index of the dynamics of the productivity of live labor t_0/t_1 (if we take the indirect expression). The savings of live labor $(t_0 - t_1)$ has to be corrected by a higher, or, in a favorable case, by a lower consumption of labor embodied in the means of production, expended on the given product in the examined sector of production. As has already been demonstrated, the saving or the higher consumption of production means per unit of output represents a proportional amount of live labor expended in those sectors supplying the means of production. The higher consumption of production means have to be,

---

V_{i_q} is the variable coefficient of the rate of the increase in production of the individual types of products,

$V_{t_0/p}$ is the variable coefficient of the ratio of laboriousness and the price of the products.

at the same time, reproduced in the supplying sectors for a continuous reproduction process. On the other hand, a lower consumption of production means decreases the demands on production and manifests itself in a decrease in the rate of employment for the same volume of final production.

In constructing an index of social labor productivity, that work time which increases or decreases the saving of live labor must be included in one of the quantities of the laboriousness of production (t_0, t_1). This must be done in such a manner that their difference will indicate socially pure saving of work time. Since the basis of the quotient of laboriousness is production in the current period, from a statistical point of view it is correct to include this saving in the numerator of the index.

The dynamics of labor productivity including calculations of changes in the consumption of embodied labor in individual cases is expressed by index (7),[7]

$$\frac{t_0 + (c_0 - c_1')}{t_1} \tag{7}$$

where c_0 is the amount of embodied labor per product in the base period expressed in units of work time (corresponds to the consumption of means of production per product in the base period), and

c_1' is the amount of embodied labor per product in the current period, expressed in fixed units of work time in the base period—thus the symbol (′)—in order to eliminate the changes in the quantity of labor embodied in the means of production, brought about by the increase in labor productivity in the sectors supplying the means of production.

Index (7) can be transferred into a formula, which has the necessary features for practical application

$$\frac{t_0 + (c_0 - c_1')}{t_0} : \frac{t_1}{t_0} \tag{8}$$

7. This relation can be derived also from the quantitative characteristic of the economic law of the perpetual increase in labor productivity, according to which the consumption of work time—live and embodied labor—per unit of production on the basis of the perpetual development and perfection of technique, technology and organization of production, by increasing the cultural and technical standard and the production qualification of the workers and the effective exploitation of all means of production and live labor, continuously decreases. This perpetual decrease is expressed by the disparity

$$c_0 + t_0 > c_1 + t_1$$

If we eliminate in c_1 the changes resulting from the increase in labor productivity in the supplying sectors, we obtain the quantity c_1' for the measuring of the productivity of labor at the examined stage and after transferring it to the left side of the

The quantity in the numerator of first relationship corresponds to the share of the physical volume of net production, which pertains to a product in the current period, the quantity in the denominator corresponds to the share of net production per product in the base period. The quantity of net production is expressed indirectly, in constant units of work time. Because the extensive records of the social costs of production in units of work time do not exist in practical use, it is necessary to replace the constant units of laboriousness by a value, specifically by fixed prices. The second ratio in the index expresses the changes in the volume of work time, of live labor expended on the product over the examined sector.

Assuming that the quantity $(c_0 + t_0)$ equals the price of the product in the base period, our practice of fixed prices makes it possible to express the index (8) as the index of labor productivity based on the physical volume of net production expressed in fixed prices.

$$\frac{\Sigma Q_1(t_0 + c_0) - \Sigma Q_1 c_1'}{\Sigma Q_0(t_0 + c_0) - \Sigma Q_0 c_0} \div \frac{\Sigma Q_1 t_1}{\Sigma Q_0 t_0} = \frac{\Sigma Q_1 P - \Sigma C_1'}{\Sigma T_1}$$

Therefore index (8) may be transformed to

$$\frac{\Sigma Q_1 P - \Sigma C_1'}{T_1} \div \frac{\Sigma Q_0 P - \Sigma C_0}{T_0}$$

where $Qt = T$ is the amount of live labor

C_1 is the consumption of means of production for the current period evaluated in fixed prices

C_0 is the consumption of means of production for the production of the base period evaluated in fixed prices.

Indexes (8) and (9) also express the requirements of measuring labor productivity for the formation of prices. The transition from index (8) to index (9) is theoretically justified only if the fixed prices of production correspond to the value, for example, the socially necessary costs of work time in the base period (o). With a change in the structure of production, any sort of deviation from the value of the fixed base period prices, in their absolute size or in the structure of their components, gives rise to distortion in the measurement of the real physical level of net production and the social labor productivity.

From the above analysis we can conclude that measurement of social labor productivity, including changes in the structure of live and embodied labor, can only be based on the physical volume of the net product.[8] Thus

disparity and by dividing both sides of the disparity by the quantity t_1 we obtain index (7).

8. To be thorough, it is necessary to note that this requirement is not met by such a method of calculation of the net production, which is used to ascertain the sampling

the social changes in the effectivity of labor, caused by technical progress and the related changes in the ratio of live to embodied labor, can be expressed in the individual sectors of social production.

At the present time the index of social labor productivity in the USSR is officially being ascertained on the level of the entire national economy. Its application on a mass scale in lower production levels requires a solution to some problems, primarily the question of interference in the formation of prices used to determine the volume of net production. Fixed prices, used for determining net production, should be as close as possible to the socially necessary costs of work time expended on the products at the time of the setting of these constant prices. These could be used as prices of the base period.

Measuring the productivity of total labor. From the practical point of view a much more complex problem at this time is presented by the determination of total labor productivity, characterized by index type (2). The main problem lies in the conversion of quantities of embodied labor T_c to quantities of work time. In practice we know these quantities only in the form of price values. In view of the considerable deviations of the prices from the values, which are intentionally created in a socialist economy, the conversions of the prices of products to work time is quite inaccurate.

We can expect that in the future it will be possible to use input-output analysis for this measurement. This method makes it possible to determine the amount of total labor expended on the product directly and indirectly in all the production sectors concerned, on the basis of the knowledge of the natural consumption of products by other products and knowing the laboriousness, that is, the consumption of live labor for the various types of products.

If we mark the unknown consumption of the social work time expended on a product Z, we need for its calculation a set of equations, the general term of which includes the factors

$$Z_j = t_j + \sum_{i=1}^{n} = a_{ij} Z_i \quad (i = 1, 2, 3, \ldots, n) \quad (10)$$

indexes of the physical volume of production and labor productivity. In this case the net production appears to be a weight, thus a constant quantity which is independent of the changes in the consumption of production means in the compared period. In Western countries it is not the net production in our sense of the word but a value added by manufacturing. This among others also contains part of the embodied labor, corresponding to the wear and tear of the means of work. Their use for index (9) is incorrect. The increase in the consumption of means of work per product, increasing the value added by manufacturing, in contradiction with reality, would overrate the increase in social labor productivity and underrate a decrease.

where $a_{ij} — Q_i/Q_j$ is the natural amount of products Q_i consumed in the production of product Q_j.

Expressed in the symbols of matrix algebra,

$$Z' = t' + z'A \qquad (11)$$

where small letter expresses the vector, symbol $(')$ the original vector.

From the formula (11) we can see that the calculation can be simplified, if we know instead of the coefficient of direct consumption—sometimes called in the input-output terminology technical coefficients—the coefficients of the total (direct and indirect) consumption b_{ij}. We can obtain the coefficient b_{ij} by the inversion of the matrix $(1 — A)$ where (A) is the matrix of the technical coefficient. This is obvious from formula (11).

$$Z' = t'(1 — A)^{-1} \qquad (12)$$

If we mark the matrix of the coefficients of the total consumption $(1 — A)^{-1}$ with a symbol (B), we can construe the index of total labor productivity (embodied in the complex of heterogeneous products) for instance in the form of

$$\frac{t'_0 B_0 q_1}{t'_1 B_1 q_1} \qquad (13)$$

Index (13) expresses the changes in the total social costs of the work time which is expended on the volume and structure of production over the examined period of time. It includes the changes in the consumption of live labor (t) in the individual stages of production and the changes in the consumption of embodied labor, expressed in the changes of elements of matrix B. By combining the individual factors of the index (13), we can analyze their influence on the total change in the index.

Although the use of highly effective electronic computers brings the possibility of making such calculations closer, for practical application we still must solve a number of organizational and technical questions. Measurements of this type, as far as they have gone, are for technical purposes limited to various groups of products rather than to individual products, and this leads to certain inaccuracies. For example, calculations of labor productivity made on the basis of this principle in the United States, Hungary, and elsewhere, are, for the time being, experimental.

We can make the following conclusions. Changes in the social division of labor, in the structure of the production forces, rapid technical progress manifesting itself in the sphere of the means of work and power and in the sphere of work objects—all these factors influence the social effectiveness of human labor. It is therefore not possible at this time, as it was at the time of scarcely mechanized labor, to characterize labor productivity merely by the changes in the consumption of live labor. In order to grasp the basic tendencies of the development of labor productivity, at least three basic types of indexes are required. These must be further worked out according to the concrete conditions of their application for use in practice and analysis.

CHAPTER 7

Measuring Labor Productivity
and Its Factors
by the Time-Sum Method

FRIEDRICH BEHRENS

German Academy of Sciences

Labor productivity is of great importance both as an economic category and as a statistical index figure because of its close connection with productive labor. It is the use-effect of productive labor, and, since only living labor can be productive, it is also the use-effect of living labor. This does not preclude consideration of the use-effect of "labor converted into product" nor its measurement as expenditure of means of production against cost of production-use, insofar as converted labor can be measured in money. Increase in labor productivity is a basic economic process, but maximum increase in labor productivity can only be one aspect of the most economical use of social work. The other aspect is maximum reduction in value (or cost). Increase in labor productivity and reduction in value or cost are two aspects of one task: the task of using social labor most economically and achieving the highest possible use-effect.

In order to arrive at the use-effect of social work, it is necessary to measure not only labor productivity but also the use-effect of the means of production. This must not lead one to conclude that the index figure of labor productivity, which relates living labor to gross production, must be expanded into an index figure for the whole of labor by relating gross production to both living labor and product-converted labor. Such a conclusion would be false, since the means of production are naturally not themselves productive but only auxiliaries thereto: this means that one cannot contrast "labor-affected" productivity and "capital-affected" productivity. The fact that productive labor consumes labor converted into product in earlier production periods increases its effectiveness, and the product-converted labor becomes a factor in labor productivity, just like other factors which must be taken into consideration in the analysis of their development (worker qualification, production and labor organization, for example). It is characteristic of technical and economic progress that the amount of product-converted labor consumed by living labor continually increases. This shows itself in the growing organic composition of capital or, under socialist conditions, in the steady increase in the basic fund in proportion to the number employed; this is expressed in the costs of production.

We thus define labor productivity as the quantity of use-values and material services produced per time unit. As a formula for the measurement of labor productivity we shall use the so-called time-sum formula:

$$
\begin{array}{ccc}
\text{Index of} & \text{Index of production} & \text{Index of the} \\
\text{labor} \quad = & \text{volume and its} \quad : & \text{work time or} \\
\text{productivity} & \text{structure} & \text{work forces}
\end{array}
$$

$$
Ap' \quad \frac{\Sigma\, q_n t_0}{\Sigma\, q_n t_n} = \frac{\Sigma\, q_n t_0}{\Sigma\, q_0 t_0} \quad : \quad \frac{\Sigma\, T_n}{\Sigma\, T_0} \tag{1}
$$

(q_n and q_0 = products of the report period or basic period; T_n and T_0 = use of living labor; t_n and $t_0 = T_n : q_n$ or $T_0 : q_0$)

The time-sum method is used for the measurement and planning of labor productivity in the German Democratic Republic. After a longer period of preparation it was introduced as binding for centrally run socialist industry in January 1961, and should be gradually introduced in the next few years in all branches of industry.

It is based upon two preconditions: (1) far-reaching comparativeness of production in the basic period and the report period, at least in the individual work phases; (2) sufficient exactness in the calculation of labor expenditure per product.

As formula (1) shows, the index figure calculated by the time-sum method creates a relation between an index of gross production and an index of work time or work force; thereby the gross production is made addable by the labor expenditure in the basic period, or, in other words, the individual indexes of the products are weighed with the labor expenditure in the report period:

$$Ap' = \frac{\Sigma \; q_n t_0}{\Sigma \; q_0 t_0} = \frac{\Sigma \; q_n t_0 \cdot \dfrac{q_n}{q_0}}{\Sigma \; q_0 t_0} \qquad (1a)$$

The product units which form the basis for the time-sum index are *not* necessarily identical with finished products, but are more products of work stages or work groups, according to the character of production and length of production cycle; particularly in the chemical industry, they correspond with the production stages in natural form, that is to say, the worked-up product. The index thus meets the demand for eliminating the influences of change in product assortment and variations in cooperation, and it also permits splitting up of index figures among the lowest production units, such as work teams, aggregates, factory sections, and so forth. In addition, the index figures calculated by the time-sum method can be used to create a close link between planning and judging labor productivity with socialist reconstruction, with the planning and implementation of technical-organizational measures, and with the planning and judging of wages, costs, and the like. They show the extent to which labor time has been productively used during a shift, a workday, a month, and, finally, a year.

The time-sum index is an index of factory labor productivity, which, in order to measure the extent of change, must be reinforced by an index which measures the structural effect and an index which measures the effect at various stages.

It has often been suggested that instead of an index of labor productivity on the basis of gross production at unaltered prices, there should be an index on the basis of net production, according to the following formula:

$$\frac{q_n p_0 - Pm_n}{q_0 P_0 - Pm_0} : \frac{T_n}{T_0} = \frac{N_n}{N_0} : \frac{T_n}{T_0} \qquad (2)$$

(*Pm* = production expenditures; N = net product; p = unchanged price.) However, this formula leads to index figures of variable structure. The changes in degrees of cooperation are excluded, and all the objections to a "price" index figure can also apply to this index. The criticism of measuring labor productivity on the basis of unchanged prices leads not to other price indexes, but to an index on the basis of time sums.

It is clear that without the most inclusive and exact analysis of factors which have led to an increase in labor productivity, it is not possible to find out if all possibilities of increasing labor productivity have been exhausted, and whether the existing reserves have been mobilized. Since all productivity-improving factors lead to a saving in human labor, there is a possibility of qualifying them by calculating the index with the use of work-time categories and employee categories that lead the development of labor productivity back to causal complexes including all possible individual factors.

The same is naturally true in connection with costs, since the raising of labor productivity is the main cause for reduction in costs. In other words, the index figures should not be concerned alone with a saving in living labor achieved by raising labor productivity. We can avoid this by collating the factors which raise labor productivity and reduce costs into two groups: (1) factors exploiting labor time, and (2) factors exploiting technology and technical progress. There is a close connection and an intensive reciprocal action between these factors. However, it is more or less possible to isolate their effect after the reduction in expenditure of living labor and the reduction of costs. This possibility is made difficult in practice because as a rule the costs are only known for industrial personnel, and we can only calculate on wage costs in the case of basic production workers and auxiliary workers. There is the additional difficulty that wage costs are generally only available for factory work time as paid work time.

The precondition for the isolation and quantification of the factors which increase labor productivity and reduce costs is the existence of index figures of the same structure. This is a task which has been solved both in the theory of index figures and in practice.

We shall present first the measure of labor productivity as it actually developed in the German Democratic Republic. It has proved useful in measuring labor productivity by factors to take as a basis the following categories of work time and persons employed:

	Symbol	Category
(1)	$Tnom$ (IP)	Nominal working time (calendar working time) of industrial personnel. Its change per unit of product reflects the effect of all factors having influence on the dynamics of labor productivity in the factory.
(2)	$Tnom$ (PA)	Nominal working time of the production worker. Its change per unit of product is due to the effect of all those factors which come into play by the activities of the production worker in the factory.
(3)	T (PA)	Actually performed working time of the production worker (productive time). Its change per unit of product is caused in the main by the following factors: the use of new technology and technical methods or better use of existing technology;

technical and political qualification; quality and dimensions of the basic materials; labor intensity.

(4) T *(PGA)* Actually performed working time for basic production work (productive time). Its change per unit of production is mainly caused by the complex of factors noted under (3), but only applied to basic production work.

By comparing the index figures for labor productivity obtained on the basis of *Tnom* *(IP)* and *Tnom* *(PA)*, the effects of a change in the proportion of production workers in industrial personnel on the dynamics of labor productivity can be shown; such evidence is finally obtained by comparing the productivity index figures on the basis of T *(PA)* and T *(PGA)*.

The use of the time-sum method to calculate the average development of productivity in various work categories and employee groups makes it necessary in principle to collate the time expenditure per unit of product of industrial personnel, auxiliary work, and basic production work. If such categorizing is not possible without difficulty in every case in connection with the actual working time for basic production work—$T/q(PGA)$—it is extremely difficult to categorize the nominal working time of industrial personnel—*Tnom* $(IP)/q$—or the actual working time of production workers —T/q *(PA)*—in relation to individual units of production in the majority of factories. For this reason, an exact calculation of the productivity index is made only on the basis of actual working time for basic production workers —T *(PGA)*—since the necessary time and details of amount are noted on the time card, the output wage card, or similar factory documents. All other working-time categories are drawn into the index calculation by means of a corrective coefficient. It has proved that the mistakes generally caused by the use of an approximation are because of a statistical lack of focus. The approximation method its based on a breakdown of the index of labor productivity into indexes of production and working time. The production index is weighted with the actual labor expenditure for basic production work in the report period, and divided by the index of those time categories or employee categories for which labor productivity should be shown. The formula for labor productivity of production workers on the basis of nominal working time (per capita output) can be written as follows:

$$Ap' \ (Tnom; \ PA) = \frac{q_n t_0}{q_0 t_0} : \frac{Tnom_n \ (PA)}{Tnom_0 \ (PA)} \tag{3}$$

If working-time categories and employee categories needed for the factor analysis which cannot be directly apportioned to the individual employee categories are included in the index on the basis of approximation, then a system of productivity index figures can be expressed as follows:

Index figure system of labor productivity

Work time category	Employee category	Industrial personnel (IP)	Production workers (PA)	Basic production workers (PGA)
$Tnom$	$\dfrac{\Sigma\ q_n t_0}{\Sigma\ q_0 t_0} : \dfrac{Tnom_n\ (IP)}{Tnom_0\ (IP)}$		$\dfrac{\Sigma\ q_n t_0}{\Sigma\ q_0 t_0} : \dfrac{Tnom_n\ (PA)}{Tnom_0\ (PA)}$	—
	—		$\dfrac{\Sigma\ q_n t_0}{\Sigma\ q_0 t_0} : \dfrac{T_n\ (PA)}{T_0\ (PA)}$	$\dfrac{\Sigma\ q_n t_0}{\Sigma\ q_n t_1}$
				$= \dfrac{\Sigma\ q_n t_0}{\Sigma\ q_0 t_0} : \dfrac{T_n\ (PGA)}{T_0\ (PGA)}$

In the factories of the German Democratic Republic, the indexes Ap' $(T; IP)$ and Ap' $(Tnom: PGA)$ are not calculated, since they are not needed for the analysis.

For planning, drawing up balance sheets, and analyzing processes in the factory and the economy, importance must be attached not only to the dynamics of labor productivity but also to the saving in labor time or increased expenditure of labor time. Since the quoted productivity quotient is the numerical expression for a comparison of time sums, their subtraction produces the greater or lesser expenditure of labor time. Such a calculation is best done on the basis of the reciprocal expression of the productivity index—that is, the labor expenditure index:

$$\frac{\Sigma\ q_n t_n}{\Sigma\ q_n t_0}$$

In the analysis, attention must be paid to the fact that these are weighted time sums, and that the economy would have been affected if in the actual development of productivity the same production structure had existed during the reference period and the report period. This type of middle-weighted index calculation is necessary to prove the dynamics of productivity. To prove the *actual* saving in labor time or labor power between the reference period and the report period, the change in production structure must be included in the calculation as well as the influence of the development in productivity. This is possible by setting up unweighted time-sum indexes.

The numerator and denominator of such indexes consist of the entire time period devoted to production in the period included in the calculation.

For the calculation of the lesser or greater demand for work time, the following formulas apply:

$$q_n t_n - q_0 t_0 = (q_n t_n - q_n t_0) + (q_n t_0 - q_0 t_0)$$
$$q_n t_n - q_n t_0 = (q_n t_n - q_0 t_0) - (q_n t_0 - q_0 t_0) \qquad (4)$$
$$q_n t_0 - q_0 t_0 = (q_n t_n - q_0 t_0) - (q_n t_n - q_n t_0)$$

The proof of lesser or greater demands for work time by the subtraction of weighted time-sums can only be shown in this way for those time categories which can be directly related to the individual units produced. In general, it is only possible to ascertain the lesser or greater demands for actual work time in basic production work including time for mistakes— T (PGA)—according to the formula

$$\Sigma \, q_n t_n - \Sigma \, q_n t_0$$

If however a weighted production index is divided by an unweighted time-sum index, the approximation formula for the calculation of the productivity development is used,

$$Ap' \, (Tnom) = \frac{\Sigma \, q_n t_0}{\Sigma \, q_0 t_0} : \frac{Tnom_n}{Tnom_0}$$

then a subtraction of numerators and denominators of the quotients is not possible. In such cases, the following process should be applied:

If, for instance

$$\frac{\Sigma \, q_n t_0}{\Sigma \, q_n t_n} = Ap', \text{ resulting in } Ap' \cdot \Sigma \, q_n t_n = \Sigma \, q_n t_0$$

one can also write

$$\Sigma \, q_n t_n - \Sigma \, q_n t_0 = \Sigma \, q_n t_n - \frac{(Ap' \cdot \Sigma \, q_n t_n)}{100}$$

If one wishes to establish the relevant lesser or greater demands for work time for all productivity indexes calculated by approximation, then the indexes are multiplied by the relevant labor expenditure in the planning or report periods which are not directly attributable, and, if the labor productivity index was expressed in percentages, then divided by 100. The difference between this time sum and labor expenditure in the planning or report periods then shows the lesser or greater demand for work time.

If the increase in labor productivity is the main source for reducing costs, then it follows that the factors which lead to an increase in labor productivity also lead to a reduction in costs. The reverse does not always apply, since there are factors which lead to a reduction in costs, without increasing labor productivity, as is often seen in savings in material, auxiliary aids, and factory materials.

The reduction in costs by the increase in labor productivity leads to cost savings composed of savings in the wage bill and savings in costs for production-use.

We are particularly interested in the costs for production-use, which are composed of: (1) the use of labor means, and (2) the use of labor objects. These most directly reflect the use of technology and technical progress.

In analyzing the factors which ensure a reduction in costs, we proceed from the index of costs which is comparable with the index of productivity by the time-sum method. Here too the starting point is the fact that the index of specific cost expenditure (the cost expenditure per unit produced) reflects the relation between the index of production and the cost volume.

$$sk' = \underset{\text{Index of average cost development}}{\frac{\Sigma\, q_n sk_n}{\Sigma\, q_n sk_0}} = \underset{\text{Index of cost volumes}}{\frac{\Sigma\, SK_n}{\Sigma\, SK_0}} \; : \; \underset{\substack{\text{Index of production} \\ \text{volumes and their} \\ \text{structure}}}{\frac{\Sigma\, q_n sk_0}{\Sigma\, q_n sk_0}} \qquad (5)$$

Since the index calculation must be based on comparable production, few difficulties are encountered in cases dealing with individual indexes for finished products. In those cases where planning and judging labor productivity deal with such production units as work stages, groups of work stages, building groups, and production steps (and for analytical purposes this should certainly be the goal), it is not possible at the moment in most factories to ascertain analogous index figures of costs. In most cases, however, bookkeeping figures in industrial undertakings make it possible to calculate index figures for basic wage costs per unit produced. All other cost index figures analogous to productivity index figures can be calculated by the use of approximation, familiar in principle from the measurement of labor productivity. In this case, in order to determine the average weighted cost index as weight for the production index one takes either the effective wage costs—$1k$—or the calculated wage costs—$1kk$—for basic production work per unit produced in the report period.

$$sk' = \frac{\Sigma\ SK_n}{\Sigma\ SK_0} : \frac{\Sigma\ q_n\mathrm{I}k_0}{\Sigma\ q_0\mathrm{I}k_0}$$

$$= \frac{\Sigma\ SK_n}{\Sigma\ SK_0} : \frac{\Sigma\ q_n\mathrm{I}kk_0}{\Sigma\ qn_0\mathrm{I}kk_0}$$

Or, by using this approximation method, it is possible to calcuate cost index figures corresponding with the productivity index figures:

Index figure system of production costs

Cost category	Employee category	Industrial personnel (*IP*)	Production workers (*PA*)	Basic production workers (*PGA*)
SK	$\dfrac{\Sigma\ SK_n}{\Sigma\ SK_0} : \dfrac{\Sigma\ q_n\mathrm{I}k_0}{\Sigma\ q_0\mathrm{I}k_0}$	—	$\dfrac{LK_nZZa\ (PA)}{LKZZa\ (PA)} : \dfrac{\Sigma\ q_n\mathrm{I}k_0}{\Sigma\ q_0\mathrm{I}k_0}$	
LK	—	—	$\dfrac{LK_n\ (PA)}{LK_0\ (PA)} : \dfrac{\Sigma\ q_n\mathrm{I}k_n}{\Sigma\ q_0\mathrm{I}k_0}$	$\dfrac{\Sigma\ q_n\mathrm{I}k_n}{\Sigma\ q_n\mathrm{I}k_0}$

For example, the productivity index calculated on the basis of *Tnom* (*IP*) shows the effect of all factors affecting the expenditure of living labor by industrial personnel, and this is supplemented by the cost index (*IP*), which reflects the influence of the main factors of the use-effect of social labor related to the named category of employees. Comparison between the two index figures allows one to determine whether, and to what degree, the increase in the productive power of the useful concrete work, and its extended application, has been compensated for, or more than compensated for, in a given period by the increase in the use of product-converted labor (material, write-offs).

The wage-cost index *LKZZa* (*PA*) shows for example the effect of all factors included in the productivity index on the basis of *Tnom* (*PA*) in the development of the breakdown into direct and indirect basic wages for production work per unit produced, including supplements and supplementary wages for all shortfall times. In this case it should be noted that the supplementary wage is not the sole comparative figure for all avoidable and unavoidable shortfall times but may also be paid for special reasons unrelated to the productive strength of living labor. These supplementary wages include bonuses for long service and allowances in kind in mining, and so forth. In the same way the productivity index on the basis of *T* can be compared to the roughly comparable wage cost index on the basis of LK and analyzed in accordance with the factor schemata.

The following points must be noted in evaluating such a comparison of corresponding productivity index figures and cost index figures: the productivity index calculated according to the time-sum method, as was foreseen, reflects only quantitative changes, without giving any information on the quality of the labor consumed, whether it be simple or complicated work. The cost index, on the other hand, shows as an expression of the dynamics of the use-effect of social labor not only quantitative but also qualitative changes (for instance, varying material costs per unit produced as the result of changes in material application, or payment in higher wage groups as a mark of improved qualifications).

This should not be regarded as a shortcoming. On the contrary, it is precisely this which makes possible the investigation and analysis of higher and more material-effective productivity factors not only in regard to quantity but particularly in regard to quality.

If the approximation method described cannot be used for the compilation of cost index figures, because the wage costs per unit produced—$_1k_0$ or $_1k_0$—are not available as weights for the production index, then an even more simple approximation can be used. This method can only be used to produce results with the necessary precision in cases where the relation between the expenditure of wages and time for the various units of production remains roughly the same. In this case, the weight—$_1k_0$—can be replaced by the weight—t_0—from the time-sum formula. The formula for the approximated average cost development is then:

$$sk' = \frac{SK_n}{SK_0} : \frac{q_n t_0}{q_0 t_0} = \frac{SK_n T_0}{SK_0 q_n t_0} \tag{6}$$

If the index of labor productivity is calculated on the time-sum formula, then a comparable index of costs can be calculated without the costs per unit produced being available. This naturally is a great help in the analysis of the connection between the development of labor productivity and costs, particularly when it is not a case of global comparisons but concerns the lowest units in the factory.

It is understandable that the number of factors influencing productivity and costs, the effects of which can be collated, will be at first relatively small. At the moment there are limits imposed by the state of mechanization in administrative work and by the organization of factory bookkeeping. It is clear, however, that it is possible and necessary to improve and extend the index-figure system of use-effect in social labor to meet the needs of planning and organizing factories, branches of industry, and the economy as a whole.

The main point is that the comparison of the two indexes—for expenditure of living labor and for costs—show the results of the increase in use-effect of living labor, and show whether it is balanced by a stronger increase in consumption of product-converted labor, or whether the saving in living labor is compensated for by the increase in other costs. If the reduction in costs, as laid out on the basis of planned and implemented increases in labor productivity, lags behind, then the reasons must be discovered.

The costs per product only drop when the wage costs resulting from an increase in average wages, and the costs for production consumption resulting from the increase in production consumption, rise more slowly than labor productivity.

The measure for the development of costs in relation to labor productivity is the coefficient Aw'/sk'.

The development of costs is therefore the more favorable the nearer this coefficient approaches 1.

In summation, we can say that the time index figures and cost index figures developed in the German Democratic Republic are not necessarily based on the relation that one unit produced $= q$. The units produced are not necessarily identical with the finished factory product, but in accordance with the character of production and the length of the production cycle, they represent the results of the labor process or the labor-process group in natural form—that is, worked-up production. One then comes to the following conclusions:

(1) The influence of changes in cooperation are completely or very largely excluded.

(2) It is possible to make an analysis in depth of productivity factors and cost-effective factors as the basis for planning and accounting.

(3) It is possible to break down the index figures for labor productivity and costs on the basis of cost proportions and allocate them to the lowest production units of the factory.

Naturally the evidence value of such index figures depends upon exact collection and preparation of the original material in the factories. It must therefore be emphasized that this can only be done rationally with the use of modern office and calculating technology. Since the introduction of modern office and calculating technology is only in its early stages in our factories, methods of approximation must be used for the time being.

The Concept of Labor Productivity

Friedrich Behrens

German Academy of Sciences

Great attention is devoted in all countries to the measurement of labor productivity, independent of production relations. It is therefore of value to check the theoretical concepts upon which the measurement of labor productivity is based. There is agreement upon the effort made to measure labor productivity, but its definitions are varied. This is not surprising when one considers that the concept of labor productivity is closely linked with the economic category of productive labor. One would not be in danger of contradiction if one described labor productivity as the practical effect of productive labor. It is, therefore, to be expected that in defining labor productivity one encounters the same differences of opinion as with the definition of productive labor.

It may be of value to recall that Karl Marx once wrote, "the critical differentiation between productive and unproductive work [remains] the basis of all *bourgeois* economics." [1] In fact there are at present the same differences of opinion on the delimitation of productive and unproductive work of which Marx spoke. But even when, for practical purposes, one measures labor productivity by a definition which fairly closely approaches

1. Karl Marx, *Theories on Surplus Value* (Berlin, 1956), vol. 1, p. 120. (This and following quotations are unofficial translations from the German.)

Marx's, there are conflicting opinions on whether one should take as a starting point gross or net production, and what should be understood as individual and social labor productivity. The differences of opinion regarding the delimitation of productive and unproductive labor are of particular importance, since they are directly connected with the question of whether one should recognize as productive only living labor, or also the work achieved in previous production periods. This is naturally more than a simple question of terminology; the issue is whether one can divide the output of production among its "causal" factors, that is to say, the so-called production factors. Since the "causal" estimation of production output among the so-called production factors on the basis of the theory of labor value is not possible, all variants of the "attribution theory" proceed from the natural character of the means of production. They "abstract" from the capital character of the means of production, just as they "abstract" from the double character of labor when they identify product value and value of product.

Thus the definition of the concept of labor productivity raises questions of principle of economic theory, closely connected with very practical questions of economic analysis and planning.

On the one hand, these conflicting opinions affect the delimitation of material production itself. Even when there is agreement that productive labor lies within material production, one school holds that material services such as publishing, radio, and film must be completely excluded from labor in production, and the others are ready to describe as unproductive not only material services such as transport and communications in production but also work in passenger traffic and certain work in communications. On the other hand, they affect the question of the limits between productive labor and socially useful labor. Since all productive labor is also socially useful labor, but not all socially useful labor is productive labor, the delimitation of the frontier between productive labor and unproductive but socially useful labor becomes particularly important under the socialist production conditions in which parasite labor disappears. It appears to me that a firm point of view on the definition of the concept of productive labor can only be gained when one holds with the distinction made by Karl Marx between its general and special aspects.

The Category of Productive Labor

Marx, in his critique of the theoreticians of the young *bourgeois* type of production, defined on the one hand the concept of productive labor of this type. On the other, he developed the two main factors of the definition of productive labor: the general factor and the special factor.

The *general factor* results directly from the nature of material production itself, in which the process of cooperation between man and nature is consummated, resulting in a product which meets human needs either directly as consumer goods or indirectly as means of production. In all types of production, material production includes those spheres in which a product is produced and takes a special form as the result of production, or in which the product is directly consumed in the production process: agriculture and industry, building, transport, communication services, and trade, insofar as they serve production directly or continue the process of production. In contradistinction to this, the activities belong to the sector of nonmaterial production which are carried out in the material sphere, but which, like statistical work, represent only an ideal reflection of the material process; this category includes all activities in the social superstructure, in the state, culture, health services, and so forth. It is thus just as wrong to extend the concept of productive labor to include *all* activities in the basis of society, such as transport and communications for individual purposes and all branches of trade, as it is to extend this concept to include all socially necessary labor. On the other hand, it is necessary to include in the concept of productive labor not only individual labor but also all labor which forms part of the total.

From the point of view of the labor process, all physical or mental work is productive when it forms part of material production either individually or as a link in a labor-divided production organism. It includes all activities of a physical or mental nature which help in the production of consumer value or material services.

This division of hand labor and head labor, originally combined in one individual, a division which goes as far as hostility, is caused by the growth of the social division of work and private ownership of means of production. The original naturally developed and primitive production organisms became divided into production organisms with division of labor, private property, and exchange of the products of labor. As a result of this development, first only the social division of work according to profession, later, under the capitalist mode of production the division of labor inside a factory, the clear and consciously distributed total labor of a naturally grown production organism has been replaced by blindly effective laws which go into effect behind the backs and over the heads of the producers.

The division between physical labor and mental labor, originally united, which finally reaches a stage of hostility under capitalist conditions, means that the same productive work is divided into various activities which in their total, as in their individual parts, retain their productive character. The division of labor does not change labor's productive character.

Taken alone, the individual part of the total work is no longer productive; it cannot be productive, since the product of labor is no longer the result of individual work, but of labor which only becomes effective cooperatively. The individual work is now only productive as part of the total work, as a link in the labor-divided production organism.

The *special factor* in productive labor results from the fact that material production always takes place in determined forms liable to historical change. The concept of productive work must therefore also cover determined social relations resulting from the form of ownership of the means of production and thus from the results of production. When the means of production belong, individually or collectively, to the direct producers, then they also possess the product of their labor. If the means of production, on the other hand, do not belong to the direct producers, then the product of their labor does not belong to them but to the owner of the means of production. Thus productive labor is always physical or mental work, a useful activity in material production done either individually or as a link in a labor-divided production organism, but, from the standpoint of the ruling type of production, not every useful activity in material production is productive labor. Under the conditions of capitalist ownership of the means of production, the means of production belong to the capitalist, and the worker has to produce surplus value in order to be a productive worker. But surplus value is only one form of the surplus production of the immediate producer, the capitalist form; this existed in other forms in the pre-capitalist type of production and naturally continues to exist in the socialist type of production. To define productive labor from the standpoint of the ruling production relations, it is necessary to answer the question—who acquires the surplus product produced in material production—since the form of the surplus product depends upon the ruling relations of production in the means of production.

When we take into account the relation of production to the definition of productive labor, then we see that on one hand not all work in material production is productive, and, on the other, labor outside material production can be productive. From the standpoint of the capitalist, the work of the simple commodity producer is unproductive, since it produces no surplus value; on the other hand a part of the production of nonmaterial services is productive labor since it serves the self-use of capital. The labor of the simple commodity producer is not wage-labor at the service of the capitalist, but labor outside material production is subordinated to the relations of capital, that is, it is converted into wage-labor at the service of the capitalists. To be productive labor from the standpoint of the capitalist has nothing to do "with the determined content of the labor, its special usefulness, or its generic use-value, in which it materializes." [2]

The materialization of a use-value (directly or by means of a material service) is thus a necessary condition for the definition of productive labor, but not a sufficient condition. To this must be added the special historically determined form in which the labor is clothed, which results from the ruling production relations.

Under socialist conditions productive labor in material production creates the product from which the whole of society lives. This is defined as specifically social work in material production. The product in socialist society is created by productive workers in material production, and the nonproductive section of the population active in the nonproductive sphere receives its income as income derived from this.

Productive and nonproductive labor under socialist conditions are always socially necessary, but they fulfill different functions in society. In capitalism the entire material production is subject to capitalist conditions, and the labor is converted into wage-labor; not only this, but the labor in the nonproduction sphere is increasingly degraded to the rank of capitalist wage-labor. In socialism, on the other hand, in which labor serves to meet human needs, nonmaterial services in the fields of culture, health services, education, art, and science cannot become subjects of private production, subjects which are bought and sold. The product of labor from material production serves in society to support and broaden the field of nonproductive but socially necessary labor. This is expressed in the large sums devoted to cultural and social purposes in the socialist states.

All labor which satisfies demands is *useful,* but it is only *productive* if it creates a demand-satisfying use-value or provides a material service. Thus not all useful labor is productive, although all productive labor is useful.

Productive labor thus includes not only the general condition of useful activity, but also a historically developed social relation, which under capitalism makes the worker the direct use means of capital. "To be a produc-

2. Karl Marx, *Das Kapital* (Berlin, 1949), vol. 1, p. 233.

tive worker is therefore not good luck but bad luck," [3] and it is clear that *bourgeois* economics never liked to dwell on this bad luck which affected the direct producers in their mode of production. In the post-classical period of *bourgeois* economy there is a double argument: first the various attempts to prove that not only labor in material production is productive, but all labor is productive; and, second, as a result of the first argument, the attempt to prove that "capital" too is productive.

Bourgeois economy makes varied efforts to prove that every labor which provides an income is productive, since it thus "contributes to the social product"; at the same time the attempt is made by means of a theory of production factors to prove that capital is productive in the sense of the means of production produced. Economists, basing themselves on the income thesis in defining productive labor, manage to inflate the definition of national income by making it the sum of all incomes both original and derivative; in the same way, basing themselves on the production factor thesis, they succeed in hiding the growth conditions of the social labor product by putting technology in the place of economy. In contemporary *bourgeois* economics productive labor is equated generally with all labor which achieves an income; and this has a tradition. This simply waters down the definition of labor productivity, which is clearly defined as the useful effect of productive labor; what remains is so diluted and so thin that it is useless for the purpose of economic analysis.

The Use-Effect of Productive Labor

It is clear that in defining the term labor productivity it is necessary to take into consideration the ruling production relations, in those cases where it is not sufficient to define productive labor on the basis of the general factor of productive labor. By expanding the definition of productive labor to include all work which achieves an income, one reaches the conclusion that the labor of the owner of the means of production is also productive. This is reflected in the definitions based upon the modern *bourgeois* measuring of productivity. Productivity is described as relation of output per unit of input, and there is talk of "factor applied" productivity, in particular "work applied" and "capital applied" productivity, but also of "material applied" productivity.

The idea of productive labor is expanded to cover all labor which

3. Karl Marx, *Das Kapital,* vol. i, p. 333.

achieves an income, and in a similar way the idea of productivity is expanded. "There is thus a machine productivity just as there is a raw-material productivity and a productivity of human labor," writes Jean Fourastié.[4]

This definition means that not only labor is productive, but also capital and land, though not all "productive contributions" are measurable, so that in practice one is confined to those portions which can be measured. In reality, however, "capital" is only a factor of productivity, of the only productivity which exists: labor productivity. In the course of production, productive labor consumes labor converted into products in previous working periods; this increases its degree of effectiveness, and the "labor converted into products" becomes a factor in the labor productivity, which must be taken into consideration in the development analysis just like the other factors: training of the labor force, and the organization of production and work. Since the living labor, as concrete productive labor, produces not only new use values, but also transfers to the new product the value of the means of production consumed in making the product, this value is greater than the value product which the living labor produces as abstract value in the production of the new use value. The gross production is on one hand the sum of the use value produced—means of production and means of consumption—and on the other hand the sum of the value transferred by the concrete labor and newly created by the abstract labor.

In accordance with the double character of labor, the use effect of the social work is expressed both as the sum of the use value produced per unit of living labor, and also as the sum of the used living labor and product-converted labor per unit of the use value produced. In order to measure the use effect of the social labor, it is thus necessary to measure on one hand the labor productivity as use effect of living labor, and on the other hand the value, or its quantitatively most important part, the cost price per unit produced. Index numbers of labor productivity, costs, and their breakdown are only of value when they make possible an analysis of the expended living labor and product-converted labor. Since one of the main means of reducing costs is the increase in labor productivity, it is particularly important to collate and analyze the productivity factors and the cost-affecting factors.

In accordance with the requirements of planned economy, the endeavor is made to draft index figures which:

(1) reflect the niveau and dynamic of the specific use of labor time and costs per unit produced;

4. *The Great Hope of the Twentieth Century* (Cologne, 1954), p. 46.

(2) exclude completely or as far as possible the influence on the labor productivity index and the costs index of changes in cooperation;

(3) offer the possibility of making a deep analysis of the productivity factors and the cost-affecting factors as the basis for planning and accounting on a factor basis;

(4) permit the allocation of the index figures of labor productivity and costs on a breakdown basis to the subsidiary production departments of a works.

The possibility of drafting such index figures is given by the so-called "Time and Cost Summation Method."

There are not only differences of opinion with regard to the definition of labor productivity, resulting from different views on the concept of productive labor, but also differences of opinion as to what should be measured: whether gross production or net production. There is a common cause both for "factor applied" productivity, that is to say the measurement of the productivity of the "factor" labor as labor productivity and the measurement of the "factor" capital as so-called capital productivity, and for the measurement of the net production instead of the gross production. It is perhaps not superfluous to point out that there is a long "tradition" in the attempt to take, instead of the clear concept of the gross production as the result of production which is a unitary process of labor and value creation, something which is described as "adjusted" gross production, or even net production. The roots of this theory were disclosed by Marx in his criticism of certain views of Adam Smith.[5]

Gross production consists on one hand of the sum of the use value produced—means of production and means of consumption—by a department, a factory, a branch of industry, industry, or the whole economy, and on the other hand, the sum of the values transferred by concrete labor and newly created by abstract labor. In our practice, the sum, measured either by volume or by value, of the product of the department or the factory, and the sum of the product of the factory is described as *gross production turnover,* and this clearly defined gross production is compared to the gross production according to the factory method and the over-all gross production. Both concepts—the gross production according to the factory method and the over-all gross production—are produced by subtracting the consumption by the factory itself or the so-called step turnover from the actual gross production resulting from production as a unitary process of labor and value crea-

5. See Karl Marx, *Das Kapital,* vol. 2, p. 379 ff.

tion. Both self-consumption of the factory and so-called step turnover are results which leave production only to return either to maintain production in the same factory, or be further worked up in the same factory or another factory. There are means of production—work objects or work means—which enter production again, either without in the meantime entering circulation, as in the case of the factory self-consumption, or after entering circulation as in the case of the so-called step turnover. If one excludes self-consumption or step turnover entirely or partly from gross production, by estimating the gross production of the factory by the factory method and the gross production of society by the method of national economy gross production, then one falsifies the index figures of labor productivity by showing the productivity of labor, both on the factory and social level, as too low.

The products which go into the self-consumption of the factory, and the products which circulate in step turnover, are the results of productive labor, and must therefore be included in calculating the index of labor productivity.

This does not mean that one should not calculate indexes of production for special purposes such as factory comparisons (resulting from subtracting the self-consumption or the step turnover from the gross production). But such "adjusted" gross production, however calculated, is not suitable as a basis for an index of labor productivity, since it does not include all the use values produced by living labor in the relevant period. The gross production of the factory and of society is economically the sum of the use values produced, that is to say the sum of the products produced in natural units of a clear dimension.

If the gross production of the factory is not found by adding together the gross production of the departments, and the gross production of the branch of industry, the industry as a whole, or the whole of the economy, is not found by adding together the gross production of the factories, then the index of gross production, and thus the index of labor productivity, will be too low. If, for instance, the yarn which goes to the factory spinning shops is not included in the gross production of the factory, but only the yarn which leaves the factory, then the niveau of gross production and labor productivity depends to a great degree upon whether a small quantity or a large quantity of yarn leaves the factory.

The nature of labor productivity as the useful effect of living work results naturally in the fact that one cannot measure this if one excludes from consideration a part of the use values produced.

Finally, there are differences of opinion with regard to so-called individual and social labor productivity.

If labor productivity is the use effect of productive labor, and if social labor appears as a division of labor between various concrete labors, then it is necessary to make a distinction between individual and social labor productivity. Individual labor productivity is the use effect of the labor of an individual worker, or a labor-divided "total worker," such as a work team, a department, or a factory. Social labor productivity, on the other hand, is the complex of the individual labor productivities of the productive strength of the work of a branch of production, of industry, or of the whole economy.

The differentiation between individual and social labor productivity is of great importance for the measurement of labor productivity, since the more complex the labor productivity, the more factors affect it. Social labor productivity is influenced not only by the use effect of the individual worker or "total worker," but also by structural changes of the most varied sort, such as changes in the composition of the work team, changes in the structure of production, and so forth, as well as by the so-called step effect. It can therefore only be measured by means of an index with variable structure, that is to say an index which shows all the factors affecting the use effect of social labor as a complex of individual labors. This may even be true in the case of factory labor productivity, if it is considered as a complex of "individual" work teams, sections, departments, and so on. Individual labor productivity, on the other hand, can only be measured by means of an index with a firm structure, that is to say an index which excludes all other factors except labor productivity itself.

We use the term "social labor productivity" in the sense of a complex labor productivity which expresses not only the productivity of concrete work in the strictest sense, but also all other factors which affect the use effect of the labor.

The differentiation between individual and social labor productivity is of importance, since the average individual labor productivity does not necessarily coincide with social labor productivity. The average of individual labor productivity can be smaller or larger than the social productivity, according to which outside factors affect the complex labor productivity.

Economic analysis has the task of determining which factors, in the individual case, had such concrete effect on the development of the social labor productivity so that it increased faster, or slower, than individual labor productivity.

It is undeniably necessary to analyze the factors and to measure the use effect of the whole work, and this arises from the demands of economic planning. One closes the path to a correct and speedy solution of this problem, however, if one bases oneself upon false conceptions. It is therefore not superfluous to fix exactly the definition of labor productivity. However, the measurement of labor productivity cannot be sufficient, even though it is of particular importance. It is necessary at the same time to develop the methods of measuring the value, or in its place the costs, and to make an analysis of all factors affecting the increase in labor productivity and the lowering of costs.

PART II

International Comparisons
of Productivity

CHAPTER 8

Methods for International Comparisons of Productivity Levels

ZOLTÁN ROMÁN

Hungarian Central Statistical Office

Introduction

The international comparison of productivity levels has been increasingly gaining ground in the economic research of recent years. The research begun twenty years ago by the Hungarian, Laszlo Rostas, which is highly appreciated even today, is counted as an experiment by a pioneer. Today, on the other hand, in the most economically developed countries and in a number of international organizations regular work is being done on international productivity comparison. In this field the number and the standards of available scientifically valuable works are growing. In Hungary the work of G. Bombach, and elsewhere the works of D. Paige, M. Frankel, W. Galenson, A. Kac, L. Rostas, V. Sztarovszkij, Sz.G. Sztrumilin and other researchers and organizations in this field are highly appreciated. This study reports some experiences gained in the course of Hungarian studies on the international comparison of industrial productivity.

This comparison may take place on the factory level which makes a rather thorough analysis of factors of productivity differences possible, but it would require a great number of studies to draw general conclusions. The international comparison of productivity levels may also be made of industries and economic sectors. The results at this level can more easily be combined with a general comparison of the countries' positions and development, but they offer the possibility of analyzing factors determining productivity levels in only a general way. Thus the two comparisons supplement each other. In Hungary our experiences have been more in the area of industries and economic sectors, and it is this field that we cover here.

Comparison by Productivity Indicators in Natural (Physical) Units of Measure

In order to avoid foreign exchange conversions, indicators of natural (physical) units of measure are usually employed for international productivity comparisons. When applying this method the following difficulties arise in the first instance: (*a*) the comparison must in most cases be confined to homogeneous branches at which production and labor input data can be directly related; (*b*) there are quality-choice differences among the products compared; (*c*) the labor inputs spent on products of the same denomination do not cover the same state of production.

Comparisons were made recently of the productivity levels in Czechoslovak and Hungarian industries by applying several methods, including productivity indicators of natural units of measure. We have learned in the course of this work to employ the following methods for overcoming the above-mentioned difficulties:

It is usually necessary to confine studies to "homogeneous" branches because production and working-time data serve as a basis of comparison by *branches,* and these data can be directly compared only in the homogeneous sectors, and even here by disregarding so-called "secondary" production. In both Czechoslovakia and Hungary the enterprises regularly report the working hours per unit of product, or production per man-hour, in natural units of measure in mining, metallurgy, the building material industry, the textile industry, and other branches. They served as a basis for our comparison of the first stage (accomplished for the year 1958) in the indexes of thirty-five products; in the second stage of the work, in the years 1959 and 1960, the list of the products analyzed has been increased by quite a number of engineering and food industrial products.

There are always more or less substantial quality differentials between products of the same denomination made in two countries. In practice the comparisons are made not in respect to products but to groups of products so that we have also to reckon with the circumstance that the different proportions of products of different labor intensity within the group impairs the results of the comparison. In our experience the problem of such quality-choice differences cannot be properly solved without the cooperation of the institutions concerned in the countries in question, rather than merely on the basis of published sources; even with such cooperation we must often content ourselves with pointing out these differences. In the course of the Czechoslovak-Hungarian comparison we tried to eliminate the differences by: (1) choosing units of measure which substantially reduce these differences or rather their impact on productivity; and (2) converting production (with the help of coefficients) into a main type of product.[1]

We can relate the stage of the production process to the product by spelling out the technological limits and intermediary cooperation. On the whole we use data of enterprises or industrial branches, but the enterprises or branches may be at different stages of the production process in creating their product. For the sake of comparability, we must identify each product at the same stage of the production process and its labor inputs (with the same technological limits). Thus, in the textile industry, an agreement must be reached on whether cross-winding is an end-operation of spinning or preparatory work for weaving; in cement-manufacturing, the proper classifications of limestone quarrying, clinker-production, and the finishing operation of sacking, and so forth, must be made. Technological limits must also be fixed in respect to the auxiliary or ancillary processes. In other words, power-stations, waste processing and packing-material production must be left out, since only some of the works perform such activities.

The definition of uniform technological limits demands that the impact of different degrees of intermediary cooperation be removed. This problem is particularly outstanding in engineering. Here we suggest making a list of the components or unit parts, for instance, in the case of machine tools the electric motors, which are as a rule procured by cooperation. The working hours spent are not to be counted in the manufacture of the products even if in a given country the branch enterprise in question produces them itself, whereas the working-time input of all other cooperation is counted in the product. Differences in cooperation must be studied and eliminated in respect to the auxiliary or ancillary operations such as repairs, tool-manufacturing, and so forth.

In the first stage of the Czechoslovak-Hungarian comparison we were still unable to meet all these requirements, yet we could ensure the com-

---

1. The conversion will not give a correct result unless both countries apply the same coefficients.

parability of the indicators with quite a close approximation. The results of the comparison in respect to a few products are shown in Table 4.

Table 4. Level of productivity in the production of some commodities in Czechoslovak and Hungarian industries in 1958.

Product			Industrial productivity indicator		Productivity of Czechoslovak industry as percentage of the Hungarian level
Denomination	Unit of measure	Type of indicator	Czecho-slovakia	Hungary	
Anthracite (hard coal)	t	a	350	169	207
Brown (soft) coal and lignite	t	a	1,210	278	435
Electric power	1000 kwh	a	1,220	635	192
Pig iron	t	b	906	305	259
Open hearth steel	t	b	603	411	147
Cement	t	b	766	575	133
Sulfuric acid	t	b	774	547	141
Cotton yarn	km	c	112.0	90.5	124
Carded wool yarn	km	c	20.0	13.6	147
Worsted wool yarn	km	c	46.9	33.4	140
Cotton cloth	shot	c	20,640	18,100	114
Woolen cloth	shot	c	2,710	2,420	112
Silk cloth	shot	c	15,400	11,100	139

Symbols for the different types of indicators:
a = production per worker
b = production per worker directly engaged in the production of the commodity
c = production per man-hour performed by workers directly engaged in the production of the commodity

This method disregards inputs of embodied labor, as do most methods of productivity measurements. To solve this difficulty, several methods can be applied. The simplest solution is offered by further supplementary study of so-called technical-economic indicators in natural units of measure, indicating the specific inputs of embodied labor. The industrial statistics of socialist countries observe a great many technical-economic indicators of this type. It is convenient to supplement our analysis with their comparison. In the given case, as could only be expected, this supplementary study indicated much smaller differences in respect to specific embodied labor inputs, than with regard to directly applied labor (working-hour) inputs, but in this case, almost without exception, the comparisons favored

Czechoslovak industry. There are other examples of the comparison of these indicators: in pig iron production in Czechoslovak industry the exploitation of the blast furnaces is 20 per cent higher, the use of metal inlets is 10 per cent lower, the use of coke is 7 per cent lower; in open-hearth steel manufacturing the exploitation of the furnaces is 16 per cent higher, the use of metal inlets is the same; in the electric power industry the fuel consumption is 8 per cent lower, and the self-use 11 per cent lower.

The productivity level ratios of different products (branches) can be determined by proper weighted averages. The average ratio can also be established for single major branches and for industry as a whole. In this connection the degree of representation requires a closer analysis; the weighting computation should be made by the structures of both countries. In the comparison of productivity of Czechoslovak and Hungarian industries a few branches have been given proper representation and for these the average level ratio can be established, as Table 5 indicates.

Table 5. Productivity in the Czechoslovak industry as percentage of Hungarian level, weighted by working time inputs.

Sector	Czechoslovakia	Hungary
Ferrous metallurgy	159	180
Textile industry	125	124
Leather and footwear industry	156	177

Although industry as a whole was not properly represented by the products examined, we have tried to establish the average ratio. It is convenient to weight the branch ratios not by the actual weights of the products observed but by those of different sectors. Following this method we have found that in 1958 the productivity level was about 70 per cent higher in Czechoslovak industry than in Hungary. This conforms quite strikingly with the results of other calculations. Thus, electric power consumption per industrial worker, eliminating the sectorial (structural) differences prevailing in the industries of the two countries—on the basis of indexes with fixed weights—was 77 per cent higher in Czechoslovak industry.

The first comparison between Czechoslovak and Hungarian industrial productivity levels, based on natural units of measure, is to be followed by more precise and detailed analyses. But even the work hitherto performed has shown that in order to obtain a reliable comparison a number of disturbing factors have to be eliminated from the indicators examined, and to this end direct cooperation of the institutions in question is required. The far-reaching, widespread data compilation of the socialist countries in the field of industrial statistics and the direct, friendly cooperation between the state bodies engaged in the comparisons warrant favorable conditions for such cooperation, but such cooperation can be fruitful even with Western countries. At the same time a *parallel* application of other methods of comparison is deemed desirable.

Comparison with the Aid of Production and Labor Input Indexes

The different methods applied for comparing productivity levels are usually classified into two groups according to whether they are based on indicators of natural or of value units of measure. The author has consciously given another name rather than a value limit of measure to the method described below. In our opinion this method is distinguished from the one discussed earlier primarily because we do not compare directly computed indicators but production and labor input indexes. It is a condition of applying the method that the countries under analysis should publish production data of a great number of products in a comparable sectoral or branch system, that there should be unit prices or other weights available, and, moreover, that there should be data on labor inputs by sectors. The direct cooperation of the corresponding institutions of the countries in question could in such a case be dispensed with, but for the sake of simplifying work and for making computations more exact they are desirable. The conditions of data-supplying are available in Hungary[2] and in the German Federal Republic: their serial publication *Die Industrie der Bundersrepublik Deutschland,* Reihe 1 and Reihe 3, contains ample data for such computations for comparing the West German and Hungarian industrial productivity levels, employing the following method.

Both countries publish production data about approximately three thousand commodities both in natural units of measure and in value, although in some cases only one of the two terms is available. The two lists can be placed side by side showing the utmost accuracy in the classification of the German branch-system because the German labor input data are available and we can also draw up the Hungarian labor input data. If the production is not surveyed in the same unit of measure, we convert Hungarian data into the German unit. Where possible, we find if the uniform

2. See *A magyar ipar, Statisztikai adatgyüjtemény* (The Hungarian Industry, Statistical Compilation).

units of measure cover substantial differences of quality-choice, and, if so, whether such differences can be quantified. For instance, we consider differences in the calorific value of coal accounted in tons. But if certain engineering products are expressed in tons or in pieces, there may be considerable quality differences, and there is no way of accounting for them.

In the next move we compute a production index from the production data of the two countries with (a) Hungarian unit prices, (b) German unit prices, (c) where such data are available computed on basis of Hungarian specific working time inputs. Thus we obtain three indexes on the production volume ratios of different branches. These indexes may incorporate the following "errors": (1) discrepancies in qualities—choices of products; (2) cooperation between the enterprises within the sector may be of different degrees, although we endeavor to eliminate this by using for our computations, whenever available, output rather than production data, including consumption in the sector; (3) the observed products may represent different proportions within the total production of the sector.

In the event of the third type of "error," we proceed as follows: We examine what percentage of the total output[3] the products observed represent. This ratio often approximates 100 per cent and is about identical in the two countries; in this case the index is void of a gross error of representation. In branches where cooperation within the sector is rather developed (and for this reason we have to compute with data including consumption in the sector—metallurgy, and the textile industry) the extent of representation cannot be checked on the basis of value of output, further data being needed. In such a case control can be effected only from the Hungarian side. In cases where the degree of representation offered by comparable products is low or different, the production index cannot be based only on these products; by using the former calculations we establish a price index, weighting with the German and Hungarian quantities respectively, and with their help we establish production indexes, converting at the same prices the value of the total production or, in certain cases, the production value of all published products. Thus we obtain two or even four further production indexes, and another two production indexes if we make comparable the value of total production or of all published products on the basis of the Hungarian specific working-time input data. In the final analysis we obtain in certain cases nine production indexes depending on whether we count on the basis of the value of (a) comparable products, all published

---

3. We must make an approach to the problem as far as the German side is concerned by sales data.

products or of the total production, and (b) with Hungarian prices, German prices, or Hungarian specific working-hour inputs. Of the variants listed under (a) we always pick out one, although each variant has an "error." When using price indexes for our computations, they may have errors of representation or the particular error arising from the fact that we do not count with actual products and prices but in most cases with groups of products and average prices. We can regard the variants listed under (b) as interchangeable. Setting as our chief aim the comparison of productivity, we must regard it best to make our computations by working our weights because the differing ratios of products of different material and labor intensity have the smallest role in this case. German working-hour or "net production" weights are not available by products; Hungarian weights are only partly available.

We wish to point out a few of the numerous problems and special solutions arrived at through computation. Hungarian industry does not produce many of the products which are important in West German industry, and, consequently, no Hungarian prices (weights) are available for such products. This was especially true in the engineering industry so that in these sectors all calculations are made only at German prices. The German publications in many cases only provide either quantitative or value data rather than both (for example in ore-mining, and the pharmaceutical industry). In such instances we try to formulate the German prices from world market prices with the aid of official foreign exchange rates. In some cases we have found it more accurate to compute the production indexes on the basis of the materials used rather than on the basis of production data. This was our course of action in the case of the flour milling and oil refining industries. In respect to some branches, none of the methods seems to offer opportunity for computing acceptable production indexes, but presumably only branches of lesser weight and importance are included in this category.

When establishing labor input indexes we try to adjust Hungarian and West German data; we have succeeded in establishing the coverage of West German manpower and working-hour data, and are now making Hungarian data comparable. Thus we are also determining Hungarian data by using the "main activity" classification which corresponds to the concept of German "beteiligte Industriegruppe"; in several cases, however, the differing ratio of the staff engaged in maintenance, forwarding, commercial, and other auxiliary activities may cause a certain distortion. We use three different expressions of labor inputs; working hours performed by operatives (in connection with the Hungarian data we include here the working hours of the so-called auxiliary staff too), man-years performed by operatives including the auxiliary staff, and man-years performed by the total staff. These three types of labor input indexes show up discrepancies in certain sectors which cannot be altogether overlooked; we determine the productivity indexes with the aid of all three labor input indexes. The results of these computations, though still preliminary, are indicated in Table 6 with respect to some branches.

Table 6. Productivity level in some industrial branches in West German industry as percentage of the Hungarian industrial level, 1959.[a]

Branch	Indexes	Production in West German industry in 1959 (Hungarian level = 100)		
		Per working hour	Per man-year of operatives	Per man-year of total staff
Coalmining[b]	1	236	208	220
	2	238	209	222
	3	277	245	249
	4		225	
Textile industry	1	120	115	112
	2	120	114	112
	3	138	132	129
Clothing industry	1	150	129	145
	2	135	116	131
	3	133	114	128
Flour milling	5	153	150	134
Sugar industry	1	272	281	272
	2	272	281	272
	3	259	269	259

a. Preliminary data.
b. Indexes 1–3 include the production of fuel cakes and coke; index 4 relates only to coal extraction.
1 = computed at Hungarian prices
2 = computed at German prices
3 = computed at Hungarian specific working-hour inputs
4 = on the basis of productivity indexes of natural units of measure
5 = on the basis of use of materials

We conclude that ample data compilation and publication in the field of industrial statistics of certain countries enable us to compare productivity levels in detail even between countries without the direct cooperation of the statistical institutions. This cooperation, however, is also desirable, and it is necessary that at least one of the countries have sufficient data to be in a position to convert her own data into the other country's statistical system.

The computation methods described above disregard differences in embodied labor (material, power, fixed funds) input levels. The method based on productivity indexes of natural units of measure can be supplemented with a comparison of technical-economic indicators. The latter method, described in this section, can be supplemented with a comparison on the basis of the value of net production, not with respect to particular branches but only for industry as a whole, and even then with much difficulty. The ratio of the productivity levels should be known by branches and by products, and by also taking into account embodied labor inputs.

Comparisons by Using the Balance of Inter-Industrial Relations

The idea of using the balance of inter-industrial relations for measuring productivity frequently arises in professional literature, and we can cite some practical applications.

In Hungary the Central Statistical Office has drawn up balances of inter-industrial relations, comprising 40 sectors for the year 1957 and 100 sectors for 1959.

Balances of inter-industrial relations offer important help in measuring productivity. On the basis of inverse matrices established from the balances, embodied labor inputs can be traced back to direct labor (working-time) inputs and can thus be used for measuring productivity. On the basis of inverse matrices and the coefficients of specific uses, we can establish the *coefficients of total inputs* per production unit of different branches, regarding primary inputs such as working hours, imports, and depreciation allowances. In this case we traced back all material inputs to these three factors of primary inputs. The coefficients of total inputs can be compared between two periods or two countries after we have made the unit of production comparable. This latter task, however, is extremely difficult; it can be solved by the insertion of natural units of measure only in exceptional cases. Balances of inter-industrial relations as a rule require price index computations, and to secure them reliably may be hard to do.

The coefficients of total inputs of the three primary inputs can also be compared separately. Since they are greatly interchangeable, it is more convenient to compare them in summarized form. Summarization in terms of money may include a lot of conditional factors and involve a further conversion into an identical price level; thus it is better to trace back imports and depreciation allowance to working-time inputs. The former on the basis of the inputs of products exported against imports; the latter on the basis of average inputs of renewals and replacements of fixed funds. I have actually made this computation on the basis of the balance of inter-industrial relations for 1957 in my article[4] jointly authored by Dr. György Cukor; the results are illustrated in Table 7.

Table 7. Total labor input of the national economy and its factors required for production in a value of 10 million forints.

Branch of industry	Share of industrial production used for final consumption (per cent)	Total working hour input					
		Man-year	Per cent	Directly in the producing branch	Indirectly in the producing branch (and other branches)	Of imports	Of depreciation
Coalmining	1.5	785	100	51	18	13	18
Iron and steel manufacturing	1.5	699	100	20	21	44	15
Engineering	11.3	391	100	38	26	25	11
Telecommunications	2.4	349	100	45	21	27	7
Electric power	1.9	488	100	20	23	30	27
Pharmaceutical	1.7	281	100	25	32	31	12
Timber	1.6	388	100	33	16	47	4
Cotton	7.7	173	100	34	9	50	7
Textile clothing	10.5	233	100	31	26	38	5
Food	33.0	353	100	10	73	11	6

The method of computing total labor inputs for the national economy is more fully discussed in my paper "Use of balances of inter-industrial relations for efficiency calculations."[5] In order to compare these indicators between two countries a common expression of the bases of reference (the production value) and proper foreign exchange conversion rates (price indexes) are required. The use of the foreign exchange conversion rates can be avoided by using the following process of approximation, once we have succeeded

4. "Az ágazati kapcsolatok mérlegének felhasználása az ipar ágazati szerkezetének vizsgálatára és tervezésére" (The balance of inter-industrial relations used for analysis and planning of inter-industrial structure), *MTA Közgazdaságtudományi Intézetének közleményei*, no. 9, 1960.
5. Paper presented for the Statistical Scientific Conference held in Budapest June 1–5, 1961. *Statisztikai Szemle*, no. 8–9, 1961.

in solving the comparison of productivities with the help of the method described in this study.

The comparison of the labor inputs directly arising in the sector is effected on the basis of labor inputs (f) directly arising in the branch f_A/f_B.

We establish by countries the f^+ total labor inputs of the national economy.

$$h_A = f_A^+/f_A \text{ and } h_B = f_B^+/f_B$$

With this coefficient we adjust the result of the original comparison:

$$\frac{f_A}{f_B} \cdot \frac{h_A}{h_B}$$

I have tried to work out indicators of the total labor input of the national economy on the basis of the Polish balance of inter-industrial relations published for the year 1957.[6] Czechoslovakia has not published a balance of inter-industrial relations. In the absence of proper basic data, I had to disregard the depreciation allowance. It follows that the Hungarian data examined and thus made comparable contain only the total labor and import inputs of the national economy summed up in terms of labor. I have examined 13 industrial branches; in 6 branches coefficient h is almost identical. Thus, in ferrous metallurgy the values are 4.2 — 4.2; in the textile industry 2.9 — 2.9; in the clothing industry 2.8 — 3.0; in the food industry 10.0 — 9.0. In five branches the deviations are 20–40 per cent. Substantial differences can be seen in the chemical industry where the Polish coefficient amounts to 2.9, the Hungarian to 5.0, and in electric power production where the coefficients are 1.7 — 3.7 respectively. The deviations are the result of several factors such as different ratios in imports, cooperation, specific embodied labor inputs, and the productivity level of other branches. The separation of these factors is a difficult but interesting task, even if it does not promise exact computation results, but it will surely offer ample possibilities for analysis.

The indicators of total labor inputs of the national economy have been used successfully for a study which is closely related to productivity. In the centralized state-owned foreign trade of the socialist countries it is of great importance from the point of view of getting favorable trade results to make so-called export and import rentability calculations. In case of exports, for instance, we compare foreign exchange received for the export

6. On the basis of the article published by K. Porwit and J. Zurkowski "Prace i materialy zakladu badan ekonomicznich," *Warszawa*, no. 18, 1960.

product and all inland work spent on the production of the commodity expressed by the coefficients of total labor input in the national economy. Such coefficients have been computed earlier by rough approximation without balances of inter-industrial relations. If we compare on the basis of this balance the total labor input coefficients of the national economy determined by branches with the foreign exchange proceeds of the branches (both data related to production per unit), and if the ratios of the branches thus obtained are put side by side we get a clear view as to the rentability of the export of different branches. If we accept the view that prices reached abroad give an approximate picture of the prices in the world market and of average productivity levels abroad, this comparison can be regarded as a particular productivity comparison. (It may be well to reiterate the point that in the total input coefficients of the different branches the productivity level of all related branches is reflected. In these coefficients including the exemplified export rentability computations, the productivity level of the national economy realized in the products of the given branch is expressed.)

We can compare the level of productivity between countries not only by sectors but also in respect to the national economy as a whole by using balances of inter-industrial relations, inverse matrices, and total input coefficients, starting from the output meant for final consumption of the different countries. The description of the methods can be found in the article of A. Stobbe together with calculations.[7]

I should like to deal briefly with another application of balances of inter-industrial relations which may play an important part in measuring the dynamics of productivity and which can also be used for international comparisons. As is well known, indexes expressing productivity dynamics disregard, almost without exception, changes in embodied labor inputs. The accounting of power and fixed fund inputs is important since the saving in labor input increases mainly by directly replacing applied human labor with the work of fixed funds actuated by natural mechanical power. The use and proper transforming of natural resources of power, and the production and operation of fixed funds also require actual human work—labor input. For this reason it would be wise to estimate how much of directly applied labor input is required for one unit of production, as well as power and fixed fund inputs—all this in terms of labor inputs. An index thus construed might be called an efficiency index; its computation is based on the calculations of working time equivalents of 1 million cal. power, 1 million kwh electric power, 1 million forint depreciation allowance, and

7. *Weltwirtschaftliches Archiv*, vol. 82, no. 2.

so forth, and on the fact that on this basis the directly applied labor, power, and fixed-fund inputs can be added together. According to the Hungarian balance of inter-industrial relations for 1957, 1 million kwh electric power correspond to 17 man-years; 1 million forint depreciation allowance to 56 man-years. Considering that depreciation allowance is not based on an altogether solid footing, we would suggest, by way of approximation, that changes in the size of fixed funds be taken as proportionate with electric power consumption.[8]

We can compute a similar efficiency index for international comparisons. We have established that in Czechoslovak industry production per worker is 70 per cent higher than in Hungary and that electric power consumption per worker, after eliminating sectoral structural changes, is 80 per cent higher. Accordingly, production per unit of electric power consumption is about 5 per cent lower. Starting from this point we can establish the proportion in the two countries between the sum of directly applied labor and of the power and fixed-fund inputs directly replacing applied labor per unit of production. We can make three calculations: we can express power and fixed-fund inputs in both countries with the Hungarian equivalents or in both countries with the Czechoslovak equivalents of each country with her own working-hour equivalents. The fullest picture is given by the third solution, but because there is no balance of inter-industrial relations for the Czechoslovak economy, we can make no such calculation unless we use the following, rather rough approximation. We assume that the electric power used per worker also corresponds to the ratio of fixed funds per worker. Moreover, in Czechoslovak industry the productivity of mining, electric power production, and manufacturing of fixed funds is also 70 per cent higher (the general average of industry) than in Hungarian industry. In this case the efficiency shows a difference of 67 per cent in favor of the Czechoslovak industry.

It would be premature to talk about the value of such analytical possibilities, but at any rate it seems both interesting and useful. The drawing up and the analysis of inter-industrial relations offer manifold possibilities for international comparisons of a new type, among others in the field of productivity studies. Such comparisons would be facilitated if a certain uniformity could be reached in the drawing up of balances among the different countries.

8. See the article of the author "Termelékenység és állóalapkihasználás" (Productivity of Labour and the Exploitation of Fixed Funds), in *Közgazdasági Szemle*, no. 9, 1961.

CHAPTER 9

Some Measurement Problems in Comparing United States and Soviet Industrial Labor Productivity[1]

GERTRUDE SCHROEDER

United States Bureau of the Census

Practitioners of the art of making international comparisons of industrial labor productivity face difficult conceptual and methodological problems. The task is particularly arduous when comparisons are being made between market and nonmarket economies, such as the United States and the USSR. Data problems are enormous, and compromises with the conceptual and methodological ideal constantly have to be made.

General Methodological Problems

International comparisons of relative levels of industrial labor productivity may be approached in two general ways. The first, termed the "price index" approach, is to measure the value of the aggregate product per unit of labor originating in industry in each country expressed in the currencies of both countries. The procedure, in essence, would be to value the gross products in the two countries in each other's currencies and then to deduct

1. The views expressed in this paper are those of the author and do not necessarily represent the views of the United States Bureau of the Census. The author wishes to acknowledge the substantial assistance provided by Murray S. Weitzman of the Foreign Manpower Research Office.

the cost of material inputs valued in the same way to obtain a measure of net output, or "value-added" in Western terminology. The principal methodological problems would be those involved in ensuring that outputs and inputs are defined and measured in the same way for both countries. Because the data problems involved in this approach are so formidable, investigators have had to resort to the second, or "quantity index" approach. In short, this method is to measure the physical output per unit of labor for as many equivalent products as possible and then to aggregate the results with value-added weights.

Both approaches yield measures of labor productivity by branch of industry, showing the differences in industrial structure in the two countries and how these differences affect over-all productivity levels. Important methodological problems are common to both.[2] With respect to the numerator of the productivity ratio, there is first the matter of the size and representativeness of the sample. When comparisons are made between an industrially advanced country and one considerably less advanced, there are likely to be many unique goods in the production pattern of the former for which no meaningful price or quantity can be found in the latter. If the sample is not to be seriously biased, techniques must be devised to convert most of these unique products into equivalent products.

Next, there arise the problems connected with differences in product quality. Where products are similar in name but different in quality in the two countries, means of adjusting for these differences must be devised, because goods of higher quality represent more "product" in an economic sense than goods of lower quality. In Country A, for example, a typical "automobile" may weigh 3000 pounds and be equipped with automatic transmission, whereas in Country B an "automobile" may weigh 2000 pounds and have manual transmission. Clearly, more resources would be required to produce the heavier automobile in both markets, and an "automobile" is thus not a homogeneous product between the two countries. The methodological problem, then, is to devise ways to convert such products into homogeneous units—that is, into equivalent products. Although the particular techniques will differ depending on product peculiarities and available data, the aim must be to measure as best one can the proportionate adjustment in costs or prices that would result in the two countries if identical products were made.

2. These problems are discussed in Milton Gilbert and Irving B. Kravis, *An International Comparison of National Products and the Purchasing Power of Currencies* (Paris, 1954).

Finally, there is the matter of the weights to be used to aggregate individual products into branches of industry and to sum the branches. One may use physical weights (employment, as did Rostas and Frankel in their investigations of labor productivity in British and American industries[3]). Or one may compute factor cost weights, as did OEEC economists in their pioneer effort to compare output and productivity in the United States and the United Kingdom by sector of origin.[4] In aggregate productivity comparisons the objective should be to obtain the closest possible approximation to net output weights. Often, however, the choice of weights is limited both by the data available and by the time and resources at the disposal of the investigator. The necessity for weighting produces the famous "index number problem." The question here is merely which country's employment or prices shall be used as weights, those of either country being equally valid conceptually. Or shall an average be calculated, and, if so, what is its economic meaning?

With respect to the denominator of the productivity ratio, the main conceptual problem is that of obtaining a measure of labor input that is consistent with the measure of output. Depending on objectives, one may divide the output measures by total employment, production workers, man-year equivalents, or man-hours. The employment measure also may be adjusted to allow for differences in skill levels (quality). With the employment measure chosen, the methodological problems are mainly those of wrestling with the data, both to ensure comparability with the product data and to make appropriate adjustments for differences between countries in the concept and measurements used to compile employment statistics.

A final point on general methodology concerns the indexes appropriate for extrapolating the base-year findings with respect to relative levels of productivity. Clearly, these indexes should be comparable between countries and conceptually consistent with the measure of relative productivity in the base year.

Recent Comparisons Made by Soviet Economists

During the past several years Soviet economists have published a number of comparisons of trends and levels of labor productivity in the United

---

3. L. Rostas, *Comparative Productivity in British and American Industry* (Cambridge, 1948); M. Frankel, *British and American Manufacturing Productivity* (Urbana, 1957).
4. Deborah Paige and Gottfried Bombach, *A Comparison of National Product and Productivity of the United Kingdom and the United States* (Paris, 1959).

States and the USSR. The first of the aggregate comparisons, made by Ya. Ioffe, was published in 1957 and showed Soviet labor productivity in 1955 to be 40 to 42 per cent of that of the United States.[5] He later published the following comparisons (United States = 100):[6] The output per person employed was 40 in 1955, 42 in 1956, 44 in 1957, 45 in 1958, and 46 in 1959; output per production worker was 44 in 1955, 46 in 1956, 48 in 1957, 49 in 1958, and 51 in 1959. Another economist, A. Aganbegyan, has published the finding that in 1957 Soviet output per person employed was half that of the United States.[7] The over-all comparison currently cited most often in Soviet literature and used in statistical handbooks,[8] however, are those apparently calculated by the USSR's Central Statistical Administration and recently described by V. Starovskiy.[9] He states that both the gross and the net value of industrial production in the two countries in 1959 were computed using ruble-dollar ratios calculated on the basis of both the Soviet product mix and the United States product mix. The value of net output in the USSR was found to be 61 per cent of that of the United States when measured in rubles and 60 per cent when measured in dollars. With respect to labor productivity, he states, "proceeding from these data (industrial production in the USSR more than half, and production workers about 30 per cent more than in the United States), we conclude that the productivity of industrial workers in the USSR in 1959 was 40–50 per cent of industrial labor productivity in that in the United States." These also are the productivity comparisons given by Khrushchev at the 21st Communist Party Congress in January 1959.[10]

Soviet economists undoubtedly spent many laborious hours in constructing these comparisons and may have made important progress in solving some of the complex methodological problems involved in comparing economies with such different industrial structures, product mix, and institutional settings as the United States and the USSR. Unfortunately, however, the authors have not provided detailed descriptions of these methodologies or the basic data from which an independent reconstruction of their results could be made.

The comparisons illustrate two of the methodological dilemmas pre-

5. *Strany sotsializma i kapitalizma v tsifrakh* (Moscow, 1957), p. 59.
6. *Planovoye khozyaystvo*, 1960, no. 3, p. 48.
7. *Sotsialisticheskiy trud*, 1959, no. 4, p. 19.
8. *Narodnoye khozyaystvo SSSR v 1959 godu* (Moscow, 1960), p. 89; *SSSR—SShA, tsifry i fakty* (Moscow, 1961), p. 29.
9. *Voprosy ekonomiki*, 1960, no. 4, pp. 103–17.
10. *Pravda*, January 28, 1959, p. 9.

viously discussed—the index number problem and the problem of the temporal extrapolation of findings concerning relative productivity levels in a given year. Besides the unanswered question of how "gross" and "net" outputs were defined and compared in the two countries, the conclusions about relative output levels cited by Starovskiy are most puzzling. The finding that the relative levels of "net" output are the same regardless of which country's prices are used implies that the price structures (or product mix) in the two economies are essentially the same (or that the differences are offsetting)—a situation that seems highly improbable theoretically and also is at variance with the findings of ruble-dollar studies made by United States economists.[11] In addition, the conclusion that Soviet output relative to the United States is higher when both outputs are valued in rubles differs from the results of international product comparisons made for Western economies, where a given country's level of output invariably was found to be considerably higher relative to the level in another country when both outputs were measured in the other country's prices. One would suppose that this general result should also be obtained for comparisons of total industrial production in the United States and the USSR.

To extrapolate their calculated levels of labor productivity, all three Soviet authors apparently used the official industrial labor productivity indexes for the USSR and a productivity index for the United States computed from the Federal Reserve Board's index of industrial production and an employment index based on Bureau of Labor Statistics data. Neither the production indexes nor the employment indexes for the two countries are really comparable. The United States production index measures changes in net output (value-added) in manufacturing, mining, and electric and gas utilities. The Soviet index measures changes in the gross value of output in "industry" defined to include a number of activities not covered by the United States index and uses price weighting procedures that are radically different from those used in computing the United States index. Differences in the definition of industry and of production workers affect the comparability of the employment indexes.

Soviet economists also have published several recent investigations of relative levels of labor productivity in individual branches of industry. The most comprehensive is A. Kats's comparison of physical output per pro-

11. A. S. Becker, *Prices of Producers' Durables in the United States and the USSR in 1955*, RAND, RM 2432, August 15, 1959; Norman H. Kaplan and Eleanor S. Weinstein, *A Comparison of Soviet and American Retail Prices*, RAND, P-901, October 3, 1956.

duction worker for 28 branches of industry in the United States in 1954 and the USSR in 1956.[12] The author claims that these branches represent about two fifths of total production workers and payrolls in the USSR. According to this comparison, Soviet labor productivity ranged from 17.1 per cent of that of the United States for margarine to 147.4 per cent for bread and bakery products, the average being 45.5 per cent when weighted by USSR payrolls and 47.9 per cent when weighted by USSR employment. Although the sample covered a wide variety of industries, almost all machine building was omitted, as were nonferrous metallurgy, electric power, and most of the chemicals industry. In a later paper, Kats reported (with no details) his findings that physical output per production worker for 25 branches of industry in the USSR in 1957 averaged 42 to 47 per cent of that of the United States in 1956.[13]

Two other recent studies pertain to the machine building industry. In one of them the authors compared productivity in specialized machine tool plants in the USSR in 1958 with productivity in all machine tool plants in the United States in 1956,[14] and found Soviet output per production worker to be 60.5 per cent of that of the United States computed in physical units and 53.7 per cent computed in "standard" units. The second study compared relative levels of output and productivity in the machinery and metalworking industry as a whole.[15] Using value indicators of some kind, the authors concluded that output per production worker in the USSR was 33 to 37 per cent of that of the United States in 1958. In another study, A. Aganbegyan, without presenting methodological details, states that Soviet labor productivity (presumably output per production worker in 1957) was 40 per cent or less that of the United States level in mining (25 per cent in coal mining), logging, and the chemical industries, and that the levels were 50 to 67 per cent in machine building, metallurgy, light industry, and the food industry.[16]

Comparisons Made by United States Economists

Three Western estimates of the relative levels of total industrial production and productivity in the two countries have been published recently, all of them in papers or testimony presented before committees of the Con-

12. *Sotsialisticheskiy trud,* 1959, no. 1, pp. 42–55.
13. *Ekonomicheskiye nauki,* 1961, no. 1, p. 132.
14. *Vestnik statistiki,* 1960, no. 6, pp. 25–32.
15. *Planovoye khozyaystvo,* 1960, no. 8, pp. 81–91.
16. *Sotsialisticheskiy trud,* 1959, no. 4, p. 15.

gress of the United States. Two of these studies were made by United States government economists. The earlier study found production and productivity in the USSR in 1955 to be about one-third that of the United States.[17] The later study found the level of production in the USSR in 1958 to be about two-fifths that of the United States, and the level of labor productivity to be about one third.[18] Unfortunately, the authors tell us neither how these figures were obtained, nor even what they mean, that is, are the relatives in rubles or dollars or do they represent geometric means? The author of the third of these studies, G. Warren Nutter, concludes that Soviet output was 22.7 per cent that of the United States in 1955 and that productivity was 20.7 per cent.[19] Nutter's estimates raise serious questions of comparability, however, because his measures clearly omit military production and a substantial part of machinery on the Soviet side, but include them for the United States.[20]

The United States Bureau of the Census has recently completed studies of comparative productivity in the logging, automobile, and mineral fuels industries. The authors of these studies made numerous adjustments in both production and employment data for the two countries in an effort to obtain comparability. The data and methodologies are spelled out in detail in the published studies. For logging the average physical output per production worker man-day in the USSR in 1956 was found to be 18 per cent of that of the United States.[21] For the automobile industry the gross value of output per production worker in the USSR in 1955 was shown to be 38 per cent (measured in dollars) of that of the United States in 1954.[22] For the mineral fuels industries the following productivity ratios (measured in standard fuel equivalents per person employed for the United States in 1954 and the USSR in 1955) were obtained: coal and lignite extraction—19 per cent;

17. US Congress, Joint Economic Committee, *Soviet Economic Growth: A Comparison with the United States,* 85th Congress, 1st Session (Washington, 1957), p. 105.
18. US Congress, Hearings Before the Joint Economic Committee, *Comparisons of the United States and Soviet Economies,* 86th Congress, 1st Session (Washington, 1960), p. 4.
19. US Congress, Joint Economic Committee, *Comparisons of the United States and Soviet Economies,* Joint Committee Print, 86th Congress, 1st Session (Washington 1959), part I, p. 113.
20. R. V. Greenslade and Phyllis A. Wallace, "Industrial Growth in the Soviet Union: Comment," *American Economic Review,* September 1959, pp. 687–95.
21. US Bureau of the Census, *International Population Reports,* Series P-95, September 1959, no. 54, p. 93.
22. US Bureau of the Census, *International Population Reports,* Series P-95, June 1959, no. 53, p. 109.

coke—34 per cent; oil and gas extraction—19 per cent; and oil and gas refining—36 per cent.[23]

Tables 8–11 present productivity comparisons made by the author of this paper for 25 branches of industry in 1956. By way of illustrating the difficulties faced by a Western economist in making such comparisons, we may examine them by reference to the major methodological problems posed at the outset. First, with respect to the nature of the sample, the comparisons (which relate to total physical output per production worker) cover branches of industry employing 22 per cent of all production workers in the United

Table 8. Physical output per production worker in selected industries, US and USSR, 1956.

Product	Units	Output per worker US	USSR	Ratio (US = 100)
Coal	Metric tons	2,036	400	20
Coke	Metric tons	2,314	793	34
Crude petroleum and natural gas	Metric tons of std. fuel equiv.	5,414	1,089	20
Petroleum refining	Metric tons	2,886	1,049	36
Iron ore	Metric tons	3,271	1,101	34
Steel	Metric tons	196.2	84.4	43
Synthetic rubber	Metric tons	156.7	19.4	12
Artificial fiber	Metric tons	15.0	2.6	17
Rubber footwear	Pairs	5,051	3,756	74
Electric power	1,000 kwh	3,118.4	582.5	19
Paper and paperboard	Metric tons	61.6	21.8	35
Lumber and logging	Cubic meters	908.6	226.6	25
Cement	Metric tons	1,530	527.8	34
Brick	1,000 pieces	255.0	67.7	27
Lime and gypsum	Metric tons	1,077	260.8	24
Cotton fabrics	Square meters	24,838	5,798	23
Silk and synthetic fabrics	Square meters	22,524	6,164	27
Woolen fabrics	Square meters	4,377	1,815	41
Footwear (except rubber)	Pairs	2,672	1,046	39
Beer	Decaliters	20,196	7,077	35
Sugar	Metric tons	86.4	33.9	39
Flour	Metric tons	503.5	251.4	50
Meat	Metric tons	50.1	19.4	39
Dairy products	Metric tons	391.3	115.5	30
Margarine	Metric tons	337.8	56.95	17

Sources: Tables 9 and 10.

23. US Bureau of the Census, *International Population Reports,* Series P-95 forthcoming), no. 60.

States and 34 per cent of this total in the USSR.[24] The sample includes every product properly measurable in physical units for which reasonably comparable output and employment data could be found. The sample is the same as that used by the Soviet economist Kats, except for the addition of crude petroleum, electric power, and sugar, and the exclusion of vegetable oil and macaroni (for which no United States data could be found), metal-cutting machine tools, bread and bakery products, and confectionery products (which are highly diverse product categories not comparable in physical units in the two countries).

A few adjustments were made to allow for differences in quality and product mix in the two countries. Thus, because United States fabrics are considerably wider than Soviet fabrics, textile outputs are measured in square meters rather than in linear meters. Manufactured dairy products are measured in milk equivalents, and the output of crude petroleum and natural gas is measured in standard fuel equivalents. Although similar adjustments are needed for other branches, they cannot easily be made with available data. In the case of rubber footwear, for example, the inability to do so probably results in an understatement of Soviet productivity relative to the United States. A large part of rubber footwear output in the United States consists of tennis shoes and sneakers, the labor requirements for which are less than those for rubber boots or galoshes. The output of tennis shoes and sneakers apparently is much smaller relative to the total in the USSR than in the United States, but we do not know by how much.

We may now turn to the problems of comparing employment. The USSR does not publish a detailed breakdown of industrial employment like that of the United States, and for only 11 of the 25 branches could independent employment estimates be made for the USSR. The rest had to be derived from Kats's productivity estimates and physical production data in the statistical handbooks. According to Kats's statements, these derived employment figures do not include employment in collective farm industry, an omission that would significantly affect the productivity levels shown for logging, lumber, and brick. In some cases the employment data clearly do not correspond exactly to the product data. Thus the employment figures for paper and paperboard include paper products in both countries; data for paper products alone are not available for the USSR.

The employment figures shown in Table 10 for the USSR include junior service personnel, guards, and apprentices as well as "workers" because all

24. These proportions are based on estimates of the number of production workers in the United States and the USSR adjusted for comparability as described later.

Table 9. Output per production worker in selected industries, US, 1956.

Branch of industry	Output Level	Output Units	Production workers (000)	Output per production worker Level	Output per production worker Units
Coal	479,696	1,000 m.t.[a]	235.6	2,036	m.t.
Coke	67,570	1,000 m.t.	29.2	2,314	m.t.
Crude petroleum and natural gas	848,376	1,000 m.t.[b]	156.7	5,414	m.t.[b]
Petroleum refining	378,100	1,000 m.t.	131.0	2,886	m.t.
Iron ore	99,448	1,000 m.t.	30.4	3,271	m.t.
Steel	104,522	1,000 m.t.	532.6	196.2	m.t.
Synthetic rubber	1,097	1,000 m.t.	7.0	156.7	m.t.
Artificial fiber	746.0	1,000 m.t.	49.6	15.0	m.t.
Rubber footwear	100,007	1,000 pairs	19.8	5,051	pairs
Electric power	684,804	Mil. kwh	219.6	3,118.4	000 kwh
Paper and paperboard	28,523	1,000 m.t.	463.4	61.6	m.t.
Lumber and logging	408.4	Mil. m³	449.5	908.6	m³
Cement	56,152	1,000 m.t.	36.7	1,530	m.t.
Brick	8,085	Mil. pieces	31.7	255.0	000 pieces
Lime and gypsum	18,954	1,000 m.t.	17.6	1,077	m.t.
Cotton fabrics	10,094	Mil. m²	406.4	24,838	m²
Silk and synthetic fabrics	2,588	Mil. m²	114.9	22,524	m²
Woolen fabrics	460	Mil. m²	105.1	4,377	m²
Footwear (ex. rubber)	591.8	Mil. pairs	221.5	2,672	pairs
Beer	1,064	Mil. decal.	52.7	20,196	decal.
Sugar	2,280	1,000 m.t.	26.4	86.4	m.t.
Flour	10,422	1,000 m.t.	20.7	503.5	m.t.
Meat	13,470	1,000 m.t.	268.8	50.1	m.t.
Dairy products	28.2	Mil. m.t.[c]	72.1	391.3	m.t.
Margarine	621.6	1,000 m.t.	1.84	337.8	m.t.

a. m.t. = metric tons.
b. In standard fuel equivalents.
c. Milk equivalent of manufactured dairy products.

Sources:
Output: All data from United Nations, *Statistical Yearbook 1959*, except:
(1) Iron ore, paper and paperboard, lime and gypsum, silk and synthetic fabrics, meat, and dairy products—from *Statistical Abstract of the United States*, 1958 and 1959.
(2) Artificial fiber—from *Textile Organon*, February 1957, p. 18.
(3) Lumber and logging—from United Nations, *Yearbook of Forest Product Statistics, 1958*, pp. 36–7, 64.
(4) Petroleum refining—OEEC, *Industrial Statistics, 1900–59*, Paris, 1960, p. 67.
(5) Rubber footwear—*US Census of Manufactures, 1954*. Extrapolated to 1956 on the basis of the change in employment, 1954–56.

these groups are classified as production workers in the United States. If data had permitted, allowance should have been made for the fact that Soviet engineering-technical personnel who are working foremen or are engaged in product development are classified as production workers in the United States and also for certain other less important differences. Adjustment of the data for dissimilarity in the procedures for measuring employment in the two countries was not considered necessary. It was not possible with available data to adjust the employment estimates for differences in the degree of product coverage and specialization in the two countries, that is, to allow for the fact that establishments classified in one branch of industry may also produce items of another branch. Such an adjustment probably would not significantly affect the employment figures for the United States, since the coverage and specialization ratios largely cancel (according to 1954 census data). Such may not be the case for the USSR; there are no data.[25]

Next, we may consider the matter of weights. Kats used Soviet employment and wage bills as weights. Because these Soviet wage bills are not available, the comparisons shown in Table 8 could be weighted only by employment in both countries. Average output per production worker in the 25 branches in the USSR is shown to be 28 per cent of United States output using Soviet weights and 31 per cent using United States weights; the unweighted average is 32 per cent.

Finally with respect to the extrapolation of findings concerning productivity levels, comparisons were also made for 9 of the 25 branches in 1940

Employment: All data from US Bureau of Labor Statistics, *Employment and Earnings,* May 1960, vol. 6, no. 11, except:

(1) Coke—estimated from data in the *US Census of Manufactures, 1954* and *Statistical Abstract of the United States, 1959.*

(2) Synthetic rubber, artificial fiber, lime and gypsum, brick, cotton fabrics, silk and synthetic fabrics, woolen fabrics, beer and flour—from *Annual Survey of Manufactures, 1956.*

(3) Margarine—from *US Census of Manufactures, 1954.*

(4) Crude petroleum and natural gas—Bureau of Labor Statistics figure for production workers in "Crude Petroleum and Natural Gas Production," less an estimated number engaged in well drilling and rig building. See Demitri B. Shimkin, *The Soviet Mineral Fuels Industries, 1927/28–1958,* US Bureau of the Census (to be published in International Population Reports, Series P-95).

25. Although Kats points out the necessity for adjusting the data for differences in product coverage and specialization ratios, it appears that he, too, did not have the data with which to do so for the USSR.

Table 10. Output per production worker in selected industries, USSR, 1956.

Branch of industry	Output Level	Output Units	Production workers (000)	Output per production worker Level	Output per production worker Units
Coal	429,174	1,000 m.t.[a]	1,073.4	400	m.t.
Coke	46,600	1,000 m.t.	58.8	793	m.t.
Crude petroleum and natural gas	134,323	1,000 m.t.[b]	123.4	1,089	m.t.[b]
Petroleum refining	75,200	1,000 m.t.	71.7	1,049	m.t.
Iron ore	78,079	1,000 m.t.	70.9	1,101	m.t.
Steel	48,698	1,000 m.t.	577.0	84.4	m.t.
Synthetic rubber	n.a.			19.4	m.t.
Artificial fiber	128.9	1,000 m.t.	49.7	2.6	m.t.
Rubber footwear	145,000	1,000 pairs	38.6	3,756	pairs
Electric power	179,453	Mil. kwh	308.1	582.5	000 kwh
Paper and paperboard	2,581	1,000 m.t.[c]	118.5	21.8	m.t.
Lumber and logging	427.5	Mil. m³	1,886.4	226.6	m³
Cement	24,858	1,000 m.t.	47.1	527.8	m.t.
Brick	21,566	Mil. pieces	318.6	67.7	000 pieces
Lime and gypsum	13,455	1,000 m.t.	51.6	260.8	m.t.
Cotton fabrics	4,366	Mil. m²	753.0	5,798	m²
Silk and synthetic fabrics	617	Mil. m²	100.1	6,164	m²
Woolen fabrics	341	Mil. m²	187.9	1,815	m²
Footwear (ex. rubber)	311.2	Mil. pairs	297.5	1,046	pairs
Beer	180.7	Mil. decal.	25.5	7,077	decal.
Sugar	4,714	1,000 m.t.	139.0	33.9	m.t.
Flour	32,000	1,000 m.t.	127.3	251.4	m.t.
Meat	2,671	1,000 m.t.	137.5	19.4	m.t.
Dairy products	17.3	Mil. m.t.	149.8	115.5	m.t.
Margarine	437	1,000 m.t.[d]	7.7	56.95	m.t.

a. m.t. = metric tons.
b. In standard fuel equivalents.
c. Net.
d. Milk equivalent of manufactured dairy products.

Sources:
   Output: All data from *Narodnoye khozyaystvo SSSR v 1959 godu* except:
   (1) Petroleum refining—Demitri B. Shimkin, *The Soviet Mineral Fuels Industries, 1927/28–1958*, US Bureau of the Census (to be published in International Population Reports, Series P-95).
   (2) Coke—*Narodnoye khozyaystvo SSSR v 1958 godu.*
   (3) Electric power—gross kwh adjusted to net kwh to allow for station use.
   (4) Dairy products—V. P. Zotov, *Pishchevaya promyshlennost' sovetskogo soyuza*, p. 161.
   Employment: All data derived from officially reported output data and output per worker given by A. Kats, *Sotsialisticheskiy trud*, 1959, no. 1, p. 46, except:
   (1) Coal, coke, petroleum refining, iron ore, steel, electric power, and lumber

and in 1950 (Table 11). The estimates for these years were constructed by using production and employment data defined and measured in the same way as they were in the estimates for 1956 shown in Tables 8–10. The productivity ratios for 1940 agree fairly well with those obtained by Galenson for prewar years.[26]

The foregoing discussion touches on a few of the many perplexing problems involved in productivity comparisons for individual branches of industry in the United States and the USSR. The remainder of the paper will consider only one methodological problem on the aggregative level—that of obtaining comparable measures of employment in industry as a whole. This is a complicated task, and only the main considerations can be sketched here. Undoubtedly the most critical problem is to standardize the employment data for difference in the definition of "industry." Because the data needed to adjust Soviet employment data to the United States definition are not available, the Western economist must try to adjust United States data to conform to Soviet definitions of scope and coverage.[27] To accomplish

---

and logging—from Murray S. Weitzman and Andrew Elias, *The Magnitude and Distribution of Civilian Employment in the USSR: 1928–59*, US Bureau of the Census, International Population Reports, Series P-95, no. 57, pp. 71–72, 74.

(2) Crude petroleum—figure for 1955 taken from Demitri B. Shimkin, *The Soviet Mineral Fuels Industries, 1927/28–1958*, p. 103 and extended to 1956 with data in Murray S. Weitzman and Andrew Elias, *op. cit.*, p. 74.

(3) Paper and paperboard—figure for 1955 taken from Murray S. Weitzman and Andrew Elias, *op. cit.*, p. 72 and extended to 1956 with production and productivity data in *Narodnoye khozyaystvo SSSR v 1958 godu*, p. 139 and *Narodnoye khozyaystvo SSSR v 1959 godu*, p. 154.

(4) Cement—estimated from production and productivity data in *Narodnoye khozyaystvo SSSR v 1958 godu*, p. 259 and Z. I. Loginov, *Tsementnaya promyshlennost' SSSR i perspektiviy yeye razvitiya*, p. 111.

(5) Sugar (figure for 1955)—from V. P. Zotov, *Pishchevaya promyshlennost' sovetskogo soyuza*, p. 57.

(6) For coal, coke, crude petroleum and natural gas, petroleum refining, iron ore, steel, paper, lumber and logging, electric power, cement, motor vehicles, and sugar—an estimate of the number of apprentices, guards, and junior service personnel (MOP) was added to the number of workers (*rabochiye*) obtained as indicated above. These estimates were based on data in V. Ye. Komarov, *Ekonomicheskiye osnovy podgotovki spetsialistov dlya narodnogo khozyaystva*, p. 70, and Demitri B. Shimkin, *Notes on the Industrial Labor Force of the Soviet Union*, US Bureau of the Census, Foreign Manpower Research Office, July 1958 (ditto).

26. Walter Galenson, *Labor Productivity in Soviet and American Industry* (New York, 1955), p. 241.

27. For purposes of productivity comparisons, if the employment data are adjusted in this manner, comparable adjustments also need to be made in the product data.

Table 11. Percentage of change in output per production worker 1940–56,
and levels of productivity, US and USSR, 1940, 1950, and 1956.

Product	Percentage of change in output per production worker				USSR level of productivity (US = 100)		
	US		USSR				
	1940–56	1950–56	1940–56	1950–56	1940	1950	1956
Coal	118	65	32	31	33	25	20
Coke	26	20	33	29	32	32	34
Iron ore	4	5	25	39	28	26	34
Steel	51	19	57	44	41	36	43
Electric power	234	79	78	55	36	22	19
Lumber and logging	—	25	—	22	—	26	25
Paper and paperboard	30	15	28	48	36	27	35
Cement	58	33	152	97	21	23	34
Footwear (ex. rubber)	45	—	5	—	54	—	39

Sources:
US
Output Indexes—all output data from *Statistical Abstract of the United States*, 1958
and 1959, and *Historical Statistics of the United States* except:
    (1) Logging—UN, FAO, *European Timber Statistics 1913–50*, Table P-2; and UN,
      FAO, *Yearbook of Forest Product Statistics, 1958*, pp. 36–37.
    (2) Footwear—National Shoe Manufactures' Association, *Facts and Figures for
      Footwear*, 1958, p. 17.
Employment Indexes—all employment data are published and unpublished esti-
mates of the Bureau of Labor Statistics except those for coke, which are from
the Bureau of Mines. Published data are from *Statistical Abstract of the United
States, 1958* and BLS, *Employment and Earnings*, May 1960, vol. 6, no. 11.
USSR
Output Indexes—all output data from *Narodnoye khozyaystvo SSSR v 1958 godu* and
Narodnoye khozyaystvo SSSR v 1959 godu.
Employment Indexes—production worker estimates are published and unpublished
estimates of the Foreign Manpower Research Office. Estimates of the number
of wage workers (*rabochiye*) are set forth principally in Murray S. Weitzman
and Andrew Elias, *The Magnitude and Distribution of Civilian Employment in the
USSR, 1928–59.* US Bureau of the Census, International Population Reports,
Series P-95, no. 57, Table 7. Estimates of the number of apprentices, junior
service personnel, and guards, added to the estimates for wage workers, are
based on *Narodnoye khozyaystvo SSSR v 1959 godu*, p. 138, and V. Ye. Komarov,
Ekonomicheskiye osnovy podgotovki spetsialistov dlya narodnogo khozyaystva,
(Moscow, 1959), p. 70.

this, using Bureau of Labor Statistics data for the United States, employment in at least the following activities must be added to the total in
manufacturing, mining, and gas and electric utilities (the groups usually
used in United States-USSR employment comparisons): cleaning and dye-

ing, fluid milk, fishing, refrigerated warehousing and storing, food lockers, railroad shops of railroad lines, auto service and repair shops, motor vehicle repair by dealers and gasoline stations, other miscellaneous repair services, water supply, and industrial activities carried on by government enterprises. All these activities are included within the scope of "industry" in the USSR and not in the United States. One must then deduct employment in the following activities, which would be classified as "industrial" in the United States but not in the USSR: publishing; drilling and exploration work; medical and educational services in industry; cafeterias operated by industrial plants; and force account construction work. It is also necessary to subtract from United States data that part of central administration office employment which would be allocated to administration under Soviet classification procedures. Finally, since BLS data cover only wage and salaried workers, estimates of the number of proprietors must be added in order to obtain comparability with the USSR. Most of these adjustments are also required to compare the number of production workers in the two countries, and in addition it is necessary to add junior service personnel, guards, and apprentices to the figures for the USSR.

Another difficulty in making employment comparisons is to obtain estimates of *total* industrial employment for the USSR. The Central Statistical Administration compiles industrial employment statistics on two different bases, termed "industry" statistics and "labor" statistics. The former are the more comprehensive, because they include employment (1) in certain small-scale industrial establishments and industrial-type activities carried on by enterprises whose major activity is classified as non-industrial (for example, a brickmaking plant of a state farm), and (2) in industrial cooperatives and in subsidiary industrial enterprises of collective farms. The "industry" statistics, however, cover only wage workers and their equivalents in industrial cooperatives and on collective farms and have not been published in detail since 1933 and only as an aggregate for 1935. In the postwar statistical handbooks such data are presented only in the form of percentage distributions by branch of industry and by republics. Therefore, one has to estimate total employment using these fragmentary data, published "labor" statistics, and other data. According to estimates made by the United States Bureau of the Census, total industrial employment in the USSR in 1955 was 22 million,[28] compared with 17.4 million reported

28. US Bureau of the Census, *International Population Reports,* Series P-95, April 1961, no. 58, p. 70.

in the statistical handbooks as "total industrial-production personnel." [29]

Finally, there is the problem of differences in the procedures used to compile employment statistics in the United States and the USSR. The annual employment data published by the Bureau of Labor Statistics represent the averages of monthly data on the number of persons who worked in or were paid for any part of the pay period ending nearest the fifteenth of the month. Soviet annual employment data represent the means of the monthly averages of daily counts of personnel carried on establishment rolls, including those on leave for a variety of reasons. Soviet statisticians consider it necessary to reduce Soviet employment figures by several per cent to allow for the fact that paid leave of all kinds is greater in the USSR than in the United States.[30] If one is comparing man-years or man-days of employment, this difference clearly would need to be taken into account. When the comparison is merely between the average annual employment figures published by the two countries, however, these differences probably do not significantly affect the comparability of the data. In the first place, workers on paid leave are counted as employed in both countries. Furthermore, although workers on unpaid sick, maternity, and other leave during *all* the reporting period are not counted as employed in the United States but are counted in the USSR, their number probably is not great in the United States and would be largely offset by the fact that (1) United States data double-count persons holding two jobs and persons changing jobs during the survey period, and (2) United States practice counts as one man month of employment a person who works only one day in the reporting period; Soviet practice counts him as working one day.

Table 12 gives the results of an attempt to estimate for 1940, 1950, 1956, and 1958 total employment and total production workers on a comparable

Table 12. Relative levels of industrial employment,
US and USSR; selected years 1940–58.
(US = 100)

Years	Total employment	Production workers
1940	115	118
1950	99	102
1956	111	119
1958	125	139

29. *Narodnoye khozyaystvo SSSR v 1958 godu*, p. 131.
30. *Voprosy ekonomiki*, 1961, no. 8, p. 51.

basis for the US and the USSR.[31] As can be seen from this table, the ratios for 1958, a year of recession in the United States, are much higher than those for the other years—indicating that the choice of year alone can have a significant effect on comparisons of the relative levels of industrial labor productivity in the two countries.

31. The sources and methodology underlying these estimates are described in detail in: US Bureau of the Census, *International Population Reports,* Series P-95 (forthcoming), no. 61.

CHAPTER 10

Comparative Levels and Movement
of Labor Productivity
in Western Europe

ANGUS MADDISON

Organization for Economic Co-operation and Development

Measures of labor productivity in the economy as a whole are subject to much greater statistical qualification than measures for certain particular sectors where output may be easier to define. However, this aggregative concept is better for judging the over-all performance of the economy, as it reflects the net impact of influences such as differing output structure, differential national resource endowment, level of technology, capital intensity, and economies of scale whose effects may be difficult to assess in a particular sector where they are felt unevenly. It is also the most appropriate policy in stimulating productivity growth. From a purely statistical point of view it has the advantage that it can be crosschecked in several ways, it avoids double-counting, and its economic meaning, though still in dispute, is at least clearer than for some lesser aggregates such as industrial production. This paper is divided into two parts. The first deals largely with the major conceptual and practical difficulties in measuring global productivity, and the second part assesses postwar productivity growth in the light of historical experience.

Problems of Measurement

The measurement of output. The concept of aggregate output used here is Gross National Product as defined in the OEEC standardized system.[1] Fortunately, there is general agreement in Western Europe as to the definition of Gross National Product, and the figures of different countries are reasonably comparable at least for the postwar years. In spite of statistical shortcomings, the figures can be used with reasonable accuracy to estimate growth trends over a period of several years. Furthermore, for several countries reasonably comparable figures are available on a continuous basis for a much longer period.

There are some snags in this concept of output from the point of view of productivity measurement, as many service activities are of a type where output is conceptually difficult to define except in terms of input. However, this also applies in practice to certain manufacturing activities which in theory have a definable "physical" flow of output. This global concept of output embraces all the activities in which workers are gainfully occupied, and the only respects in which it includes activities in which labor is not a factor of production are the imputation of a flow of services arising from the occupation of dwellings and the gain (or loss) rising from improvements in the terms of trade.

Trends in output. The major problem in obtaining international comparability in measuring output trends is to ensure that the year whose prices are chosen as the *numeraire* is the same, or similar, in the different countries. Fortunately, most of the series used here for postwar years have a reasonably similar weighting base. But for the longer-term comparisons this is not always the case and is a source of incomparability in the figures. In general, the best practice for long-period comparisons is to choose several representative years and link the results. One cannot hope to get a single representative year for really long periods or for very large increases in output as the structure of output and relative prices change too rapidly. The use of weights for early years will nearly always lead to a higher figure for the growth of output than weights for later years because those outputs which have expanded fast have generally shown smaller increases in price than those which have expanded slowly. The problem of intercountry comparison of growth trends is generally soluble by picking weighting bases which are close together in time since the structure of output, the level of

1. *A Standardized System of National Accounts* (Paris, 1959).

technology, and factor costs tend to change in the same direction over time in different countries.

Levels of output. The measurement of differences in levels of GNP is much more complicated than that of differences in growth rates. It is impossible to measure with any precision in countries where there are wide differences in the structure of output and level of technology. Fortunately, a great deal of research has been done in Western Europe to make such comparisons possible, more in fact than on comparisons of growth trends. For eight European countries and for the United States the OEEC has made a detailed study of comparative real income levels and of the purchasing power of currencies.[2] This was done by looking at GNP from the point of view of expenditures, comparing in detail the quantities of different goods and services purchased by consumers, investors, and governments, and weighting each country's quantitative expenditures by another country's price weights. This produces a set of figures of relative real GNP at each others' prices.

Unfortunately, there are no comparative studies for European countries of GNP from the point of view of output. The OEEC has, however, made such a study for the United States and the United Kingdom[3] which, in general, confirms the findings of the comparison based on expenditure, though giving a somewhat smaller difference between the output of the two countries (the output of the United Kingdom is 15 per cent higher at United Kingdom weights and 6 per cent higher at United States weights on this basis). In the author's view, this was likely to be a systematic characteristic of such studies.

The Measurement of Labor Input

Labor force. In most European countries annual figures for the labor force have been traditionally derived by interpolation from decennial population censuses. In only a few countries are there regular sample surveys of the labor force on the lines developed in the United States. Figures on employment, therefore, need to be handled with considerable care if estimates are made for long periods, since there have been some changes in the scope of censuses over time, particularly in the treatment of juveniles, women, part-

2. Milton Gilbert and Associates, *Comparative National Products and Price Levels* (Paris, 1958).
3. Deborah Paige and Gottfried Bombach, *A Comparison of National Output and Productivity of the United Kingdom and the United States* (Paris, 1959).

time, or family workers. Adjustments can usually be made to secure reasonable comparability, but there are some major countries such as France where the problem is virtually insuperable for long-period comparisons. It is, incidentally, easier to get a reasonably comparable series of the growth of the labor force for the economy as a whole than for particular sectors.

Unemployment. Figures on unemployment are usually derived from the registers of social security schemes. In the postwar years the social security schemes have been greatly widened and are now a good direct source for employment estimates in several countries, or they at least provide the authorities with much better guidance for such estimates. There are fairly substantial variations in the scope of unemployment figures over time, and these often need substantial adjustment. The figures are reasonable enough for measurement of longer-term growth trends, although in some countries such as Italy the figures are too poor to use in productivity measurement. For the postwar period the figures are satisfactory for most countries.

Working hours. The measurement of working hours is very difficult for the economy as a whole. Reliable and comparable figures are usually only available for manufacturing. Movements in manufacturing may well be representative for the economy as a whole in a highly industrialized country like the United Kingdom, but in countries like Germany, France, or Italy, which have a much larger agriculture, the relation of changes in manufacturing to that for the economy as a whole will obviously be different. The movement of working hours over long periods of time is probably similar in direction and approximate magnitude in different sectors within each economy, but in the space of a decade there may well be a much more rapid movement in manufacturing, which certainly has more volatile working hours in the short run than other sectors. It is therefore possible to use output per man-hour figures for comparisons of rather long-term trends (although the figures for the years before 1913 are shaky), but for shorter-term analysis the figures on working hours are of limited validity.

Use of the available estimates of labor inputs for comparing absolute levels in different countries is hazardous. There is a considerable variation in the census treatment of certain categories of workers, of which the most important is women in agriculture. These differences are apparent from Table 13, where it can be seen that activity rates for males aged twenty to sixty-four range from 90.3 per cent to 96.8 per cent, but for females in the same age group the range is from 12.0 per cent to 57.9 per cent. The range is wider for females in the other two age groups as well. The table does, of course, reflect real variations in activity in different age and sex groups, but there is a large element of purely statistical discrepancy in the wide range shown for female activity. The measurement of comparative levels of unemployment and working hours is also subject to major snags.

Table 13. Labor force participation rates in Western Europe as shown in population census.

Country	Year of census	Males by age group			Females by age group		
		15–19	20–64	65+	15–19	20–64	65+
Austria	1951	83.3[a]	92.6[b]	31.3	63.9[a]	47.8[b]	13.4
Belgium	1947	66.8	90.3	24.7	41.8	24.7	5.4
Denmark	1950	84.2	95.9	35.9	83.2	43.2	8.4
Finland	1950	74.2	95.0	56.7	53.4	57.9	20.6
France	1954	80.0[c]	93.0[d]	36.1	43.3	44.0	13.5
Germany FR.	1955	87.0	94.3	26.5	79.1	42.4	8.1
Saar	1951	89.9	92.0	22.4	59.6	28.2	10.1
West Berlin	1950	72.9	93.0	21.5	63.3	45.6	4.2
Greece	1951	70.8	93.5	61.5	24.6	16.9	4.9
Iceland	1940	79.9	96.4	55.4	61.1	32.6	12.6
Ireland	1951	74.4	95.7	58.4	55.3	30.1	17.0
Italy	1955	75.5[a]	91.8	33.0	42.5[a]	26.8	4.9
Netherlands	1947	70.5[a]	95.0	35.5	52.5[a]	25.4	6.3
Norway	1950	72.3	95.3	42.1	48.1	26.8	8.6
Portugal	1950	75.5	92.3	67.2	34.4	21.3	12.2
Spain	1940	89.1	94.7	56.7	13.7	12.0	6.3
Sweden	1950	74.4	94.7	86.1	54.3	31.6	7.8
Switzerland	1950	73.8	96.0	50.7	64.0	34.2	11.9
United Kingdom	1951	82.9	96.8	32.0	78.2	36.0	5.3

a. Estimate from data for a wider age group.
b. 18–64 years.
c. Official figure is 59.2, but excludes armed forces.
d. Official figure is 91.0, but excludes armed forces.

Source: All census figures from *I.L.O. Yearbook 1956*, p. 8, except for Greece, where figures taken from *U.N. Demographic Yearbook 1956*, and for Germany, from *Wirtschaft und Statistik*, August 1956, p. 398.

Level of Productivity

It is obvious from the foregoing analysis that we must treat comparisons of absolute productivity levels with a certain skepticism. Nevertheless, the results do warrant some general conclusions, and they are in line with more detailed studies which are more firmly based.

It is fairly clear that productivity levels are quite similar in the advanced industrial countries, Belgium, France, Germany, the Netherlands, Norway, and the United Kingdom. The statistical discrepancies are such that it is not really possible to distinguish between the levels in these countries. The level in Italy seems clearly below that in the more industrialized countries, and the level in the United States is very clearly higher than in Europe.

Table 14. Comparative levels of real income, employment, and output per man, 1960.

Country	GNP at U.S. relative prices ($ billion)	GNP at average European relative prices ($ billion)	Employment (millions)	Output per man at U.S. relative prices (U.S. = 100)	Output per man at European relative prices (U.S. = 100)
Belgium	13.3	11.2	3.5	62	52
Denmark	7.0	5.8	2.2	52	43
France	67.4	52.2	19.9	55	42
Germany	88.9	68.2	25.0	58	44
Italy	51.0	34.7	20.0	41	28
Netherlands	16.1	12.7	4.3	61	48
Norway	5.7	4.7	1.5	63	51
United Kingdom	84.5	67.3	24.6	56	44
United States	425.2	425.2	68.9	100	100

Source: Columns 1 and 2 derived by extrapolating the 1955 figures in Milton Gilbert and Associates, *Comparative National Products and Price Levels* (Paris, 1958), p. 86. Extrapolation was done with the aid of figures for GNP at constant prices published in the January and March 1961 OEEC *General Statistical Bulletins*. Employment figures were also derived from OEEC *General Statistical Bulletins*.

I believe the following points are the major reasons for the higher level of productivity in the United States than in Europe.[4] In the period 1870–1929 the forces of demand in the United States were much stronger than in Europe because of rapidly rising population, an expanding frontier, and much better natural resource endowments. For this reason the level of investment was much higher in this period than in Europe. This higher capitalization, and the simple fact of more or better land and better natural resources, particularly energy, led to higher productivity. There were also certain advantages from the larger scale of production possible in an economy which has for at least the twentieth century been bigger than any European country in population. Another important factor has been the much better facilities for mass education in the United States, particularly in science and technology. The American lead in this respect has been noteworthy since the

4. "Industrial Productivity Growth in Europe and the United States," *Economica*, November 1954.

American revolution, and, of course, still exists. The First World War provided no check to United States productivity growth, and the Second was a positive stimulus which made possible a recoup of the stagnation in the 1930's. In most European countries by contrast these two wars and their aftermath caused ten to fifteen years' stagnation in productivity which has never been fully regained. In spite of the fact that the United States has been generally subject to greater cyclical instability than European countries, structural adjustments have usually been easier because the pace of growth has been more rapid, and the United States has, in any case, had fewer erratic external shocks because of its smaller dependence on international trade.

Table 15. Rates of growth of GNP per man-hour, 1870–1960.

Years	Denmark	Germany	Italy	Nether-lands	Norway	Sweden	United Kingdom	United States
1870–1913	2.5	2.3^a	1.2	1.2^b	2.2^b	2.8	1.7	2.2^c
1913–1950	1.6	0.7	1.6	1.1	2.3	2.0	1.4	2.3
1950–1960	2.9	6.1	4.2	4.0	3.8	3.2	2.2	2.5

a. 1871–1913
b. 1900–1913
c. 1873–1913

Source: Figures for European countries are from A. Maddison, "Economic Growth in Western Europe, 1870–1957," Banca Nazionale del Lavoro Quarterly Review, March 1959. They have been brought up to date and revised where necessary. Figures for the United States are derived from John W. Kendrick, Productivity Trends in the United States, forthcoming study of the National Bureau of Economic Research. It has been assumed that working hours in the United States moved in the same way as in Europe between 1873 and 1913.

Rates of Productivity Growth

The postwar rates of productivity growth in Western Europe have everywhere been well above their long-term trend, even in the United Kingdom and Denmark which have been laggards compared with the others. In several countries growth has reached really remarkable levels which compare favorably with nearly all recorded historical experience in the West. This is certainly true in Austria and Germany where output per man-hour increased at 5.3 per cent and 6.1 per cent per annum respectively from 1950 to 1960.

Some of this faster growth was due to once-for-all elements of recovery, and in all the countries in which growth has been particularly rapid some recovery elements have been present. This is particularly true in Austria, Germany, and France. In the underdeveloped countries, such as Italy and Greece, there have also been certain elements of backlog which tended to raise the rate of growth.

Table 16. Rates of growth of GNP per man, 1870–1960.

Years	Denmark	Germany	Italy	Nether-lands	Norway	Sweden	United Kingdom	United States
1870–1913	2.0	1.9[a]	0.8	0.7[b]	1.7[b]	2.3	1.2	1.7[c]
1913–1950	1.1	0.4	1.0	0.7	1.6	1.5	0.9	1.7
1950–1960	2.4	5.2	4.5	3.7	3.3	2.8	2.0	2.1

a. 1871–1913
b. 1900–1913
c. 1873–1913

Source: As for Table 15.

However, there has been some convergence of productivity growth rates in recent years. In the period 1955–1960 there were lower rates of growth in all the fast growing countries such as Austria, France, Germany, Italy, the Netherlands, Switzerland, and Greece than there had been in 1950–1955. Conversely, higher rates of growth were achieved in the slower growing countries such as Denmark, Norway, Sweden, the United Kingdom, and possibly in Belgium. The only case in which a slowly growing European country has clearly reduced its pace in the past five years is Ireland. The figure around which the convergence seems to be taking place is 3.5 per cent annual growth in output per man-hour. There are, of course, still wide variations around this figure, with the United Kingdom and Ireland as laggards, and Austria and Germany in the lead. This general picture is not changed much if the analysis is done in terms of output per worker instead of per man-hour, although the leading position of Germany is somewhat reduced.

Causes of Postwar Acceleration in Productivity

The rate of investment. A major factor contributing to the accelerated growth of productivity in the postwar period has been the very high rate of capital investment. In every country where it is possible to make historical

Table 17. Rates of growth of output per man and output per man-hour, 1950–1960.

Country	Compound rate of growth GNP per man-hour			Compound rate of growth of GNP per man		
	1950–55	1955–60	1950–60	1950–55	1955–60	1950–60
Austria	5.6	5.0	5.3	6.2	3.5	4.9
Belgium	2.2	3.3	2.7	2.5	2.3	2.4
Denmark	1.2	4.6	2.9	1.3	3.6	2.5
France	4.1	3.2	3.7	4.0	3.2	3.6
Germany	6.1	6.0	6.1	6.2	4.3	5.2
Greece	n.a.	n.a.	n.a.	5.9	4.8	5.4
Ireland	3.3	1.5	2.4	3.3	1.4	2.4
Italy	5.1	3.4	4.2	5.4	3.5	4.5
Netherlands	4.3	3.7	4.0	4.3	3.2	3.7
Norway	3.2	4.3	3.8	3.3	3.4	3.3
Portugal	n.a.	n.a.	n.a.	2.3	2.7	2.5
Sweden	2.7	3.7	3.2	2.7	2.8	2.8
Switzerland	4.8	3.4	4.1	4.7	2.9	3.8
Turkey	n.a.	n.a.	n.a.	4.0	2.7	3.3
United Kingdom	1.5	2.9	2.2	1.8	2.1	2.0
Canada	3.6	1.6	2.6	2.9	1.2	2.0
United States	2.9	2.1	2.5	2.8	1.5	2.1

Source: OEEC, *General Statistical Bulletins.*

comparisons the rate of investment has been much higher than in any previous period. This is clear from Table 18. In Germany and Norway the rate of investment has virtually doubled since before the war, and in the United Kingdom and Sweden it is up by about half.

There is, in fact, some relation between the rate of productivity growth and the rate of investment. The countries with the lowest productivity growth—Ireland and the United Kingdom—are those with the lowest rates of investment, and all the countries with a high rate of growth have a high rate of investment. Higher postwar rates of investment do therefore seem to be a major explanation for accelerated productivity growth. However, the relation is not linear, and there do seem to be diminishing returns beyond a certain point, as indicated by the situation in Norway.

The productivity of investment. In analyzing the impact of investment on growth, it is, of course, highly interesting to look at its productivity. It is not possible to measure the capital stock at all accurately in individual countries, let alone make international comparisons. It is, however, possible to compare the increment in capital stock over a given period in order to arrive at an estimate of the incremental capital/output ratio. This is done in

Table 18. Gross domestic investment as a proportion of gross national product at current prices.

Years	Denmark	Germany	Italy	Nether-lands	Norway	Sweden	United Kingdom	United States
1870–1913	13.6[a]	—	11.2	—	12.7[c]	8.1	12.8[d]	20.7[f]
1920–1938	12.0[a]	13.6[b]	16.3	—	15.1	13.3	10.2[e]	15.6
1950–1959	16.6	23.7	20.7	24.0	29.9	21.1	15.3	17.9

a. Excluding inventories
b. 1925–1934 and 1936
c. 1900–1913
d. Including foreign investment, otherwise the figure would be 9.2
e. 1924–1938
f. 1869–1913

Source: A. Maddison, "Economic Growth in Western Europe, 1870–1957," *Banca Nazionale del Lavoro Quarterly Review*, March 1959, p. 74, for 1870–1938 for European countries. Prewar figures for the United States are derived from John W. Kendrick, *Productivity Trends in the United States*. They are not quite comparable with the other figures, as they include munitions purchases by government. Figures for 1950–1959 are derived from OEEC, *General Statistical Bulletin*, 1961. The average rate of investment in 1950–1959 for Austria was 21.8 per cent, Belgium 16 per cent, France 18.8 per cent, Canada 24.9 per cent.

Table 19. It differs from some other measures of the capital/output ratio, in that capital is measured gross of depreciation. However, we are really interested for our purpose in measuring capital net of replacement, and this is not a concept for which figures exist. In any case, replacement itself will nearly always lead to some productivity increase even if replacement is simply defined in terms of the maintenance of production capacity replaced rather than the replacement by new assets of particular items of the capital stock which are worn out.

In the countries for which there is historical evidence (Table 19), the productivity of capital seems clearly to have increased in the postwar period in Denmark, Germany, and Italy, and this is probably true for France and Austria as well. However, the productivity of capital has decreased in Norway and Sweden and possibly the United Kingdom.

It is obvious that there is a wide range in aggregate capital/output ratios. A breakdown of capital/output ratio by type of capital is given in Table 20 in an attempt to throw light on the reasons for intercountry variations in the global ratio. It is obvious that housing investment has only an indirect relation to productivity growth, and this part of the capital/output ratio varies widely from country to country because of differences in social

Table 19. Gross incremental capital output ratios, 1870–1960.

Years	Denmark	Germany	Italy	Norway	Sweden	United Kingdom	United States
1870–1913	5.6[a]	—	6.9	5.2[c]	—	6.0[e]	5.6[g]
1920–1938	6.4[a]	4.9[b]	7.3	5.2	3.9[d]	4.5[f]	6.6[h]
1950–1960	5.1	3.2	3.6	8.3	6.2	5.9	5.5

a. Figures adjusted upwards to include inventories, by adding postwar inventory/ output ratio of 0.4
b. 1925–1938
c. 1900–1913
d. 1921–1938
e. Includes foreign investment. Without foreign investment the figure would be 4.3. In other periods foreign investment was negligible.
f. 1923–1938
g. 1889–1913 (includes military investment)
h. 1920–1937 (includes military investment)

Source: As for Table 18. The figures are calculated in the same way as described in Table 20, except for Germany and Sweden for the interwar period, where data on investment are not available at constant prices—for these two countries the average rate of capital formation at current prices was divided by the rate of GNP growth for the period concerned.

policy and housing needs. In the case of nonresidential construction, there is wide variation in the capital/output ratio not only for reasons of climate, but also because the life of assets is fairly long, and the impact of inherited overcapacity or undercapacity from fairly remote periods in the past can be considerable. One would think there would be less scope for variation in the ratios of machinery and equipment investment to output, but they also vary considerably between countries and are not more closely clustered than the aggregate capital/output ratio.

It would be interesting to break down the capital/output ratio by sector of the economy. At the moment, it is not possible to do this with any great degree of accuracy, but there is some evidence that intercountry variations are not primarily due to differences in industrial structure. Germany, for instance, appears to have a lower capital/output ratio for nearly all parts of the economy, whereas in Norway the ratios appear to be high throughout the economy.

The higher postwar productivity of both capital and labor in some countries is due partly to recovery elements persisting from earlier periods of slow growth. For Germany and the Netherlands, there is evidence of retarded growth of labor productivity between 1913 and 1950, and this is

Table 20. Gross incremental capital output ratios by type of capital, 1950–1960.

Country	Ratio of total cumulated investment to GNP increment	Ratio of cumulated residential investment to GNP increment	Ratio of cumulated non-residential construction to GNP increment	Ratio of cumulated machinery and equipment investment to GNP increment	Ratio of cumulated inventory formation to GNP increment
Austria	4.0	0.7	1.1	1.9	0.3
Belgium	5.7	1.5	1.5	2.6	0.2
Denmark	5.1	0.8	1.4	2.6	0.4
France	4.6	0.9	1.2	2.0	0.4
Germany	3.2	0.7	0.7	1.5	0.3
Italy	3.6	0.8	1.1	1.5	0.1
Netherlands	4.8	0.8	1.3	2.2	0.4
Norway	8.3	1.3	2.3	4.5	0.3
Sweden	6.2	1.5	2.3	2.2	0.2
United Kingdom	5.9	1.1	1.5	2.9	0.3
United States	5.5	1.4	1.9	1.8	0.4
Canada	6.9	1.3	2.9	2.3	0.4

Source: These figures are derived from the OEEC, *General Statistical Bulletin*, 1961. They were calculated by dividing the absolute increment in GNP in constant prices for the ten-year period between 1950 and 1960 by the relevant type of cumulated capital formation in constant prices for the ten-year period 1950–1959 inclusive.

probably true of France as well. In Italy, the prewar productivity of capital seems to have been low. However, there are limits to the growth we can expect from recovery or backlogs because stagnation in labor productivity over a period of decades cannot be fully recouped, and although a good deal of capital has a long life there are also obvious limits on the usefulness of capital which was invested several decades ago. The theory of recovery becomes more and more difficult to sustain as the years go by without any appreciable slackening in growth. There are, in fact, grounds for believing that something fundamental in the economy has changed which tends to accelerate the rate of productivity growth and to reduce the capital/output ratio.

The higher rate of investment in Western European countries since the war has been largely induced by the buoyant state of demand. Evidence of the high level of demand is contained in Table 21 which shows the average 1950–1959 level of unemployment to have been below 2 per cent in most countries compared with 10 per cent before the war. In Germany and

Denmark, where it was higher, it has fallen considerably in the past two or three years and is now comparable with that in other countries. Further evidence of the high and rapidly rising demand could be easily adduced from figures of rising prices and rising imports. In Canada and the United States, where the postwar level of demand has been generally lower than in Europe, the rate of investment and productivity growth have not improved so much compared with historical experience. Investment has been profitable in Europe because markets looked promising, labor was scarce, and labor costs were constantly increasing.

Table 21. Unemployment as a percentage of the labor force.

Country	Average annual level		
	1904–13	1925–38	1950–59
Denmark	5.0	10.5	4.9
Germany	1.7	8.8	4.5
Netherlands	2.1[a]	10.0	1.6
Norway	1.6	11.4	1.1
Sweden	2.5[a]	6.9	1.3
United Kingdom	3.5	10.7	1.6

a. 1911–13

Source: A. Maddison, "Economic Growth in Western Europe, 1870–1957," p. 89.

When the war ended, there were many spontaneous forces which raised demand to a high level. Fortunately, governments had learned a good deal about economic policy since prewar days, and they ensured that these high levels of demand were maintained by active fiscal and monetary policies. In many countries, governments have also taken a number of special measures to stimulate the supply of capital by channeling increased resources into investment, either directly or by creating incentives which have made private investment more profitable.

The climate of high demand and high investment has given a substantial boost to the productivity of capital and labor in economies which had been through decades of stagnation and the dislocation of two major world wars. But a further stimulus has been provided by the disappearance of major downward fluctuations in demand as can be seen from Table 22. In the postwar period there have been only two mild recessions in Europe, in 1952 and 1958, and in most countries they simply checked the pace of growth and did not cause a decline. Only four European countries have had a single ex-

perience of a postwar decline in aggregate production, and in each case
the fall was no more than 1 per cent. It is noteworthy that postwar productivity growth and investment rates have been lowest in Belgium, Denmark,
and the United Kingdom where activity had been most affected by the
postwar recessions. All European countries have, however, had a better
record of stability than in the prewar years. The record of stability in Canada
and the United States compares less well with long-term trends, and this is
also true of productivity in North America. The greater stability of the postwar European economy stimulates investment and permits capacity to be
more fully used over its whole life, enables production schedules to be
better organized to achieve economies of scale, and permits a better use of
labor.

Table 22. Trends and cycles in GNP.

Country	Percentage average annual growth			Number of years below previous peak		
	1901–1913	1925–1938	1950–1960	1901–1913	1925–1938	1950–1959
Austria	n.a.	n.a.	5.9	n.a.	n.a.	0
Belgium	n.a.	n.a.	2.8	n.a.	n.a.	1
Denmark	3.4	2.6	3.3	2	4	1
France	1.0	fall	4.2	n.a.	10	0
Germany	1.9	2.8	7.5	0	9	0
Italy	2.2	1.8	5.8	4	7	0
Netherlands	2.6	1.3	5.0	1	7	0
Norway	2.6	3.4	3.6	2	3	0
Sweden	n.a.	3.0	3.3	n.a.	4	1
United Kingdom	1.5	2.5	2.6	5	2	1
United States	3.4	1.0	3.3	2	8	3
Canada	5.1	1.8	3.7	1	9	2

Source: A. Maddison, "The Postwar Business Cycle in Western Europe," *Banca
Nazionale del Lavoro Quarterly Review*, June 1960, p. 101, for prewar years. Figures for
France are derived from Colin Clark, *Conditions of Economic Progress* for 1901–1913, and
from Svennilson, *Growth and Stagnation in the European Economy* for 1925–1932. Figures
for U.S. from O. J. Firestone, *Income and Wealth*, Series VII. 1950–1959 from OEEC,
General Statistical Bulletin.

Thus we conclude that only part of the acceleration of postwar productivity growth was due to special once-for-all recovery factors, and that an important role has been played by government policies to stimulate full employment and reduce fluctuations. The impact of these policies in growth
has been felt largely by raising the level of investment.

CHAPTER 11

Anglo-Soviet Labor Productivity Comparisons

ALEXANDER NOVE

London School of Economics

Introduction

The object of this paper is to discuss some problems of measurement which arise in comparisons of British and Soviet labor productivity. The primary purpose of the paper is not to arrive at definite numerical conclusions. Indeed, a major and deep study, which alone could provide a satisfactory basis for such conclusions, would require over a year's work and several hundred pages of text, as well as the collaboration of statisticians of both countries. However, it is hardly possible to discuss problems of measurement except in the context of actual attempts to measure. Therefore, here I have attempted a few comparisons for particular commodities, conscious that these may contain errors and inaccuracies. The object is essentially one of encouraging a critical examination of the available figures, to draw attention to conceptual and methodological differences, and to stimulate further work on this complex subject.

We are all acutely aware of the many difficulties which stand in the way of meaningful international comparisons of productivity. The "normal" difficulties of international comparison are bad enough. Comparisons with the USSR, however, are further impeded by lack of information. Walter

Galenson, in his admirable study of Soviet-American comparisons, drew almost entirely on data relating to 1937 or earlier. Since his study, Soviet publication of statistics has become very much more generous. Unfortunately, this generosity has not gone very far in the field of labor statistics. For example, the statistical digest *Narodnoe Khozyaistvo SSSR v 1959 godu* (hereinafter referred to as *N.Kh.59*) provides not a single figure for the labor force of any industry which can serve as a basis for comparison. Thus, while there is a total for light industry, there is not even a figure for textiles, let alone for the cotton or wool industries. There are figures for coal output per worker, and also for particular metallurgical and textile processes, of which more will be said. There are a few indexes, which do not help us much for our present purpose. In the statistical digest *Promyshlennost SSSR*, we find productivity figures for 1955 for electricity generation, lumber, and cement, in addition to the above. This exhausts the available information on particular industries, so far as systematically published statistics are concerned, though other figures are sometimes to be found in various specialized studies.[1]

The Soviet figures lack explanatory notes, which makes it hard to identify significant differences of coverage.

The British figures are certainly not perfect either. Census of production statistics often fail to agree with other information, or do not distinguish between productive and other workers; some figures vary bewilderingly in geographical coverage between the United Kingdom, Great Britain, or sometimes England and Wales. For some industrial sectors, information is often inadequate or insufficiently detailed. There are inconsistencies: for instance, the figures published by the Iron and Steel Board exclude workers absent on holiday and through sickness, while nearly all other sources and industries include them. There is ample scope for friendly cooperation between scholars and statisticians of both countries to clarify each others' terminology and definitions, to the mutual advantage of all.

There are a few differences of importance which it is desirable to mention at this stage. In general, Soviet figures of industrial workers confine themselves strictly to those engaged in actual industrial production, omitting those persons, employed by the industrial enterprise, who work on loading, unloading, construction, repairs, canteens, and the like.[2] British statistics

1. Notably in the work of A. Kats, "Comparison of Physical Output per Production Worker for 28 Branches of Industry in the U.S. in 1954 and USSR in 1956," *Sotsialisticheskiy trud*, 1959, no. 1.
2. But there are instances, in some industries, when some loading and unloading and

usually include them, if they are employed by the industrial enterprise,[3] although in some cases canteen workers are separately given and can be deducted. Then it is known that "workers" (*rabochiye*) in the Soviet definition exclude learners (*ucheniki*) and auxiliaries (*mladshii obsluzhivayushchii personal,* including watchmen, janitors, and cleaners). British statistics generally include them as workers (operatives). For these reasons, it seems likely —though our Soviet colleagues could correct me here—that comparisons will tend to understate British productivity relative to that of the Soviet, both for particular industries and for industry in general, unless this is allowed for.

From *N.Kh.59,* p. 138, we have, for Soviet industry as a whole, the relevant figures in 1959 (in thousands):

Workers	16,791
Learners	341
Engineer-technical	1,803
Employees (white-collar staffs)	804
(Auxiliaries)	(466)
Total industrial–productive personnel	20,205

These figures exclude industrial workers on collective farms and in co-operative establishments. The term "industry" covers manufacturing, mining, and public utilities. "Auxiliaries" are calculated as a remainder, since they were not given as such in the listing. (This category includes watchmen.)

Unfortunately, no breakdown along the above lines is available for any industry. Learners plus auxiliaries were, as can be seen from the list, 4 per cent of the total. Presumably one could adjust all the figures by this percentage, but this would be a very rough estimate and will not be attempted in the analysis by industry. One should merely bear the point in mind.

Comparisons between Soviet and American labor figures generally have to be adjusted to take into account the omission from American figures of persons absent (through illness or holiday) who appear in the Soviet data. The British figures are, in this respect, similar to those of the Soviet, and no adjustment is necessary.[4]

---

even some repairs are included in the labor force. Careful inquiries need to be made in each individual instance.

3. But, perhaps illogically, excludes them if they perform exactly the same tasks, but for a specialized enterprise which works on contract.

4. Except, as mentioned above, in respect to statistics published by the Iron and Steel Board.

I shall now proceed to examine particular industries for which some basis of comparison is possible.

Coal. In Soviet Russia, in 1959,[5] in deep-mined coal there were 33.9 tons (406.8 per annum) produced per worker per month; in open-cast coal there were 227.2 tons (2726 per annum) produced per worker per month. In Great Britain[6] in the same year, in deep-mined [7] coal, 665,000 workers were employed (including surface workers). There were between 195 million and 3 million long tons produced. Per miner, it came to 294 long tons per annum (299 metric tons per annum). In open-cast mining there were 7119 employed people and 10.8 million long tons produced. About 5400 of the total employed were productive workers;[8] output per worker was about 2000 long tons per annum, or 2025 metric tons per annum.

The British labor figures for deep-mined coal exclude workers engaged in canteens and in "repairs to miners' houses." They include those employed in pithead baths and also a number of workers who may well be treated by Soviet statisticians as engaged in repairs or building and not mining. For this reason, and also because the Soviet figures exclude learners and auxiliaries, the British figures are relatively better than they look.[9] They would look better still if the calculation were in terms of calorific value rather than in gross tonnage, since in 1959, out of a total Soviet production of 506.6 million tons, 141.4 was lignite. On the other hand, a relatively much higher proportion of Soviet coal was obtained from open-cast mines, so that the comparison would be more favorable to the USSR if all coal mining were taken together.

Cement. In 1955 in the USSR, 504 tons per worker per year were produced in the cement factories of the Ministry of Building Materials.[10] In the United Kingdom in the same year 12.5 million long tons were produced by 10,012 workers. Output per worker per year was 1250 long tons (1270 metric tons). The total of workers includes some engaged in the "extraction of materials," which may or may not be in the Soviet figures. The census of production covered only those establishments employing 25 persons or over.

5. *N.Kh.59*, p. 183.
6. No production in Northern Ireland.
7. *Statistical Digest, Ministry of Power*, 1959, pp. 25, 31, and 52.
8. According to the Census of Production (not strictly comparable data). According to unofficial information, the annual average number of open-cast workers employed is significantly higher than at the date of the Census of Production, in which case the productivity figures given here are overstated.
9. See Table 23 breakdown of the British labor force. Thus there are over 12,000 "trainees" in the total.
10. "Cement," Census of Production, 1958, p. 5.

Even if one were not to allow for the differences in definition of industrial worker, the British productivity figures are very much higher. Comparisons with America have shown that cement is one of the most productive of British industries. On the other hand, the Soviet cement industry doubtless increased its productivity since 1955. (No index is available.)

Iron and steel. In the USSR[11] in 1959 in pig-iron production (blast furnaces) 2696 tons per annum per worker were produced. Figures exclude "the output of metallurgical shops of machine-building plants." In Great Britain,[12] in March 1960 there were 11,970 workers connected with "blast furnaces and sintering plants—process workers." This excludes general and maintenance workers. There were 15.76 million long tons of pig-iron produced—1316 long tons per worker (1337 metric tons).[13]

No annual average figure of the labor force in blast furnaces is available, but the figures at this period were reasonably stable and can be taken to be close to the year's average.[14]

There are a number of reasons for regarding this comparison as unduly "favorable" to the USSR. The British figures include some materials handling (for instance, the movement of ore from the dockside to the plant if the blast-furnace is by the quay, or the handling of ore which arrives by railway wagon).[15] The British figures also include so-called "foundry iron," much of which is made in small shops for special purposes and which is probably omitted in the Soviet data. Much labor goes into the process of "sintering," and the preparation of the ore and the sintering process itself is included in the British labor figures. It is not known whether, or how much, of this process in the USSR is included in their labor statistics for blast-furnaces.

An important factor adversely affecting British productivity is the low ferrous content of British iron ore. Figures for particular firms show that even the most efficient of those which use British ore cannot exceed an output of 1500 tons per worker, whereas those using the richer imported ores often exceed 2000, and the newest blast-furnaces even reach 3000. But the

---

11. *N.Kh.59*, p. 175.
12. No production in Northern Ireland.
13. *Iron and Steel monthly statistics,* vol. 6, no. 4, p. 26.
14. Strictly speaking, one can obtain an annual average by adding up each month's figure and dividing by twelve. However, since this source omits holidays and other absences from the labor figure, the inclusion of holiday months would lead to a considerable understatement of the labor force for purposes of comparison.
15. But not those engaged in transporting it by lorry from a port to the factory, even if the transport workers are employed by the factory in question.

average is weighed down by a number of obsolete blast-furnaces using domestic ore. Their gradual replacement, and greater efficiency generally, is leading to an improvement. Productivity per head has in fact increased by over 20 per cent in the period 1956–60.

Steel. In the USSR in 1959, 1217 tons per annum per worker were produced in open-hearth steel shops.[16] Of the total output of 59.95 million tons, 51.1 million was open-hearth. In 1960 in Great Britain the total steel production was 24.3 million long tons.

Workers engaged in all "steel melting furnaces and ancillary processes" (excluding melting for manufacture of steel castings) amounted to 22,790 in March 1960. The "melting of steel castings" provides only about 2 per cent of the total output of steel. The figures for both output and workers include steelmaking other than open-hearth which accounts for almost 20 per cent of the total output and an unknown proportion of the labor force.

Assuming, for lack of information to the contrary, that these facts do not unduly distort the intended comparison, the British figure is 1066 long tons per worker (1083 metric tons).

As in the case of pig-iron, the March labor figure has been used as a substitute for the annual average.

Allowing for the narrower definition of "worker" in the USSR, it seems reasonable to regard the steel industry productivity figures in the two countries as very close to one another. The British labor figures include small foundries in engineering works. The Soviet figures specifically exclude these, although they account for about 15 per cent of total steel output (15.7 per cent in 1955, according to *Promyshlennost SSSR*, p. 109), and doubtless have below-average productivity. A sizable proportion of British outputs consists of the comparatively labor-intensive—but valuable—alloy steel. The British labor figures include materials handling, sorting and moving of scrap and limestone handling, which are probably partly omitted from the Soviet figures. When all this is allowed for, British productivity may even be a little above the Soviet, but further information is obviously needed.

Rolled steel. In 1959 in the USSR rolled steel meant "rolled ferrous metal products, excluding pipes (and tubes) and forgings from ingots, per worker in rolling mill shops." There were 417 tons produced per annum.[17]

The list on p. 146 represents something approximating the Soviet coverage.

This figure, however, is quite unusable in a serious comparison. It in-

16. *N.Kh.59,* pp. 165, 175.
17. *N.Kh.59,* p. 175.

Great Britain[18] (1959)

Output (In long tons, thousands)		Labor (Number of workers in February)	
Plates	2329	Rolling mills	48,990
Other heavy rolled products	2645	Sheet mills	14,140
Light rolled products	5557		
Sheets (coated and uncoated)	2477		
Total	13,008	Total	63,130

cludes, firstly, *all* workers engaged in all processes from the delivery of materials to loading the products into train or truck. These activities require many workers, and are thought to be omitted from the Soviet data. But there is even a "weightier" reason for skepticism: the figures are in tons, and this is a poor measure of productivity, when various finishing processes add value and use labor without adding to weight. The cruder products tend to be heavier, and it is in fact possible that a high figure of tonnage per worker could reflect not so much higher productivity as waste of metal through making unnecessarily heavy goods. Finally, the Soviet figures exclude production in engineering plants, which, judging from criticisms in Soviet journals, are important and relatively inefficient. In 1955, this constituted 10.6 per cent of total production (*Promyshlennost SSSR,* p. 109). Their equivalents are included in the British statistics.

Electric generation. In the USSR in 1955 this included electricity generated in power stations operating under the then-existing Ministry of Electric Power Stations (excluding power stations operated by industrial enterprises, and rural generators, and so forth). The result was 1103 thousand kwh per worker per year.[19] The production figures include use of current at power stations. In Great Britain in 1958[20] total production "in the (electricity) industry" (excluding power stations owned and operated by other industries outside the nationalized electricity boards) was 98,498,000 kwh (including use in power stations). The total workers in generation were 37,167; in main transmission 1684; in distribution 41,148; making a total of 79,999 workers.[21]

The above figures *exclude* "meter reading and collection" (4956), and also "commercial, accounting, secretarial, legal, canteen," which presumably are

---

18. *Iron and Steel: Annual Statistics,* 1959, pp. 63, 83. This made 206 long tons per annum per worker (209 metric tons).
19. *Promyshlennost SSSR,* p. 170.
20. Detailed labor figures do not cover Northern Ireland, and therefore the production figures are also for Great Britain only.
21. Ministry of Power, *Statistical Digest,* 1959, p. 91.

omitted from the Soviet calculation. Also excluded are over 24,000 workers engaged on "capital projects," since those would be treated as building or capital repairs workers in Soviet statistics. All the labor figures are for September, no annual average breakdown being available, but there is little variation through the year.

It is far from clear whether the workers engaged in "distribution," which covers "operation and maintenance" by area boards (that is, the practical work of connecting and maintaining sub-stations and wires to houses, and so forth) ought to be part of the comparison.

If the above labor figures are the right ones for purposes of comparison, then British productivity in 1958 was slightly ahead of the USSR's in 1955, being 1231 thousand kwh per worker. By 1958, presumably the USSR would be about equal. However, if, as is quite possible, the Soviet figures include only generation and main transmission, as well as excluding workers engaged in loading and unloading at power stations, many of which are in the British totals, then in fact British productivity is *fully twice as high*. In this instance, we cannot come to useful conclusions without more information on the Soviet definition of productive worker. Thus, the comparable figure may be not 1231 thousand kwh but more like 2400–2500 thousand kwh per worker.

The Soviet data, however, include an unknown number of workers in "auxiliary industrial enterprises of electrical energy authorities." Presumably these are workshops which make various tools and components.[22] If these are appreciable, this should lead (*ceteris paribus*) to an understatement of the Soviet figure of output per head. There is no means of knowing, on the basis of present information, what correction should be made for this.

A further relevant point is that a large number of Soviet thermal power stations provide heat for nearby houses and other buildings, while only one such scheme exists in Great Britain. Obviously, this is a form of additional output, which requires additional labor inputs.

An alternative way of measuring labor in electric generation is to relate it to installed capacity. According to the Soviet source (*Promyshlennost SSSR*, p. 170) there were seven "productive-industrial" personnel to 1000 kwh of capacity at the end of 1955, of which five were workers in electricity plants under the jurisdiction of the former Ministry of Electric Power Stations. The comparative British figures can be calculated as 3.5 and 2.85 respectively, for 1958, if one were to assume that "distribution" is to be included in the

22. Also hydrogen for generator cooling, according to the British electricity delegation report.

comparison (97,500 persons, of which 79,999 workers, and 28,000 megawatts capacity).

The Soviet figures permit a rough calculation of numbers employed. The power stations under the ministry provided 82.4 per cent of total current in 1955. Since they were used very much more intensively than other power stations, the installed capacity must have been a smaller percentage of the total; let us assume it was about 75 per cent. Total installed capacity was 37,200 megawatts, so their share was 27,900 megawatts. If this is approximately correct, the total "productive-industrial personnel" was 195,000, of which 139,000 were workers, but there is a sizable margin of error possible due to rounding. However, it will be shown that these figures omit the large majority of those engaged on electricity generation in the USSR.

An interesting point is the much larger proportion of persons other than workers (managers, technical, clerical, but also auxiliaries) in the Soviet labor force in the electricity industry—28 per cent approximately, as against 17 1/2 per cent in Great Britain. The significance of this, however, depends on the extent to which the Soviet figures include commercial clerical staffs.

Since many Soviet power stations suffer from poor quality coal with high ash content, or use bulky fuels like peat, they probably require far more workers for handling fuel than their British equivalents. It is not quite clear, however, how many of those who handle the fuel are included in the Soviet labor figures. Information on this point would be helpful.

The USSR has a much higher proportion of hydro-electric stations (over 15 per cent of the total capacity, as against 3 per cent in Great Britain). There was also a much larger use of oil, which should save much labor. Both these factors should facilitate relatively higher productivity. Since 1955, a great deal more natural gas has been used in Soviet thermal power stations, which should help productivity statistics to rise further.

There is, however, another very important factor: the exclusion of small power stations of local or industrial significance from the Soviet figures involves the omission of the predominant part of the labor force employed on electric generation, which the analogous exclusion from the British figures does not. The Soviet data recently appeared in an article by A. Stepankov (*Voprosy ekonomiki,* no. 5, 1961). He pointed out that in 1955 there were 105,000 small generating plants in the USSR, that their numbers had grown by 1959 to 157,000, and that "the personnel employed at these generating stations exceeds 800,000." He himself makes the contrast with the fact that 197 thermal power stations, producing five times the amount of current than do all these small stations taken together, employed only 85,000 persons in 1955. This state of affairs has arisen because of the fact that most Soviet territory is not connected to any national or even regional systems of electricity distribution. The effect of these facts is to make the figures quoted earlier totally unrepresentative of the real state of affairs for electricity generation as a whole.

Cotton spinning. In the USSR in 1959[23] the Soviet figures are only available in the following form: Yarn per worker per hour, "kilo-counts" (*Kilonomer*) was 120.4; the average count was 39.4. Since kilo-counts represent weight times count, by dividing 120.4 by 39.4 one arrives at output per worker per hour in weight terms: just over 3 kilograms. Assuming a forty-six hour week, this would be 138 kilograms per week. It is not known how many hours an average worker was deemed to have worked in a year, but if one were to allow three weeks for holidays and sickness, the annual output would be about 6760 kilograms per annum. The margin of error here must be painfully obvious. Nonetheless, it checks reasonably with prewar calculations. Thus Galenson gave a figure of 2825 kilograms per worker for 1937, while the present method, assuming forty-nine weeks at forty-eight hours per week, gives about 2950 kilograms for 1940, using the *kilonomer* figure for that year in *N.Kh.59*.

In the United Kingdom in 1958 the British figures are not given in a combination of weight and count, though there do exist detailed figures of counts in other sources, from which an average can be calculated and might serve as a comparison—on the assumption that the English "count" and the Soviet *Nomer* are the same measure, which is not clear, at least to the author of this paper.

The figures in weight are given in the *Census of Production*[24] in the form of a table (for enterprises employing at least 25 persons):

Type	Sales (thousand lbs.)	Workers (September or October)
Spun cotton yarn	467,453	56,534
Cotton waste yarn	77,287	4,866

To this it would be necessary to add those engaged in doubling, if work on doubling is included in the Soviet labor force (which is not known). Un-

23. *N.Kh.59*, p. 256.
24. *Census of Production, 1958, Spinning and Doubling of Cotton, Flax, and Man-made Fibers.*

fortunately, British statistics do not distinguish between doubling cotton yarn and doubling various other fibers and mixtures (artificial fibers, for example). At a rough guess, some 6000 operatives are engaged in cotton yarn doubling. There is also a risk of error arising from the fact that some of the workers mentioned in the above figures do not spend all their time in spinning cotton yarn, while some workers not included in these figures do produce some cotton yarns (they work in enterprises predominantly engaged in something else). In the time available, it has not been possible to determine which of these distorting factors is the larger. There is also a considerable amount of *part-time labor,* for which a downward allowance ought to be made, but has not been made here.

Bearing in mind all these unknowns, the averages work out as follows:

If doubling is excluded: 8872 lbs., or 4024 kilograms per annum.

If doubling is included: 8204 lbs., or 3721 kilograms per annum.

The usual provisos must be made concerning definition and coverage (exclusion by the Soviets of learners, auxiliaries, transport workers, canteen workers, and so forth). On a comparable basis, it seems probable that the British are not far behind, but much depends on just what it is that the Soviet figures represent.

Some Conclusions

In the preceding pages, some effort has been made to compare productivity in a few sectors of industry for which output data in physical terms are available, as well as some figures on the labor force. There are no reasons to suppose that the industries analyzed are typical or representative, and so no generalized conclusions should be based upon them. Let us now attempt to generalize about the difficulties which have emerged.

(*a*) The list of such commodities is short. There is a serious shortage of information, particularly of labor statistics from the USSR and of explanatory notes regarding the few figures which are published.

(*b*) It is obvious that physical-output data will not be enough if a more representative cross-section can be adequately analyzed. Despite some ingenious "quantitative" attempts,[25] the machinery and metal-working sector does demand the use of money as a measure of production, and the same is true of many other multi-product industries. To do this, it is necessary to calculate price-ratios, a laborious but essential task. Even as between Western

25. For example, K. Kuznetsova and G. Sergeyeva in *Vestnik Statistiki,* no. 6, 1960, in respect of machine tools.

countries, whose price-systems are at least based on similar principles, the use of the official exchange-rate leads to quite misleading results.[26] The more so is this true in comparisons between a Western country and the Soviet Union. Careful work has been done in this connection in the United States, but it has yet to be applied to Anglo-Soviet comparisons.

(c) It would be very instructive to use the existence of detailed American-Soviet and Anglo-American comparisons of productivity as a cross-check, both for particular commodities and for aggregates. Wide disparities would suggest the need for further inquiry into methodology or statistical coverage. With so substantial a risk of error, this would be of real value for purposes of analysis. Indeed, this can be extended beyond these three countries. For example, there exist also some Polish calculations, which often contrast Polish productivity with a number of Western countries, including Great Britain.[27] Clearly, we would all gain by closer collaboration and increased awareness of each other's work.

(d) The definition of "worker" is a source of difficulty. There is the question of auxiliaries and trainees, and also the further problem of the point at which a worker is categorized as a clerk or technician, which unavoidably differs in various countries. There is much to be said for comparing the total number employed, without dividing the labor force into "workers" and "nonworkers," except for the purpose of analyzing how many are employed in particular tasks within the given industry. One would also like to be clearer about the statistical treatment of part-time workers, which are of importance in the British textile industry.

(e) Serious doubts arise about the dividing line in the two countries between *"industrial"* labor and labor employed by an industrial enterprise on tasks which are non-industrial. There seems little doubt that Soviet statisticians are able to make the distinction more logically than the British, but unfortunately the precise definitions are not available. At what point does loading and unloading become "transport"? How are repairs and maintenance treated? The British Census of Production for 1958 provides explanations, which help us to see what is supposed to be "in." Thus the volume on cotton spinning contains the following definition of an operative: "All manual wage-earners. They include those employed in or about the factory or works; operatives employed in power-houses, transport work, stores, ware-

26. See the work of Gilbert and Kravis, and the Anglo-American comparisons of Paige and Bombach, undertaken for OEEC, Paris.

27. For example, J. Gwiazdzinski, in *Gospodarka planowa*, no. 10, 1959, where he compares machinery and metal-working for Poland, France, West Germany, and the United Kingdom.

houses and, for 1958, canteens; inspectors, viewers and similar workers; maintenance workers and cleaners. Operatives engaged in outside work, erection, fitting, etc. are also included," but those working at home with the firm's materials are excluded. Some other British statistical sources use slightly different definitions, as we have seen. It would be useful to have a Soviet definition in equal detail.

(f) There is frequent doubt about the definition of the processes covered in the comparison. Is chalk procurement considered part of the Soviet cement industry for purposes of employment statistics? Is the connection and maintenance of lines to private consumers included in the labor force of the electric power industry? Does spinning include doubling?

(g) In some sectors, the definition of the product presents difficulties. This is particularly so in the textile industry, with its many types of yarn and cloth, including mixtures. British statistics are often confusing, and Soviet statistics are scarce and ambiguous. The collaboration of statisticians in both countries with expert knowledge of the textile industry would be required for an adequate analysis.

Finally, there are many aspects of Anglo-Soviet comparisons, hardly touched upon here, which would certainly merit close study. These include the employment of women, the relative importance of clerical and engineer-technical personnel in industry, the use of power (energy) per worker, the extent of the shift system, hours and holidays, the relative magnitude of industrial employment in the total occupied population, the relative size of the labor force occupied in what (in Soviet terminology) are known as unproductive sectors, and so on. The recent publication of census data by the USSR makes possible some very interesting contrasts (though differences in definition may confuse the analysis). For example, it appears that, in relation to the occupied population, the number of civil servants in the United Kingdom greatly exceeds those in the USSR, despite the much wider field of Soviet state activity. But to proceed to detailed discussion of any of these points would mean exceeding the limit on length of papers at our conference, which would be rightly regarded by the organizers of the conference as a breach of labor discipline.

Table 23. Occupational classification of wage-earners in "deep mines"
operated by the National Coal Board in Great Britain.[a]

Occupation at main places of work	1959 (in thousands)
Underground officials	
Overmen[b]	5.2
Deputies	22.2
Shotfirers	11.6
Other underground officials	2.9
Face workers	
Mechanical, electrical and maintenance workers—classified as face workers	2.9
All other face workers	231.1
Face trainees[b]	5.3
Workers elsewhere underground	
Developments at roadways	21.7
Transport	101.8
Roadway repairs	32.8
Special work	2.5
Engineering services (including mechanics, electricians, other craftsmen and other maintenance workers)	31.2
Reconstruction (including capital work)	5.8
Trainees[b]	1.2
Other underground labor	40.1
Total	518.3
Surface workers	
Weekly paid industrial staff	5.3
Winding and banking	15.9
Traffic[b]	13.4
Coal preparation	20.9
Power	5.5
Maintenance (including mechanics, electricians, other craftsmen and other maintenance workers)	31.6
Reconstruction[b] (including capital work)	1.5
Trainees	5.7
Other surface labor	27.0
Total	126.8
Grand Total	645.1

a. The figures relate to the end of September. Mines operated by the National Coal Board account for 99 per cent of the total number of wage-earners employed at all coal mines.

b. These categories are probably omitted, in whole or in part, from the Soviet total of "workers" in this industry.

CHAPTER 12

Indexes and Methods of Comparing International Labor Productivity

A. G. Aganbegyan

Moscow University

The System of Labor Productivity Indexes Used in International Comparisons

There are many facets to the system of comparing international labor productivity indexes. Comparisons of individual labor productivity indexes may suffice for particular purposes, but to obtain a full and objective picture it is essential to compare a set of interrelated indexes. In this system, particular indexes of labor productivity sound more convincing. They supplement and verify each other. This is because there are intimate connections—and, more important, dual connections—between particular labor productivity indications. First, the weighted average of the sum of productivity indexes for enterprises (industries and branches) yields the productivity index for an industry or branch. Second, particular indexes often act as components of more general indications (hourly labor productivity as a component of annual productivity and the index of labor per unit of production as a component of aggregate labor outlay, and so forth). This connection may also be expressed quantitatively.

Important though it may be to compare particular labor productivity indexes by countries, the main purpose is to compare the entire set of indexes, just as in science it is more important to study the interconnected system of particular laws and categories than to study them in isolation. Because of this dialectical requirement, summary international comparative inquiries into labor productivity based on a set of corresponding indications are all embracing and conclusive.

The system of labor productivity indexes used in international comparisons may include the following basic sections:

(1) Enterprise (shop), group of enterprises, line of production, branch of production, group of branches of production, branch of economy, and national economy as a whole. This vertical section yields a comparative picture from top to bottom and requires that the indexes correspond. We attach considerable importance to the comparison of labor productivity by groups of production branches in the fuel industry as a whole, for example (with due consideration to the structure of fuel balance), in the extracting and manufacturing industries, in heavy and light industries, in plant-growing and animal husbandry (in agriculture), and so forth, since comparisons of that sort give a better idea of the structure of labor productivity indications in the economic branches of the countries concerned.

(2) Outlays of live labor, current outlays of living and past labor, aggregate outlays of living and past labor (including capital outlays), and social outlays of all labor with due regard to the degree of use of available manpower. This horizontal section mirrors the economic content of indexes used as indications of the efficiency of labor outlays. The preceding index is included in the succeeding one, thus yielding an interdependence of the chain of indexes under review.

(3) Hourly, daily, monthly, and yearly productivity of labor. From the standpoint of a single enterprise the hourly and daily labor productivity indication is preferable, but, from the standpoint of society as a whole, the indication of annual labor productivity which registers the use of labor time for the year is most important. When productivity is calculated solely by outlays of labor per unit of production it may be broken down for the basic workers, all workers, and aggregate personnel.

(4) Measurement of labor productivity: in kind, in conventional units, by the labor method, and in terms of value. These different ways of measuring labor productivity supplement each other and are widely used in international comparative studies.

(5) Indexes of the level, differentiation, rates and factors of labor productivity. Indications of the level of productivity are, naturally, the keystone of all comparative international productivity studies. But they are not

enough. It is desirable to supplement the average level indications with indexes of the differentiation of productivity by groups of enterprises (advanced, medium, backward, and so forth), so as to obtain a more conclusive picture of the aggregates compared. It is unquestionably essential, when comparing the levels of labor productivity, to make a special study of the actual and possible rates at which labor productivity changes, in order to establish the stability of comparisons over time and to determine trends and prospects. Soviet economists regard it as one of the fundamentals to make their comparative international studies of economic indexes not only static, but also dynamic, from the standpoint of the historical development concerned.

A comparative inquiry into the factors of labor productivity by countries is highly important. It is extremely difficult to accomplish, but of utmost importance for an understanding of the substance of the indexes obtained, which, after all, is the purpose of the comparisons.[1]

Methods of Comparing Labor Outlays in Different Countries

In its general form the index of labor outlays per unit is given as T/Q, and the corresponding index of labor productivity by the reverse formula, Q/T, where T is the outlay of living labor and Q the production.

The following basic methodological requirements may be listed for comparisons of labor outlays and productivity in different countries.

Comparability of production by enterprises and by quality. The comparability of production by enterprises is especially important when the correlation of aggregate output in an industry (the automobile industry, for example) is determined by comparing the physical indexes of production (the output of automobiles), since enterprises of a given industry usually produce subsidiary items. Moreover, the share of the basic product in the output of an industry differs greatly from country to country. To avoid errors, the comparisons for the basic product may be extended to the aggregate production of the industry, provided an appropriate adjustment is made based on indexes of the share of basic product in the aggregate product by countries.

Comparability of production by quantity is important when aggregate outputs are compared in physical units. Since in many cases it is impossible

1. "A Few Methodological Propositions on Comparisons of Labor Productivity in the Industries of the USSR and the Capitalist Countries," *Sozialistichesky trud* (Socialist Labor), no. 6, 1956.

to eliminate differences in the quality of the products compared by countries, special provisions should be made to that effect, backed by appropriate data (for example, different percentages of electric steel and grade steel in the aggregate steel output, indexes for different structures of machine tools, and the like). In more thorough calculations different qualities of the product may be reduced to one quality by means of conversion coefficients calculated in accordance with the relation of labor outlays that go into the manufacture of a unit of the products of these qualities, or in accordance with their production costs, or, ultimately, by their respective prices. This gives rise to difficulties, deriving from the difference of conversion coefficients in different countries, but they may be eliminated by a double calculation (using the coefficients first of one country and then of the other) or by selecting a mean coefficient.

When international comparative studies are made of the aggregate output, first for industry as a whole, or by branches, it should always be borne in mind that errors may creep in due to a duplication of outlays of material in the aggregate output. The aggregate output of the automobile industry, for example, may duplicate the cost of parts (the cost of the parts as such, and their cost as elements of the automobile) whenever these parts are produced at independent enterprises. If these parts are produced in a shop of the motor works they are only set down once in the aggregate output. It stands to reason that the varying degree of specialization of production from country to country has a substantial effect on the volume of aggregate production. To avoid this error wherever it is likely, the volume of the final product—a product of the branch in a different line of goods—should be compared. Comparisons may also be made conditionally by registering the net output (aggregate output minus raw and other materials), which is free from duplication.

Comparability of labor outlays ascribed directly to output. To begin with, it is necessary to ensure comparability of labor outlays (number of workers) for the labor processes involved, since workers doing various ancillary jobs are listed with the workers of the given branch in some countries and under separate subheads in others, depending on the varying levels of development of the ancillary branches. In comparing the number of industrial workers in the USSR and United States of America, for example, railway rolling-stock repair workers and workers repairing tractors and agricultural machines, motor transport workers, waterworks employees, and the like, should be excluded from the Soviet total of industrial workers.

It is furthermore essential to ensure comparability of the number of workers by categories of personnel. When calculating labor productivity for the basic workers, economists should verify whether the breakdown of workers into basic and ancillary is the same in the countries concerned, and when calculating labor productivity for all workers they must verify that the term "workers" is identical in the statistics of the countries concerned, and so forth. The general indication would, of course, be the index of labor productivity for all workers engaged in a given branch—workers, engineers, technicians, office workers. (In industry, they make up the productive personnel.)

There should also be unification of the listed labor outlays and employees. It would be an error, for example, to compare an average listed number of employees in one country with the number reporting to work in another.

Comparison of labor productivity levels in different countries by different methods. It is desirable, too, to verify indirectly the results obtained by comparing other indexes related to labor productivity. This methodological requirement is especially important when labor productivity comparisons are based on the aggregate output of groups of production branches, a branch of the economy (such as industry on the whole, building, and the like) or the national economy. The results of such comparisons are never more than approximate, since they do not yield a precise and equivalent index if only because the structure of production varies from country to country or because all calculations in effect contain too many assumptions.

More of these assumptions derive from comparisons of aggregate outputs by estimating them in one currency for the different countries, which involves purchasing capacity indexes for the various currencies concerned in the various classes of goods calculated as representative and then applied to the entire class of goods. It is usual that the summary purchasing capacity index of currencies for the production line varies, depending on what currency is converted into another and on the weights employed in a country to obtain particular indications of the purchasing capacity. For purposes of precision, therefore, comparisons of physical output or labor productivity by aggregate production often entail two indexes—the maximum and the minimum. Comparative labor productivity indexes by countries, even for large branches, may avoid indirect estimates of aggregate outputs in terms of one currency by employing the method of aggregating the physical indexes of labor productivity measured by the number of workers employed. A. Kats, a Soviet economist, used this method in his comparative study of industrial labor productivity in the USSR and the major capitalist countries.[2]

A brief outline of this method follows. Wherever possible in branches of production, output is compared physically (or in conventional physical units) and by the number of workers employed. This enables the economist to compare the level of labor productivity. To obtain the respective indexes for the branch as a whole (and not only for the basic product under review), economists employ data concerning the share of the given branch directly employed in the production of the given basic product (coefficient of range) and data concerning the numerical share of workers in the given branch in the production of the basic product (coefficient of range) and data concerning the numerical share of workers in the given branch directly employed in manufacturing the given basic product (coefficient of specialization). Weighting the particular productivity indexes thus obtained by the numerical strength of workers in the given line of production, we thus secure the summary results for industry as a whole. The possibilities of this method are great, because physical indexes of labor productivity may be obtained for production lines manufacturing more than 50 per cent of the product and employing more than 50 per cent of the workers, and a proper selection of these lines will yield good representative summary indexes. Naturally, by using weights of different countries for the number of workers, we get somewhat different over-all indexes, and it is, therefore, desirable to show the "extremes" in the comparative levels of labor productivity. But it is difficult to determine physical labor productivity indexes for the engineering and chemical industries (which are basic lines) by this method, and that is its weakness.

Labor productivity comparisons by means of the above two methods should be paralleled, and the closeness of the results obtained should indicate that the resulting indexes are valid. (Comparative studies of labor productivity in socialist countries follow the same two methods.)[3] Comparative studies of labor productivity in Soviet industry and that of the leading capitalist countries by a few different methods have yielded an approximately similar result. Labor productivity in Soviet industry in 1959, for example,

2. A. Kats, "Comparison of Industrial Productivity in the Soviet Union and Some Capitalist Countries," *Sozialistichesky trud,* no. 1, 1959, "Comparative Study of Labor Productivity in Soviet and US Industry," *Trud i zarabotnaya plata* (Labor and Wages), no. 7, 1959.
3. V. Gelbraz and N. Zarubov, "Some Methodological Questions Related to Comparisons of Labor Productivity in the Industry of Socialist Countries," *Trud i zarabotnaya plata,* no. 11, 1960.

amounted to from 40 to 50 per cent of the level attained by United States industry, and slightly exceeded that of West Germany, Britain, and France. For practical purposes, it is desirable to employ one average index for the various indications obtained, rather than a set of "extreme" indexes.

The index of power and electricity consumed per worker in industry as a whole and in its branches is often used as an indirect check of the competence of comparative data obtained for labor productivity for various countries. In so doing, it is advisable for the sake of thoroughness to calculate these indexes solely in relation to motive power, since the varying share of power used for technological purposes usually derives from the varying content of production. It is also advisable to deal with similar branch structures when calculating the index for industry as a whole, so that they do not affect the index. It stands to reason, moreover, that the data is not to be based on the capacity of the machines (since the degree of use of machinery differs from country to country; it is considerably greater in the USSR, for example, than it is in the United States) but rather on the actual consumption of power.

In some lines of production, data of output per unit of equipment combined with indexes showing the norms of servicing (such as metallurgy, power stations, the textile industry) serve as good indirect checks for the comparative level of labor productivity in various countries. Other technico-economic indexes may also be compared, provided it is ascertained that labor productivity is largely dependent on the size of these indexes.

A comparative study of labor productivity by countries should be combined with a comparative study of the rates of change of these indexes.

Furthermore, it is desirable for a number of reasons (to escape structural factors) to compare the indexes of the permanent composition of labor productivity based on sub-indexes for the various branches in accordance with weights used in the country concerned. It is also useful to calculate the rates by countries not only as relative accretions of productivity but as a comparison of the absolute increases.

The question of correlating factors of labor productivity in international comparative methods is the question of questions. This is a field in which progress has been poorest, because it is extremely difficult. It is therefore my opinion that the basic aim of the subject reviewed in this paper should be an inquiry into the methods in different countries.

In making this comparison of factors it should be first noted that: (a) each factor should be quantitatively measurable and its quantitative influence on productivity should (at best) be ascertainable; (b) there should be a set of factors which would, as a whole, establish the level of labor productivity more or less accurately (mathematically, so that the coefficient of the multiple correlation of the productivity level to the set of factors amounts to not less than 85–90 per cent). The ideal case would be if the level and factors of labor productivity given for countries in their quantitative correlation were presented in terms of a single economico-mathematical model. Development of such a model, whose parameters should indicate the degree of influence which each factor has on the level of labor productivity, is obviously a most important theoretical and practical task facing economists dealing with labor productivity.

A model of that sort is being developed in the USSR, and the first few experiments made have been promising. The economic and industrial planning research laboratory of the Kharkov Engineering and Economic Institute (E. G. Liberman and V. P. Khaikin) has suggested the following model of correlation between labor productivity (x_1) and the factors on which it depends $(x_2, x_3, \ldots, x_n)$

$$x_1 = b_1 x_2^{b_2} x_3^{b_3} \cdots x_n^{b_n}$$

in which b_1 stands for the parameters denoting the degree of influence which the changes of the said factors exert on the level of labor productivity. Singling out 9 factors for a start, the laboratory used an electronic computer to calculate by the method of least squares the concrete parameters for a group of Kharkov engineering plants, and it turned out that the coefficient of the multiple correlation was 0.98, and the mean quartile deviation of the calculated data from data reviewed was 0.032.[4]

The following are the factors of labor productivity common to all branches and measurable quantitatively in international comparisons: (1) indexes of concentration—the size of enterprises by their output; size of basic assets and number of workers; (2) indexes for outlays of living labor —power and electricity per worker, funds per worker, organic structure of funds, proportion of fixed and circulating assets (including implements of labor as part of fixed assets), proportion of mechanized jobs, proportion of mechanized labor, and so forth; (3) indexes for use of production funds, output per unit of funds, and so forth; (4) structure of the labor force— proportion of basic and ancillary workers, numerical relation of workers, engineers, technicians, and office employees, and the like; (5) length of

4. E. Liberman and V. Khaikin, "Theses of Reports Made at Conference on the Use of Mathematical Methods and Latest Computers in Intramural Planning by Engineering Plants," Moscow Engineering and Economic Institute and Moscow Economic Council, 1961.

production cycle; (6) indexes for the use of the labor force—number of working hours per week, number of working days per year, and so forth; (7) indexes of proficiency—level of general and specialized education, years of service, and so on.[5]

In Q/T, the index of labor productivity, T stands for physical outlays of labor time not reduced to simple labor of average intensity. It may be presented as cofactors:

$$\frac{Q}{T} = \frac{Q}{T_0} \times \frac{T_0}{T}$$

where T_0 is the outlay simple labor and T_0/T is the coefficient of reduction of average labor to simple labor (labor of higher intensity to light labor of normal intensity). The index Q/T_0 may be used for a number of purposes in international comparisons, but it is hard to obtain, because it involves measuring the coefficient of reduction.

Methods of Comparing Productivity of Social Labor in the National Economy as a Whole in Different Countries

Besides the index of labor productivity for the aggregate social product, use is also made of the index of labor productivity for the net product (the national income). In dealing with the national economy as a whole, this is desirable because the national income represents the total ultimate output of society newly created in a given year, and may therefore rightly serve as an indication of the efficiency of labor employed. Concurrently, the volume of the produced national labor qualifies the degree of use of past labor, since, given the same volume of the social product, a reduction of the norm of material outlays will serve to increase the dimensions of the national income.

Comparative international studies of labor productivity in the national economy may follow two methods: (a) the value method, involving an assessment of the total product or the national income (depending on the chosen index) in comparable currency; (b) by the factor method, involving a comparison of factors determining the level of labor productivity.

Thus, when using this method to compare productivity by national in-

5. E. Liberman, "Report at Conference on Labor Productivity, December 1956," from *Statistical Methodology for Study of Labor Productivity in Soviet National Economy* (Moscow), 1956.

come in different countries,[6] we first calculate the correlation of the levels of labor productivity for the social product by weighting the comparative indexes of labor per unit in the individual branches of the national economy. Then we calculate the possible influence exerted on productivity by the norms of material outlays in the countries concerned and the different numerical structure of manpower by branches (owing to the different output of net products per worker in different branches). By combining these factors we obtain the initial index.

Both methods are used in the Soviet Union, and we have obtained close results when comparing the labor productivity in the national economies of, say, the USSR and the United States.[7]

When comparing the productivity of social labor for all society, the degree of use of manpower must also be taken into account. The efficiency of social labor in the broad and true sense of the word depends largely on what portion of the population is directly employed in the production of material wealth. To obtain these factors in the case of capitalist countries, the numerical strength used in the calculation of labor productivity of social labor should also include the number of unemployed. It is worthwhile calculating and comparing production indexes per able-bodied member of society or per able-bodied member of society minus those employed in education, public health, science, and so forth.

When comparing the productivity of social labor for all society, the consumer value of the products must also be recorded. This may be done by excluding from the social product or the national income (used in calculating labor productivity) all military production, for it is not consumed and does not augment a country's wealth.

6. A. Aganbegyan, "Use of Mathematical Methods and Electronic Computers in the Field of Labor and Wages," *Sozialistichesky trud,* no. 1, 1961.
7. I. Joffe, "Productivity of Labor in the USSR and USA," *Planovoye khozaistvo* (Planned Economy), no. 6, 1960; A. Aganbegyan, "Overtake USA in Productivity of Labor," *Sozialistichesky trud,* no. 4, 1959.

CHAPTER 13

Comparative Productivity
in the Steel Industry

Erik Ruist

Jernkontoret, Stockholm

A comparative study of productivity in the steel industry in several countries can have different objectives. In some cases, the planning aspect is predominant. An estimate is then desired of the number of workers required to get a planned tonnage of steel. The figures for other countries are of interest to guide a forecast of the ton-per-man-hour development in the country concerned.

A more common objective of productivity comparisons is to get an idea of the relative efficiencies of the steel industries in different countries. Such a study can be of great value to those countries which turn out to be on the lower end of the efficiency scale, since it shows what can be achieved, and, in fact, what has already been achieved elsewhere. This is an incentive to improvement and points out where better methods could profitably be studied.

Since no doubt the efficiency aspect is always in the picture, the following study will have as its goal to illustrate the possibilities and difficulties in calculating a labor productivity measure that could be used together with other data in assessing the efficiency of the steel industry.

For several reasons, comparisons will be made not in terms of productivity, but in terms of inputs per unit of output. Difficulties in measuring unit labor input are discussed before figures are presented. In fact, the steel industry in a very illustrative way shows quite a few of the difficulties associated with productivity measurements.

In order to make the following discussion understandable it may be necessary to give a very brief description of the processes in a steelworks.

Technical Processes in the Steel Industry

Iron ore is first melted with coke in a blast furnace, the product of which is pig iron. The ore may have been pretreated by grinding and enriching (which is usually done at the mine) and then by agglomeration (in the sintering plant at the blast furnace). The coke used in blast furnaces may or may not have been produced in a coke-oven plant at the works. Thus, the degree of preparation of raw materials as well as of fuel is not uniform, which no doubt is reflected in differences in the amount of labor and of capital required for the production of one ton of pig iron.

Part of the pig iron produced is sold to iron foundries which are not considered as belonging to the steel industry. There is also a considerable trade in pig iron between works inside the steel industry.

The next processing stage is steelmaking. The raw materials used in the steelworks are pig iron—hot in liquid form or cold in the form of pigs —and scrap. Part of the scrap has arisen in the further processing departments, but part of it may have been bought from outside. The proportion of bought scrap in the charge of the steel furnaces may vary from 0 to something like 70 per cent. Quite a few steelworks have no blast furnaces of their own but have to rely upon bought pig iron and scrap. This is of course a further complication in measuring productivity.

There are several different ways of making steel, the principal processes being the Bessemer, the open hearth, the electric, and the oxygen processes. The normal composition of the charge (ratio scrap/pig iron) is widely different in these processes. Labor requirement per ton of steel is also different.

The steel produced in the steel furnaces is either forwarded to the foundry to make steel castings or directly cast into ingots. Total production of ingots and steel for castings is usually referred to as crude steel production. The further processing of the castings is in many countries not considered to belong to the steel industry and is excluded here. The ingots are rolled in several stages, into different shapes, such as bars, plates, sheets, and strips, or forged. Like casting, forging is not always included in the steel industry and is not counted here.

In some countries, there exist rolling mills which are not locally integrated with steelworks, but rely on purchased ingots or semis (the semi-finished product obtained from the first rolling of the ingot).

In the rolling mills, the amount of labor required per ton of finished product not only depends upon the type of mill (strip, plate, and so forth), but also on the type of steel used. Thus, for certain purposes, steel with special properties is required. It usually takes much more time to go through the rolling mill and its ancillary departments. Thus, labor requirement for a ton of finished stainless steel is approximately five times as high as for a ton of ordinary steel.

Total or Departmental Measures

Now, the computation of labor input per unit of output could be performed in different ways. Thus, in principle, it would be possible either to take each of the three stages of production (blast furnace, steelworks, and rolling mills) separately, or to compute an over-all figure for the entire steel industry, taking due account of the differences in degree of integration that exist between countries. Each of these methods has its advantages. The first one gives figures which are easy to interpret and which could be easily supplemented by data on the consumption of raw materials, fuel, and perhaps also capital. It is often used in Eastern European countries, which give figures on output in tons per worker (in blast furnaces and open hearth furnaces, for example).

The method of course also has its disadvantages, especially in international comparisons. It is very sensitive to differences in worker classification. Thus, in one country certain jobs are done by workers belonging to the relevant production department, while in another country the same jobs are performed by workers in an auxiliary department. In this case, it is of course of no interest to compare the tonnage produced per worker in the production departments of the two countries.

In this respect, the over-all method has an advantage, in that it takes account of all workers. It is also practical, since it concentrates all available information into one figure, easily managed in comparisons. This method has often been used when comparing the rate of productivity growth in the steel industry in one country with that of other industries or of the steel industry in other countries. In that case, the problem of different concepts of what is included in the steel industry is not so important, as long as the definition within each country is kept unchanged during the period of comparison.

In fact, the two methods referred to are not competing but rather supplementing each other. In the following section, both methods will be used as far as possible with respect to available data.

Measure of Output

For an over-all measure of labor used per unit of output, several output measures can alternatively be used. The simplest one is the tonnage of crude steel produced. This measure may be relevant since all material goes through a stage when it is relatively uniform. However, it is not very well suited for a comparison of absolute levels in different countries, since the ratio of pig iron produced to steel produced is not the same in all countries, and since the proportion of different rolling mill products, requiring different amounts of labor per ton, is very dissimilar.

The standard method recommended—at least in Western countries— for measuring output in connection with labor productivity is to take the sum for all items sold of the tonnage produced multiplied by a conversion coefficient, which is proportional to the labor required per ton during some base period or in some base country. Without modifications, this method is not very well adapted to the steel industry because of the varying amounts of raw materials coming in at different stages, and particularly because of the different amounts of scrap being used in different countries. With some slight modifications, this difficulty could be taken care of, and this method is used in what follows.

Still another output measure can be used in productivity calculations, namely, some net value of production. However, in international comparisons it is very difficult to choose the relevant exchange rates to convert all figures to a common currency. For these reasons, this method has not been used.

In order to adapt the "man-hour weighted tonnage" method to the peculiarities of the steel industry, two approaches have been used. The first and more straightforward is described below, while the other will be used later in connection with the discussion of the differences in the first modification.

Since the difficulty is in the passing in and out of material at several stages during the production process, a proper way to handle it is to consider the products at each stage as end products, and, when calculating the conversion coefficients, to take account of the man-hours used in one stage only. Thus, pig iron is considered as an end product and receives the weight calculated on the man-hours used in the blast furnace. In the same way, crude steel is also an end product, weighted by man-hours in the steelworks. Finally, the weights for rolling mill products take account of the man-hours in the rolling mills only. This is the method used in studies performed by the U.S. Bureau of Labor Statistics[1] and by the Iron and Steel Board in the United Kingdom.[2] From the point of view of need for data this is a convenient method, since it requires only total number of workers or of man-hours in the steel industry of each country to be analyzed, plus one set of weights to be applied to the data of all countries.

The Set of Weights Used

The weights used in the present investigation have been taken from the American study just referred to. The reason for this is that it seems to be the only set of weights based on unit labor requirements that has been published in recent years. However, for special steels the American weights have not been used. There are two reasons for this. The more compelling one is that in most countries, unlike the United States, there are no published statistics on the production of rolling mill products of special steels, only on crude special steel production. Moreover, the American figures seem to over-emphasize the difference between special and ordinary steels in respect to man-hour requirements per ton.

Account is taken of the higher labor-intensiveness of special steel products by the following method.

There is supposed to be no difference in man-hour requirements per ton in the steelworks, assuming that furnaces are identical. Moreover, for rolled products of a certain type of steel the coefficients are supposed to be proportional to the coefficients for similar products of ordinary steel. Thus, if the number of man-hours required to roll a ton of stainless strip is five times the corresponding number for ordinary strip, the ratio between the man-hours required to roll a ton of stainless heavy plate and a ton of

1. *Man-Hours Per Unit of Output in the Basic Steel Industry, 1939–55* (Washington, 1954).
2. *Development in the Iron and Steel Industry, Special Report* (London, 1961), p. 103.

ordinary heavy plate should also be five. This seems to be a rather realistic assumption, according to Swedish experience.

It is, however, also necessary to make another assumption which is less realistic. Since no information is available on which products are rolled from special steels, an estimate has to be made. The simplest one is that the special steel products form a constant proportion of all rolled products. This is in no way realistic since, for example, it is only seldom that railway track material or heavy sections are rolled of special steels.

If, however, in absence of better data, this assumption is made, a multiplicative correction could be applied to the weights for rolled products. It has been thought necessary to consider stainless steels and other special steels separately, in view of the much higher labor requirements as well as the scrap rate for stainless steels.

Unfortunately, the definitions of special steels used in countries' production statistics are not uniform. For the countries included in the following calculations, the main lack of uniformity appears in the United Kingdom, where only alloy steels are taken into account, while for the ECSC countries and for Sweden high carbon steels are also included. This means a negative bias for the correction that is applied to the British output data. The correction factors used are based on figures collected from Swedish steelworks and are for:

France	1.05
Federal Republic of Germany	1.05
Italy	1.10
Sweden	1.23
United Kingdom	1.04

For the remaining countries, no correction was necessary, because of the small percentage of special steels produced.

Before we can start calculations, it is necessary to define the limits of the steel industry. This is of great importance, since in all countries steel production is often locally integrated with other activities, and it is possible to find a variety of definitions being used in European countries. Among departments included in some countries and excluded from others are coke ovens at blast furnaces, steel foundries, forging shops, and tube rolling mills. For practical reasons we shall mainly use the limits drawn up by the treaty of the European Coal and Steel Community which excludes all the above-mentioned departments with the exception of coke ovens.

To be sure that the production figures used should be as comparable as possible, they are all taken from the *Quarterly Bulletin of Steel Statistics,* issued by the U.N. Economic Commission for Europe. The items included and the weights chosen for them are given in the list.[3]

Coke produced at steelworks	0.6
Pig iron (and sponge iron)	1.0
Crude steel	1.4
Semis for tubes or for sale	0.3
Railway track material	1.7
Heavy sections	1.5
Light sections	2.8
Wire rods	2.0
Strip	1.5
Heavy plates	1.1
Medium plates	1.3
Sheets, hot rolled (incl. for cold-rolling)	1.5
Sheets, cold rolled (in addition to 1.5 for hot-rolling)	1.3
Tinplate (in addition to 1.5 + 1.3)	3.6
Galvanized sheets (1.5 + 1.3)	1.5
Other rolled products	2.8

Measure of Labor Input

The man-hour figures to be compared with the output measures so defined should only include workers in the relevant departments mentioned. For firms which also include other departments, it is necessary to estimate the amount of work done in auxiliary departments that refer to the "steel industry" as we have defined it. Within the ECSC, returns are regularly collected from the firms, giving certain rules for this subdivision. The total number of man-hours worked within the limits of the treaty are published for each member country in the *Statistical Bulletin of the High Authority.* For the United Kingdom, a similar calculation has been made by the Iron and Steel Board and published in the special report referred to. For Sweden, the author has regrouped available man-hour data collected for the wage statistics in the same way. This estimate is probably less reliable than for the other countries. Finally, for Poland and for Eastern Germany estimates are taken from the statistical yearbooks of the two countries. It is however not clearly stated which activities are in fact included in these man-hour figures. Since the production of seamless tubes seems to belong to the steel industry of these countries, production of that item

3. Production data derived from various sources; for Poland and Eastern Germany, consumption figures.

has been included in their output figure. It is still uncertain whether input and output data actually match each other.

Over-all Figures on Labor Input per Unit of Output

The data refer to 1959, except for Sweden, where the period used is the first half of 1959. The resulting man-hours per unit of output are given in list form. Since absolute figures have no relevance, all results are expressed in percentages of that of Western Germany.

Belgium	104
France	119
Saar	108
Eastern Germany	(194)
Western Germany	100
Italy	115
Luxembourg	75
Netherlands	62
Poland	(217)
Sweden	104
United Kingdom	157

When analyzing these figures, the varying degree of reliability should be kept in mind, as well as the arbitrariness of the weights.

It may also be argued that the variance between the results is partly due to differences in choice of steelmaking processes. This choice has in turn been directed by economic considerations of the local availability of coal, iron ore, scrap, hydro-electric power, and so forth. Thus, the existing combination of steelmaking processes in each country may be economically rational under the prevailing conditions, in spite of the fact that the man-hour requirements per ton of crude steel are widely different.

Thus, it may be natural to allow for the existing differences, and to treat the steel coming from each process as a separate product. The coefficients for these products have been estimated from an observed number of workers per ton of steel produced in different types of steelworks in the ECSC, the open hearth coefficient being fixed at 1.4 as above. (In the United States, the source of the coefficients, open hearth is the predominant method):

Bessemer (acid and basic)	0.7
Open hearth	1.4
Electric	2.3
Other	0.8

Some experts would consider the coefficient for electric steel as unduly high, but no information is available to improve the estimate.

By using these coefficients, the results are somewhat modified, as will be seen from Table 24. In both cases, the figures for the Federal Republic of Germany are taken as 100.

Table 24. Man-hours per unit of output for the steel industry, 1959.
(Federal Republic of Germany = 100)

Country	Over-all (per cent)	Including different processes
Belgium	104	111
France	119	121
Saar	108	114
Eastern Germany	(194)	(179)
Western Germany	100	100
Italy	115	99
Luxembourg	75	84
Netherlands	62	59
Poland	(217)	(198)
Sweden	104	89
United Kingdom	157	146

The effect of the change in weights was mainly to increase the index for countries with a high proportion of Bessemer steel (Belgium, Saar, Luxembourg) and to lower it for those with a high proportion of electric steel (Italy, Sweden). Since the differences are not negligible, this is really a test case for the question of how productivity data should be used. According to one school of thought (represented in the Western discussion by Farrell),[4] it is necessary to take account of all factors of production in a measure of production efficiency. In that case, man-hour requirements should be calculated without regard to the production process used. The relative advantages of the processes will be apparent through low requirement figures for different factors, and thus the advantages and disadvantages are duly weighted one against the other.

The other school which may be represented by Vanden Abeele[5] says that it is unrealistic to hope to get quantitative measures of the require-

4. M. J. Farrell, "The measurement of productive efficiency," *Journal of the Royal Statistical Society*, 1957, vol. 120, p. 253.
5. A. M. Vanden Abeele, "A method for analysis and comparison of labor productivity in cotton spinning mills," *Productivity Measurement Review*, Special Number, October 1957.

ments of all factors of production. It is better to concentrate on labor, but to make corrections in the measure of labor productivity for known differences in machinery equipment, and so forth. In principle, the figures should be corrected so as to refer to identically equipped firms or industries.

The first of these approaches is, in the mind of the author, theoretically much preferable to the second. However, it is very seldom—at least in international comparisons—that it is possible to find appropriate data to apply this method. The second approach is better in this respect, in that it is possible to take into account existing pieces of information, even if they do not entirely cover the ground. However, it seems difficult to interpret such partially corrected indexes. It is also difficult to know which differences should and which should not be accounted for. Thus, in the steel industry, should a correction be made for the fact that in some countries the number of man-hours per ton of pig iron in the blast furnace is higher than in others because they are using lower grade—and thus cheaper—iron ore?

Whichever point of view is preferred here, there is an additional point to be considered concerning the above calculations, in that their result is different from the "ordinary" method which takes account of end products only of the industrial sector under consideration. This would be true even if the integration of all firms were similar, all raw materials were put in at the beginning of the process, and no semi-finished products were sold. The point is that the method is *not* sensitive to differences in the requirements of pig iron for steelmaking and of crude steel for rolling. If one country would require 1.20 tons of ingots for 1 ton of a certain kind of rolled product and another country 1.25 tons, the method used would, other things being equal, give identical results for the number of man-hours per unit of output. The "ordinary" method would give a greater figure for the country with 1.25 tons of ingots, since more man-hours have to be spent in order to produce 1 ton of finished (rolled) product.

Rather than try to correct the results obtained in order to take account of this difference—which would indeed be very difficult—it seems better to study the raw material requirements at each stage of production together with the corresponding labor requirements.

Separate Measure for Each Stage of Production

To get a connection between the "over-all" measures demonstrated above and the study of each stage or process separately, it may be of interest to see how the over-all measure can be broken down into a weighted sum of measures for the separate departments. The detailed data necessary for this decomposition are, however, available only for a few countries, and even for those only as the number of men, not of man-hours. Thus, the results will be somewhat different from what was obtained above. The calculations have been carried through for France and for the Federal Republic of Germany. In spite of the fact that both countries are members of the ECSC, whose high authority has tried to coordinate statistics in the field, employment data do not seem to be quite equivalent. In order to reach the highest possible degree of comparability, the totals are derived from ECSC statistics, while subdivisions are obtained from the more detailed national statistics.

In calculating the number of workers per unit of production at each stage, only process workers at each stage could be included. Workers in auxiliary departments have to be treated separately. Here the ratio of total number of workers over total number of process workers is used as a general multiplicative factor in the breakdown. If, to begin with, the three sectors—blast furnace, steelworks,[6] and rolling mills—are shown separately, the results are:

Country	Factor for indirect labor	Blast furnace		Steelworks		Rolling mills
France	1.86	$(33\ w_1$	$+$	$50\ w_2$	$+$	$79\ w_3)$
F.R. of Germany	1.78	$(33\ w_1$	$+$	$43\ w_2$	$+$	$82\ w_3)$

Here w_1, w_2, and w_3 are the weights of different stages, while the figures represent number of workers per unit of output at each stage. The figures for the two countries could be compared at each stage. The comparison of, say, a blast furnace figure with a steelworks figure is less relevant.

Now, if the weights are also inserted, the full result is:

France	$1.86[(33 \cdot 0.26) + (50 \cdot 0.27) + (79 \cdot 0.47)] = 109$
F.R. of Germany	$1.78[(33 \cdot 0.25) + (43 \cdot 0.35) + (82 \cdot 0.40)] = 100$

The total French figure is less in comparison to the German one when calculated on the basis of workers than on the basis of man-hours, depending upon the larger number of working hours per man-year in France.

6. The fact that figures are lower for blast furnaces and steelworks than for rolling mill indicates, however, that by American standards (American weights) the European works are doing better in the first-mentioned departments than in the last one.

The results for each department are not too unequal, the main difference being located in the steelworks. The lower rolling mill figure for
France almost exactly corresponds to the higher proportion of indirect
labor.

The data may be further subdivided. As an example, the steelworks
part is shown, divided into processes. The input figures may now be
expressed as number of men per thousand tons of steel. However, the
correction for special steels must be kept into the general coefficient and
cannot be distributed to the processes.

Workers per 1000 tons of steel in France number 0.59 in Bessemer; 1.40
in open hearth; and 2.94 in electric and other. In the Federal Republic of
Germany it is 0.54 in Bessemer; 1.24 in open hearth; and 1.80 in electric
and other. Although expressed in another unit, these figures may be weighted
and added to give the same sum as the steelworks' term.

France	$50 \cdot 0.27 = (0.59 \cdot 8.1) + (1.40 \cdot 4.0) + (2.94 \cdot 1.1)$
F.R. of Germany	$43 \cdot 0.35 = (0.54 \cdot 6.3) + (1.24 \cdot 7.4) + (1.80 \cdot 1.4)$

Here, the weights (8.1, 4.0, 1.1, etc.) are proportional to the tonnages
produced of each kind of steel.

In this connection, it may be of interest to include data on number of
workers per 1000 tons of open hearth steel which are available for a few
other countries:

Czechoslovakia	1.66
France	1.40
F.R. of Germany	1.24
Hungary	2.43
Poland	1.62
USSR	0.82

Since it is not known how large a part of the total staff is counted as
"indirect" labor, it is difficult to know the relevance of the figures for the
Eastern countries in comparison with the Western ones.

Supplementary Measures Necessary

The preceding calculations have been devoted entirely to the input
of labor. However, in the steel industry labor cost is only a rather small
part of total cost. Equal consideration must therefore be given to the

amounts of raw materials, fuel, electrical energy, and capital that are used in the production. A high labor input per unit of production may be compensated by a small input of some other factor, resulting in a low total cost or a good over-all efficiency. A study of the relative efficiencies of the steel industries of several countries must therefore study all factors of production. Unfortunately, and in spite of the fact that the steel industry is unusually well equipped with statistics, information is insufficient to permit an over-all study.

In conclusion, the figures on labor requirements are certainly elements in measures of total efficiencies by which the steel industries could be compared, but they do not by themselves give the complete picture of the situation. We have not been able to supplement these figures by any other kind of relevant quantitative information. This being so, the author would like to finish with a question: Are the figures as calculated of any use except as new toys in the economists' playground?

CHAPTER 14

International Productivity Comparisons for Managerial Decisions

Joel Dean

Columbia University

Productivity, or output per man-hour, measures and reflects all the various determinants of cost behavior, including economies of scale, rate of use, homogeneity of product mix, managerial competence, and technological progress.

Output per man-hour is therefore the result of many forces in addition to, and in most instances more important than, the personal efficiency of the man himself. Hence, increases in labor productivity do not have the monistic or explanatory significance that might be implied by the term.

Productivity is generally a descriptive statistic used to dramatize the rise of income levels by expressing output in terms of that input factor which is scarce in the United States economy, namely, labor. Professional economists understand the difficulties of measurement and the conceptual shortcomings of output per man-hour so well that they make little use of the concept of productivity in formal economic analysis. Is there anyplace for productivity concepts in managerial decisions?

In a free enterprise economy, unlike a socialized economy, output per man-hour is not, *per se,* of great managerial interest. Gains in labor productivity usually result, but they are inadvertent. Management's focus is not on increasing labor productivity, but on maximizing the profits of the enterprise. Since the focus of management is on the incremental profits associated with a decision, and value theory, capital theory, and marginal analysis are the appropriate and accepted tools, productivity of capital, tangible or intangible, is more likely to control a decision than is labor productivity.

Nevertheless, American management does make some use of productivity analysis. Productivity projections are used in sales-forecasting by predicting income levels for the distant future. American management in recent years has become increasingly concerned lest the United States product be priced out of world markets. International productivity comparisons can show labor and management what international competition they face and how this may influence the job-elasticity of wage rates. For companies which face foreign competition, productivity analysis may be a useful first step in evaluating this competition.

For example, a large United States manufacturer of consumer durables recently made two kinds of "productivity" studies to answer these overlapping questions:

(1) What competition did this manufacturer face, both at home and abroad, from competitors in Germany and England?

(2) What were the comparative costs of obtaining certain of the components for its U.S. manufactured products from abroad?

Underlying both studies was the conviction that the important determinant of the firm's future competitive position is comparative costs of labor. International disparities in the cost of capital, at least between Western Europe and the United States, are likely to diminish in the long run as a result of increased capital mobility, lower barriers to commerce, and more homogeneity of risks. International disparities in the cost of major materials also appear likely to diminish over time. For example, efficient new European tide-water steel mills will lower European steel prices and set ceilings on United States prices. Moreover, international dissemination of managerial competence and technological know-how is leveling cost disparities.

International disparities in labor costs may, however, last for a long time. A strong union in the United States, by reason of its large ocean-sheltered market, has power to raise and maintain wages far above those of an industry's European competitors. Consequently, despite the recognized analytical weaknesses of output per man-hour, international comparisons of the level and trend of labor productivity proved useful in appraising the company's probable competitive predicament.

Study 1: Comparative Trends in Wages, Productivity, and Unit Labor Costs

The first study is a three-nation comparison of trends in wages, output per man-hour, and unit labor costs in the United Kingdom, West Germany, and the United States for a consumer durable goods industry. This study has four parts: (1) hourly labor costs, (2) productivity, (3) unit labor costs, and (4) consistency with competitive experience.

Table 25. Hourly labor costs,[a] production workers in industry X in the United Kingdom, West Germany, and the United States, 1952–1960.

Years	UK as percentage of US	W. Germany as percentage of US
1952	28	31
1953	29	33
1954	31	31
1955	33	32
1956	34	32
1957	34	31
1958	32	31
1959	34	31
1960	35	32

a. Excluding incentive and overtime premiums. Exchange rates used were the current ones. Between 1950 and 1960 value of the pound in dollars varied from $2.78 to $2.81; and the value of the mark varied from .2375 to .2398 cents.

Hourly labor costs. The series on hourly labor costs was derived from records of the company's own operations in the United States, the United Kingdom, and West Germany. Table 25 shows that in 1960 hourly labor costs of production workers in England averaged 35 per cent of that of the United States; in West Germany they averaged 32 per cent of that of the United States. Between 1952 and 1960, the United Kingdom wage relative to that of the United States increased from 28 per cent to 35 per cent; during the same period there was virtually no change in the West German wage relative to that of the United States.

Productivity. Annual indexes of productivity for this industry are published by the West German government. For the United Kingdom, and the United States, industry data were more limited. By piecing together company data, and several published studies, some productivity relatives were nevertheless obtained. The results are summarized in Table 26.

Table 26. Industry X productivity in the United Kingdom,
West Germany, and the United States.

| | Output per production worker man-hour | |
Year	UK as percentage of US	W. Germany as percentage of US
1950	25	21
1951	—	23
1952	—	24
1953	—	25
1954	32	30
1955	—	32
1956	—	33
1957	—	35
1958	—	38
1959	33	40

As shown in Table 26, 1950 output per man-hour in the United Kingdom in this industry was estimated at 25 per cent of the United States level. The application of benchmark data for 1954 and 1959 indicates that United Kingdom productivity per employee reached 33 per cent of the United States level in 1959.

Output per man-hour rose by over 10 per cent per year in the West German industry from 1950 to 1959, compared to 3.6 per cent in United States industry. This faster rate of productivity growth enabled the West German industry to advance from 21 per cent of the United States level in 1950 to 40 per cent in 1959. By 1959, German productivity had surpassed the estimate level in Great Britain.

Unit labor costs. Tables 27 and 28 show the effects of these trends in relative wage rates and productivity upon unit labor costs in this industry.

From the scattered data of Table 28, it appears that there was little change in the United Kingdom's cost position vis-à-vis the United States between 1954 and 1959. The modest increase in relative United Kingdom productivity was more than offset by a rise in relative United Kingdom hourly labor costs. Meanwhile, German industry was experiencing rapid gains in productivity associated with greatly expanded volume and the adoption of United States technology. As is shown in Table 28, these productivity gains, coupled with hourly labor costs that rose no faster than they did in the United States, pushed down German unit costs from 129 per cent of the United States level in 1952 to 78 per cent of the United States level in 1959.

Table 27. Industry X unit labor costs in United Kingdom
as per cent of United States.

Year	Hourly labor costs	Est. output per man-hour (per cent)	Est. unit labor costs (per cent)
1950	n.a.	25	n.a.
1951	n.a.	—	—
1952	28	—	—
1953	29	32	97
1954	31	—	—
1955	33	—	—
1956	34	—	—
1957	34	—	—
1958	32	33	103
1959	34	—	—
1960	35	—	—.

Table 28. Industry X unit labor costs in West Germany
as per cent of United States.

Year	Hourly labor costs	Est. output per man-hour (per cent)	Est. unit labor costs (per cent)
1950	n.a.	21	—
1951	n.a.	23	—
1952	31	24	129
1953	33	25	132
1954	31	30	103
1955	32	32	100
1956	32	33	97
1957	31	35	89
1958	31	38	82
1959	31	40	78
1960	32	—	—

Consistency with competitive experience. Data on output per man-hour had to be pieced together from diverse sources, and this raised doubts about comparability. Unit labor costs, derived from these productivity estimates, did however conform to the firm's international competitive experience. Consistent with the unit cost data, West Germany is a stronger competitor in the firm's world markets than is the United Kingdom, and has been growing more formidable throughout the decade.

Export-import experience also confirmed the findings of the unit labor cost calculations. West German unit labor costs in this industry as computed were at parity with the United States by 1955. After this they fell below the United States. About 1955, this firm's exports from the United States began to shrink, and imports, particularly from Germany, began to increase.

Computed changes in unit labor costs in All-Manufacturing in the United Kingdom, West Germany, and the United States were also validated by comparison with price-level changes in the three countries, and with changes in exports and imports. Again the results seemed to be reasonably in accord with other experience.

The advantage in productivity-derived unit cost for West Germany was not nearly so sharp in All-Manufacturing as it was in this industry. Export-import data indicate that, vis-à-vis West Germany, United States difficulties as an international competitor are not across-the-board problems, but rather are confined to particular products.

Study 2: Comparative Long-run Incremental Production Costs

Study 1 illustrates a conventional productivity analysis that is frequently used in the United States to support positions that require quite different concepts and measurements. Our firm's main purpose for this study was to see whether the competitive advantage which the firm had in the United States because of size of market, economies of scale, capital intensity and standardization, was being eroded by similar developments in the United Kingdom and in West Germany, where wages relative to those of the United States were still low. Such a trend was suggested by the industry's decline in United States exports and increases in imports. The productivity analysis of Study 1 further supported the hypothesis of a long-run decline in the United States competitive position at least versus West Germany.

Study 2 illustrates a different approach to a similar, but more specific problem: namely, in which country can we by expanding capacity of existing plants manufacture at lowest, long-run incremental costs?

The forecast of future costs was based on the following assumptions:

(1) *Volume*—a specified and identical added volume of production was assumed for each location.

(2) *Processing*—the best known processing for each location was assumed, rather than identical processing for all locations.

(3) *Integration*—the make-or-buy pattern would differ among the three locations, since continuation of existing patterns of purchasing components and vertical integration was assumed.

(4) *Operating Pattern*—use of existing facilities was assumed. Required peak capacity would be obtained through maximum use of overtime, third shifts, and so forth. Detailed operating patterns differ among locations because of local working practices, different degrees of overtime availability, and so forth.

(5) *Prices*—factor prices assumed to continue at same relative levels.

Based on these assumptions, the amount of added investment required to produce an identical added volume of the component in the United States, in England, and in West Germany was estimated. Full-accounted, unit incremental costs were then computed for each country. These long-run incremental costs, if this component was produced in England, were estimated as 25 per cent below United States costs and if in West Germany, 22 per cent lower than the United States.

Most of the European cost advantage was explainable by lower labor costs. For certain types of steel, the United States had lower costs than England or West Germany. For most raw materials, however, the cost advantage lay with England. And this English raw material advantage was, in this case, sufficiently great to counterbalance the lower unit labor costs of West Germany.

The Mechanization Riddle—A Managerial View

These two studies indicate one role of international productivity comparisons for managerial decisions. Productivity analysis can provide a rough indication of a company's international competitive position and can be a springboard for more specific analysis of where to buy or manufacture products. In the final analysis, however, it is not labor productivity but rather capital productivity (profitability) which is the management guide to greater economic efficiency.

The concept of physical labor productivity is essentially technocratic rather than economic. It conceives of efficiency as reduction in the ratio of physical inputs to outputs. The managerial problem, however, is economic rather than technocratic; namely, to find the combination of inputs (labor, machine-hours, and so forth) most profitable for the firm. For this decision, physical efficiency ratios are inadequate because relative prices, which can be decisive, are ignored.

In the second study, management's approach to the problem was more traditionally economic. The analysis was not framed in terms of a single input factor; attention was, instead, focused on incremental costs; explicit recognition was given to the effect of volume on costs; and some allowance was made for differences in technology among countries. However, the second study itself raises questions relating to international investment.

Presumably, within the bounds of substitutability, input combinations are determined in large part by relative prices. Study 1 showed that physical labor productivity in the United Kingdom and West Germany was, in this industry, much lower than in the United States. In West Germany, however, lower wage rates more than compensated for lower productivity. Study 2 implied that notwithstanding wide differences in input prices (wages, for example) between Europe and the United States, productivity of European labor would nevertheless be brought up to the United States level by capital investment.

These divergent views of productivity lead to an interesting question. Why do mechanization levels not differ more among nations to reflect international differentials in the prices of labor and other inputs?

In an enterprise economy, the correct economic criterion for mechanization decisions is clear. The criterion is profitability, and the minimum acceptable profitability should be the firm's cost of capital. Specifically, the pertinent profitability is the rate of return on the additional investment that will be produced by future cost savings (or other added earnings) flowing from the mechanization. Thus for managerial decisions on capital formation, the relevant concept is not labor productivity. It is capital productivity.

For firms operating internationally, mechanization decisions should be made in the same way. The same criterion should, however, produce different levels of mechanization in different countries. A mechanization investment which is barely justified by cost of capital in the United States must in Germany save three times as much labor to produce the same money profit. Only if the machine costs a third as much, and the minimum acceptable rate of return is identical in Germany, would a United States level of mechanization appear economic. How then do we explain the mystery of this apparent insensitivity of capital investment to the relative scarcities of factor inputs in the different countries? Seven hypotheses warrant consideration:

Hypothesis 1: Future labor costs (including fringe benefits and job security) warrant a higher level of mechanization than is justified by labor costs of the present.

Hypothesis 2: A low level of mechanization requires greater numbers of skilled workers, which are often more scarce than indicated by their wages rates (presently in West Germany).

Hypothesis 3: World-wide standardization of mechanization at the high United States level facilitates the transfer of United States executives abroad, training, and supervision.

Hypothesis 4: Mass-produced equipment which over-mechanizes is cheaper than custom-tailored equipment whose degree of mechanization is just right for the relative prices of labor in a low wage-rate nation. Equipment that is appropriately labor-intensive has been entombed by progress, and the cost of disinterring it is too high compared with the price of standardized equipment that is too capital-intensive.

Hypothesis 5: Technocracy thwarts economics: the dream of the engineer and the production manager is to have the most modern (highly mechanized) operation known to man. Only when a top management fully oriented to profits insists on the full cooperation of technical executives will the combination of inputs be economic, that is, be governed by relative prices rather than by "efficiency" in a technocratic sense.

Hypothesis 6: Tax incentives, designed to stimulate modernization, have been stronger in low-wage nations than in the United States. The excess results from a mistake at the national level: under-guessing the power of the tax stimulant, or striving for over-mechanization as a national status symbol.

Hypothesis 7: Fear of future prohibitions of job displacement from increased mechanization (because it appears to destroy jobs) causes excessive mechanization in new plants.

These seven hypotheses, disquieting as they are to a managerial economist who would wish the world more computable, nevertheless point the way to a ploddingly imperfect future for international productivity comparisons as a basis for managerial decisions on capital expenditures.

CHAPTER 15

Problems Involved in International Comparisons of Labor Productivity in the Automobile Industry[1]

AUBREY SILBERSTON

Cambridge University

Introduction

It is never an easy task to make sure that our measures of comparative labor productivity are well founded, and in automobile industry comparisons it is particularly difficult to do so. One of the main problems is the degree of comparability of vehicles produced in different countries, and in order to get around this difficulty some writers have made productivity comparisons in terms of gross value of output[2] or of value added[3] per worker. However, this approach raises the thorny problem of what exchange rates to use when converting the value of output into a common currency. To avoid this, an attempt will be made in this paper to make a comparison in terms of physical units of output, but some broad adjustments will be made to take account of the different proportions of automobiles and trucks manufactured in different countries.

1. I am greatly indebted to Mr. C. F. Pratten, Assistant in Research in the Faculty of Economics at Cambridge, for assistance in collecting statistical material and making calculations for this paper.
2. Walter Galenson, *Labor Productivity in Soviet and American Industry* (New York, 1955), pp. 164–172.
3. Barney K. Schwalberg, *Manpower Utilization in the Soviet Automobile Industry* (Washington, 1959), pp. 96–121.

Problems of Calculation

Choice of time period. The first question here is whether to compare output per man-hour or output per man for some longer period, normally a year. The latter period is the easier to take, since it is cruder and requires no detailed knowledge about hours of work, but for this reason it is less accurate as a basis for productivity comparisons. Fortunately, if one starts with figures for a year, it is not difficult in principle to make a correction for hours of work, although it may not be easy in practice to gather the necessary information. In the present paper, output per man-year will be used for the calculations: it has not yet been possible to collect sufficient information to enable man-hour comparisons to be made.

Another problem concerning time periods relates to the particular years to be taken for making international comparisons. In the automobile industries of countries like the United Kingdom and the United States of America, it is unusual in years of low vehicle production for the number of operatives to be cut down by the same proportion as the number of vehicles produced. The result, other things being equal, is that output per man falls in years of low vehicle production and rises in years of high vehicle production. To compare labor productivity in two countries in a particular year would give a distorted picture of the "normal" relationship if one of the countries had enjoyed a boom in vehicle sales in that year, while the other had suffered from a slump. To overcome this difficulty, one can attempt to confine the comparisons to years of generally high production: among Western countries 1950 and 1955 were generally good years, and 1959—the last year for which full figures are available—was also a good year, except in the United States. Lack of data limits the choice of years to some extent, however. The most reliable data for employment, in particular, are available for those years in which Censuses of Manufactures were taken. It is unfortunate that recently (1954 in the United States, for example) several Censuses have been taken in years in which vehicle production has been particularly low. In the actual comparisons to be attempted later, the years 1950, 1955, and 1959 will be taken whenever possible, although these years will be departed from on occasions, usually because of lack of data.

The measurement of output. This is one of the most difficult problems to be faced. The final output of firms mainly engaged in the automobile industry consists of automobiles, trucks, buses, agricultural and other tractors, spare parts for vehicles, and a host of other manufactures ranging from refrigerators to machine tools. In the present context we are interested only in the production of automobiles, trucks, and buses and the number of employees engaged in making these.

It is often possible to obtain some estimate of numbers employed in the production of non-motor trade products, although this calculation is not an easy one to make when workers in a plant which also produces vehicles are involved. It is much more difficult to estimate the number of workers engaged in the manufacture of spare parts for vehicles, especially as the manufacture of spare parts for current vehicles usually takes place on the same production lines as parts for the vehicles themselves. It is difficult enough to obtain estimates of the value of spare parts as a proportion of the total value of output, and even when this figure has been obtained it cannot be assumed that it applies to the proportion of workers engaged in the manufacture of spare parts. Fortunately, from the point of view of comparisons, spare parts output does not appear to be of great importance in several countries (the United Kingdom and the United States), although it is more important in Soviet Russia.[4]

Another problem concerns the manufacture of agricultural tractors. In some countries the bulk of these are produced by automobile manufacturers. Since the number of tractors produced is generally known, there is no difficulty in separating the production of tractors from that of automobiles and trucks. However, a corresponding separation has to be made between those employed on the manufacture of tractors and the manufacture of other vehicles. This can usually be done for years for which a Census of Manufactures exists. It is sometimes difficult to do for other years.

When one concentrates attention on the production of automobiles, trucks, and buses, there are a number of formidable problems to be faced when making international comparisons. Perhaps the chief of these concerns the proportion of automobiles to trucks. In all Western countries, the number of automobiles produced is far higher than the number of trucks. In Russia it is the other way around, although the proportion of automobiles has been rising in recent years. In order to make a fair comparison between Russia and the other vehicle producing countries taken as a group, one needs to know whether trucks require more labor per unit than automobiles, given identical production conditions in all important respects.

---

4. In the case of one British vehicle manufacturer, revenue from sales of spares was one sixth of total revenue in 1954. G. Maxcy and A. Silberston, *The Motor Industry* (London, 1959), p. 69. The Russian data for 1955 suggest that spare parts represented nearly one quarter of total revenue. The United States proportion was much lower. Schwalberg *Manpower Utilization*, pp. 81, 98 and 104.

Galenson noted that the gross value weights that he used when comparing United States and Soviet productivity implied a two to one ratio between trucks and automobiles.[5] In order to gain more information on this point, enquiries were made of a large British vehicle producer who makes medium trucks as well as cars and light vans. He gave figures for direct labor costs in the production of each of these vehicles, but pointed out that, although the range of manufacturing operations carried out on each was broadly comparable up to the stage of body production, only a small proportion of the trucks he produced were fitted with the firm's own standard body-work. His figure for direct labor costs on trucks ought therefore to be written up to allow for the labor involved in making bodies for most of them. Unfortunately, no factor could be given for this. The figures of direct labor costs in 1961 were: (passenger cars = 100) vans 67.3, trucks 102.7.

When it is remembered that the standard truck body is not usually very elaborate, it may perhaps be deduced that the ratio of direct labor costs on trucks fitted with standard bodies to direct labor costs on passenger cars is not greater than, say, 1.25. However, a large number of trucks have specialized bodies fitted by coachbuilders, and these involve much more labor in their production than standard bodies. Where bodies of this sort are concerned, the ratio of two to one quoted by Galenson is likely to be much nearer the mark, and for vehicles like buses, with elaborate coach-work, the ratio of direct labor cost must be very much higher than this. In general, also, it is probable that the larger the trucks or buses involved the greater is the direct labor content as compared with passenger cars of a given size.

Even when attention is concentrated on passenger cars or on trucks alone, the problem arises of how far the vehicles produced in different countries are comparable. Rostas noted[6] that the average United States passenger car was much bigger than the average United Kingdom car before the war— this of course is still the case—but that the average United Kingdom truck tended to be bigger than the average United States truck. It is interesting that the average Soviet truck produced in 1956 was considerably larger than its American counterpart.[7] This is of especial importance to any comparison of labor productivity between Soviet Russia and the United States because of the predominance of truck production in the Soviet Union.

A final problem connected with the measurement of output concerns

5. Galenson, *Labor Productivity in Soviet and American Industry,* p. 171.
6. L. Rostas, *Comparative Productivity in British and American Industry* (Cambridge, 1948), p. 167.
7. Barney K. Schwalberg, "The Soviet Automotive Industry: a current assessment," *Automobile Industries* (January 1, 1958), p. 18.

military vehicles. There is indirect evidence that these vehicles are not included in the Soviet statistics.[8] On the other hand, they appear to be included in the British statistics, although they are not shown separately. In so far as Western countries include the output of military vehicles and the Soviet Union does not, this is a factor tending to underestimate comparative productivity in the Soviet.

The measurement of employment. In many ways this is the most difficult problem of all. It arises principally from the fact that no vehicle manufacturer makes all the parts and accessories that he uses for his vehicles. The percentage of factory costs represented by bought-out parts and components varies from firm to firm. In the United Kingdom, where there is a highly developed parts industry, there is a great deal of vertical disintegration, and the percentage of costs represented by bought-out parts, and so forth, can be as high as 80 per cent.[9] On the other hand, some British firms have bought-out proportions of 50 per cent or less. In the Soviet Union, the proportion of costs represented by bought-out parts and materials appears to be of the order of 60 per cent.[10] Figures for a number of firms in different countries are given in the table. They reflect the relatively high degree of vertical integration found in France and Italy and, to a lesser extent, in the United States of America, as compared with the United Kingdom and Germany.

These figures are mainly for the year 1958. It should be remembered that year-to-year changes in the proportion of bought-out parts and materials are often appreciable, so that even in the case of the same firm no figure for any one year can be taken as standard. For any country's automobile industry taken as a whole, the variations from year to year may be considerable.

It follows from the fact that degrees of integration vary between automobile firms in different countries, that simply to calculate the number of employees in these firms and use this figure as a basis for comparisons is not very helpful. If some estimate could be made of the numbers engaged in producing parts and accessories for vehicles in these firms, so that the numbers engaged directly on vehicle production could be isolated, that would be a different matter, but it is rarely possible to obtain much information on this point.

8. Schwalberg, *Manpower Utilization,* p. 22.
9. Maxcy and Silberston, *The Motor Industry,* p. 62.
10. N. S. Preobrajenskaya, "Measures of Labour Productivity in Automobiles," *Automobilnaya promyshlennost,* no. 9, 1960, p. 6.

Table 29. Automobile purchases as a percentage of
total costs, 1958.

Country	Automobile	Percentage
U.K.	Ford	70.4
	Ford	74.3[a]
Germany	Volkswagen	70.1
	Daimler Benz	71.5
France	Renault	54.5[a]
Italy	Fiat	54.0
U.S.A.	General Motors	60.0
	Chrysler	65.3

a. 1959 figures.

Source: Company accounts.

Another approach is to attempt to compute the total number employed in the industry, that is, in all firms making parts and accessories as well as in vehicle manufacturing firms themselves. To do this properly, one would have to attempt to estimate how many of those engaged in industries like steel were employed in producing iron and steel to be used in the automobile industry rather than in other industries. In practice, some information about numbers employed in producing parts and accessories for motor vehicles is usually available from Censuses of Manufacture and the like, but it is difficult to get anything like a full coverage of supplying industries (firms making tires or electrical equipment are often excluded, for example), and there is usually a particularly difficult problem in these industries in separating those working for the motor industry from those working for other industries.

Because of these difficulties it is impossible to be sure of comparability when making international comparisons of the numbers employed either in vehicle manufacturing alone or in the automobile industry as a whole. Indeed one can be sure that there is *lack* of comparability, although one can do one's best to reduce it.

A comparatively minor question connected with the measurement of employment is whether to include all employees (clerical, and so forth) or simply to take the number of operatives. The choice depends mainly on the purpose of the productivity comparisons being made. Whichever measure is preferred, however, it is not difficult to calculate what the effect of taking the other measure would have been. For the present purpose, we shall use the figures for the total number of employees, including clerical and salaried staff.

Comparative Productivity by Countries

Full details of the information regarding employment and vehicle production that has been assembled are given in the Appendix. It will be only too evident from what is said there that all the difficulties of measurement that have been referred to above have been encountered in practice. Additional problems have arisen because of a scarcity of statistical material: in particular the fact that Censuses of Manufactures are only available for a limited number of years—often for years of comparatively low vehicle output. This has made the computation of the numbers employed in years of high vehicle output a difficult task. Another thing that will be evident from the Appendix is that it is virtually impossible in many countries to separate those employed directly on the manufacture of vehicles in vehicle producing firms from those employed in these firms in producing parts and accessories. In view of this, it has been decided to make comparisons involving, as far as possible, all employees in the automobile industry, including those making parts and accessories in both vehicle producing firms and supplying firms.[11] An attempt has been made to ensure comparability as far as possible and to point out differences of coverage where these are known.

Bringing together the figures for employment contained in the Appendix, we obtain Table 30.

The figures for vehicle production are subject to many fewer difficulties as far as obtaining crude information goes. The production figures contained in the Appendix are shown in Table 31.

Table 31 shows clearly the relatively low level of production in Italy, Japan, and the Soviet Union, and the high level of production in the United States.

Dividing the figures in Table 31 by those in Table 30, to get a first crude measure of labor productivity, we obtain the information in Table 32.

Even this crude measure of productivity throws up an interesting point about the changes that have taken place. This is the rapid increase in output per head in France, Germany, Italy, and Japan during the 1950's, as compared with the comparatively slow increase in the United Kingdom and

11. Those employed in producing non-automotive products have been excluded, but those producing spare parts for vehicles have had to be included because of lack of information about the numbers involved.

Table 30. All employees in the automobile industry—estimated number
engaged on automotive operations.
(In thousands)

Country	1950	1955	1959
France[a]	160[c]	188	228
W. Germany	148	240	316
Italy	77	93	107
Japan[b]	81[d]	121	167[e]
U.K.	250	310	315
U.S.A. (excl. electrical)	770	820	630
U.S.A. (incl. electrical)	825	880	675
U.S.S.R.[a]	180	218	250

a. Includes employees producing electrical equipment.
b. Includes employees producing motor bicycles.
c. 1952.
d. 1951.
e. 1958.

the lack of increase in the United States and in Soviet Russia. This difference appears to be closely associated with the different rates of growth of
vehicle output in the countries concerned.

The relationship between the increase in vehicle output and in crude
productivity is quite close. It is interesting that Italy has achieved the most
rapid rate of growth in productivity, although her rise in output has not been
the greatest. However, her productivity was apparently very low in 1950.
The United States, it would appear, has just about managed to keep produc-

Table 31. Passenger car and commercial vehicle production.
(In thousands)

Country	1950	1955	1959
France	499[b]	724	1283
W. Germany	306	909	1718
Italy	128	269	501
Japan[a]	109[c]	302	528[d]
U.K.	784	1238	1560
U.S.A.	8003	9169	6728
U.S.S.R.	363	445	495

a. Includes motor bicycles.
b. 1952.
c. 1951.
d. 1958.

Table 32. Number of vehicles (unadjusted) produced per employee per year.

Country	1950	1955	1959
France[c]	3.1[d]	3.85	5.65
W. Germany	2.1	3.8	5.45
Italy	1.7	2.9	4.7
Japan[a]	1.35[e]	2.5	3.2[f]
U.K.	3.1	4.0	4.95
U.S.A.[b]	10.4	11.2	10.7
U.S.A.[c]	9.7	10.4	10.0
U.S.S.R.[c]	2.0	2.0	2.0

a. Includes motor bicycles.
b. Dividing by employees excluding those producing electrical equipment.
c. Dividing by employees including those producing electrical equipment.
d. 1952.
e. 1951.
f. 1958.

tivity constant, in spite of the fall in her output. Soviet productivity does not appear to have risen, in spite of some increase in output.

Table 32 is not very useful when comparing the level of output per head in different countries until some correction has been applied for the different types of vehicles produced. This is particularly important in the case of Soviet Russia because of the predominance of heavy truck production in that country. As was seen earlier, it is very difficult to know what correction to make—infinite degrees of refinement are possible to allow for different

Table 33. Indexes of output and crude productivity, 1950–1959.
(1950 = 100)

Country	Vehicle output	Crude productivity
France	257[a]	182[c]
W. Germany	562	260
Italy	392	276
Japan	494[b]	237[b]
U.K.	199	159
U.S.A.	84	103
U.S.S.R.	136	100

a. 1952 = 100. On the basis 1950 = 100, the index would be 360.
b. 1958 as a proportion of 1951.
c. 1959 as a proportion of 1952.

sizes of cars and trucks as well as for the over-all distinction between them. Looking at the information on vehicle size contained in the Appendix, it would appear that French and Japanese trucks are, on the whole, of low carrying capacity, and this is probably the case in Italy, where truck production is, in any event, very small. German and British trucks appear to be rather heavier on the average (25 per cent of the commercial vehicles produced in both countries are of over 3 tons carrying capacity), and United States truck production also includes a high proportion of heavy trucks. However, all these countries produce a very large number of light vans (50 per cent of the total number of commercial vehicles produced in several of these countries). The labor content of these appears to be only two thirds that of cars. Soviet trucks are almost certainly the heaviest of all on the average, and comparatively few light vans are produced in Russia.

As a crude approximation, taking cars as 100, a weight of 110 will be given to French, Japanese, and Italian commercial vehicles (including vans), and a weight of 120 to German, British, and United States commercial vehicles (including vans).[12] A weight of 200 will be given to Soviet commercial vehicles. In the case of Japan, motor bicyles will be given an arbitrary weight of 50, and three-wheeled trucks the same weight as cars. No attempt will be made to differentiate between the types of cars produced in different countries.

When these adjustments have been made, the productivity comparison appears in Table 34.

If this table is compared with Table 32 it will be seen that the figures for Italy have not been affected, and the French figures have risen only a very little. The Japanese figures have been reduced in 1955 and 1958 because of the low weight given to motor bicycles whose production was much higher in those years than in 1950. German and United States figures have risen by about the same proportion, and United Kingdom figures by very slightly more. The Soviet figures have, of course, risen most of all. The slight fall between 1950 and 1955 is accounted for by the fact that in 1955 an appreciably higher proportion of cars was produced than in 1950. By 1959 the proportion of cars produced was higher still.

If Table 34 has any validity at all,[13] it suggests that in 1950 labor produc-

12. Assume vans have a weight of 70 and trucks of 170 in Germany, Britain and the U.S.A. Given equal numbers of both, an average weight of 120 is arrived at.
13. If other weights had been taken, and they had been very different ones, some of the results would of course have been considerably affected, particularly those for

Table 34. Adjusted number of vehicles produced per employee per year.

Country	1950	1955	1959
France[b]	3.2[c]	3.9	5.7
W. Germany	2.2	4.0	5.6
Italy	1.7	2.9	4.7
Japan[f]	1.6[d]	1.9	2.5[e]
U.K.	3.3	4.2	5.2
U.S.A.[a]	10.7	11.5	11.0
U.S.A.[b]	10.0	10.7	10.3
U.S.S.R.[b]	3.6	3.5	3.5

a. Dividing by employees excluding those producing electrical equipment.
b. Dividing by employees including those producing electrical equipment.
c. 1952.
d. 1951.
e. 1958.
f. Includes motor bicycles.

tivity in France, the United Kingdom, and the Soviet Union was at approximately the same level—about 35 per cent of that of the United States.[14] By 1955, Germany had, broadly speaking, caught up with the French, British, and Soviet levels of productivity. By 1959 France and Germany were both somewhat ahead of the United Kingdom with Italy catching up fast. Aided by the comparative stagnation of American productivity, because of low output in that country, the European producers had achieved a level of labor productivity something like that of 50 per cent of the United States by 1959. There is no doubt that, were United States industry to produce at anything like its total capacity, it could achieve very much higher levels of productivity than is suggested by the figures given here. Whether its productivity could rise to three times the European level, as it was before the war,[15] is, however, doubtful.

---

the U.S.S.R. Indeed, it might be argued that the weights taken are unduly favorable to the U.S.S.R. On the other hand, no adjustment has been made for the high proportion of workers engaged on spare parts production in that country. On balance, it is difficult to believe that any reasonable alternative adjustments would have appreciably altered the general picture given by Table 34.

14. Schwalberg, in "Manpower Utilization" estimated Soviet productivity in 1954–55 at 31 per cent of the United States level, measured by value added, and at 38 per cent, measured by the gross value of output (pp. 115 and 109). He points out that Klimenko and Galenson both arrived at a figure of 40–50 per cent, measured by gross value, when making a comparison of United States/Soviet productivity for the period before World War II (p. 117).

15. Rostas, Comparative Productivity, p. 171.

Conclusions

The most obvious conclusion that can be drawn from our figures is that the level of labor productivity in the automobile industry of any country is closely related to the number of vehicles produced in that country: this is scarcely surprising in view of the well-known connection between mechanization and scale of production. Bearing in mind the high proportion of motorcycles produced in Japan, the Japanese motor industry is the smallest of those considered here, and its productivity is apparently the lowest. The next industry in terms of productive size is that of Italy, and Italy's productivity is next but one to the lowest, although it is true that by 1959 Italian productivity was not appreciably below that of other Western countries. Bearing in mind the high proportion of commercial vehicles produced, Russian industry is rather larger than the Italian and, if our figures are broadly correct, productivity per head in the Soviet Union was higher than that of Italy in 1950 and 1955, although this was no longer true in 1959. The relationship between size and productivity is clearly not invariant. France, in particular, now has high productivity per head, although her output was appreciably smaller in 1959 than that of the United Kingdom or of Germany. Obviously other factors are at work.

One of the most important of these factors is almost certainly the degree of standardization achieved in the motor industries of various countries. United Kingdom industry has always been famous for the large number of different models of vehicles that have been produced by it, although since the war the degree of variety has been appreciably reduced.[16] In France and Germany, on the other hand, the degree of variety is less, partly because there is greater concentration of production in the hands of a comparatively small number of manufacturers. Volkswagen is, of course, the outstanding producer in Germany, accounting for 41 per cent of total vehicle production in 1959, and Renault in France, accounting for 39 per cent of production in 1959. More important, both companies, particularly Volkswagen, are noted for their concentration on a very small range of models, as are most other French and German companies. Concentration of this sort is bound to increase productivity per head, other things being equal. In Italy, the concentration of production is even greater. Fiat alone accounted for 86 per cent of Italian vehicle production in 1959. Fiat, too, concentrates on a comparatively small number of models, and this perhaps helps to explain why Italian pro-

16. Maxcy and Silberston, *The Motor Industry*, pp. 119 ff.

ductivity is so high in relation to that of countries whose total vehicle production is two or three times as great. Soviet productivity benefits also from a concentration on a comparatively small number of basic models.

The last major factor affecting productivity in the countries under consideration is the degree of capital intensity for any given scale of production which is general in these countries and in their automobile industries in particular. In this respect, the United States is, of course, the country where capital intensity is by far the highest, and this is undoubtedly the principal reason for its high level of productivity.[17] An interesting article by a Soviet writer[18] recently examined the differences in productivity between the United States and the Soviet Union in steel and engineering, including automobile production. He found that the chief explanation for the differences was the very much larger number of workers in Russia engaged on auxiliary work —repair work, transport, and so forth. In the basic processes, the Soviet industries employed a relatively smaller number of extra workers compared with that of the United States. The main cause of this seemed to be greater mechanization in auxiliary processes in the United States, although faults in Russian organization were also blamed.

It is almost certainly true that this contrast exists also between the United States automobile industry and those of European countries. In basic processes there is undoubtedly greater mechanization and automation in the United States, but the degree of mechanization is comparatively higher in auxiliary activities, particularly in materials handling.

It is interesting that in the basic processes, especially machining, there has been a considerable growth of mechanization in Europe in recent years. Automation is now fairly widespread in the British motor industry, and Renault has been the pioneer in France.[19] In Germany, Volkswagen was at first slow to introduce automation, but has now begun to do so. In the Soviet Union, the basic production shops of the automobile industry contain a high proportion of Russia's automatic machine-tool lines and are outstanding technically in Russian industry.[20] This growth in mechanization in Europe and the Soviet Union has partly been a natural consequence of increases in scale. In part, however, it has resulted from technological advances and, in Western countries at least, from a changing ratio of labor to capital costs.

17. Maxcy and Silberston, *The Motor Industry*, pp. 210–212.
18. S. Kheynman, "Certain economic problems of the organization of industrial production," *Voprosy ekonomiki*, no., 1. 1960, pp. 36–50. The picture he gives is confirmed by Schwalberg in "The Soviet Automotive Industry," p. 32.
19. Maxcy and Silberston, *The Motor Industry*, pp. 56–61.
20. Schwalberg, *The Soviet Automotive Industry*, p. 32.

One can undoubtedly expect the trend to greater mechanization to continue.

These developments have enabled levels of productivity in other countries to compare more favorably with that of the United States level than was the case in prewar years. With the growth of vehicle production since the war, productivity has increased everywhere. But, generally speaking, production and mechanization have both increased faster outside the United States than within it, and this is reflected in the changes in comparative labor productivity that have taken place.

Appendix: Problems Involved in International Comparisons of Labor Productivity in the Automobile Industry

France

Employment. Table 35 is made up of figures obtained from the Federation Nationale de l'Automobile. According to the Federation, they include all those employed by vehicle manufacturers, together with employees of firms producing 95 per cent of bought-out parts, and so forth. Manufacturers

Table 35. Total employed in vehicle manufacture in France, 1952–1959.
(In thousands)

December 31	Operatives	All employees
1952	131	166 (160)[a]
1953	128	163
1954	145	184
1955	151	192 (188)[a]
1956	165	208
1957	175	219
1958	180	225
1959	184	230 (228)[a]

a. Approximate figure for calendar year.

of electrical equipment are included, but manufacturers of tires and motor bicycles are excluded.

The Federation does not publish separate figures for vehicle manufacturers and supplying firms because, in their view, this distinction has no significance because of the way it varies from year to year. They say that on the average, however, supplying firms account for about one quarter of the total number employed. A check on this figure is provided by the 1954 Census of Population which shows the number of employees in May 1954, as follows:

Construction of automobiles	128,740	(73%)
Manufacture of parts for automobiles	46,660	(27%)
Total	175,400	(100%)

It will be noted that the average of the Federation's figures for December 1953 and December 1954 is 173,500, so that the two sets of figures agree well.

Table 36. Vehicles produced in France, 1950, 1952, 1953, 1955–1959.
(In thousands)

Vehicles	1950	1952	1953	1955	1956	1957	1958	1959
Cars	257	370	371	560	663	738	969	1128
Commercial vehicles	100	129	126	164	164	190	159	155
Total	357	499	497	724	827	928	1128	1283

Source: Society of Motor Manufacturers and Traders; Motor Industry of Great Britain.

An idea of the breakdown by types of vehicle is given in a list of figures for 1955 (in thousands):

Cars	560	Commercial vehicles	164
Less than 6 h.p.	240	Vans, up to 1 ton carrying capacity	91
6–8 h.p.	200	(1–2 tons)	31
10–12 h.p.	77	Trucks, 2–3½ tons	18
Over 12 h.p.	44	3½–5 tons	1
		5–7 tons	9
		7–10 tons	6
		Over 10 tons	2
		Buses and coaches	3
		Other	2

West Germany

Employment. Table 37 figures, from the Verband der Automobilindustrie E.V., include only those working on motor vehicles in the firms concerned (excluding those working on non-motor trade products in these firms). They exclude those producing electrical equipment, for which separate figures are not available.

Table 37. Total employed in motor vehicle manufacture in Germany, 1950–1959.
(In thousands)

Year	Vehicles	Parts	Bodies and trailers
1950[c]	114[a]	(39)[b]	(22)[b]
1953	136[a]	47	25
1954	151[a]	50	27
1955	177[a]	60	30
1956	164	67	28
1957	176	67	28
1958	190	68	28
1959	209	76	30

a. Including motorcycles.
b. Based on figures for January 1950 and January 1951.
c. The figures for 1950 agree well with those derived from the Census of Workplaces (1950).

Separate figures for those engaged in producing motor-bicycles are available from 1956 onward. The number fell from 26,000 in 1956 to 12,000 in 1959. Deducting an estimated figure for those producing motor-bicycles in 1950 and 1955, Table 38 is arrived at.

Table 38. Total employed in motor-bicycle manufacture
in Germany, 1950, 1955, 1959.
(In thousands)

Section	1950	1955	1959
Vehicles	87	150	209
Parts	39	60	76
Bodies, etc.	22	30	30
Total	148	240	316

Vehicles produced. Table 39 reveals the number of vehicles produced during the stated period.

Table 39. Number of vehicles produced in Germany, 1950, 1955–1959.
(In thousands)

Category	1950	1955	1956	1957	1958	1959
Cars	216	706	848	1040	1307	1503
Commercial vehicles	90	203	228	172	188	215
Total	306	909	1076	1212	1495	1718

Production by types of vehicle was as follows in 1955 (in thousands):

Cars	706	Commercial vehicles	203
3-wheel, etc.	14	Utilities	57
Other	692	Goods vehicles, up to 1 ton	61
		1–2 tons	24
		2–3 tons	5
		3–4 tons	13
		4–5 tons	20
		Over 5 tons	17
		Buses	6

Italy

Employment. The Italian employment figures are very incomplete, other than for the year 1950. The following figures in Table 40 were supplied by A.N.F.I.A. They exclude those employed in firms producing parts and accessories but not vehicles, but include those employed in producing parts in vehicle manufacturing firms. They appear to exclude those producing non-

Table 40. Employees directly engaged in automotive operations in Italy, 1954–1959.
(In thousands)

Year	Operatives	All employees
1954	60	73
1955	60	73
1956	63	76
1957	64	79
1958	62	77
1959	68	84

automotive products in vehicle manufacturing firms. Figures before 1954 are not available from this source.

For the year 1950, the following information from Consimento Generale dell'Industria et del Comercio is available in Table 41.

Table 41. All employees engaged in automotive manufacture in Italy, 1950.

Section	In thousands	Percentage
Cars, lorries and vans	46	60
Bodies and trailers of cars and lorries	14.5	19
Parts and accessories of cars, vans, and lorries	16.5	21
Total	77	100

Other evidence suggests that the 1950 figure comparable to those given in Table 41 for 1954–59 was 60.5 thousand (including those employed in body manufacture). Using the proportion of those employed in parts production in 1950 (21 per cent) for 1955 and 1959 the following very tentative estimates are arrived at in Table 42.

Table 42. Total employment in automotive industry in Italy, 1950, 1955, 1959.
(In thousands)

Section	1950	1955	1959
Vehicles and bodies	60.5	73	84
Parts	16.5	19.5	22.5
Total	77	92.5	106.5

Vehicles produced. The total number of vehicles produced in 1950 and from 1955–1959 are given in Table 43.

Table 43. Total number of vehicles produced in Italy, 1950, 1955–1959.
(In thousands)

Section	1950	1955	1956	1957	1958	1959
Cars	101	231	280	318	370	471
Commercial vehicles	27	38	36	33	34	30
Total	128	269	316	351	404	501

Japan

Employment. The Japanese employment figures include those engaged on the manufacture of motor-bicycles: there seems to be no reliable way of estimating the number of employees producing these.

Table 44. Total employed in automotive manufacture in Japan, 1951–1959.
(In thousands)

Year	Motor vehicles (incl. motor bicycles)	Bodies for cars and trucks	Motor vehicle parts and accessories	Total
	Establishments with more than 4 persons			
1951	27	21	34	82
1952	34	19	41	94
1953	45	18	53	117
1954	46	20	57	123
1955	43	17	61	121
1956	40	18	73	131
1957	50	20	90	160
	Establishments with more than 30 persons			
1957	49	18	67	135
1958	49	20	73	142 (167)[a]
1959	54	28	99	181 (210)[a]

a. Estimate for establishments with more than 4 persons.

Source: Ministry of International Trade and Industry, Census of Manufactures.

Vehicles produced.

Table 45. Total vehicles produced in Japan, 1951, 1955, 1958.
(Units as monthly average)

Category	1951	1955	1958
Cars	285	1,113	4,220
Buses	339	401	636
Trucks, large	1,886	1,715	3,285
Trucks, small	698	1,793	7,554
Trucks, 3-wheel	3,643	7,312	8,241
Motorcycles	1,180	8,161	10,643
Motor scooters	1,067	4,728	9,435
Total	9,098	25,223	44,014

Source: Japanese Economic Statistics (Ministry of Trade and Industry).

Annual output in 1951 was 109,000; 302,000 in 1955; and 528,000 in 1958.

United Kingdom

Employment. The Census of Production is the most reliable source of employment figures.

Table 46. Total employed in automotive manufacture
in the United Kingdom, 1954, 1958.
(In thousands)

Category	1954[a]	1958[b]
Cars, taxis, and delivery vans[c]	70	96
Commercial vehicles[c]	27	32
Motor bodies	58	65
Trailers	5	6
Internal combustion engines	12	15
Parts and accessories	64	65
Other	64	50
Total	300	329
Cars, comm. vehicles, and bodies only	155	193

a. Firms with over 10 employees.
b. Firms with over 25 employees.
c. These figures include those producing parts and accessories in factories making motor vehicles.

Source: Census of Production.

The Census of Production figures exclude those producing tires and electrical equipment for vehicles. They include those employed on other products than the principal products of industry. The gross value of these other products amounted to approximately 7 per cent of gross output in 1954. Deducting this percentage from total employment in 1954 and 1958 in order to make an approximate adjustment for this factor, we can estimate that employees engaged on automotive products numbered 280,000 in 1954 in total industry and 305,000 in 1958; for firms producing cars, commercial vehicles, and bodies only, the total was 145,000 in 1954 and 180,000 in 1958.

The Ministry of Labor figures for the years in which we are principally interested produced Table 47.

Using these figures and those from the 1954 and 1958 Censuses of Production, employment in 1950, 1955, and 1959 may be very roughly estimated as 250,000 for total industry in 1950; 310,000 in 1955; and 315,000 in 1959. In

Table 47. Total employed in automotive manufacture in the United Kingdom, 1950, 1954, 1955, 1958, 1959.
(In thousands)

Years	Motor vehicles and cycles	Parts and accessories	Total
June 1950	297	115	412
End May 1954	312	157	469
End May 1955	331	173	504
End May 1958	319	179	498
End May 1959	330	181	511

firms producing cars, commercial vehicles, and bodies only, the total was 130,000 in 1950; 185,000 in 1955; and 185,000 in 1959.

Vehicles produced.

Table 48. Number of vehicles produced in the United Kingdom, 1950, 1954–1959.
(In thousands)

Category	1950	1954	1955	1956	1957	1958	1959
Cars	523	769	898	708	861	1052	1190
Commercial vehicles	261	269	340	297	288	313	370
Total	784	1038	1238	1005	1149	1365	1560

Source: Society of Motor Manufacturers and Traders.

Production by types of vehicle was as follows in 1955 (in thousands), from S.M.M.T.:

Cars	898	Commercial vehicles	340
		Trucks-carrying capacity	
Under 1600 c.c.	684	Under 15 cwt.	188
1600–2200 c.c.	23	15 cwt.–3 tons	68
Over 2200 c.c.	191	3–6 tons	49
		Over 6 tons	24
		Buses, etc.	10

United States

Employment. The Census of Manufactures is a comprehensive source of information. Detailed figures for 1954 are available, but only preliminary figures for 1958.

Table 49. Total employed in automotive manufacture in the United States, 1954, 1958. (In thousands)

Section	1954	1958
Passenger cars	203	—
Trucks and truck chassis	40	—
Parts, etc.	406	—
Total, motor vehicles and parts	649	529
Truck and bus bodies	19	—
Truck trailers	16	—
Automobile trailers	11	—
Total	695	—

The list gives an estimate of those employed on shipments to the automotive industry only.

Diesel engines	2
Carburetors and pistons	40
Bearings	5
Hardware and stampings	65
Lighting equipment	10
Electrical equipment	40
Tires and tubes	74
Glass	20
Grand total	951

The figures for motor vehicles and parts (only parts actually made in the factories concerned are included) also take in those employed in motor vehicle factories on products other than motor vehicles and parts. In 1947 and 1954 the proportion of workers employed in primary products of the industry was over 90 per cent. Hence the number of those engaged in producing motor vehicles and parts was approximately 649,000 in 1954 and 529,000 in 1958. In motor trade products alone, it was 600,000 in 1954 and 485,000 in 1958.

In order to make the figures as comparable as possible with those for other countries, it is necessary to exclude those producing a number of products excluded, or apparently excluded, from the employment statistics of other countries. These include hardware and stampings, tires and tubes, and glass. Lighting and electrical equipment is included in the figures of some countries and excluded in those of others.

The estimated number employed on producing motor trade products in 1954 (in thousands) is as follows:

Motor vehicles and parts	600
Bodies and trailers	43
Diesel engines	2
Carburetors and pistons	40
Total	685
Lighting and electrical equipment	50
Total, incl. electrical	735

Figures for other years are published in the *Survey of Current Business*. They show that the number of employees in motor vehicles and equipment are as follows:

1950	702,000
1954	624,000
1955	746,000
1958	480,000
1959	574,000

Using these figures and the Census figures, and assuming that these figures represent the trend of employment in the industry reasonably well, we can obtain the following estimates for 1950, 1955 and 1959. Approximately 770,000 were employed in the industry (excluding electrical) in 1950; 820,000 in 1955; and 630,000 in 1959. In the industry (including electrical) there were 825,000 in 1950; 880,000 in 1955; and 675,000 in 1959.

Vehicles produced.

Table 50. Number of vehicles produced in the United States, 1950, 1954–1959. (In thousands)

Category	1950	1954	1955	1956	1957	1958	1959
Cars	6666	5559	7920	5816	6113	4258	5591
Commercial vehicles	1337	1042	1249	1104	1101	877	1137
Total	8003	6601	9169	6920	7214	5135	6728

Production by types of vehicle was as follows in 1955: Cars (in thousands), 7,920.

Commercial vehicles (in thousands)	1249
Trucks (gross vehicle weight in lbs.)	
Under 5,000	586
5–10,000	213
10–14,000	47
14–16,000	226
Over 16,000	174
Buses	4

The Soviet Union

Employment. Published Soviet employment statistics for the postwar period are very incomplete. Estimates have been made by Barney K. Schwalberg in *Manpower Utilization in the Soviet Automobile Industry* (Washington, 1959), pp. 24–49. His figures cover those employed in vehicle producing firms, in specialized component producers, and in smaller plants producing electrical equipment, gauges, and so forth, for the automobile industry. Those employed in producing glass, tires, and so forth, are excluded. Total production personnel for 1937 was 100,000; 1950, 180,000; and 1955, 215,000. Actual workers were 75,000 in 1937; 135,000 in 1950; and 175,000 in 1955.

These figures exclude non-industrial personnel. It was reported in 1955 that this group represents about one tenth of employment in industrial establishments in general. To make the Soviet figures comparable with those for other countries an estimate for non-industrial workers must be added. Assuming that this figure of 10 per cent was applicable to the automobile industry in the years being considered, we get 200,000 in total employment in 1950, and 240,000 in 1955.

There is apparently a considerable amount of non-automotive production in the Soviet automobile industry. According to Schwalberg, roughly one eighth of the industry's 1955 gross value of output consisted of non-automotive production. Deducting this percentage, in the hope that it applies roughly to numbers employed as well as gross output, we arrive at 175,000 employees engaged in automotive operations in 1950, and 210,000 in 1955. If apprentices, and so forth, are added to get the closest possible comparability with United States figures, the final figures are 180,000 employees in 1950, and 218,000 in 1955.

Schwalberg has not produced estimates of employment in 1959. However, it is stated by Kheynman (*Voprosy Ekonomiki,* 1960, no. 1, p. 39) that the total employment of basic-production workers in the Likhachev (ZIL) Gorkiy (GAZ), and the Moscow small-car (MZMA) plants was 113,000 in 1958–1959. This compares with a figure for these plants of 95,000 for 1955, quoted by Schwalberg (*Manpower Utilization in the Soviet Automobile Industry,* p. 76) as coming from Soviet sources. An increase of employment of 18,000 workers, or 19 per cent, is therefore indicated between 1955 and 1959. If it is assumed that the number of workers in the entire Soviet automobile industry increased by a rather smaller percentage than in these three plants between 1955 and 1959, say by 15 per cent, an estimate for 1959 of 250,000 employees is arrived at.

Vehicles produced.

Table 51. Number of vehicles produced in the Soviet Union, 1950, 1955–1959.
(In thousands)

Category	1950	1955	1956	1957	1958	1959
Cars[a]	64	108	98	114	122	125
Trucks	294	329	367	382	389	371
Total	358	437	465	496	511	496

a. Includes buses.

Source: Industry of the U.S.S.R.—a statistical handbook (1957). National Economy of the U.S.S.R. in 1959—a statistical annual.

Complete figures of production by types of vehicle are not available. Schwalberg reports that the output of GAZ, which accounts for about half the total Soviet automotive output, consisted primarily of 2.7 ton capacity GAZ =51 trucks and Volga passenger cars in 1957. ZIL, another large plant, concentrated primarily on the 4.4 ton capacity ZIL-150 truck, MAZ, a smaller plant, concentrated on the 7.7 ton capacity MAZ-200. YaAZ, the sole large-scale producer of automobile diesel engines, concentrated on the 13-ton capacity YaAZ-210. Over 90 per cent of annual truck production was accounted for by the GAZ-51 and the ZIL-150.

PART III

Wages and Productivity

CHAPTER 16

Productivity and the System of Labor Remuneration

MAKSIMILIAN POHORILLE

Central School of Planning and Statistics, Warsaw

The remuneration system cannot be isolated from an examination of the general principles of distribution in force in a given economic system, or from the production relations prevailing in that system. Under socialism the guiding principle is distribution according to amount and quality of the work done. This has universal character and is carried out under the conditions in which distribution of the whole national income is exclusively subordinated to the interests of the working class.

I shall not dwell at length on this subject, since the questions of the economic system are not on the functions of this paper. It is necessary, however, to emphasize the fact that conclusions of a methodological nature follow from this approach to the problem.

Fetishism with regard to the forms of remuneration should not be indulged in, although these forms are of vital importance to labor productivity. Behind the façade of external similarities of certain forms of remuneration in different socio-economic systems one should discern essential differences in the social gist of this notion. The effectiveness of the several forms of remuneration depends, to a large extent, upon the total of production relations and the social stimuli behind it.

The main source of the dynamism of a socialist economy is its planned character and the fact that its development serves the interests of the whole community. In these circumstances the labor remuneration system is most effective when it strengthens the principle of planning and helps the employees in understanding the relationship between their personal and social interests.

The influence of the system of labor remuneration on productivity can be considered in its three aspects:

(1) To what extent it is conducive to improving the qualifications of the employees to meet changes in the occupation structure and the necessary transfers of labor power; all of which speed up the general economic growth and increase the social productivity of labor;

(2) To what extent it induces the worker to intensify his individual efforts; in his job;

(3) To what extent it is conducive to the development of the employee's initiative in perfecting the production process and in a better use of the factors which increase labor productivity in the enterprise.

Wage Ratios

In considering the effect of the labor remuneration system on improving trade qualifications and on the supply of manpower in particular industries, the problem of wage ratios is of foremost importance. The wage-rate system is the basic tool of the socialist wage policy. It constitutes a means of differentiating wages depending on how complex and hard the job is, and on working conditions. The wage-rate schedules should reflect, at any time, the actual level of technology and organization in industry.

In coal mining and in the metallurgical industry in Poland the discrepancy in wage rates as fixed in schedules can be seen in Tables 52 and 53.

The changes in wage-rate schedules indicate that there is a tendency in Poland to allow more effectively in the labor remuneration system for dif-

Table 52. Coal mining in Poland—discrepancy in wage rates as fixed in schedules.

Area	1945	1947	1949	1952	1957	1960
Upper Silesia	5:1	2.41:1	3:1	3.6:1	4.8:1	4.8:1
Lower Silesia	—	—	—	—	—	5.4:1

Table 53. Discrepancy in wage rates in the
metallurgical industry in Poland.

1953–1957	1960	1960[a]
2.7:1	2.8:1	4.4:1

a. This concerns factories with wages
based on the new system.

ferences in the level of the qualifications of particular workers. It should be
emphasized, however, that the level of actual earnings is determined not
only by the basic wages, but also by a number of allowances for hard work
and difficult working conditions, as well as by the "moving" portion of
wages, comprising piecework, surpluses, and bonuses.

Table 54. Changes in the level of discrepancy of real wages in the fuel industry
and the metal and machinery industries in Poland, 1953, 1956, and 1959.

$$\left(\text{Coefficient of variation} = \frac{\text{standard deviation}}{\text{arithmetical mean}}\right)$$

Industry	1953			1956			1959		
	Manual workers	Engineering and tech. staff	Admin. and office workers	Manual workers	Office workers	Change in wage discrepancy (1953 = 100)	Manual workers	Office workers	Change in wage discrepancy (1956 = 100)
Fuel industry	52.5	55.6	36.2	51.6	52.3	98.3	41.1	47.6	79.4
Metal and machine industry	44.7	44.0	38.1	42.2	42.9	94.4	39.7	33.3	94.0

Figures represent percentages.

The discrepancy of wage rates in the metal and fuel industries somewhat
decreased in the period 1953–1959 in spite of the greater emphasis placed on
the level of skill. This was due, to a large extent, to the tendency to raise the
minimum wage level.

Apart from the differentiation in wage-rate schedules within each industry, achieved by the application of an appropriate wage rate, there also appears a wage-rate differentiation depending on the importance of the several
branches of production and on the working conditions which prevail in
them.

It should be mentioned in this connection that differences in average
wages in the whole industry are usually greater than differences in wage
rates.

The difference between average wages in particular industries in Poland
decreased slightly between 1956 and 1960, as we see in Table 55. This state-

Table 55. Changes in the level of discrepancy of average wages in
particular industries in Poland, 1956–1960.
(Percentages)

	Coefficient of variation		
Year	Employed in industry	Workers	Engineering and technical staff
1956	24.8	25.6	23.8
1960	23.6	25.3	—

ment, however, cannot be generalized, since the period under investigation
is too short.

During the period of industrialization the processes taking place in the
national economy are very complex. The development of a whole number of
new branches of production, the resultant appearance of new trades, and a
large influx of unskilled workers to industry from rural areas—all these
factors require an effective system of incentives which will encourage the
workers to raise their qualifications and thus bring about a greater differentiation of wages. A pressure in the same direction is also exerted by the
concentration of dynamic trends conducive to the maximization of the rate
of growth of social labor productivity. On the other hand, experience has
proved that preferential promoting of development of certain industries has
many drawbacks (it causes an unjustified lack of proportion in wages and
distorts the relationship between the costs of production). Therefore, this
policy should only be considered a temporary measure.

The influence of the development of techniques on wage ratios is no less
complicated. There is a widely accepted view that, as industry develops, the
demand for highly skilled workers relatively decreases, while the percentage
of semi-skilled workers employed in production increases. This view is only
partly correct. The situation is different with regard to qualifications required
in newly created industries, different in introducing direct-line production
in already existing industries, and different again in switching over from
direct-line to automatic-line production. It is universally recognized today
that organization of the production process which reduces the function of
the worker to rapid, repetitive motions is not a proper way to increase labor
productivity. The worker rebels. He does not appreciate this degradation of
his trade, and wants to derive some personal satisfaction from it. If the theory
of the "semi-skilled" worker now raises doubts in the West, it is bound to be
even more at odds with development trends in socialist production. These

trends point to a many-sided development of man, and not to inflicting injury upon his personality.

The total additional demand for skilled workers in Poland in the current five-year period—1961–1965—amounts to approximately 597 thousand. Included in this figure is the demand for 331 thousand persons, resulting from an absolute increase in employment. This amounts to 44 per cent of the total planned increase in employment.

The plan envisages a substantial absolute and relative increase in the number of employees with university and high-school education. (See Table 56.)

Table 56. Number of persons with university and high-school education employed (and to be employed) in the socialized economy in Poland, 1958–1965.

Particulars	1958	Targets for 1965
Population	29,000,000	32,051,000
Employment of personnel		
With university education	240,000	420,000
With high-school vocational education	440,000	826,000
Per thousand employed there are		
With university education	37.0	54.4
With high-school vocational education	69.4	107.1

The differentiation of salaries and wages in accordance with qualifications is, of course, only one of the factors conducive to the raising of the level of skill among industrial employees. The principal part in speeding up this process is played by the development of university and high-school education, the improvement in the organization of elementary schools, the introduction of technical subjects into the curriculum, and the development of factory training courses. The fact that education in a socialist system is free of charge cannot be without its influence on the wage-rate ratios for skilled and semi-skilled workers. Of basic importance, however, is the gradual diminishing of the differences in the level of qualifications resulting from the general improvement in education. The prospect of the gradual disappearance of essential differences between manual and clerical work is connected with this process.

It could be expected, therefore, that the tendency—appearing in the initial period of industrialization—toward greater differences in wages within the several industries and in the whole of industry will gradually give way to the tendency toward the flattening of the wage rates.

The wage structure must be periodically corrected and adapted to the current and future economic objectives. These corrections are necessary, both because certain changes take place in qualification requirements and in the distribution of manpower, and because wage ratios are influenced by some secondary factors which threaten to distort the proper wage structure (differences in norms). For this reason great importance attaches to the division of the total planned wage increase into a part connected with the autonomous wage movement, that is, changes in wages resulting from increased production and productivity and connected with the wage-rate system, and the part destined for wage control.[1] The latter part is used for carrying out planned wage increases, which take into consideration the improvement of wage ratios between the several groups of workers and the several sectors of the national economy. The planned and centralized method of implementing wage policy creates a possibility of influencing the wage policy in the national economy as a whole, in the way most desirable from the point of view of raising the social labor productivity.

To transform such a possibility into reality, however, is both difficult and complicated. The correct achievement of this objective in Poland has been hampered by a number of serious difficulties, both of an objective (the difficult beginnings of the wage policy because of tremendous war destruction) —and of a subjective nature (deficiencies in planning methods). A serious effort has been made recently to put the question of wages in order and to improve some wage ratios.

A comparison of wage ratios in 1955–1960 is interesting because a substantial increase in wages and labor productivity occurred in Poland at that time.

The question arises in this connection: What relationship is there between the rate of growth in labor productivity in the several industries and the changes in wage ratios?

Changes in wage ratios in 1955–1960 in Polish industry were decisively affected by wage controls. Those industries in which the rate of growth in labor productivity was lower have gained more by such controls than other industries. This statement refers to observations covering only a relatively short period of time and, therefore, cannot be generalized.

An attempt at such generalization can be made, however, on the basis

1. In socialist countries real wages are often raised by planned reductions in the prices of consumer goods. These reductions create a favorable climate for striving for greater productivity but exert no influence on wage ratios and the incentive system affecting the employment structure. For this reason this method is not discussed here.

Table 57. Wage ratios in Polish industry, 1955–1960.

Industry	Socialized industry (Total = 100)	
	1955	1960
Machine building and metal construction	108.9	104.4
Coal mining and briquetting	146.0	148.9
Non-ferrous metallurgical	129.8	127.5
Ferrous metallurgical	126.2	124.2
Transportation equipment	108.7	106.6
Electrical engineering	101.3	96.7
Electric power	101.3	117.0
Chemical	96.5	96.7
Construction materials	95.6	91.2
Glass	94.9	90.7
Rubber	94.3	91.8
Printing	92.3	96.7
Salt	88.9	102.7
China, pottery	88.4	88.5
Food products	84.5	82.4
Paper	84.0	84.6
Timber	83.2	83.5
Textiles	76.3	84.6

of the knowledge of how the mechanism of wages works in our economy.

In my opinion the following general theses may be formulated: the material basis for wage increases is, of course, an increase in labor productivity. However, as far as changes in wage ratios for various industries are concerned, these are not so much the effect of different rates of growth in productivity in the several industries, as an incentive for speeding up this rate of growth and for the real location of manpower.

In other words: increases in labor productivity in the several industries automatically bring about a certain increase in wages in these industries. However, if this were the only decisive or main factor influencing wage ratios in industry, preference could be given not accessarily to those industries that should enjoy a preferential treatment.[2]

It is, therefore, a planned regulation of wages, and not their automatic increase,[3] that should have a decisive influence on changes in wage ratios.

2. When I speak about wage ratios in this context, I always have in mind ratios between average wages in the several industries.
3. A distinction should be made between an increase in labor productivity resulting from the introduction of new techniques and improvements in organization, and

The development of the social service system is of essential importance to the problem of wage ratios and labor productivity. Social service benefits are not related to the effort of the worker or to the material results of his labor, and, therefore, cannot be a direct incentive to greater efficiency on his part. Their indirect effect, however, is tremendous. Free medical care, workers' holidays, free education, a well-developed system of grants and scholarships for university students, and mother and child care are of great importance from the point of view of the betterment of the general health level of the community, for the development of its culture, and for the satisfaction of the most basic needs of the working people.[4]

The amount of social welfare funds in Poland—as is the case in the other socialist countries—has been showing a steady growth. Should, however, the specific weight of social security benefits increase in relation to wages? There is no unequivocal answer to this question. In individual periods the need for stimulating the growth of production and of labor productivity may justify a stronger emphasis on remuneration, directly related to work and its results, at the expense of limiting the growth of social security benefits.

At other times the first priority may be given to the need for satisfying the collective wants of the workers. There is no doubt, that in the long run the latter form of raising the standard of living of the community will play a more and more important part.

At the present stage in the development of our economy, social policy to some extent reconciles the contradiction between the necessity of maintaining certain differences in wages, required for the development of production, and the striving for a rapid increase in the standard of living of the lowest income groups, which, at a given size of the total wage fund, must result in some flattening of the wage-rate structure.

Forms of Remuneration

The best way to raise labor productivity is through a wage system in which wages depend directly on work and its results. This condition is satis-

---

an increase resulting from greater efforts on the part of the workers. Only the latter should, as a rule, be accompanied by automatic wage increases. It is difficult to agree, therefore, that it would be justified considerably to differentiate the rates of automatic wage increases in the several industries. If such a differentiation appears in practice it is usually caused by the fact that the norms have not been revised at the proper time.

4. See Figure 1, p. 223.

fied by the <u>piecework</u> system. It should be noted that in a socialist economy this system is free of a number of negative effects which appear in a capitalist economy. It does not lead, as a rule, to an excessive increase in the intensity of work, nor does it result in too much competition among workers and thereby damage the morale of the employees of an enterprise. A tendency toward a collective effort is now a dominant trend in the organization of work, and it is expressed by group, rather than individual, piecework,

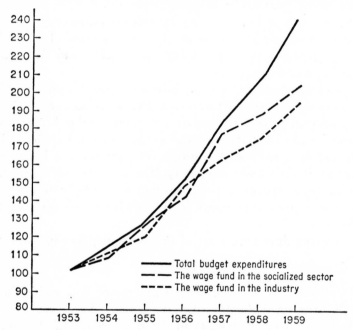

Fig. 1. Budget expenditures for social and cultural services and the wage fund in Poland, 1953–1959.

and by the granting of bonuses to production teams for collective achievements. This does not mean that the piecework system in a socialist economy is free of drawbacks. Frequent dangers are: a lowering in the quality of the product, differences in the "intensity" of norms for several jobs, and so forth.

There is, therefore, not absolute merit in the piecework system, whether on a group, or on an individual, basis. The use of this form of labor remuneration is only justified when (1) the worker has to have a decisive influence on the effects of his work, because the incentives only work within the limits of this influence; (2) the labor outlay has to be measurable; (3) it is necessary to establish standards that would permit an objective evaluation of the expenditure and the effects of labor—scientifically motivated norms.

Whether these conditions are satisfied depends primarily upon the development of techniques and the organization of labor.

In 1953–1955 the percentage of piecework labor increased considerably; in 1959–1960 its share somewhat diminished. This was a result of a revision of the view which prevailed in the preceding period, that the piecework system is the best way of implementing the socialist principle of distribution according to work, and a consequence of a more purposeful adaptation of remuneration forms to the actual production conditions in the several industries and groups of enterprises.

The use of the piecework system creates a number of complex problems. Differences in the intensity of norms should be prevented, norms should be constantly adapted to new techniques and improvements in organization, care should be taken lest the incentive system affect the established trade hierarchy and the correct wage structure. The day-rate and bonus systems create problems of no lesser complexity. The most difficult question is to establish the bonus system on principles that will preserve the role of the bonus as an incentive and prevent it from becoming a mere permanent addition to the wage.

The following three factors are of decisive importance in solving these problems:

(1) Gradual improvements in the organization of work and in the methods of the technical norm-setting procedure.

(2) Increased share of workers in the management of the enterprise, active participation of employees and their organizations—workers' self-government—in revising the norms and wage rates in the enterprise.

(3) The control of autonomous wage movements.[5] This control is exercised, on the one hand, by the bank, and on the other, by the management of the enterprise and by the workers' self-government.

---

5. It should be noted that the national economic plan takes these movements into account by determining percentage increases in wages that should accompany the planned increases in labor productivity.

Profit-Sharing in an Enterprise

A great advantage of a remuneration system is the dependence of wages on individual efforts, qualification, and efficiency of the worker. At the same time, however, these features of wages are the reason wages cannot be the one and only form of stimulating an increase in social labor productivity.

Individual efficiency cannot grow to a very large and unforeseen extent nor, as a rule, is it individual. An increase in productivity depends upon the cooperation of large teams—comprising both workers and the technical and engineering staff; it depends upon the labor of the "collective worker."

Neither do wages usually allow for—or, at any rate, not to a sufficiently large extent—the economic effects of savings in raw and other materials, and in the tools of labor. For this reason the role played by economic incentives connected with the operating results of the enterprise as a whole is of great importance. These incentives are also important from the point of view of education and of the strengthening of the spirit of solidarity and loyalty to the enterprise, the sense of responsibility, and the feeling of the dependence of one's own future upon the future of the enterprise. In a socialist economy they may become powerful factors consolidating the workers in fulfilling their production goals, because—in consequence of the socialization of the means of production—there is no basic conflict between the personal interest of the worker and the interests of the community.

Since 1957 the main economic incentive in Poland—apart from wages—has been the factory fund, which is a form of the workers' participation in the profits of the enterprise. The amount of profit on which this fund is based is checked every year. Windfall profits, independent of the enterprise —caused by changes in prices, in profit margins, and so forth—and so-called irregular profits, obtained by methods contrary to the public interest (deterioration in quality of product, arbitrary changes in range of products, delays in repairs, and so forth) are eliminated. It is also forbidden to increase profits by lowering wages. Thus, profits reflect the real achievements of the enterprise in the sense of increasing production and lowering costs. In these circumstances it may be said that economic incentives are designed not simply to increase the profit of the enterprise, but, first and foremost, to raise the social labor productivity.

The way of implementing the idea of profit sharing in Poland provides interesting examples of solution which may be worth mentioning.[6] This is particularly true with regard to the principles of writing off the amounts earmarked for the factory fund and its distribution.

(*a*) The factory fund depends upon actual economic progress expressed in better results achieved in a given year in comparison with the preceding year. The strictness of this requirement is somewhat toned down by splitting the amounts into two parts: the fund proper, connected with the attainment of results equal to those of the preceding year, and the supplemented fund—for improving results.

(*b*) In order to make the economic performance of the enterprise comparable and to eliminate the impact of change in product range, the notion of "base" has been introduced. The "base" is used in calculations instead of the actual results of the preceding year in cases where changes in the profit of the enterprise were due to reasons beyond control.

(*c*) The factory fund is expressed in differentiated percentages of the wage fund and is a function of the number of employees and their average wage. In this way the employees of different enterprises are, in principle, ensured an equal start. The total profit, which, as a rule, is a quantity independent of a given team of employees, does not effect the size of the factory fund.[7]

(*d*) The mechanism of the system works in the following way: the rate of the basic fund in all enterprises amounts to 2 per cent of the wage fund. The supplemental factory fund is differentiated depending upon the degree of difficulty in attaining the postulated improvements in operating results. As a consequence, the several enterprises get the same rates—expressed as percentages of the wage fund—for different percentage improvements, requiring, however, the same amount of effort.

On this basis of the preliminary factory fund index a supplemental fund table is compiled. This table contains, on the one hand, percentage improvements in profit shown in consecutive intervals, and, on the other hand, the write-offs to the supplemental factory fund—in percentages of the planned wage fund—corresponding to definite percentage improvements in profitability.

(*e*) The higher the percentage improvement in profit resulting from the technical and economic plan, the higher the position of the enterprise in the table.

---

6. This method was worked out for the first time in this form in 1960.
7. Thus profit is only a source of financing bonuses for the employees and not a quantity to be distributed among the enterprise and the employees.

A progressive scale for the amounts to be written off to the fund for the planned improvement in operating results provides an incentive to planning high, but reasonable, targets. Thus the method of calculating the factory fund ensures the greatest advantages to enterprises disclosing their reserves and mobilizing them for planning their targets as high as possible. Both planning "with reserves" and planning "for growth" result in a reduction in the supplemental fund.

The resources of the factory fund may be used for the following purposes: 25 per cent of the total for housing; the remaining amount up to the value of 8.5 per cent of the wage fund for bonuses and grants to the employees. These amounts are distributed by the workers' self-government only; the employees should participate in the payments from the fund according to the amount of work they contribute. When there are no appropriate direct criteria, the most frequently accepted principle is a division proportionate to the basic wage; factory fund surpluses may only be used for housing or social investments that benefit all employees.

The concept behind the employees' profit-sharing scheme described above is characterized by the following features: it eliminates the danger of substantial wage fluctuations—for payments out of the fund cannot exceed 8.5 per cent of the wages; it encourages the development of initiative among workers in working out planned targets, and mobilizes the employees for the task of the realization of these targets; It strengthens the principle of distribution according to work—this principle is the only basis for differentiating both supplemental funds in particular enterprises and payments to particular employees out of these funds.

Tables 58, 59, and 60 show some statistical data on the formation and distribution of the factory fund in Poland.

Table 58. Factory fund in the whole national economy in Poland, 1957–1959.

Year	Amount (millions of zlotys)	Index	Percentage of wage fund
1957	4.120	100	5.9
1958	5.124	124.4	5.8
1959	5.141	124.8	5.2

Table 59. Distribution of the factory fund in industrial enterprises[a]
in Poland, 1959.

Ministry	Factory fund as percentage of wage fund	Percentage of factory fund used for housing	Percentage of factory fund used for bonuses and grants	Percentage of factory fund used for social investments
Mining and power	9.9	25.6	64.0	10.4
Heavy industry				
Iron and steel metallurgy	—	25.0	67.8	7.2
Other enterprises	—	25.6	70.2	4.2
Chemicals	12.3	26.5	66.5	7.0
Construction and				
construction materials	9.5	24.4	66.0	9.6
Light industry	7.9	25.0	73.2	1.0
Food products	8.2	27.9	66.1	6.0
Timber	7.2	24.5	58.0	17.5
Committee for handicraft				
production	4.7	22.1	76.2	1.2
Totals	8.7	25.5	67.1	7.4

a. Data based on a statistical sample comprising 17 per cent of all enterprises. The investigations were done by the Central Council of Trade Unions.

Table 60. Distribution of bonuses among the several groups of employees in Poland.

Group of employees	Percentage of employees	Share of the group receiving bonus	Percentage share of the group in total bonus
Manual workers	81.7	81.7	77.5
Technical and engineering staff	7.9	8.5	14.0
Clerical staff	4.6	4.9	5.0
Other employees	5.8	4.9	3.5
Total	100.0	100.0	100.0

Conclusions

In the light of the information contained in the present paper, necessarily brief and fragmentary, concerning the methods of raising labor productivity through the labor remuneration system, we can now describe a general outline of the approach to the problem.

In a socialist system the material incentives used for raising the productivity of particular employees and teams play a very important role. The perfecting of those incentives is an important element of the economic policy of the state. It is strictly connected with the process of improving the whole mechanism of the planned economy, the perfecting of the methods of planning, and the management of the economy.

The problem of wage organization is transformed from a psychological problem of influencing an individual or a group into a problem subordinated to the organization of social labor in the national economy.

The stereotype *Homo economicus* whose behavior is determined by the weighing of utility and disutility, a being completely isolated from society and influenced by a complex and elaborate system of incentives, is replaced by the concept of social man who consciously participates in the social process of production and in its effects.

The problem of man in the production process must be treated collectively. It is inseparably tied in with the question of the new hierarchy of social values and, especially, with the new position of labor and the working man in a socialist society, the development and formation of moral and cultural attitudes, education, the creation of an equal start for everybody, and the satisfaction of the basic needs of the community.

CHAPTER 17

Postwar Development of Productivity in Italy

Pietro Merli Brandini

Italian Confederation of (Free) Trade Unions

Per capita income at constant prices in Italy has increased from 209,000 lire in 1951 to 324,000 lire in 1960. The rate of average annual increase is therefore 6.1 per cent. Industrial and commercial activities have contributed in large measure to this increase. It has been accompanied by notable structural changes within each branch of economic activity.

In agriculture, the relative importance of cereals has diminished, and that of wine, garden produce, and livestock raising has increased. In industry, the relative importance of food and textile industries has decreased, while that of the metal industries, chemical, and paper industries has increased. Where services are concerned, the importance of activities connected with transport and communication tends to increase.

Because of these structural modifications, changes in the structure of the labor market have also taken place. The dominating phenomenon is the exodus from agriculture. The labor force engaged in agriculture in 1954 was 39.5 per cent of total employed labor. In 1960, this decreased to 31.2 per cent. On the other hand, industry went up from 32.5 per cent to 37.8 per cent, and services from 28 per cent to 31 per cent.

The general advance of per capita income hides the existence of grave problems in the process of Italian development. Cultural and historical factors have caused the existence of a marked economic and social divergence between the southern and northern zones. The process of development over the last decade has not served to reduce this divergence. The relationship between per capita income in the south and that in the north decreased from 51.8 per cent in 1951 to 41.8 per cent in 1960. In fact, investment has remained mainly attracted by existing development areas, thereby contributing to a further rapid development of economically progressive zones.

It must, however, be pointed out that the problem of regional divergences is the central problem both of economic policy and of the country's national conscience. This factor was the driving force that helped create the Cassa del Mezzogiorno in 1950, an instrument designed to initiate a massive plan of public investment over a fifteen-year period, with the purpose of improving the framework of the communications systems to ports, to land reclamation areas and their irrigation systems, and the aqueducts. It is generally held that this policy has contributed notably to the development of the country.

Yet this has still not succeeded in solving the problem of regional disequilibrium, even though massive investments from both private and public sources have been made in the south in recent years for industrial activity, and others are planned in the steel and chemical industries for the near future.

Factors of Internal and International Economic Policy That Have Speeded Up Productivity

The expansion of the home market, the freeing of international trade, and the entry of Italy into the European Economic Community have been factors of extreme importance in the increase of productivity. The expansion of the home and foreign markets have brought about a double impulse: a) toward the extension of the production scale and b) toward fiercer competition of Italian industries with foreign counterparts.

In the last three or four years, Italy's balance of payments has shown a credit for the first time in the history of the country, in the presence of noteworthy increases of exports in recent years. This shows that the extension of the scale of production has permitted economies which have allowed Italian products to compete with success on the international market.

In fact, the growth of productivity has its origin in the opportunities offered by the extension of the market's dimensions, which happens as a result of freeing international trade and European economic integration. The process of European economic integration, especially, has brought Italian industry face to face with that of other European countries, and it is no accident that the most sensational increases in the productivity of the country have taken place since 1958, the year in which this process began.

Light and Shade in Italian Economic Development

This summary picture of the general situation of the country opens the way to certain conclusions and to the formation of certain questions.

First of all, the rhythm of increase of per capita income is notable and in excess of the normal development rates for industrialized countries. However, this result is in line with the development of European countries linked to the European Economic Community, whose development rhythms are near to, or equal to, that of Italy.

But Italy's development encounters difficulties caused by a disequilibrium deeply rooted in history. From one point of view, this disequilibrium is between one region and another, and, from another point of view, between one industry and another. The cause of this may be that productivity does not naturally grow harmoniously, that is, so as to reduce existing divergences.

On the economic plane, various reasons are put forward to explain this lack of harmony. Among these, the extent of monopoly or oligopoly, with administered price practices, is said to be one of the most important. However, examination of the facts leads one to suppose that this price stiffness has a much less general effect than is supposed, and that it cannot be the whole explanation.

In Italy, there is discussion as to the advisability of working on income distribution, shifting the terms of trade in an appropriate manner between one economic activity and another, and between income brackets, in order to obtain a more harmonious distribution of productivity. There are other minor reasons, however, connected with fiscal policy, that makes this extension difficult. Because of these uncertainties, the right answers to the problem of an equitable diffusion of technical progress must be sought on a plane not strictly economic. To what extent do insufficient cultural and professional levels bar technical progress? How far does the defense of traditional production methods hinder this progress? How far does insufficiency of information as to data of technical progress hinder its diffusion?

The Trend of Labor Productivity in Italy

In this section we will try to analyze the why and how of the development of Italian productivity. It should be mentioned that in 1960 an important study convention was held on "Technological Progress and the Italian Society" during which every economic and social effect of technical progress was exhaustively examined.[1]

To evaluate the progress of productivity, two different yardsticks have been developed. The first is that of the average gross productivity revenue in every branch of activity per labor unit employed. The second is the calculation of the average physical productivity per man-hour in twenty-four branches of industry. These are necessarily rough estimates because of the limitations of the available data.

For the computation of average gross productivity revenue, reliable data are obtainable for net product, while over-all employment is estimated through the sample surveys made by the central institute of statistics for some weeks each year. Furthermore, the reduction of the net product to constant prices on the basis of the price dynamics of each sector has presented some difficulties.

The statistics for the over-all production of each industry and those for the employment of manual workers compiled by the ministry of labor have been used for calculating the average physical productivity per man-hour. The latter covers the employment of manual workers in 18,500 establishments having more than ten employees, and it comprises about 55 per cent of the employed workers.

Since over-all production indexes are only correlated with employment indexes in the larger concerns, the productivity indexes obtained are inaccurate, being too high.

Table 61 shows us that from 1954 to 1960 gross productivity rose 12.7 per cent in agriculture, 22.2 per cent in industry, and 18 per cent in tertiary activities.

Table 62 shows the increases in physical productivity in twenty-nine industrial sectors. The most notable increases were in the extraction, sugar, chemical, glass, cement manufacture, iron, railroad materials, and the automobile industries. However, the increase of productivity in railroad materials and shipyards should not be evaluated as too positive a factor. These

1. The convention which was promoted by the Centro Nazionale di Prevenzione e Difesa Sociale was held in June 1960 at Milan. Information in this paper has been drawn from contributions made at the conference.

are industries which in Italy are linked to public consumption which is subject to fluctuations, whereas the level of employment in the factories tends to be stable.

Discussions of the "why" of the growth of productivity focus on two questions: (*a*) whether the variations in the terms of trade of labor versus capital have favored a substitution between labor and capital, and (*b*) whether the substitution is due to the extension of the products market and the scale of production.

Table 61. Average gross productivity revenue per man in Italy, 1954, 1960.[a]
(In lire per man at 1954 prices)

Year	Agriculture	Industry	Tertiary activities
1954	360,000	710,000	509,000
1960	406,000	868,000	601,000
$\frac{1960}{1954} \times 100$	112.7	122.2	118.0

a. Gross productivity revenue per man has been calculated relating the values of the net product and the labor force employed. Correcting coefficients to reduce the net product to constant prices, 1954, have been obtained thus: agriculture 108.8; industry 99; services 126.2.

Source: Data on the net product in the economic sectors and on the labor force employed in April–May 1954 and 1960 are from the figures of the Central Institute of Statistics.

The increase in real and monetary wages does not seem to have been a decisive cause in the process of substituting capital for labor. Furthermore, the most notable increases in productivity are recorded in highly concentrated sectors and corporations which are for the most part self-financed. Consequently, these concerns are not sufficiently sensitive to variations in the rate of interest on the capital market versus the wage rate to decide on the substitution.

A more consistent reason in favor of the substitution may be found in the fact that the terms of trade of capital goods versus labor have changed to the disadvantage of capital goods. Actually a lathe cost only 40 times more in 1958 than in 1938, whereas the cost of labor had risen 100 times in the same period. The same arguments hold true for electric power. In this way the field where the substitution of capital for labor is expedient is expanded. Numerous indexes point to the fact that in the last twenty years there have been variations of the terms of trade of labor and capital that have fostered the substitution of the former by the latter.

Table 62. Production, employment, productivity in 29 industries in Italy, 1953–1960.
(Index numbers 1953 = 100)

Sectors	Production (1)	Employment (2)	Hours worked (3)	Productivity Per man (= 1:2) (4)	Per hour (= 1:3) (5)
Mining and quarrying					
1954	110	94	94	117	117
1955	123	89	90	138	137
1956	139	86	90	161	156
1957	156	86	85	181	184
1958	159	77	72	206	221
1959	171	67	65	255	263
1960	180	63	61	286	295
Mills and factories					
1954	102	91	91	112	112
1955	104	89	90	117	116
1956	105	91	89	115	118
1957	102	92	89	111	115
1958	102	89	86	115	119
1959	97	85	82	114	118
1960	100	94	94	106	106
Sweets and cakes					
1954	105	103	103	102	102
1955	108	107	108	101	100
1956	112	111	109	101	103
1957	122	115	113	106	106
1958	125	115	113	109	119
1959	134	116	113	116	119
1960	150	115	112	130	134
Sugar					
1954	115	103	104	112	110
1955	157	109	114	144	138
1956	131	99	95	132	138
1957	113	85	84	133	135
1958	150	88	84	170	179
1959	189	87	93	217	203
1960	134	78	79	172	170
Paste					
1954	105	97	98	108	107
1955	108	95	95	114	114
1956	114	97	96	118	118
1957	114	96	93	119	119
1958	116	95	93	122	122
1959	117	97	94	121	121
1960	120	97	96	124	124
Textiles (in general)					
1954	103	97	99	106	104
1955	95	91	89	104	107
1956	100	89	89	112	112

Table 62. Continued.

Sectors	Production (1)	Employment (2)	Hours worked (3)	Productivity	
				Per man (= 1:2) (4)	Per hour (= 1:3) (5)
Textiles (continued)					
1957	110	87	90	126	122
1958	105	83	84	127	125
1959	116	83	88	140	132
1960	127	87	93	146	137
Cotton					
1954	107	97	100	110	107
1955	92	90	85	102	108
1956	98	86	84	114	117
1957	109	82	86	133	127
1958	105	77	79	136	133
1959	112	73	78	153	143
1960	124	75	81	165	153
Wool					
1954	103	99	98	104	105
1955	94	95	91	99	103
1956	99	94	93	105	106
1957	106	95	94	112	113
1958	98	90	87	109	113
1959	112	92	93	122	120
1960	122	97	99	126	123
Hosiery					
1954	96	102	100	94	96
1955	100	107	106	93	94
1956	109	117	116	93	94
1957	129	131	127	98	102
1958	121	131	125	92	97
1959	136	134	133	101	102
1960	143	151	150	95	95
Stockings					
1954	99	92	88	108	112
1955	95	83	80	114	119
1956	105	80	81	131	130
1957	108	81	83	133	130
1958	102	77	76	132	134
1959	121	75	77	161	157
1960	144	81	85	178	169
Flax and hemp					
1954	115	95	104	121	110
1955	88	85	84	103	105
1956	84	77	80	109	105
1957	88	74	78	119	113
1958	82	63	65	130	126
1959	80	57	61	140	131
1960	86	57	64	151	134

Table 62. Continued.

Sectors	Production (1)	Employment (2)	Hours worked (3)	Productivity Per man (= 1:2) (4)	Per hour (= 1:3) (5)
Jute					
1954	107	87	89	123	120
1955	112	77	83	145	135
1956	112	73	80	153	140
1957	113	75	76	151	149
1958	106	67	70	158	151
1959	117	65	72	180	162
1960	122	67	74	182	164
Footwear					
1954	105	104	104	101	101
1955	102	106	104	96	98
1956	109	114	113	96	96
1957	126	126	124	100	102
1958	136	133	129	102	105
1959	143	142	140	100	102
1960	157	155	155	101	101
Wood					
1954	104	110	114	94	91
1955	110	115	119	96	92
1956	95	117	117	81	81
1957	98	110	110	89	89
1958	98	112	113	88	87
1959	105	114	116	92	91
1960	105	119	121	89	86
Paper and newsprint					
1954	104	100	110	104	94
1955	114	99	109	115	104
1956	125	99	106	126	118
1957	138	100	107	138	129
1958	140	98	103	143	136
1959	157	98	105	160	150
1960	176	111	122	159	144
Leather					
1954	106	97	91	109	116
1955	101	92	87	110	116
1956	106	88	81	120	131
1957	117	86	81	136	144
1958	123	82	78	150	158
1959	139	83	81	167	172
1960	146	90	87	162	168
Rubber					
1954	117	102	104	115	103
1955	122	105	105	116	116
1956	113	104	100	109	113

Table 62. Continued.

Sectors	Production (1)	Employment (2)	Hours worked (3)	Productivity Per man (= 1:2) (4)	Per hour (= 1:3) (5)
Rubber (continued)					
1957	118	102	98	116	120
1958	117	94	91	124	128
1959	135	89	90	152	150
1960	173	98	100	177	173
Chemical industries					
1954	122	105	106	116	115
1955	135	109	109	124	124
1956	148	113	111	131	133
1957	154	119	117	129	132
1958	175	114	113	154	155
1959	209	116	115	180	182
1960	242	123	122	197	198
Minerals other than metals					
1954	108	106	107	102	101
1955	130	111	113	117	115
1956	141	110	108	128	131
1957	151	112	110	135	137
1958	160	110	107	145	150
1959	178	110	109	162	163
1960	207	115	114	180	182
Glass					
1954	104	102	101	102	103
1955	125	101	104	124	120
1956	137	103	103	133	133
1957	151	103	103	147	147
1958	160	99	99	162	162
1959	176	103	104	171	169
1960	213	110	112	194	190
Cement					
1954	112	102	102	110	110
1955	136	105	106	130	128
1956	145	105	102	138	141
1957	151	105	102	144	148
1958	161	99	94	163	171
1959	180	96	93	187	193
1960	200	88	86	227	233
Iron and steel					
1954	122	98	99	124	123
1955	156	100	102	156	152
1956	172	106	105	162	163
1957	195	106	105	183	185
1958	182	107	103	170	177
1959	197	103	101	191	195
1960	247	109	108	227	229

Table 62. Continued.

Sectors	Production (1)	Employment (2)	Hours worked (3)	Productivity	
				Per man (= 1:2) (4)	Per hour (= 1:3) (5)
Non-ferrous metal industries					
1954	104	102	104	101	100
1955	111	103	102	107	108
1956	115	109	105	105	109
1957	118	108	103	109	114
1958	119	104	100	114	119
1959	124	102	99	122	125
1960	136	108	107	126	127
Mechanical industries					
1954	102	104	105	98	97
1955	113	109	110	103	102
1956	118	116	114	101	103
1957	127	121	118	104	107
1958	128	116	114	110	112
1959	137	116	113	118	121
1960	164	127	127	129	129
Shipbuilding					
1954	56	96	91	58	61
1955	107	96	96	111	111
1956	158	105	108	150	146
1957	196	118	121	166	162
1958	196	114	112	177	175
1959	166	104	97	160	171
1960	137	100	91	137	151
Building and repair of railway materials					
1954	86	94	95	91	90
1955	112	95	96	117	116
1956	133	97	96	137	138
1957	127	88	86	144	147
1958	209	88	86	237	243
1959	223	81	83	275	269
1960	225	77	80	292	281
Automobile industry					
1954	124	102	103	121	120
1955	136	108	108	125	125
1956	156	110	107	141	145
1957	160	114	111	140	144
1958	175	119	115	147	152
1959	212	121	119	175	178
1960	289	134	135	215	214
Pedal cycles					
1954	111	97	98	114	113
1955	111	93	90	119	123
1956	99	86	84	115	117

Table 62. Continued.

| Sectors | Production (1) | Employment (2) | Hours worked (3) | Productivity | |
				Per man (= 1:2) (4)	Per hour (= 1:3) (5)
Pedal cycles (continued)					
1957	93	84	79	110	117
1958	121	110	109	110	111
1959	119	116	113	103	105
1960	138	127	125	108	
Electricity					
1954	109	104	104	104	104
1955	117	106	105	110	111
1956	125	108	106	115	117
1957	131	109	108	120	121
1958	139	110	107	126	130
1959	149	111	107	134	139
1960	170	112	108	125	157

However, the most important factor has been the expansion of the scale of production caused by the expansion of the home markets and by the liberalization of international trade.

The influence of the scale of production on the increase of productivity is great. In a large Italian factory producing typewriters and calculating machines, a 78 per cent increase in productivity has been recorded in the last eight years in the typewriter department, and 150 per cent in the calculating machine sector. Given equal technological levels, equal technical capacity, and equal work methods adopted, the explanation of this difference is found only in the scale of production which increased six times in calculating machines and twice in typewriters. The economies of scale have had an important effect on the pace of productivity growth. Since the general progress of productivity in Italy is rendered possible by technology and work methods already known in the past, it can be concluded that: (a) the incentives to the substitution of labor by capital have been notable because of the worsening of the terms of trade between capital goods and labor; (b) that there have not been increases in the cost of labor which has rendered substitution absolutely necessary; (c) that the use of improved technology and more efficient work methods (which are already available) is being hastened and made necessary only by the change in the scale of production caused by the expansion of the markets.

The proof of this theory is to be seen in the fact that it was only when the markets expanded and the scale of production began to change that recourse was had to the existing accumulated technical progress, and productivity began to develop. Nevertheless, examination of the data in Table 62 proves that productivity is higher in the expanding industries.

The second query concerns the features of the process of the development of productivity in Italy. The dominant feature is to be found in the technological field, in the substitution of universal machines by machines with a single use and the creation of assembly lines, particularly for the mass production of consumer goods. This substitution was brought about with a relatively low capital output ratio. This form of substitution combined with expanding investments could supply a satisfactory explanation of the high rate of growth in the Italian economy.

Now we must face the question as to whether capital investments have entered or are entering a phase of diminishing returns. In this connection the general data given in Table 63 which shows growing investment per

Table 63. Marginal capital output ratio in Italy, 1951–1960.

Year	Net domestic product a (millions of lire)	Net investment b	Investment rate $\frac{b}{a}$ 100	Marginal capital/ output ratio $\dfrac{bn - 1}{an - an - 1}$
1951	8.503	1.104	12.9	3.9
1952	8.782	1.033	11.7	1.4
1953	9.656	1.311	13.6	4.3
1954	9.958	1.523	15.2	2.2
1955	10.665	1.783	16.7	6.5
1956	10.939	1.842	16.8	3.0
1957	11.543	2.089	18.1	4.4
1958	12.013	2.175	18.1	1.7
1959	13.275	2.360	17.7	3.1
1960	14.041	2.970	21.1	
1951–1955 Additional net product Net investment	2.162	4.971	—	2.3
1955–1960 Additional net product Net investment	3.376	10.249	—	3.0
1951–1960 Additional net product Net investment	5.538	15.520	—	2.8

Source: Central Institute of Statistics.

unit of output are of but slight help and might be misleading. Reliable data can only come from the concerns, but the possibility of obtaining them is still far off. On the basis of the judgment and opinions of technologists it is only with the automation of the plants in some industries that the capital invested enters a phase of diminishing returns. And since the number of factories and industries where these procedures have been introduced is still limited, it appears that the technical progress that has caused the increase of productivity in Italy has come about during a phase of increasing returns on the invested capital. Furthermore, recent studies in some mechanical industries seem to confirm that the investments made have increased both the productivity of the capital and that of labor.

This would seem to lead to the following conclusions: (*a*) the basic explanation of the development of productivity in Italy is to be found in the changes in the scale of production rather than in the variations of the terms of trade between capital and labor; (*b*) there are convincing reasons for holding that the increase in productivity is predominantly due to the adoption of technology and productive methods that were already known rather than to new technical knowledge; (*c*) available capital is therefore invested in this body of technical knowledge that has been accumulated during the last twenty years, just as soon as its use proves to be expedient; (*d*) this investment has brought about an increase in both the productivity of labor and in that of capital; and (*e*) there are not yet any obvious signs —particularly of a statistical nature—proving that capital investments in technical progress are entering a phase of diminishing returns.

Organizational Factors in Labor Productivity

The evolution of industrial organization in Italy is a factor that has exerted an undoubted influence on the productivity process development. Between the two world wars a strong tendency was seen toward the "divorce" of ownership and the control of the operation of the concern. For reasons of varying natures many family enterprises were converted into corporations. It may be said that in the most traditional industries (textiles, mechanics, foodstuffs, clothing, leather, construction, and so forth) this stage is not yet widely accomplished. The relatively new industries (chemicals, cement, electricity, and the like) were born corporations. In the traditional Italian industries this process is still going on. Particularly the textile industries, which up till recently were directly family owned, are rapidly being transformed.

The process of transformation marks a definite stage of transition in managerial methods. The new management which is composed of a class of technocrats follows different policies from those of the owner-manager in regard to (*a*) finance, (*b*) organization and control of production, (*c*) marketing, and (*d*) personnel management. The factors that serve as an impetus are furnished by the comparison with managerial methods in similar enterprises or in other industries, and the profit motive is accompanied by the efficiency motive. The functions of staff and line are defined, and consequently a new organizational structure is created: marketing management, planning and control of production, and personnel management. The function of command flows evenly along the line.

Alternative methods of financing are studied (self-financing, increase of capital, recourse to the capital market); the problem of the organization of the production process is studied as are the correlated problems of labor organization; the product is studied as are possibilities of simplification and reduction of types.

As soon as the work is sufficiently distributed, new work methods are studied, and incentive schemes launched. The production process is studied systematically, and the markets are surveyed with the proper methods. In this connection scientific and applied research are coming more to the forefront. Industries which devote much of their energies to research are especially those of chemicals, automobiles, electronics, electro-mechanics, typewriters and calculating machines, machine tools, rayon and artificial fiber, and oil and petrochemicals. Many companies in this field are aiming at freeing themselves from the bonds of foreign industrial patents.

These transformations of management are more marked in industries where there is mass production that enables a complete rationalization of the productive process. Actually this evolution of management is conditioned by (*a*) the scale of production, (*b*) the variety of the products, (*c*) the accumulated technical knowledge that can be employed, and (*d*) the possibility of "innovations" through scientific and applied research. As a result the function of management is less rational (with a loss of productivity) in the trades or the companies where these conditions do not exist.

Effects of Technical Change

Wage rates. Statistical sources in Italy covering wages give the figures for the average hourly earnings of the manual workers in individual industries. They have no data on the average earnings according to the degree of skill.

First of all, it should be noted that average monetary earnings increase more rapidly than productivity in the industries where progress is slower, whereas in the high productivity sectors the increase in earnings is below that of productivity. This is certainly because of the spreading influence of trade union pressure which, obtaining benefits (less than those sought) in the high productivity industries, stimulates an equal pressure in those where productivity lags.

From 1953 to 1960 average hourly earnings have risen, in real terms, 7 per cent in the chemical industry, 30 per cent in the electrical industry, 5 per cent in the timber industry, 5.5 per cent in the metallurgic industries, 9 per cent in the mineral industry, 9 per cent in textiles, and 4 per cent in transports. This average does not, however, take into consideration the changes that have occurred in job classifications. Consequently, the above-mentioned increases are less than reality where there has been substitution of skilled labor for unskilled labor; whereas they are above reality in the event of an inverse substitution. It must be pointed out that it would be arbitrary to credit this increase in earnings solely to technical progress inasmuch as it stems to a certain degree from overtime and from the competition of employers in the labor market (a competition which has become particularly keen during these last two years).

Wage structure. Technical progress alters job classifications. It tends to expand the scope of the classification and changes the proportion of each degree of skill. As will be pointed out later, collective bargaining provides four grades of classification of manual workers, and the difference in terms of wages between the bottom and top grades is 25 per cent. Actually this very slight wage difference is wider in company wage structures, following adjustments made by the management either because of the difference in job content or the influence of the labor market.

The sex differential tends to shrink both from the impetus of technical progress and from the pressure of the trade unions. An agreement has recently been reached in this connection with the associations of employers. A certain contraction in the wage differential in regard to age is also taking place.

In spite of the diversities in the increase of productivity between the different industries, the inter-industrial wage differential does not seem to be accentuated. Actually, measuring the differences between pairs of equidistant values in the 1953 and 1960 series of hourly earnings, there are no significant divergencies.

It may therefore be concluded that wage differentials due to skill tend to expand and those due to sex and age to reduce, while there are no significant changes in the inter-industrial differential.

Organization of work methods. Technical progress has had a considerable influence on the organization of labor within the firm. The most notable changes are as much the result of the use of improved technologies and work methods. This process normally determines a greater division of labor accompanied by the following variations: a) development of new managerial responsibility in work methods and b) study and improvement of work methods and time and motion studies.

The execution of the job is no longer the responsibility of the worker, but of the management, which, through method study, imposes upon the worker the sequence of operations to be followed. The determination of the methods is followed by the determination of production standards. Pay assumes the form of an incentive.

In Italian experience, the hourly pay rate is determined as a function of the degree of worker qualification. (For manual workers there are four job grades.) The manual worker keeps his basic pay even when doing jobs inferior to those to which his qualifications apply. This situation is much upset by the introduction of new systems of job evaluation which grade pay according to individual jobs, or the position held rather than the worker's qualifications. This technique is used because (*a*) division of labor tends to accentuate differences in relative values of jobs; (*b*) classification of labor grades laid down in collective bargaining are outdated, and it is felt necessary to redetermine the company wage structure owing to the variations that have arisen in relative values of jobs and positions; (*c*) with the introduction of job evaluation (which pays for the job done and not for the qualifications of the worker), employers mean to attain a greater mobility of workers between one job and another. This is strongly hindered by Italian collective bargaining.

There are also forms by which workers may share in the benefits of increased productivity through productivity bonuses.

In the integral or partial automation phase of the plant, the qualification level of the employee assumes greater importance. In fact, new trades' (professions) are developed, and the worker is no longer required to abide by work method regulations established by the management. He must use his ability and trade qualifications to control the production process and not to carry out little repetitive movements. As will be pointed out later, these workers tend to associate in craft unions and to determine the basic wage for multi-employer groups.

The characteristics resulting from technical progress in labor organization and wage structures are summarized below.

Under mechanization and marked divisions of labor

(1) Management receives the responsibility of fixing work methods.
(2) Fixing of standards and payment by results (the methods most widely used are the Barth Merrick and the revised Bedaux). There is no lack of methods time measurement.
(3) Introduction of job evaluation to redetermine wage rates in the gamut of jobs.
(4) Determination of productivity bonuses to share the benefits of productivity increase.

Under partial or integral automation

(1) Determination of new professions.
(2) Payment by results declines.
(3) Payment is by time rates, supplemented by productivity bonuses.
(4) Wage level is often influenced by competition among employers.

Bargaining units. In Italy until 1954 there were two different bargaining units. The first was made up of inter-industrywide agreements covering all the branches of industry in the country, and the second was the internal plant committees. Until that date, these agreements covered the entire wage structure of the country, and, therefore, all the average differentials due to (*a*) branch of industry, (*b*) zone, (*c*) skill, (*d*) sex, and (*e*) age. Since that date, differentials due to zone still remain unchanged, but the national unions may stipulate agreements which provide other bases for wage differentials.

Technical progress has brought about a crisis in this centralized system of industrial relations. Firms have become the real points of reference in the interflow of relations between employers and employees. Wages actually paid diverge from those established on an industrywide basis. The CISL (one of the Italian trade union organizations) put forward the necessity of developing a system of plant bargaining units, to exist side by side with the national bargaining units from 1953 on. The other trade union organizations in Italy have since adhered to this point of view. In fact, since 1957, and especially in the years 1959 and 1960, there has been a massive development of plant agreements (more than a thousand).

Together with this substantial change in bargaining units, there are profound changes in the content of collective agreements. Company agreements lay down regulations in regard to: a) time and motion study, b) incentive schemes, c) job evaluation and merit rating, d) productivity bonuses, and so forth.

The resulting job of the trade union is to establish grievance procedures within the companies. This is the result of the more extensive reasons for disagreement between management and employees brought about by changes due to technical progress. The system of industrial relations in Italy is summarized below.

Plant level	The agreements linked mainly to the specific situation determined by the dynamics of technical progress in the firm.
Industry level	The agreements fix minimum wages and general conditions of work, annual holidays, public holidays, dismissal, and supplementary benefits.
Economic system as a whole	There is consultation with government and employers' associations on general problems of political economy (economic development, full employment, and so forth).

Union structure and tactics. It is well to remember that the Italian Trade Union organizations have the following structures.

National level	They operate on the basis of several industries linked to the same branch (the National Union of Metalworkers represents workers in the shipbuilding, automobile, electrical and mechanical industries, and so forth).
Local level	There are local unions for every branch. Coordination of the various branches is carried out by the provincial unions.
Company	There are the internal committees (delegates elected by all workers, whether union members or not). Since

1954 there have been company union sections (shop
stewards) elected by union members only.

In any case, Italian trade unions have no craft unions. The existing
structures are suitable for representing the mechanization phase, which produces a lowering of average skill level, but they are not suitable for dealing
with the requirements of higher qualified trades resulting from automation
processes. These workers, owing to their cultural level, the nature of their
work, and the need to exchange working experiences show an increasing
desire to associate themselves with craft unions. These needs, even if felt
by the unions, have not been met. The result is that these workers do not
join existing unions.

The very strategy of the unions has undergone changes under the impulse of technical progress, particularly in the tactics of disputes at company
level. In communist-controlled unions, interesting disputes may be noted
between political doctrinaires, union leaders, and communist workers. The
former reproach the latter for thinking it sufficient to make union claims
in order to achieve "democracy and socialism," and maintain that the communists in the unions should be instruments of political action toward a
non-capitalist society.

As time passes, it is easy to see that the fragmentation of disputes and
the general ability of workers to obtain an increasingly large share of general well-being reduces the political value of union action. Strikes tend to be
longer, and public demonstrations of those typical of communist action
five or six years ago are becoming increasingly rare. Substantially, disputes
are becoming more responsible and less violent, in spite of the strong ideo-
logical and political proportion of communists among Italian workers.

CHAPTER 18

Wage Structure and Productivity in Great Britain

K. G. J. C. KNOWLES

Oxford University

In Britain, productivity is only one of the principles of wage determination, and it operates haphazardly and imperfectly. Wages are by now highly "structured": in each industry, there exists a framework of wage payments agreed to by workers and employers. Agreement, as distinct from coercion, implies some comparability of bargaining power—and also that whatever is agreed on is felt to be justifiable by some standard of equity or fairness. The simplest form of wage structure is that of the parable of the laborers in the vineyard, under which every worker, irrespective of time spent and output produced, was to receive exactly the same sum. The equity of this is comprehensible at a subsistence level; but above this level it is felt equitable to differentiate between one worker and another in respect of the effort each exerts—time spent and output each being regarded as crude measures of effort. Hence the two main systems of payment, by time and by results; but further differentiation has come to be made according to age, skill, and other attributes.

Wage structures today consist of a wage rate, or a scale of rates (related to a standard week of a set number of hours worked at acceptable times), graded by occupation and skill, as well as, to some extent, by age. Women have separate scales; so, in some cases, do workers in different regions. The rates are sometimes "standard" rates but more often minima which may be greatly exceeded in practice. Pieceworkers' wages are usually covered (except where there are specific price lists because the product is homogeneous, and technological change is rare) by a percentage figure—by which the wages of a pieceworker "of average ability" ought to exceed the bare time rate. In addition to these prescribed or implied payments, there are rules governing payment in particular circumstances—for instance, for working at inconvenient times, for working under difficult conditions, for enforced idleness, and for vacations. Thus wage structures impose complex but rigorous limits on the kind of wage changes which can be made at any time.

Given this complexity, ensuring equitable payment is by no means simple. The two main problems confronting those who settle wages are to achieve fair relativities between industries on the one hand and within industries on the other. Obviously these problems can never be posed in a vacuum, but always in the atmosphere of history: what will be done tomorrow depends on what is the case today, and this in turn has been determined by yesterday and the day before.

Let us begin with fair wage relativities between industries. Half a century ago, when many British workers were living nearer the subsistence level (and some of them below it) than they are today, the question of establishing minimum subsistence wages was paramount, and inter-industrial relativities had hardly come to the surface of consciousness. The question of fairness between industries could, in fact, hardly arise except in the form of raising wages in "sweat shops" and casual trades to a level at which their workers could physically survive. Moreover, there was no national negotiation as we know it now, and therefore no nationally agreed "general wage level" which characterized an "industry." But, after forty years of national negotiation and twenty years of economic prosperity (on most definitions) with near-full employment and expanding social benefits, subsistence levels have been left behind, and we look at our neighbors rather than at the specter of starvation: "We are more interested," wrote Barbara Wootton,[1] "in keeping our distances above other people than in the actual level at which our earnings make it possible for us to live."

Now if our prime concern is to keep our distance, our main appeal is to history: "Printers, police and railwaymen, though they have not yet matched the firemen in digging up evidence from the nineteenth century, are all prepared to treat the relationships of thirty years ago as relevant to

1. *Social Foundations of Wage Policy* (New York, 1954), pp. 139–140.

the pattern that in their view ought to obtain today." [2] Those sections that have been able to hold their station may attribute their success to the regular use of a "League Table" of wage rates in negotiation. The appeal to history is itself, in a sense, an appeal to fairness: the continued acceptance of a wage relationship is taken as a pragmatic sanction for its equitability.

When historical relativities are disturbed, the stock arguments are pressed home with even more vigor—still on grounds of equity. Thus, "it is only fair" that wages should accompany rising productivity (even though employers retort that the increased output is due to improved technology, new machines, and wise capital investment). If, however, the productivity argument is accepted, other groups—such as busmen and railwaymen—will protest that, as they have less opportunity to raise their productivity, "it is only fair" that they should be compensated for a disability which is not their fault. They may indeed, if they have fallen behind, sometimes lead wage movements and—since some service industries are nationalized and therefore unhampered by competition—are credited with a better chance of success. Again, if profits are rising, "it is only fair" that these should be shared; if they are not, "it is hardly fair" that workers should be penalized as in the bad old days of selling-price sliding scales. Finally there is the cost-of-living argument; but this affects everyone alike, and to tie wages to the cost of living is, once the movement is general, merely to preserve historical differences intact. But the cost-of-living argument is two-edged; if living costs fall sharply, everyone will resist a consequential cut in money wages, while if they rise sharply the fear of accentuating inflation will infallibly be used to counter wage demands. If historical relativities are preserved, however, these further arguments lose much of their force—except as a means for an opportunist industry to steal a march on its fellows.

Historical wage relativities are not invincible (witness the rise of miners and agricultural workers); but they are nevertheless strong. They have, moreover, been powerfully buttressed by the increasing standardization of wage-settlement practices, to the point where the "wage round" is taken as a commonplace. Thus "the conduct of wage claims is nowadays as rigidly stylized as the classical ballet";[3] "the wage claims which have been submitted over the whole field of industry have conformed to a certain pattern irrespective of the profitability of individual industries or of their productivity . . . if any group of employers offers stubborn resistance to a wage claim which is part of a series of similar claims affecting the entire economy

2. *Ibid.*, p. 135.
3. *Financial Times*, December 4, 1959.

the result is that friction is generated and industrial relations seriously strained."[4] Similar pronouncements have come from the British Employers' Confederation, the Council on Prices, Productivity and Incomes, and many other official and unofficial observers.

One can easily exaggerate the cohesiveness, homogeneity, and importance of the wage round, and the power of the forces believed to generate it;[5] but it is hard to deny the *tendency* to uniformity in wage settlements and even the growing interdependence of wage and salary bargains. Uniformity and interdependence are products of increasing institutionalization: the "omni-presence" of the general workers' unions in the negotiations of different industries, the "interlocking" personnel of wages councils, the sensitivity of arbitrators to their own previous decisions and to those of others in the search for precedent, and the elaboration of "comparative" procedures such as that of the Post Office Engineers are enough to illustrate the point. Outside industry, there has also been a growing acceptance of "fair comparison" —a principle enunciated by the Priestley Commission on the Civil Service in 1955, the Grigg Advisory Committee on Recruiting for the Armed Forces in 1958, and the Pilkington Commission on Doctors' and Dentists' Remuneration in 1960. The Guillebaud Committee, in settling railwaymen's wages in the same year, took the same line.

The net effect of this "institutionalization" of wage settlements was that from 1948 to 1959 between two thirds and three quarters of some 220 wage rates listed by the ministry of labor rose by between 60 and 80 per cent (very few rose by more, and about a quarter by less). Unskilled rates tended to go up by rather more than skilled—another small sign of increasing uniformity. This is admittedly quite a broad range; and it must be remembered that we are talking of wage rates—some standard, some minimum—whose importance as components of actual paypackets can be very different. But there are obviously tendencies causing wage rates to keep roughly in step over a period. In so far as the picture is orderly, the so-called wage round is partly responsible in that it tends to generalize particular increases—to award them both to those whose productivity has risen and to those whose productivity has not and whose wage rates would otherwise have been lagging. The apparent egalitarianism of this process is not so

4. *Report of a Court of Inquiry* (engineering), *Cmd. 159,* May 1957, paras. 55, 57.
5. K. G. J. C. Knowles and E. M. F. Thorne, "Wage Rounds, 1949–1959," *Oxford University Institute of Statistics Bulletin,* February 1961. OEEC report on "The Problem of Rising Prices," 1961, 426–430 ff., presents a simplified view.

much a product of principle as of "free collective bargaining" under which every group tries for at least as big an increase as its neighbors.

If this is not to have an inflationary effect, the increases secured by groups whose productivity has risen must be less than proportionate to the rise—if an equivalent increase will go to those whose productivity has not risen. But in practice strong groups are sometimes able to get increases fully in proportion to their increased productivity and, when others follow suit regardless, inflation pressure builds up—although this pressure is not continuous, if only because wage rounds do slacken. But pressure on wage rates through successions of nationally negotiated increases is far from being the only wage pressure: earnings are continuously being pushed up by local negotiation—which widens the earnings gap or exerts an additional pull on rates. Any national wages policy (which, to be justified, would involve profit and price control) is felt to imply the abandonment of trade union autonomy—not to mention others' autonomy. Trade union autonomy and "free collective bargaining" are sacred cows *par excellence,* and, in the world of practical politics, we are living on the farm.

If the dead hand of history lies heavy on wage relationships between industries, it lies heavier still on wage relationships within industries; for all wage structures are historical monuments. When, at the end of the First World War, national wage structures were first established, they were inevitably based on existing differences. Many, indeed, of the differentials frozen then have persisted until now, impervious to technological and organizational change.

At first sight, this seems paradoxical or untrue. Thus we know that many wage differentials have narrowed in relative terms: that between skilled and unskilled, for example, which had stuck at around 50 per cent for a long time before 1914, has by now been whittled away to 20 or 15 per cent. But the very narrowing in percentage terms has reflected a sticking (over a period of rising money wages) in money terms; and it has been due to the practice (dating from the First World War, when it was introduced in the name of simplicity and, as usual, of equity) of granting uniform flat-rate increases to all grades to keep pace with the cost of living. Flat-rate increases may be regarded as no more than the immediate cause: one may rationalize the relative gains of the unskilled by reference to their increased bargaining power since they organized in the 1890's, or one may prefer the explanation that there has been a reduction in the ratio of skills required. Yet not all relative skill differentials have narrowed (as in steel, cotton, and coal); and, in addition, other differentials (piecework, sex, and regional differentials) have narrowed as well. If one resorts to justification (as negotiators regularly do) in terms of equitability, one can safely support equal money increases or equal percentage increases: that is, it is just as fair to *narrow* relative differentials as to *maintain* them. And when, as recently, skilled workers in some industries feel that narrowing has gone too far, no less equitable a case can be made for giving skilled workers proportionately bigger increases to reestablish some earlier relativity—that is, for *widening* relative differentials. Any justification of fair relativities proves shaky if one moves far from the criterion of acceptability-by-historical-sanction. What, at any rate, seems to have been happening within industries is a more or less uninterrupted whittling of relative differences—the same sort of process, in effect, as appears to operate between industries. The existing machinery of national wage negotiation is thus not very receptive to the injection of productivity considerations as a fuel: it has developed so much momentum that it can almost be said to run without fuel at all.

This double tendency to uniformity in wage rates—between and within industries—has not, however, had the effect on actual earnings that might be expected: it does not follow that earnings levels are being homogenized. What we have seen is the marked, if highly uneven, development of an earnings gap—a progressive divergence between nationally negotiated wage rates and actual earnings. In manufacturing, the gap has become so large that negotiated rates often bear little or no relation to levels of earnings, so that negotiators seem to be arguing about unreal abstractions—wage rates which virtually nobody is actually paid, since they are overlaid and augmented by innumerable other payments given by individual firms and have no place in national negotiation.

This is not to say that national wage negotiations are unimportant. Not only may wage rates, as has been suggested more than once, have sociological importance as status symbols or "social labels," not only may they also have potential economic importance as "floors" to earnings in a slump, but these "floors" have the unique property that, when they are raised, the ceilings go up as well. An increase in wage rates secured by national negotiation will, in practically every case, raise earnings levels throughout an industry, by however much these levels may already exceed those of wage rates. National wage negotiation, although it is so largely concerned with the fixing of "unrealities," is a powerful instrument for jacking up the entire edifice of earnings.

The earnings gap is no recent phenomenon, although it seems to have been a postwar discovery. It was growing in the engineering industry (the biggest single section of manufacturing) before the second interwar depression, and it is tempting to regard it as a consequence of institutionalized wage settlement: as bargains became centralized they became less sensitive to market pressures and more subject to institutional momentum or inertia, but were redressed by an increasing divergence of earnings. There is by now a great variability of earnings in engineering,[6] not only between occupations but within occupations from one firm to another. It is true that any large occupational category is bound to include workers of different degrees of skill exerting different efforts; but in so far as such differences seem insufficient to account for the variability of earnings, further explanation is needed. Hicks has suggested that much of the earnings gap may be due to the pull of the labor market, and on the whole he approves: "The economist could look with some satisfaction upon an arrangement by which basic agreed rates are kept in relation with the differentials that are appropriate in the long period, while short-period scarcities are reflected in (no doubt relatively disorderly) bonuses above the agreed minima."[7] In the same vein, Roberts commented: "This bifocal wage policy gives employers a convenient degree of flexibility, since they can adjust their actual wage payments to the level demanded by a competitive market situation."[8]

"Flexibility" may be excellent in principle, even though it has to be purchased at the price of equity. But while earnings are extensively adjustable upwards, they are hardly so at all downwards: can a ratchet be called "flexible"? Again, differentials are undoubtedly established for long periods; but in what sense are they "appropriate"? Is it only "short-period scarcities" which are reflected in the earnings gap? Are wage payments adjusted with any precision to "the level demanded by a competitive situation"? There is clearly a risk of begging the very questions one should be answering. Certainly some of the differences between firms in occupational earnings can reasonably be attributed to differences in labor supply and demand, and some to heterogeneity in respect of skill and effort; but, when all this has been said, the variability found in practice seems too great for all of it to be explained in these ways.

How much direct effect, by and large, has productivity on earnings? A

6. K. G. J. C. Knowles and T. P. Hill, "The Variability of Engineering Earnings," *O.U.I.S. Bulletin,* May 1956.
7. J. R. Hicks, "Economic Foundations of Wage Policy," *Economic Journal,* September 1955.
8. B. C. Roberts, "Employer and Industrial Relations in Britain and America," *Political Quarterly,* July–September 1956.

study by Nicholson and Gupta,[9] comparing for more than 90 industries the rise of productivity with that of men's hourly earnings between 1948 and 1954, suggests little or no correspondence—a finding confirmed by other enquiries.[10] Advances in earnings were found to be much more uniform than changes in productivity: in particular, there appears to have been no tendency for industries where productivity had risen greatly to secure correspondingly large increases in earnings. This effect—or lack of effect—is hardly paradoxical. Payment by results is hard to control by national agreement: the detail of piecework prices and times, and of more or less complex bonus systems, has almost inevitably to be settled by individual firms, national agreements usually offering no more than a "minimum percentage" as a guide. Almost anything may happen within firms: piecework prices may be set "loosely" ("tight" prices are seldom tolerated for long); they may deliberately be set generously to attract particular grades of labor; minor changes in working may be introduced enabling output (and earnings) to be increased without the job being able to be redefined, and so on. The net result is the familiar tendency of pieceworkers' earnings to "run away"; and the result of this in turn is that timeworkers tend, before long, to demand compensation. Thus a national "production bonus" based on the output of a whole works, a "merit rate" awarded to an entire department in order "to keep them in line," special "lieu rates" to timeworkers (in "lieu" of piece rates or, to use a polite fiction, "for working at piecework speed") are often introduced simply to avoid anomalies and frictions. The sanction, again, is pragmatic rather than economic.

Piecework itself is a highly diverse phenomenon. The ministry of labor estimates the proportions of those paid by results for each industry, but no such classification can be very rigorous. Virtually no pieceworker is a "pure" pieceworker: for practically all of them there is some time-rate element in their earnings. In a big steelworks (to take an extreme example) it was found [11] that, for those paid by results, the piecework element in pay ranged from 8 to 85 per cent; moreover, many workers changed from timework to piecework in the course of a single week. If the piecework element can fluctuate so widely for individuals, mustn't its incentive effect vary too? More important perhaps, the "incentive" element in the worker's paypacket (that

9. R. J. Nicholson and S. Gupta, "Output and Productivity Changes in British Manufacturing Industry, 1948–54," *Journal of the Royal Statistical Society* (Series A), IV, 1960.

10. C. H. Feinstein, *London and Cambridge Economic Service* (*Times Review of Industry*, December 1960); also W. E. G. Salter, *Productivity and Technical Change* (Cambridge, 1960), pp. 129, 167.

11. S. W. Ostry, H. J. D. Cole, and K. G. J. C. Knowles, "Wage Differentials in a Large Steel Firm," *O.U.I.S. Bulletin*, August 1958.

part of his pay which was responsive to his productivity) could in practice be swamped by other elements relating to matters outside his control—such as the premium for working on a particular shift. In general, a number of other principles enshrined in traditional wage structures can compete very strongly with that of rewarding the worker according to his productivity. Again, the hand of history is heavy, and, if the question "why are these rigidities tolerated?" is asked, the answer is that industrial peace itself seems to depend on not breaking with tradition.

How far the incentive effect of piecework is important in raising the productivity of the workers concerned is, indeed, a debated question.[12] Presumably experience differs a good deal in different industries: in some (though not of course in all), incentive payments may be swamped by other established forms of payment unrelated to effort, and in any case the force of tradition will be likely to prevent any wholesale recasting of existing wage structures. It seemed, moreover, as if piecework and payment by results had reached their peak in Britain a few years ago. They had, it is true, enjoyed a strong burst of popularity after the war; but no sooner had the exhortations been uttered than it was learned that in the United States, where productivity was highest, piecework appeared to be going out of fashion. In Britain too it was stagnating by the mid-fifties, and declining slightly by the end of the decade—although the latest figures indicate some apparent revival.[13] It is tempting to interpret any marked decline as a reflection of increasingly automatic production: the more automatic processes become, the more the pace of work is set by the machine and the less by the worker. For some time, probably, payment by results has increasingly tended to be calculated on the "results" achieved by groups rather than by individuals; but the bigger the group the more questionable the efficacy of the personal incentive. Except in so far as production methods are still relatively primitive, any marked extension of payment by results would seem to be attributable to the desire of employers to keep their workers earning good money under conditions of tight labor supply than to any renewed faith in its incentive efficacy. A decline in the prevalence of payment by results would undoubtedly lighten the work in firms' wages offices by eliminating the need for detailed bonus calculations; more important, it should also help to relieve the national wage structure of an industry from one of the internal pressures causing wage levels to rise.

12. For an examination of the relationship of productivity to earnings in coal mining, see T. P. Hill and K. G. J. C. Knowles, "Wages in Coal Mining," *O.U.I.S. Bulletin,* May 1961.
13. "Payment by Results," *Ministry of Labour Gazette,* September 1961.

If there is substance in the preceding discussion, the following points emerge.

There is a marked tendency toward the preservation of existing (historical) money differences in wage rates and—in an era of rising wages—a movement toward greater relative uniformity and the narrowing of all differentials both between and within industries. This trend seems unlikely to be decisively reversed, and the exceptions unlikely to do more than prove the rule. Various impulses to uniformity have been noted, of which the so-called wage round is only the most notorious.

If most workers' wages are to rise by more or less similar amounts at more or less regular intervals, it ought to be ensured, from the standpoint of the national economy, that the current increase in wages is not greater than the current rise in over-all productivity[14]—which implies that industries where productivity is rising will have to secure increases less than proportionate to the rise in their own productivity, so that industries where productivity is not rising may enjoy an equivalent increase without contributing to further inflation.

Policymakers have concentrated mainly on the rate of increase in wage rates (if only because these alone are subject to some sort of national control), and actual earnings have received secondary attention; the problem of the earnings gap remains with us. The reasons for the gap lie—almost by definition—outside the province of national wage agreements: it depends on such factors as the amount of overtime which is being called for, the extent of above-standard payments being made by individual firms, and the generosity of piecework pricing (as well, of course, as increased earnings resulting from improved productivity on existing jobs). Some of these "inflators" of earnings are due to labor-market pressures, although what are sometimes called "bribery rates" can hardly be defended *in toto* on these grounds.[15] Others are due to pressures inherent in the piecework system,

---

14. Strictly speaking, the rate of increase in wages should not exceed that in the productivity of *consumption goods*. (More strictly speaking still, it is the rate of increase in the demand for consumption goods resulting from increases in wages that should not exceed the rate of increase in the productivity of consumption goods.)

15. The British Employers' Confederation, in their *Bulletin* for July 1961, gave figures purporting to show that a substantial proportion of the national wage bill consisted of "extra payment made to attract the right kind of labor":

(1) Agreed rates (time and piece) for a
    normal working week (in £ million)   6500
(2) Overtime   600
(3) Excess payments over and above
    agreed rates   1500

and these at least would be alleviated if the popularity of payment by results were to decline decisively.

With the advance of automatic production, payment by results is in any case less appropriate in some industries than it has seemed hitherto. (Other incentives—if not wages, then "net advantages" such as fringe benefits, non-monetary improvements and industrial privileges—may therefore have to be used more widely.) Any pronounced decline in payment by results would be an administrative gain, since it would not only lighten the work of wages offices but would also reduce the considerable time expended in disputing about prices and times. It should also relieve one of the internal pressures on wages, and in the long run make settlements more "realistic" by removing one of the forces causing earnings to pull away from rates.

Moreover, payment by results complicates the problem of gearing wage increases in particular industries to the productivity increase in industry as a whole. For since pieceworkers are continuously getting wage advances in response to *their own* productivity increase, any general wage rise should, strictly speaking, discount for these advances. This would mean either (*a*) a reduction to insignificance of any "permissible" percentage increase in wage rates on the score that many workers had already "taken their bite" in earnings, or (*b*) an announcement that in piecework industries the negotiated increase would be smaller than elsewhere at a time of general advance. But if (*a*) the "permissible" percentage were set appreciably below the modest level of the current rise in over-all productivity, it would almost certainly be rejected; while the apparent anomaly of (*b*) might well induce workers paid by results to limit their output—and hence, self-frustratingly, their future productivity.

In any case it is questionable whether the unions would agree to a formal national wages policy (as distinct from a strictly temporary "restraint," "freeze," or "pause"). The same is probably true of current proposals to "atomize" wage negotiations in the interests of economic order:[16] it seems unlikely that the unions, after struggling for a century and more to enlarge

But (waiving all doubts about the reliability of such a breakdown) one must remember that (3) will inevitably include payments related to increased productivity. (2) and (3) together may give some indication of the current size of the earnings gap; but the existence of the gap is not "inflationary" *per se*— only in so far as it is unrelated to increased productivity or tends to pull wage rates up irrespective of increased productivity.

16. The Council on Prices, Productivity and Incomes toyed with the idea of subdividing the engineering industry for purposes of wage negotiation "so as to get more homogeneous and manageable bargaining units" (*Fourth Report,* July 1961, p. 27).

the coverage of negotiations, would willingly jettison their successes in favor of disintegration. Nor is it certain that such a cure would not aggravate the disease.

One possible alleviant, which amounts to settling wage rates with reference to actual earnings, is the somewhat exceptional type of agreement known as the *pro tanto* agreement. Normally, any negotiated increase in wage rates will result in an increase in the earnings of everyone covered; but a *pro tanto* agreement awards the full increase only to those whose earnings are fairly near the minimum rate, while those with higher earnings receive progressively smaller increases. The case for such agreements (they appear, on the whole, to have failed in engineering and succeeded in coal mining) has been argued elsewhere;[17] but in so far as they can help to reduce the variability of earnings within industries, they should surely not be neglected as a possible method of relieving one of the pressures tending to widen the earnings gap and to pull wage rates up in the wake of the highest earnings.

In the long run, the problem of gearing wages to productivity may diminish in obtrusiveness. The more automatic processes become, the more the pace is set by the machine, the more reasonable it is for workers to be paid by time, the smaller do labor costs become as a proportion of total costs; but the more, also, the wage bill tends to become a fixed charge on industry irrespective of output.[18] But maximum mechanization ("automation") does not appear overnight: it proceeds unevenly, and pockets of labor-intensive methods are likely to persist for a long time to come. Twin problems therefore remain: to prevent the momentum of existing wage-fixing mechanisms from raising wages unrestrainedly in excess of over-all productivity increases; and to increase productivity so that the expected demands can be safely met. There need be no harm in systematic and repetitive wage increases (so long as they *are* systematic), provided productivity rises sufficiently to meet union demands without the need for price rises; indeed, to attempt to restrain wage claims because of the supposed dangers of excess demand could be self-defeating if production were curtailed and the necessary rise in productivity inhibited.[19]

17. K. G. J. C. Knowles and T. P. Hill, "Wages in Coal Mining."
18. Frederick Pollock, *Automation* (New York, 1957), pp. 197–198.
19. G. D. N. Worswick, "Prices, Productivity and Incomes," and T. Balogh, "Productivity and Inflation," *Oxford Economic Papers*, June 1958.

CHAPTER 19

The Establishment of Norms under Incentive Systems in the Basic Steel Industry in the United States

LAWRENCE FENNINGER, JR.

Bethlehem Steel Company

Background

About 65 per cent of all production and related workers in the basic steel industry are paid some form of incentive in addition to their basic hourly wage rates. Average incentive pay amounts to 22 per cent above the wage rates of workers who participate in the incentives. In all cases, the basic wage rate serves as a guarantee that a worker's daily earnings will never be less than his basic rate multiplied by the number of hours worked per day.

In general, incentives relate as closely as possible to the activities of the individual worker. However, operations in steel require the services of closely coordinated crews. Incentives for those operations are based on the activities of the entire crew. Incentive workers in occupations such as crane operation, maintenance work, and so forth, providing service for several production processes are frequently paid on the basis of the performance of the men whom they service. In each case, however, the incentive is designed to reflect, as closely as possible, the consequences of the participant's own performance. Broad incentives or bonuses covering all workers in a large department or entire plant are rare.

Prior to 1947, incentive earnings were characteristically based on hourly rates less than the rates for non-incentive work. For many years, base rates used for incentive purposes were not increased by the amounts of general wage increases, but those amounts in cents per hour were added to incentive earnings. This meant a gradual erosion of incentive earnings as a proportion of total pay and a decline in the effectiveness of incentives.

Beginning in 1947, the basic wage structure throughout most of the steel industry was revised under a uniform system of job evaluation.[1] The resulting hourly rates were defined as the appropriate rates of pay for a normal day's work. One implication of that definition was that incentive pay for more than a normal amount of work should be related to the basic hourly rates. Pressure on the companies to develop methods for establishing that relationship was increased by the fact that the new hourly rates were, in many cases, equal to or greater than former average hourly earnings including incentive pay. In those cases, the incentives were abandoned because they were ineffective. In my own company, the proportion of hours worked by incentive employees to hours worked by all wage employees dropped from about 75 per cent to less than 50 per cent with the adoption of the new hourly rates.

There has been much speculation about the effect of increased mechanization and automation on incentives. Some students have concluded that as the individual worker exerts less and less control over the speed of an operation or the quality of its product, incentives of the traditional type have decreasing validity. That view explains the interest in some quarters in development of departmental or plant-wide incentives. Others, however, believe that the efficiency of the individual operator becomes more important with increased mechanization, because the cost of idle time rises as equipment becomes more expensive. Those holding that view, and they are in the majority among steel management and labor union people, think that incentives can be engineered so as to encourage individual initiative, good teamwork, and improved worker efficiency under conditions resulting from any degree of mechanization which may be achieved in the predictable future.

Underlying Theories of Incentives

In the development of incentives based on evaluated basic hourly wage rates, the industrial engineers can look on incentive pay as a reward for

1. For a detailed study of this system and its application, see Jack Stieber, *The Steel Industry Wage Structure* (Cambridge, Massachusetts, 1959).

(1) greater individual effort or (2) achieving a high rate of efficiency in the operation of equipment. Of course, the achievement of a higher rate of efficiency ordinarily involves an increase in effort in the case of a particular piece of equipment. But it is difficult, if not impossible, to take both points of view into account in one incentive plan.

It is, of course, natural to feel that if one works harder one should be paid more. Thus, most people are predisposed toward incentives based on effort. Moreover, although the theoretical basis for many of the incentives used in the steel industry in 1947 was obscure, many of them recognized increases in effort. Consequently, a number of companies, including the largest, decided to base new incentives on effort, or work measurement. Under those incentives, earnings are proportionate not only to increases in production above a norm but also to the ratio of productive to total available time.

Other companies, including my own, believe that in an industry characterized by heavy capital investment the primary interest of management is to ensure the most efficient use of the equipment provided by that investment. Whether or not a man puts out greater effort is of no consequence in and of itself. There are other considerations. The tendency in steel toward greater mechanization usually means less effort on the part of operators. Work-load incentives strictly applied would reduce incentive earnings in spite of increasing output. Not only do workers resist a permanent reduction in pay, but also most labor contracts in the United States provide that incentive earnings opportunity will not be reduced because of a technological change. The only alternative would be to compromise the work-load principle, knowing in advance that it would be lost altogether in the long run, but only after incentive earnings had ceased to bear any intelligible relationship to the original concept. Adopting from the beginning the theory known as "equipment utilization" avoids this problem. Incentives constructed on that theory are geared to practical capacity of equipment, and performance is measured as a percentage of that capacity. Thus operators of equipment having different capacities have the same opportunity to earn incentive pay. Further, the level of incentive earnings is not affected in either direction by changes affecting the capacity of the equipment.

Equipment utilization also has unattractive features. Increases in machine capacity may require increased efforts by operators to maintain a given level of performance in terms of capacity. But an equipment utilization incentive provides exactly the same earnings opportunity after the change as before. That is equally true where a worker who has been operating two machines is given a third to operate in addition to the original two. Work-load incentives provide greater earnings opportunities in both those cases. The problems presented by the use of equipment utilization incentives in those cases could be solved by substituting work-load incentives for them. That, however, would result in substantial differences between the incentive earnings opportunities for workers on different units. The two theories cannot be used simultaneously in the same plant for the same type of work. Finally, equipment is a minor factor in certain types of work. The efficiency of a carpenter who is building forms for pouring concrete cannot be expressed in terms of the capacity of his hammer. Here we are dealing with the capacity of the man, and, consequently, incentives applying to that type of work cannot be strictly equipment utilization incentives.

In setting norms for incentives, the distinction between the work-load and equipment utilization concepts is of considerable importance. Under the work-load theory, attention is directed primarily to the activities of the man, and, therefore, studies of the activities of particular men must be evaluated against some concept of "normal" or "base" performance. This involves "pace-rating," and the process contains difficulties introduced by subjective judgments.

On the other hand, in equipment utilization incentives, the emphasis is on the practical capacity of the process rather than on subjective considerations such as "normal" or "standard" rates of operation. Of course, activities of men are involved and must be evaluated if they occur *outside* the cycle of the machine process. But in most steel plant operations, that is normally a small proportion of the total cycle. This is equally true of much of the work in central maintenance shops. Consequently, subjective considerations are kept to a minimum in this type of incentive.

Setting of norms. I shall discuss the setting of incentive norms only for equipment utilization incentives. That is because my own experience has been with that kind of incentive and because I am convinced that, over the next decade, true work-load incentives will decline in importance. The discussion will be limited further to equipment utilization incentives based on a measurement of maximum possible production. Such incentives can be based on other concepts, such as normal or average production. However, many benefits of the equipment utilization theory are lost or weakened by the introduction of subjective determinations.

The method of setting norms is clearer if it is described in terms of a particular operation. Let us, therefore, examine the case of a rolling mill which produces concrete reinforcing bars. The raw material for such a mill consists of semi-finished steel, called billets, having a square cross-section of 2 to 4 inches (5.1 to 10.2 centimeters) and varying in length up to perhaps 40 feet (12.2 meters). Billets are heated in a furnace and then pushed into the first of a series of rolls which reduce the cross-section area, change the shape of the section, and elongate the billet. The finished bars are discharged from the last set or stand of rolls and are cut into lengths which allow them to fit on the cooling beds. There they are cooled sufficiently to be removed from the mill for straightening, cutting to lengths specified by the customer, and stored for shipment. Normally, all operations, beginning with the billet storage yard and ending with the storing of finished bars, are covered by one incentive plan, since all those operations are closely coordinated.

Figure 2 (page 266) shows the general arrangement of such a mill and the relationship of its components.

A rolling mill represents a series of engineering compromises. The cost of building a mill which can produce an equal quantity of all the different products made on it would be prohibitive. The mill which we are examining is designed to produce concrete reinforcing bars ranging from ¼ inch to 2¼ inches (.64 to 5.7 centimeters) in diameter. Those bars are made of five different grades of steel, each having different heating and rolling characteristics. The quantities of the various products of the mill purchased by our customers vary considerably. Thus, the mill is designed to be most efficient when it is rolling bars of sizes and grades in greatest demand. The heating furnace, mill stands, shear and cooling bed have characteristics properly coordinated for producing those bars. When bars of larger diameter are produced, the heating furnace limits the output of the mill, because the furnace transfers heat to the billets at a constant rate. Thus, the heavier the billet, the longer the time required to heat it to rolling temperature. The furnace can hold only a limited number of billets, and it can, obviously, hold fewer heavy billets. However, when bars having small diameters are being rolled, the entire operation may have to be slowed down because the cooling beds cannot accommodate all the bars which can be heated and rolled.

Thus the capacity of the entire mill differs for each size range and grade of product. Consequently, the first step in establishing norms for an incentive is to determine exactly how much of each size and grade can be produced within a specified period of time if the entire operation is at maximum efficiency and is not interrupted. This involves determining the maximum number of billets of each size and grade which can be heated, rolled, sheared and cooled within the stated period. Those determinations

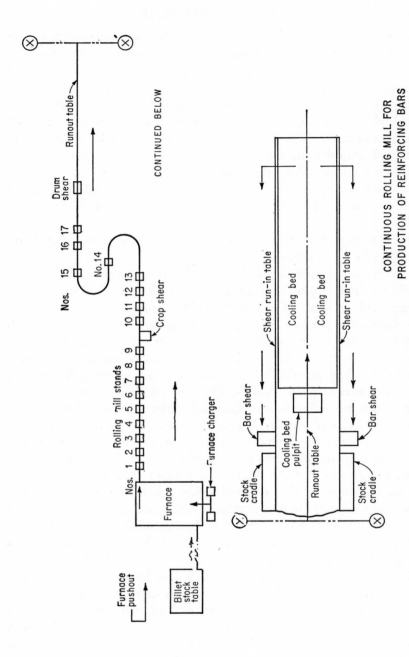

Fig. 2. The general arrangement of a rolling mill and the relationship of its components.

can be made originally for this type of mill by means of theoretical calculations. However, we know that rolling mills have peculiarities which require that the calculations be checked by observations of the actual rolling of various product sizes.

Rolling speeds are affected by the diameters of the rolls. Mill rolls become worn as material passes through them. A new roll revolving at a given rate passes material faster than a worn roll because it has a greater diameter. Attempting to adjust capacity figures for roll wear, which is not uniform on all mill stands, would introduce complexities unjustified by the higher degree of accuracy. We, therefore, calculate mill speeds in terms of mean diameters of the rolls; that is, the diameters halfway between those of new rolls and rolls ready for scrapping.

From the calculations described above, we can determine how fast each kind of product can be produced if the mill is operating at maximum speed, if the members of the crew do not become fatigued, if the size or grade of the product is not changed, if material is supplied to the mill without interruption, if the finished product is removed without delay, and if all mechanical and electrical equipment functions properly. Those are not, however, maximum *possible* speeds. Obviously, they cannot be attained for more than a short period of time, and so factors must be introduced to compensate for time lost because of changes of rolls and related equipment, fatigue, normal delays resulting from imperfect delivery of material or removal of product, and delays because of normal mechanical or electrical failures.

Each time the size of product is changed, guides which direct the bar into the proper grooves (or "passes") in the rolls must be moved. In addition, it is frequently necessary to change one or more sets of rolls. Those operations cannot be performed while the mill is operating. However, a number of guides and sets of rolls may be changed simultaneously. The time allowed for a guide change or a roll change thus depends on several factors, the most important of which are the locations of the guides and rolls, the numbers of guides and rolls being changed at the same time and whether or not spare mill stands are available so that another crew can prepare them for a new size while the mill is rolling. The minimum practical times required for such changes are determined by observation, and those times, factored in the manner described below, become incentive rates for the changes to encourage speed in making those changes.

One can determine with reasonable accuracy the maximum rate at which a product of good quality can be processed through a particular piece of mechanical equipment. There are, of course, variables which must be taken into account, because even machines do not always behave as their designers intended. But variations in machine behavior are insignificant compared with those in human behavior. This suggests that determining the maximum possible performance of workers for purposes of establishing norms for work elements characterized by human rather than machine activity, such as guide and roll changes, would be exceedingly difficult. However, the working habits of an experienced worker are remarkably consistent as to each component activity of his total job. Thus, if work elements are identified properly and in sufficient detail, a number of observations will show a strong concentration of times used in the performance of a particular element toward the lower end of the scale. There is far more uniformity to those times approaching *minimum* than there is to *average* times for individual elements or to total times for entire cycles. This is true even when the worker is intentionally working at a slow pace. Apparently it is nearly impossible for an experienced worker to slow down consistently throughout an entire work cycle. Almost invariably he performs some elements of the work at or near a maximum rate. Thus, it is possible to determine quite accurately his consistent minimum times for each work element. And, of course, consistent minimum times measure maximum possible performance.

Allowances for crew fatigue and normal delays are applied as percentages to base times for actual rolling or for guide and roll changes rather than as separate rates. Fatigue occurs over the entire day and cannot rationally be assigned to particular hours or pieces of product. Delays occur irregularly and unpredictably and are of varying duration. To a mill crew, ten delays of two minutes each affect incentive earnings as much as one delay of twenty minutes. However, it is difficult to record accurately very short delays. To reduce accounting problems and yet give workers proper credit for recurrent, minor delays, we treat those delays as occurring uniformly throughout the day. This means that delay allowances may be excessive on one day and inadequate on another, but over a week or two discrepancies tend to disappear. Major delays, in our case delays lasting longer than 30 minutes each, are covered by incentive only to the extent of the first 30 minutes. Beyond that, they are paid for at basic hourly rates.

Fatigue allowances are determined from standard tables widely used in steel manufacturing and in other industries. Special allowances are sometimes developed for conditions not covered by the standard tables, but this is rare. Allowances for delays, however, are based on extensive observations of mill operations and examination of routine records of delays maintained by those in charge of the mill. Unusual delays and the excess over 30 minutes of any common delay are eliminated from the data, and the remainder, which we call "inherent delay time," is converted into a percentage of total observation time.

We now have all the essential elements for the establishment of an incentive norm: (1) ideal or base time for processing each type of product, (2) base times for roll and guide changes and any other work elements which occur outside the rolling process, (3) a factor for fatigue of the crew, and (4) a factor for delays which can be expected in the normal operation of the mill. Base times increased by factors for fatigue and delays represent the minimum practical time required to produce a unit of product or to perform a work element. They are, therefore, practical measures of maximum possible production.

This description of the process of establishing incentive norms is, of course, much oversimplified. The mill used as an example produces a very simple range of products compared with other mills, some of which are able to roll several thousand different sizes and shapes. Obviously, the task of establishing norms increases in difficulty as the variety of products rises. Other operations in the steel industry present a bewildering variety of special problems in the determination of maximum possible production quite unlike those encountered in comparable determinations for rolling mills. But the basic principles involved are essentially the same.

Application of incentive norms. While the minimum practical time value is the norm for a unit of product or a work element in terms of maximum possible production, supervisors and workers are more likely to think of the norm as the time allowance (or standard time) for the performance of the work. The difference between the two figures is determined by the amount of pay which is associated with maximum possible performance and the level of performance which is associated with the basic rate. In our own case, a worker whose job directly affects the rate of output is paid an amount in excess of his basic rate in direct proportion to the amount by which actual output exceeds 72½ per cent of maximum possible output. Thus, a worker's pay for maximum possible output is 137.9 per cent of his basic rate, and, for output equal to or below 72½ per cent of maximum, his pay is his basic rate. A minimum possible time value for a unit of output or an element of work is converted to a time allowance (or standard time) by dividing it by .725 (or multiplying it by 1.379) so that standard time can be translated into money by multiplying it by the worker's basic rate.

Accordingly, the time allowance for an element of work which can be performed in a minimum of one hour is 1.379 hours. A worker whose basic hourly rate is $2.50 is paid $3.448 for the work if he performs it in one hour. If he performs the work in 1.1 hours, his performance is 1.379 ÷ 1.1 or 125.4 per cent, and his pay is at the rate of $3.448 ÷ 1.1, or $3.135 per hour worked. Because a worker is guaranteed his basic hourly wage rate, if he uses more than 1.379 hours for the job, he is paid $2.50 per hour.[2] If the work is performed by a four-man crew consisting of one worker having an hourly wage rate of $3.50, two men having hourly wage rates of $3.00 and one man having an hourly wage rate of $2.50, the allowed time is 5.516 hours, and the time of 1.1 hours spent by the crew on that work totals 4.4 man-hours. The performance is calculated as a ratio of allowed hours to actual hours worked (5.516 ÷ 4.4), and the result (1.254) multiplied by the respective basic rates. Thus, the total hourly earnings of the respective members of the crew are $4.389, $3.762 and $3.135.

Because time allowances for delays in the incentive rates are averages, incentive earnings can exceed those for maximum possible output on days when actual delays consume less than the average amount of time. Those earnings are, of course, balanced by other days on which delays consume more than the average. However, earnings can be consistently above maximum only if errors were made in the determination of norms.

Performance data as a management control device. Performance data expressed as percentages of base performance (base equals 72½ per cent of maximum) inform management as to labor efficiency on a particular operation. That is because actual performance (total man-hours used in producing a given output) is measured against a man-hours standard representing maximum possible sustained performance. Thus, if incentive performance rises from 105 per cent to 125 per cent, we know that output per man-hour has risen about 19 per cent on that operation. Furthermore, performance of 105 per cent indicates that efficiency is relatively low and should be improved.

If any of the conditions under which the operation is performed are changed (mechanical alterations, changes in crew size, and so forth), the incentive norms are also changed. We can thus determine from incentive performance data whether or not the men involved are working with the

2. The guarantee is actually applied on a daily basis. The worker is paid the greater of his total incentive earnings for the day or an amount equal to his basic hourly wage rate multiplied by the number of hours he worked on that day.

same relative efficiency after the change as they were before. Incentive performance data do not, however, tell us anything about the effect of the change on the efficiency of the operation itself.

Because incentives for different operations are based on the same "maximum" concept, incentive performance data tell management whether the men engaged in one operation are more or less efficient than those engaged in other operations. For example, if the incentive performance of the crew of an open hearth furnace is 125 per cent and the performance of a rolling mill crew is 110 per cent, we can say that the open hearth crew is using its equipment about 14 per cent more efficiently than the mill crew. Or, if two open hearth crews have incentive performances of 125 per cent and 110 per cent, respectively, one crew is about 14 per cent more efficient than the other. Those figures do not tell us anything, however, about the relative efficiency of the two open hearth furnaces.

Effects of applying the new incentive norms. The final test of incentive pay systems is how they encourage workers to improve their performance. Our experience with the system described above has convinced us that it is generally effective. We found, when we began to apply our concept of maximum possible production to specific operations, that there was a wide variation in levels of efficiency. There has been a tendency for workers who were performing well to continue to do so and for workers whose performance was poor or mediocre to improve it. We have had cases, however, of continued poor performance and other cases of deliberate reductions in performance for the purpose of trying to force management to change norms.

Our new measures have shown us that the opinions of operating supervision about the efficiency of workers are not reliable. Those opinions are, of course, affected by customary levels of performance and by the natural human desire to convince superiors that an operation is efficient. For example, at one of our plants, performance on a group of rolling mills had been unsatisfactory for a number of years. Studies for the purpose of establishing new incentive norms indicated that performance was about 90 per cent of the level equated with the hourly wage rate. Supervisors agreed that performance could be better but were convinced that the new norms could not be achieved. However, isolated cases of good performance had occurred, and the industrial engineers and top management were sure that the norms were proper. After a drive by management with the cooperation of the union to improve performance, the workers decided to see whether they could consistently equal or exceed the norms. As a result, performance on those mills has gone up to an average of 127 per cent. This represents, of course, a 40 per cent improvement in efficiency. Most of our gains have been less spectacular, but they have been substantial.

Some General Observations

The incentive system used here as an illustration provides a uniform rate of gain for increases in performance at any level. This is common practice among American steel incentive systems based on the entire basic hourly wage rate regardless of the type of incentive. That practice seems fairer than any other to the American worker. Past experience with progressive and regressive piecework systems has convinced him that a constant rate of gain is more intelligible and less subject to manipulation than any other earnings-performance relationship.

A worker under this incentive system is never paid less than his basic hourly wage rate. That guarantee is applied over an entire day or cycle, if the latter is longer, rather than to each hour or unit of work. This practice is universal throughout the steel industry in the United States.

Our incentives generally are based on output of acceptable product and do not, therefore, include factors or premiums for quality. Under many incentives, product which does not pass inspection is not counted for incentive purposes. Furthermore, under many systems, the worker who makes an unacceptable product which can be salvaged by further work corrects his error without additional time allowance. If another worker performs the salvage work, the worker who made the error may be charged for the other's work.

All members of a coordinated crew under our incentive system are paid the same rate of gain for a given job. Differences in skill and responsibility as between members of a crew are reflected in their basic rates. Because incentive pay is calculated by applying performance, expressed as a percentage, to the workers' basic wage rates, those differences are reflected automatically in their incentive pay.

Equipment utilization incentives distinguish between categories of jobs which affect output directly and those which have only an indirect effect on output or involve activities the output of which cannot be measured economically and with reasonable accuracy. Included among those jobs classified as "indirect" are service and maintenance jobs and jobs associated with processes, such as coke ovens and blast furnaces, controlled to such an extent by metallurgical and other requirements that workers can affect output only to a limited degree. Under our system, workers in such jobs are paid as their incentive above basic rates 67 per cent of the amount by which actual performance exceeds 72½ per cent of maximum possible performance. The measure of performance of service and maintenance workers is usually the actual performance of the operation or operations serviced. In the case of workers associated with processes controlled by metallurgical or similar requirements, incentive norms are determined and applied in the normal manner.

The success of incentives depends largely upon the workers' being convinced of their fairness. Relating incentive pay to basic hourly wage rates seems fair to the workers only if they are convinced that the hourly wage rates for the various occupations are properly related. This is accomplished by evaluating each occupation by means of a system agreed to by the union. That system has been in effect for fourteen years and has greatly reduced conflict over the proper rates for the respective occupations.

Conclusions

To anyone not accustomed to incentive systems relating to the performance of individual workers or crews, those systems may appear to involve unduly large administrative costs. Some operations are, of course, too small to warrant the establishment of properly designed incentive systems, and we do not apply incentives to those operations where the administrative cost exceeds any possible saving through the use of incentives. However, incentives for large producing units representing substantial capital investment usually result in major cost savings and justify the required administrative expenditures. In addition, the measure of the efficiency of a process provided by records of incentive performance is a valuable management tool. The types of studies required for the determination of accurate incentive norms are useful in indicating improved operating methods and work assignments. Often studies initiated for the purpose of establishing incentive norms have revealed inefficiencies in the way work is being performed, the correction of which fully justified the cost of the studies. And after the incentives are put into effect, records of incentive performance provide management with accurate and sensitive indicators of the efficiency of each operation to which an incentive applies.

CHAPTER 20

Wages and Labor Productivity in the System of Planned Direction of Czechoslovak National Economy

ANTONÍN ČERVINKA

Czechoslovak Academy of Sciences

Work is the natural condition for the existence and the development of every individual as well as of the entire society. Socially useful labor along with nature are the sources of society's wealth. Increase in social wealth, provided there is full employment for all able members of society, depends on the increase in labor productivity. This dependence of society's wealth on the level of labor productivity would seem to be a natural inducement to work and to increase productivity. However, this dependence does not act directly, regardless of the economic and social system of the country concerned; on the contrary, it makes itself felt through the social relations between people, among which economic relations play a decisive and determining role. As long as the means of production are produced, distributed, exchanged, and consumed with the interests of a certain class in mind, and as long as the finished product again becomes the property of only one part of society, increased labor productivity will concern only the owners of the means of production, while the producers will only be indirectly interested because of their need for subsistence. This indirect interest is not, as we shall show, sufficient incentive for increase in labor productivity under socialism.

In Czechoslovakia where all the means of production passed into the hands of society and where their ownership by the entire society has been established, the means of production are produced, distributed, exchanged, and consumed in production to satisfy the identical, fundamental interests of all members of society, and the resulting products are also distributed and exchanged in the interest of all. At least two conclusions follow from this: the basic interest[1] of every member of a socialist society coincides with interest in the growth of social wealth, and this creates a personal interest in each individual to increase labor productivity. The second conclusion is that these favorable conditions can only be used by a planned directive activity realized by organs representing the society. If this directive activity on the part of social bodies is to be effective and successful, it must be based on scientific knowledge and on a system of public administration which permits the activities of social organizations to be controlled. Distribution of national income is regulated by social organizations in the interest of the development of production, and increased production under socialism is best assisted by distribution that enables all members of society to develop and maintain their abilities as universally as possible. It is obvious that under such conditions, in addition to individual material interests, a considerable role is played by social moral interests.[2] Satisfying the requirements of the entire society thus becomes the general interest of all its members. These social interests are linked increasingly with individual interests. The more closely and more consistently social interests are linked with individual aims, the more do individual members of a socialist society identify social interests with their own and, by their activity, ensure their realization.

Development of social interests is assisted by the socialist state which ensures that a number of basic requirements are satisfied, free of charge and regardless of the amount of work done by individuals. This mainly concerns gratuitous health service, gratuitous school attendance, payment of 90 per cent of the wages during illness (treatment, including hospital expense, is free of charge), payment of pensions to superannuated persons, gratuitous school requisites for all school children, very reasonable communal meals, inexpensive holidays in sanatoria and recreation establishments with a guaranteed four weeks' holidays, and so forth. These benefits are accorded to all those who want them and are entitled to them. This, of course, in turn

1. By the term economic interest I mean particularly pronounced and relatively stable focusing of attention on satisfying certain economic needs.
2. Social moral interests are interests which have become part of the people's morale, where not any interest in oneself and in securing one's means of subsistence, but interest in others, in society, and in creative application of one's abilities in socially important work is predominant.

creates and continuously reproduces social moral interests in the development of socialist production and increased labor productivity.

Although we have so far stressed the importance of social moral interests in increasing labor productivity, and although experience has shown that some tasks could not be solved at all without the development of moral interests, in our economy the principle still applies that moral interests cannot develop at the present stage unless they are closely linked with personal material interests[3] in socially useful work. Since our citizens secure 75 per cent of all their requirements by buying for money gained by socially useful work, personal material interests must as yet be considered the most important factor influencing the increase in labor productivity. However, personal material interests can play an active part in relation to labor productivity only in connection with the existence of social moral interests.

Wherever social moral interests are totally lacking or are insufficiently developed, tasks are fulfilled only mechanically and for the sole purpose of earning money. This, however, is an insufficient, incomplete, and weak incentive for increasing labor productivity. Socialist economy requires that every able member of society take an active part, in a creative manner if possible, in controlling the economy, and that is impossible without the development of social moral interests. Conversely, however, people's participation in directing the national economy creates and strengthens social moral interests in their minds.

Our task is to discuss the relation between wages and labor productivity. Within the above-defined limits, wages are the decisive form of personal material interest, the most important incentive for using personal material interests. Other forms of remuneration have been abandoned recently, for example, in agricultural cooperative production, in favor of forms of remuneration very similar to wages in industry.

We consider wages in socialist production to be the share of the working people, determined by society and expressed in money terms, in the national income, proportional to the expended work. To simplify our explanation we shall narrow down the term wages to mean remuneration for work to productive workers. To define wages under socialism, a short explanation is required. Wage under socialism is chiefly a form of distribution according to work. Under what conditions can the work by an individual be a criterion of his share in the social wealth? It is a criterion only when there is social ownership of the means of production and the finished products and when

3. Personal material interest is to be understood to mean interest in the greatest possible quantity of use-values for individual consumption.

social organs elected or selected by the people act in the interest of public prosperity and are under the people's control. Where there is private ownership of factories, enterprises, soil, and so forth, the work of an individual—the producer—cannot be a criterion of his share in the social wealth, and under those conditions the wage is always the result of the struggle between those purchasing labor power and those selling it. In other words, it is an expression of the value of labor power.

Distribution according to work under socialism is not only possible but necessary. This necessity is a consequence of the fact that so far it has been impossible to eliminate completely the former division of labor, that the lifelong chaining of people to one trade still exists, and also that production has not yet secured an absolute abundance of consumer goods. In the second place, wage under socialism is the share in national income determined by society. Without all the means distributed among enterprises concentrated in the hands of the social organs, the socialist principle of distribution according to quantity, quality and social importance of work, could not be realized. Planned direction of wage policy together with planned direction of price policy by one center is the basic pattern of the entire control system of socialist economy under the conditions of commodity production. What is the role of the central social organ in controlling wages? The organ representing society as a whole does not and cannot determine the actual wage to be paid to each individual worker. The fixing of actual wages is in the hands of individual enterprises which alone are able to take into consideration all the peculiarities of working conditions. Of course, enterprises cannot fix wages arbitrarily because the central planning organ determines, from the total fund at society's disposal, the share for each branch of national economy and enterprise and also fixes the wage level in individual branches by means of tariffs and average wages. Under these conditions every actual wage is determined in general by organs of the entire society and definitely by the respective enterprises. Finally, the term wage is the money form of distribution, which means that remuneration as the share in the social product, determined by society according to work done, is paid in a special commodity—money. This money every individual then uses to buy consumer goods to satisfy his requirements.

We have now defined the role of wages in a socialist economy and explained our concept of the term wage. We may therefore pass on to the analysis of the influence of wages on the increase in labor productivity.

Proceeding from the definition of the term wage under socialism, we find that the influence of wages on labor productivity is considerable. Wages do not become a factor affecting labor productivity only in enterprises; since productivity of social labor is to a large extent determined by correct proportional labor distribution according to economic branches, wages begin to affect the level of social labor productivity at the stage when by their differentiation they influence the distribution of labor power according to branches and trades.

Because of the existing division of labor, our economy contains diverse types of work, different from each other by their specific character or the environment in which they are being performed. There are fundamental differences which form the basis of wage differentiation and preference. Wage differentiation cannot reflect all the differences which exist between various kinds of actual work. We are concerned only with basic differences. The basic traits distinguishing different kinds of work are complexity and laboriousness. In determining wages in individual branches we have to take these traits into account. If, for instance, we did not pay higher wages in a branch where complex work prevails, requiring greater physical and mental exertion, or where the environment is unfavorable, new workers would lose interest, and the result would be a shortage of products in that branch. At one time there was a shortage of labor in the mining industry. In view of the key position of that branch, it became necessary to raise wages there more perceptibly than in other branches of the economy. If that measure had not been taken, the shortage of coal might have caused serious disproportions in the entire national economy and eventually considerably slowed up the rise in social labor productivity. Wage planning, however, can avoid such unfavorable consequences. Taking into account the complexity and difficulty of the work, the central social organs adjust the wage level in individual branches so that the work is still attractive. In addition, the social organs, in determining average wages in a branch, also weigh the question of wage preference. The point is not only to ensure that all socially required work, stemming from the given degree of social division of labor, is carried out, but it is carried out proportionately. Although experience so far has shown that wage preference was usually applied in an unfavorable environment, we assume with a view to future development that it is not absolutely necessary to apply preference only in such cases. Preference may also be used for different reasons, but it is always connected with a relative shortage of labor. In this connection we want to add that preference is chiefly concerned with decisive trades in the various branches. To illustrate this point we quote examples of differences in workers' wages among branches of Czechoslovak industry from 1948–1960 in Table 64.

From Table 64 it is obvious that the main branches receiving preference are fuel, metallurgy, ore mining, power engineering, and heavy engineering. They occupy key positions. Experience has shown that the existing state of wage differentiation ensures on the whole a sufficient incentive for work in all trades. Although there is still a certain shortage of labor in some branches, it is precisely this differentiation which assists in overcoming such a shortage. It is necessary to add that these proportions of average wages did not develop spontaneously. They are the result of purposeful and planned activities of the socialist organs of society and are connected with the relative importance to our economy of the various industrial branches. Proportions concerning average wages in the capitalist prewar period were

Table 64. Index of workers' average gross wage in Czechoslovak industry.
(Consumer goods industry = 100)

Branch	1948	1954	1958	1960
Fuel	143	169	164	172
Metallurgy and ore mining	136	149	145	143
Power and hydraulic engineering	148	139	139	138
Heavy engineering	130	132	132	133
Building	126	125	128	124
Chemicals	117	121	118	119
General engineering	116	114	113	114
Foodstuffs	120	108	106	108
Consumer goods	100	100	100	100

utterly different. In 1935 the highest wages were paid in the leather industry, and miner's wages were lower than wages in the printing and clothing industries and in heavy engineering. The development of an independent socialist economy in our country also enforced a substantial change in wage differentiation, and Table 64 shows the results of this process. The new wage differentiation assisted the proportional development of Czechoslovak economy and considerably speeded up the increase in social labor productivity. It must be pointed out that we do not consider this wage differentiation to be permanent and immutable. We bear in mind that with the changed technical basis of production and with the attendant changes in proportions of trades required for the social production process, new trades emerge and others became extinct. In existing trades, the number of workers required changes because of increasing labor productivity and because of the changing requirements of society. Wage differentiation as a material incentive must therefore adapt itself to this development and act continuously to ensure the required number of workers in every trade in accordance with the development of society's forces of production.

Wages affect social labor productivity at the stage when, with a view to the requirements of the entire society, proportions of average wages in economic branches are being decided on. Wages differentiated according to economic branches influence the distribution of labor power toward the required proportions, and that has a considerable influence on the speed with which the entire economy develops in addition to assisting redistribution of labor power and increasing workers' qualification.

Another question altogether is the connection between increase in labor productivity and rising wages. Assuming differentiation among branches to have been already determined, the problem of a further rise in wages must be solved. In that, we proceed from two points of view. The first is that wages should rise in connection with increased labor productivity, not, however, at the same rate but slower than labor productivity. The second point is that in view of the non-uniform increase of labor productivity in different branches and even enterprises it would be wrong to fix the same relative increase of wages on a national scale. If, for instance, we assumed a yearly increase of labor productivity of 9 per cent and fixed the average wage increase for all branches and enterprises alike at 3 per cent, wage differentiation among economic branches might be wiped out within a few years since some branches have better possibilities of increasing labor productivity than others. In the direction of our national economy certain methods of relating increased labor productivity to wages have gradually emerged. An example of such a solution is the introduction of long-term norms determining the dependence of the increase in wage funds on the increase in labor productivity. In consequence of the validity of these norms, average wages also increase in connection with increased labor productivity. In view of the non-uniform increase of labor productivity, these norms cannot be the same for all branches of the economy or for all enterprises. They are therefore differentiated as to branches. For example, for the mining industry the norms of wage increase in connection with increased labor productivity have been fixed by the coefficient 0.5. That means that an increase labor productivity of 10 per cent permits a wage increase of 5 per cent. For light industry, wage increase in connection with increased labor productivity is determined by the coefficient 0.15, which means that if labor productivity rises by 10 per cent, wages may rise by 1.5 per cent. Differentiated long-term norms of wage fund increases dependent on the increase in labor productivity according to branches are based on calculations pertaining to the possibilities of the increase in labor productivity in different branches, and they are required to ensure the existing wage differentiation in spite of the difference in the rate of increase in labor productivity. Within individual branches of the economy the adopted norms are not being mechanically passed on to all enterprises alike; they are also being differentiated according to the existing reserves capable of use in the increase of labor productivity. The above-mentioned long-term norms create on the part of enterprises and collectives an interest in increased labor productivity since this arrangement puts financial means for increased wages at the disposal of enterprises. In addition to that, we want to point out that in view of improved proportionality of our economy and better uncovering of reserves, the coefficient of wage increase is raised in case an enterprise should take on a greater share of increasing labor productivity than the state plan requires. However, if the tasks are not fulfilled, the coefficient of wage increase is lowered. This practice has in recent years been introduced into our economic life and has already yielded favorable results. The unified system of directing socialist economy makes it possible to link the enterprises' material interest with increased labor productivity, to eliminate transitory and accidental fluctuations resulting in disproportionately large profits achieved by individual enterprises and branches, and to prevent in principle any violation of the wage differentiation among branches. The norms of dependence of wages on labor productivity introduced in our economy in 1959 have proved to be a suitable means of strengthening the interest of enterprises in increased labor productivity.

The nominal wage of an individual worker depends on the amount and the complexity of his work and also on the branch of economy in which he is working and what norms of wage increase dependent on increased labor productivity have been fixed for that branch. It goes without saying that measures taken by planning organs representing the entire society cannot solve every detail connected with the mutual relations of individual wages and labor productivity. They only state the principles involved. However, individual activity of workers is of great importance for an increase in social labor productivity. The means gained by enterprises because of increased labor productivity must not, therefore, be evenly distributed among all employees. In the first place, there are differences in wages among individuals. These differences exist, no matter whether productivity rises or not. However, the fact that more complex work demands higher wages creates an endeavor on the part of individuals to increase their qualifications. This is very important especially at the moment when complex mechanization and automation are being-introduced in Czechoslovak industry.

Learning several trades and increasing qualifications make it possible to avoid the detrimental consequences of automation. In addition, we want to arouse the people's interest in suggestions for improvements and innovations which, in detail, provide only small increases in labor productivity but in the whole enterprise lead to a high effectivity of production. Average wages increase in connection with increased labor productivity, but individual wages do not increase uniformly, they increase according to the contributions made by individuals. Experience has shown that a suitable form is the payment of bonuses for the fulfillment of tasks which increase labor productivity or for improvement suggestions by workers and other employees. This has meant that people who contributed to increase labor productivity received a lump sum according to the merit of their suggestions. In addition to this, we have also tackled the problem of incentives for workers who begin a new kind of work on machines and with equipment which enable labor productivity to be increased. Workers who change over to jobs on more efficient machines receive a guarantee that their wages will not be lowered, and for a certain time they even share in the savings achieved by these new machines.

In socialist society the chief means of increasing labor productivity is technical advance. During the period of transition from capitalism to socialism, labor productivity could to a large extent be increased by drawing on reserves inherited from capitalist economy, such as the use of idle production capacities, work for the unemployed, and so forth. However, as soon as the building up of socialism was completed and full employment and permanent use of production capacities were ensured, the main source of increased labor productivity became technical advance and, connected with it, application of scientific results in production. Support for technical advances cannot remain solely a matter of personal material incentives. The subject of this article, however, requires us to concentrate mainly on the way personal material interest influences technical development. Technical advance must be promoted by a deliberate system of material incentives affecting collectives as well as individual members of these collectives. Our relevant decisions are based on our conviction that under socialism increase in labor productivity is the result of the active participation of the broadest mass of working people and that every worker should therefore be personally and materially interested in this increase. Awakening and encouraging this participation is the task of personal material interest. The main form of personal material incentives promoting technical advance are bonuses and bonus systems. The giving of bonuses as personal material incentives to promote increased labor productivity has the advantage, in relating bonuses to the fulfillment of certain indexes, that material incentives succeed where it is of decisive importance in a given enterprise. With a bonus system, all three aspects of technical advance can receive an impetus: introduction of techniques connected with improved means of production, their use in the production process, and increased qualification of the workers. With bonuses it is thus possible to influence all the working people. It must be realized, however, that bonuses cannot have a social role (raise lower wages to the level of higher ones), they have an economic task (as an incentive to increase labor productivity). In this connection, we wish to point out that the consistent application of the principle that bonuses fulfill an economic task must also be in the interest of individuals. In addition to bonuses, basic wages also offer certain possibilities as incentives for increased labor productivity, especially concerning minor technical and organizational changes realized by the worker himself and in his interest in increased qualification. Experience proves that both piecework and time-work rates are suitable forms of incentives to raise labor productivity. Yet piecework ensures a better incentive for increased productivity in production, which is not continuous and where results depend mainly on the worker. On the other hand, in belt production and where emphasis is on the quality of products, time rates are more suitable. These assertions are supported by factual data from our economy.

Table 65. Distribution of wage forms in Czechoslovakia, September 30, 1959.
(In percentages)

Branch of economy	Piecework wages	Time-work wages with bonus	Plain time-work wages
Fuel	49	36	15
Metallurgy	44	38	18
Power engineering	1	97	2
Chemical industry	24	56	20
Heavy engineering	49	43	8
General industry	63	26	11
Consumer goods production	62	30	8
Foodstuffs	64	31	5

Table 65 shows clearly that in economic branches where the level of mechanization and automation is highest, the proportion of piecework wages is smallest. In power engineering, for instance, it is only 1 per cent, and in the chemical industry 24 per cent. It can therefore be assumed that with future technical development, the proportion of time-work wages with bonus will increase, and the proportion of piecework wages decrease. However, this process must not be precipitated, it must take its course in connection with the development of the technical basis of socialist society.

The foregoing exposition on the influence of wages on labor productivity may be summed up as follows: Wages in the system of the planned direction of Czechoslovak economy affect the level of labor productivity on the one hand by ensuring proportional distribution of labor power according to branches of economy and trades. On the other hand their increase is dependent on increased labor productivity, and this connection is achieved in regard to individual working collectives (norms of dependence of wage fund increase on increase in labor productivity) as well as in regard to individual workers (bonuses for increasing labor productivity and increase in basic wages). Wages are so far the most important incentive to increasing labor productivity but are by no means the only incentive under socialism.

CHAPTER 21

Wages as an Important Condition for the Growth of Labor Productivity in the USSR

E. I. KAPUSTIN

Moscow Research Labor Institute

The socio-economic content of wages as a form of distribution of material and spiritual values among the working people is determined by the nature of the relations of production in a given society and above all by the form of ownership of the means of production. It therefore differs fundamentally in capitalist and socialist countries.

In socialist countries, where the means of production are publicly owned and there is no exploitation, society determines the wage fund. The wage fund swells as the national income increases and is distributed among wage and salaried workers in accordance with the quantity and quality of their work in social production. Until such time as productive forces can ensure an abundance of the material and aesthetic values needed for switching over to distribution according to needs and when work has become the prime necessity of life for all members of society, distribution according to work is an objective necessity in socialist society. The main form of distribution according to work are wages and salaries, which under socialism are used as the principal way of advancing the material welfare of wage and salaried workers, and for giving workers a material interest in the results of their work.

In this paper we shall confine ourselves to setting forth the Soviet

Union's experience in using wages as a cardinal condition for materially stimulating the growth of labor productivity.

Growth of labor productivity is, as we know, determined by a series of complicated circumstances, among which technical progress, improvement in workers' qualification, rational and total use of labor time, improved work organization, and the strengthening of discipline on the job are major factors. Of great importance for the development of these factors in the Soviet Union is material incentive in the form of wages.

The organization of wages cannot be permanent, effected once and for all. It is being improved all the time, taking into account the changes that have taken place in the development of production, technical equipment, location of plants, work organization, the ratio of skilled workers to total labor power, and the gradual transformation of work into man's prime need. That is why substantial changes have been made in the USSR in recent years in the organization of wages and salaries, changes which have proceeded in two interdependent directions: (1) greater material incentive for workers, engineers, technicians, and office employees, through improving the system of wages, and (2) more exact reflection in wages and salaries of the quality of the work, the required skill, the conditions of work, the importance to the country of the branches of industry or of the national economy, and reduction in the difference in the pay levels. The wages of the lower-paid wage and salaried workers are being raised as the cultural and technical standard of the working people rises and their labor productivity increases.

The piece-rate system was widely used in the national economy of the USSR in the early five-year plan years. Directly linking workers' wages with the results of their work, the piece-rate system played an important part in ensuring a high rate of growth of labor productivity; it furnished material incentive for workers. By 1936 more than 75 per cent of the workers were on the piece-rate system. It was extensively used in those years because work organization in the industrial reconstruction period was characterized by a high proportion of manual labor (with the use of a hand tool), mechanized manual labor, considerable fluctuations in individual output, and workers specializing in specific operations.

Today, the ratio of piecework in the wage system has considerably declined, as individual branches of industry illustrate. While in the iron and steel industry the percentage of piece-rate workers in 1936 was 79.2 today it is 51.9 (including those paid the progressive piece rate). In the coal industry the percentage of piece-rate workers went during the same period from 80.7

to 48.8 in coal mines and to 51 in pits; in the chemical industry the decline was from 68.3 per cent to 45; in the oil industry it is down to 13 per cent; and in the machine-building industry to 57 per cent.

There is thus a very appreciable shift from piecework to time work, and underlying this process are a number of reasons, the most important of which is over-all mechanization and automation. In highly mechanized and automated industry the function of the workers is reduced more and more to watching the technological process, which proceeds automatically, and setting up and fixing the machine system. In automated production the functions of inspection and control are partly or wholly shifted to devices operating without direct human participation; all that is left for the worker to do is to start and adjust the operation and watch and check the work of the automatic installations. Automation eliminates fluctuations in output, and, thus, the differences in the output of individual workers and in collective output as well, gradually disappear and the use of piecework for stimulating higher output becomes inexpedient.

Another condition is wider application of chemical technology in industry. Chemistry in industry means strictly regulated technological processes by means of apparatus, processes lending themselves to the greatest degree of automation. But even where there is no automatic apparatus in the chemical process, the function of the individual workers operating the apparatus is, as a rule, not to turn out a specific number of articles but to keep to the established regimes and parameters. The material incentive for keeping to these showings by means of time work plus bonus is what ensures maximum output—in other words, the largest growth of labor productivity. This is confirmed to a certain extent by the high rate of increase in labor productivity in recent years in the chemical industry, with a considerable drop in the proportion of pieceworkers and a corresponding rise in the proportion of those paid time work plus bonus.

Of importance too is the growing smoothness in the functioning of plants, shops, and sections, as the technical level of production rises, and line production methods spread. Where every production group functions smoothly, overstock at the bench and varying output by workers are pointless. This can be fully seen today on conveyor belts operating with a fixed rhythm. Stimulation of this rhythmic pace and a schedule of output or production quota in the set unit of time become more expedient than to pay for each unit produced.

Playing a part in solving this question are the qualitative indexes. Such indexes reveal the rate of the technological process, the precision and the accuracy of the machining of the articles, the temperature regime, and so on. Successful production and, in particular, the quality of output, depends a good deal on keeping to these indexes. Under the piece-rate system the indexes are often upset. Besides, account must be taken of the expanding volume of experimental work, which does not lend itself to the usual rate setting, making it difficult to pay by the piece. An inseparable element of testing and experimental work is creative technical effort by workers for which no rate can be set in the ordinary way.

The reasons listed are not in effect only temporarily. On the contrary, as technical progress grows, their effect on the form of wages will gradually become greater.

The rise in the proportion of workers paid time work will stem from the decline in the number of pieceworkers in all branches of industry, but it is the machine-building, chemical, iron and steel, and food industries that apparently will exercise the chief effect.

This does not of course mean a purely mechanical shifting of workers from piecework to time work. Piecework will for a long time continue to play an important role in stimulating higher labor productivity in our country. It should also be borne in mind that in the Soviet Union the motive for freezing wages, as a reason for giving up piecework, does not exist, as it does in capitalist enterprises.

In view of this, the question arises: What are the conditions of production in which the piece-rate system produces maximum effect with respect to labor productivity?

The first condition for applying the piece-rate system is the existence of quantitative output indexes which correctly show labor input by the workers. Increased or decreased output or volume of work should correspond to the increased or decreased labor input. While this condition is, as a rule, found to exist in relation to basic, production workers, it does not in many cases affect auxiliary workers. For instance, there are no indexes for repair personnel on duty, and paying for work done by this personnel on the basis of output by the basic workers they serve is inadvisable because the output indexes of the basic workers do not properly reflect the labor input of the repair personnel. The repair personnel, for instance, might perform a very large volume of work when the output of the section served by them is small.

The other condition for using piecework is when there is a practical possibility of higher output by the workers with the particular machinery and the technology applied and when the possibility must not conflict with the interests of production. Where the worker has attained the planned productivity or output and he cannot exceed it because of the specific conditions of work, there is no longer any reason for stimulating a rise in output. Under these conditions the need arises for keeping output at the optimum level, and more suitable for this purpose is time work plus bonus, with the bonus paid either for turning out the set quotas or for qualitative indexes provided the planned quantities are turned out.

In some cases, because of specific production conditions, there is no need for increasing output of a particular product. An example is the production of steam for technological purposes at factories making reinforced concrete articles. In such plants the steam serves to maintain a certain temperature in the hardening chambers. To stimulate an increase in the quantity of the steam by means of the piece-rate system would only lead to using up more fuel than is necessary.

In industry we also find a large contingent of workers whose volume of work is constant to a considerable degree and is not directly related to the fluctuations in output. These are storekeepers, tool crib men, janitors, and so on, who cannot change the volume of work at will. Nor is there any need for increasing their work volume.

In all the enumerated cases piecework must yield to time work plus bonus.

Piecework requires fixing sound output quotas and keeping a record of their fulfillment, a record of individual articles turned out, or of units of output. To switch from time work to piecework is, as a rule, accompanied by a greater outlay on rate setting and accounting. That is natural and cannot in itself serve as a basis for holding that the piece-rate system is inefficient. Piecework becomes inexpedient only in cases where the outlays needed for making up proper rates and keeping records are higher then the expected or actual savings derived from the higher labor productivity because of payment by the piece. This is characteristic of experimental, maintenance, and a number of other jobs.

Recent years have witnessed the collective piece-rate system increasingly spreading in different branches of industry in the USSR. Serving as a basis for calculating pay under this system is not output of the individual worker but the collective output of the workers. Work is paid for either by collective rate or by individual piece rates. In the former instance, first the earnings of the whole collective of workers are calculated, and then the pay of each worker is determined, and the earnings are allotted accordingly. In the latter instance each worker is paid on the basis of fixed piece rates for the work performed by him, but the record of output is based on the last operation. In other words, the pay is calculated on the basis of the final results of the work performed by the workers collectively.

Indicating how widespread this form of piecework is are the following data. In the Donbas flat-seam coal mines, in which combines are widely used, 70 per cent of the miners are paid under the collective piece-rate system, and in the timber industry roughly 65 per cent of the workers employed on logging and some 50 per cent of those employed at the lower depots are paid this way. This is also true for most of the production workers in the iron and steel industry and a considerable number of pieceworkers employed in some machine-building plants.

Underlying the development of the collective piece-rate system are the substantial changes taking place at the present time in machinery, technology, work and production organization, and in cultural and technical standards, and skill of the worker, which more than anything else have determined the high rate of growth of labor productivity in the national economy of the USSR. Here we should note the introduction of large and highly mechanized machines and units, the development of apparatus-operated processes, and the extensive introduction of line-production methods. The higher general cultural and technical standards of the working people and their higher skills make it possible to begin training workers in a number of trades, permit working at more than one trade, and to switch workers in the work process. All of which, in turn, constitutes the basis for extensive development of the collective forms of work organization, to which the collective form of wage organization should correspond, and without which wages will lose their importance for stimulating the growth of labor productivity.

Collective piece rates with the application of general piece rates spur workers to learn different trades and to shift from one to another in the process of work. Under this system of payment, workers' specialization in performing particular operations is gradually eliminated, trades of broad scope arise, and workers' qualification grows. All this helps efficient planning of the working day and cutting down unproductive working time, and makes it possible freely to shift the working force around. It helps to develop in workers a sense of collective responsibility and mutual assistance on the job, to develop a communist attitude toward work. Under this system of payment for work, labor and production discipline rises, and workers develop mutual control. The collective piece-rate system is an incentive for workers not only to add to their experience and improve their skill but also to pass on the experience, skill, and knowledge to less qualified and less experienced workers. In other words, it provides an extended front for raising labor productivity.

Proper application of the collective piece-rate system results in increased output and higher labor productivity, better quality, and lower cost of production.

Substantial revisions have also been made in the bonus system. Showings for bonus purposes have been changed as follows: there has been a shift from paying bonuses for individual results to paying for the collective results of teamwork, section or shop; from chiefly for quantitative showings to quantity and quality, or even for quality only, and from using indexes chiefly applicable to large masses of workers to differentiated indexes.

Widely current now are bonuses for fulfilling production plans, since the plan for the sector, unit, or team is the basic production index, which is a component part of the state plan for the plant as a whole. Its fulfillment ensures normal work under the plan of all production operations with the particular production sector at the given enterprise and not infrequently in other enterprises as well, ensuring the growth of labor productivity not only in the particular section, but also throughout the enterprise, in the branch of industry, and in the national economy.

Acquiring great importance for increasing productivity of social labor is improved quality of output, which saves both living and material labor. This is why, in perfecting the bonus system, special attention has been given in our country to improving and extending the giving of bonuses for quality showings. Moreover, it should be underscored that quality showings for bonus purposes are always linked with the character and specific features of each branch of industry, each enterprise, and every production sector.

Improvement of the bonus system is also accompanied by change in the contingent of workers awarded bonuses. The introduction of a new bonus system in the course of improving the organization of wages has led to a considerable extension of the group of workers awarded bonuses, their number increasing in all branches of industry. In a large number of industries they make up more than 80 per cent of the total labor force.

In view of the decisive influence of technical progress on the growth of labor productivity, bonuses were introduced in 1960 for workers, engineers, technicians, and office workers employed in industrial enterprises, construction, transport, communications, geological prospecting, scientific research, and designing organizations for carrying out work on new techniques. Bonuses are awarded for developing and introducing new techniques, improved and economical machines, mechanisms, apparatus, instruments and other articles, new types of raw and auxiliary materials, for working out and introducing highly productive technological processes and advanced working methods. Bonuses for developing and introducing new techniques are fixed on the basis of the savings effected in the national economy as a result of this.

An important factor of increased labor productivity is the rise in the general cultural and technical standard of the workers—in other words, the higher quality of their labor. To what degree the quality of the work is reflected in workers' wages depends primarily on improvement of the wage-scale system and the role it plays in wages.

It is by means of the wage scale that pay reflects the complexity of the work and worker's skill, the conditions of work, and its importance for the national economy. And the improvement of the wage scales during the adjustment of wages followed the line of reflecting quality features more fully and more correctly.

This improvement was apparent in the making up of wage scales for branches of industry instead of for departments. Moreover, the number of industrial scales was cut down from roughly 2000 to 12. The number of salary scales was cut from 700 to 35, and rates of wages from several thousand to 43 (taking into account the different scales accorded different conditions of work). Thereby an end was put to the diversity in pay which earlier had existed in some industries and plants.

In line with narrowing the gap in the pay level of the lower- and higher-paid workers, the old wage rates, in which the rate for the highest category was 2.5 to 3.5 times the rate for the lowest-paid category, were supplanted by new rates, which, as a rule, reduced the gap 1.8–2 times. This required cutting down the number of categories themselves so as not to diminish but to increase the material incentive for workers to advance their skill. The introduction of six-category wage rates provided for a 12 to 14 per cent difference between categories, which is quite enough to have the worker palpably appreciate the extra money in his pay envelope on being promoted to the higher category.

A very big and difficult job was done at the same time in compiling new or fundamentally revising the old schedules of skills so as to take into account the changes which, in connection with technical progress, have taken place in the complexity of particular trades, the emergence of new types of jobs, and the disappearance of or radical changes in a number of old jobs.

Also, differences in scales of pay based on conditions of work conform more truly to the differences in the latter. In spheres of production where a large proportion of the jobs are time work, the differentiation in the scales of wages was retained in piecework and time-work scales.

However, the accounting of the quality of work in the pay does not depend merely on the perfection of the wage-rate system; it also depends on how much of the pay accrues under the wage schedule. The higher the proportion of the base wage rate and scale in pay, the greater is the effect of the wage-rate system and of the principles underlying its organization. It also influences workers to advance their skill, and it creates conditions which attract personnel in particular spheres of production and districts and inspires them to stay there. That is why in regulating wages a major problem was to have workers' pay conform to the wage scale to a larger degree.

The newly worked out wage rates and scales have made it possible to lift the proportion of the base wage rates in the pieceworkers' pay from 45–55 per cent to 70–75 per cent and of time workers' to 80–85 per cent. Experience has shown that such a proportion ensures optimum harmony between technically based output quotas and incentive systems of pay for high labor productivity. It also underscores the regulating role of the rates and scales system.

The revision of out-of-date output quotas and sharp increase in the proportion of technically based quotas brought uniformity into the pay of workers doing similar work, eliminated the elements of wage-leveling in remuneration for work done by workers of different skills, and established a close connection between pay and the results of the workers' labor.

The application of all these important measures in the wages system has increased the workers' material interest in higher labor productivity, lower production costs, fulfillment and overfulfillment of work quotas.

The growth of labor productivity in the Soviet Union is accompanied by a continuously rising material welfare of the people. For example, between 1950 and 1959 labor productivity in industry went up 86 per cent, real wages increased by 62 per cent, and money wages 26 per cent. Both money wages and salaries go up regularly as well as real income, the increase in which is due not only to rising money wages and real income but to the regularly growing benefits and allowances provided by the state budget and by enterprises from their own funds. These benefits and other payments, which include pensions, sick benefits, paid vacations, free or reduced-rate maintenance of children in children's institutions, allowances for children to parents of large families, extended installment payments on homes, free or reduced charges for accommodation in sanatoria and holiday homes, free tuition in all schools including higher educational institutions, stipends given students in colleges and secondary schools, free medical service, upkeep of clubs, and so on, are now already equal to one third the average earnings, and by 1980 will constitute half the workers' real income.

In analyzing the Soviet economy it is therefore necessary not to confine oneself to the ratio of growth of labor productivity to money wages, but primarily to examine the ratio of labor productivity to real income.

Today, a rise of 10 per cent in labor productivity in Soviet industry corresponds to approximately a 9 per cent increase in wage and salaried workers' real income and a 5 to 6 per cent increase in money wages. In other words, the other 3 to 4 per cent increase in real income comes from further cuts in prices, gradual abolition of taxes, and more benefits and allowances paid from public funds. To illustrate, the 1959–1965 seven-year plan envisages a 45–50 per cent rise in labor productivity in USSR industry for the seven years, and a 40 per cent rise in the real income of wage and salaried workers. Money wages will go up roughly 26 per cent on the average.

The new program of the Communist Party of the Soviet Union, on the basis of 4–4.5 increase in labor productivity in the coming twenty years envisages a more than 3.5 rise in real income per head of population, and this with further cuts in working day and week.

CHAPTER 22

The Movement of Labor Productivity and Wages in France and Germany from 1950 to 1960

FRANÇOIS SELLIER

Université d'Aix-Marseille

The effects of productivity on the movement of wages and on distribution differ according to the economy—whether it is one with a tight labor market or one with an abundant reserve of manpower. France and Germany are being compared to study this difference. During the period 1950 through 1960, France indeed faced a short labor supply, while Germany (at least until 1957–58) had impressive reserves of labor power.

In both countries, the real income of the workers has generally followed the growth of labor productivity. In France, however, the tightness of the labor market has resulted in disparities of movement—to the particular advantage of semi-skilled workers in certain industries, and of wage earners in the more industrialized areas—that exist much less in Germany. In Germany, the movement of wages seems to have been much more independent of the movement of productivity than in France from year to year. It would seem, therefore, that in a growing economy the labor market situation constitutes an important factor in determining the movement of wages and their distribution.

Germany

Average gross hourly wages of industrial workers have increased with the cost of living (more markedly between 1950 and 1951). In the years 1952–53, the cost-of-living index decreased, and wages increased. From 1954 to 1958, the cost-of-living index increased by 9 per cent, while hourly wages were rising by about 40 per cent. From 1950 to 1958, money wages rose by 85 per cent; real wages by 65 per cent. The interpretation of these figures requires an analysis of the structural shifts behind them.

The professional structure of labor. The professional structure of labor underwent a shift between 1951 and 1957, years for which precise sample surveys have been conducted.[1] However, this modification does not amount, as one might expect, to a general upgrading. (See Tables 66 and 67.)

Men. The per cent of unskilled workers fell in the aggregate and within the principal sectors between 1951 and 1957. However, it remained stable in the processing and production of metals. The percentage of semi-skilled workers increased in all activities and in all sectors except mining and power. In contrast, the number of skilled workers in the latter sector rose, while it decreased everywhere else and in the aggregate.

There is thus a noticeable concentration in the intermediate, semi-skilled groups.

Women. Here a different process is observed: On the whole there is a rise in the percentage of unskilled workers, a relative stability of the semi-skilled, and a considerable decrease of the skilled (from 11.3 to 5.1 per cent). In individual sectors, the professional structure is stable in mining and power, but the general tendencies can be seen everywhere else. They are particularly marked in construction, where the percentage of unskilled workers rose from 74 per cent to 90.5 per cent.

We have therefore a downgrading for women and a concentration toward the intermediate group for men. If the trend observed from 1951 to 1957 did extend to 1960, the average wage increases cannot be imputed, especially for women, to an upgrading factor. This factor has been active for men only in the mining and power sectors. Shifts in professional structure do not therefore explain the rise of the average wage.

The geographic structure of hourly earnings. A modification of the geographic structure of employment or of wages can explain the rise of a

1. *Wirtschaft und Statistik,* June 1959, p. 285; *Ergebnisse der Gehalts und Lohnstrukturerhehung,* October 1957.

Table 66. Sample distribution of male workers according to industry and skill categories in Germany,[a] October 1951 and 1957.

Industry	Number, 1957	Percentage of workers in each branch according to skill class					
		1957			1951		
Mining, construction materials, power	98,893	56.3[b]	26.8[c]	16.9[d]	49.7[b]	27.6[c]	22.7[d]
Iron and metal products and processing	209,679	53.5[b]	35.2[c]	11.3[d]	57.6[b]	30.5[c]	11.9[d]
Manufacturing	144,774	49.4[b]	33.7[c]	16.9[d]	55.6[b]	26.0[c]	18.4[d]
Construction[e]	119,707						
Total	575,053	55.0[b]	28.8[c]	16.2[d]	57.5[b]	23.9[c]	18.6[d]

a. Excluding the Saar and West Berlin.
b. Skilled.
c. Semi-skilled.
d. Unskilled.
e. Construction was omitted in the original table.

Table 67. Sample distribution of female workers according to industry and skill categories in Germany,[a] October 1951 and 1957.

Industry	Number, 1957	Percentage of workers in each branch according to skill class					
		1957			1951		
Mining, construction materials, power	1,924	1.4[b]	9.8[c]	88.8[d]	1.7[b]	9.6[c]	88.7[d]
Iron and metal products and processing	38,288	1.2[b]	40.2[c]	58.6[d]	1.9[b]	43.0[c]	55.1[d]
Manufacturing	107,146	6.5[b]	49.0[c]	44.5[d]	13.8[b]	46.6[c]	39.6[d]
Construction	264	2.3[b]	7.2[c]	90.5[d]	16.3[b]	9.7[c]	74.0[d]
Total	147,622	5.1[b]	46.1[c]	48.8[d]	11.3[b]	45.3[c]	43.4[d]

a. Excluding the Saar and West Berlin.
b. Skilled.
c. Semi-skilled.
d. Unskilled.

weighted average of wages, if employment in low wage areas falls relative to employment in high wage areas. On the other hand, if, given a stable structure of employment, wages in high employment areas grow relative to those in low employment areas (widening of the geographic distribution of wages), the average wage increases.

Table 68 gives a picture of the geographic structure of male and female wages, with base 100 in September 1950–51, for Northern Rhineland and Westphalia where 39 per cent of all industrial workers are located. At that time, the highest male wages were in Hamburg (+9.2 per cent) and the lowest in Bavaria (−10.1 per cent). In 1957–58, the lead of Hamburg wages over those of the Rhineland was only +5.1 per cent. However, the lag in Bavarian wages had worsened (15.8 per cent). For other regions, where average gross hourly wages are always inferior to those of the base region, the gap decreased slightly in Schleswig-Holstein and remained more or less stable in Lower Saxony, thanks to manpower migrations which made possible a reduction of the relatively high unemployment rate in these two regions. Everywhere else, the lag increased. (Hesse: from 1.2 per cent to −8.5 per cent; Rhineland Palatinat: from −8.7 per cent to −12 per cent; Baden-Wurtemberg: from −2.9 per cent to −9.8 per cent; Bremen: from −1.3 per cent to −3.8 per cent). Thus we have a rather general widening of differences between the high employment zone where the major investments have taken place, and all others where the lesser pace of investment has caused a relative depression of male wages (with some exceptions due to migration). Except for Hamburg, Schleswig, and Lower Saxony, it can be said that the average gross hourly wage for men has gone up most where it already was highest. Furthermore, employment has increased more in high wage areas than in others.

Table 68. Average gross hourly wages in Germany for industrial workers.[a]
(Northern Rhineland and Westphalia = 100)

Section	Men			Women		
	September 1950–1951	August 1953–1954	August 1957–1958	September 1950–1951	August 1953–1954	August 1957–1958
Schleswig-Holstein	91.4	91.8	92.5	91.0	90.0	93.2
Lower Saxony	91.9	91.6	91.5	94.6	97.1	97.3
Northern Rhineland and Westphalia	100.0	100.0	100.0	100.0	100.0	100.0
Hesse	98.8	95.7	91.5	97.3	98.0	94.0
Rhineland	91.3	90.2	88.0	85.5	86.4	88.9
Baden-Wurtemberg	97.1	94.7	90.2	98.6	99.4	97.7
Bavaria	89.9	88.5	84.1	97.6	97.9	94.0
Hamburg	109.2	106.6	104.9	106.9	107.4	106.1
Bremen	98.7	97.4	96.2	100.0	104.4	102.8

a. Mining excluded.

The structure of hourly earnings by skill and sex. From 1951 to 1957, the structure of earnings according to skill has remained approximately stable for men, while for women the gap between skill classes has increased. (Table 69). However, the increase of average gross hourly earnings has been of the same order of magnitude for men and women (47.7 per cent and 47.9 per cent respectively). These seemingly contradictory results (different evolution of skill differentials, parallel evolution of the average wage) are explained by the different movements of male and female professional structures between these two dates: relative stability among skilled men workers, for whom wage increases are the largest, and fewer skilled workers among women. One may conclude that modifications of the professional structure have exactly compensated for changes in differentials, or that the downward shift of women has left the best paid among them in the skilled and unskilled groups and downgraded the least paid from the skilled group to semi- and unskilled. It is probable that the shift in professional structure has not led to a fall in individual earnings. It has perhaps been effected through classifying women who entered the labor market on a new basis.

(1) The wages of men and women have increased on the average at the same rate.

(2) For each sex, the wages of categories with decreasing membership (skilled and unskilled for men, skilled for women) have increased *more* than the wages of categories with increasing membership.

(3) Nevertheless, for men as for women, the wages of unskilled workers have increased more than the average. It is the reverse for semi-skilled workers. The wages of skilled workers have increased approximately like the average (although a little more) among men and definitely more among women.

The structure of hourly earnings by industry. There was relative stability of inter-industry differentials between 1950 and 1960. This does not exclude special patterns of behavior in certain industries. Construction and metal processing follow the average trend of increase. However, the patterns of behavior of the steel industry relative to the mean would justify taking 1955 as the pivot year between a period of widening and a period of shrinking of the differentials. As it is, the importance of 1955 is revealed essentially in the movement of unemployment. From 1,597,766 unemployed in 1950 and 1,220,607 in 1954, we go to 928,328 in 1955. The figure for unemployed males falls by 17.7 per cent between 1954 and 1955, that for females by 8.5 per cent.

Table 69. Average hourly earnings of workers in Germany,
November 1951 to October 1957.
(In pfennig)

Skill class	Men			Women		
	Nov. 1951	Oct. 1957	Increase (per cent)	Nov. 1951	Oct. 1957	Increase (per cent)
Skilled	173.6	256.6	47.8	105.1	169.2	61.0
Semi-skilled	159.8	231.4	44.8	108.8	158.6	45.8
Unskilled	139.7	208.6	49.3	99.9	149.2	49.3
Total	163.9	242.0	47.7	104.5	154.6	47.9

Nineteen fifty-five is also the year when the first signs of resistance to longer working hours appeared.

We may conclude that in the German case the movement of increasing labor productivity paralleled an increase in the proportion of the semi-skilled and even of the unskilled (women, in this case), whereas the wages

Table 70. Unemployment in Germany, 1950, 1954–1960.

Year	Total	Men	Women	Percentage change from preceding year	
				Men	Women
1950	1,579,766	1,126,064	453,702	− 4.7	+ 0.3
1954	1,220,607	806,458	414,149	−29.2	+13.6
1955	928,308	570,631	357,677	−17.7	−18.5
1956	761,413	469,855	291,558	−11.5	−15.4
1957	662,334	415,796	246,538	+10.5	− 9.2
1958	683,117	459,351	223,766	−30.1	−31.0
1959	475,725	321,252	154,473	−50.5	−50.6
1960	237,428	160,543	76,885	—	—

of the semi-skilled grew relatively less than the others. Industry differentials were unaffected by the trend of productivity but reacted more to the trend of employment.

German statisticians rely on two distinct factors, one in relation to labor productivity in the industrial sector, the other corresponding to the productivity per worker in the whole economy.

Labor Productivity in the Industrial Sector and the Movement of Wages

Average wages and average productivity. Industrial labor productivity moved almost the same way between 1950 and 1955, whether measured per man-hour, per manual worker, or per wage and salary earner; however, the curve of production per earner began as early as 1955 to part from the other two. Starting with 1956, a gap appears between production per hour on the one hand—(growing at about the same rate as before) and production per manual worker or per active earner—(shifting to a lower level between 1956 and 1958). The curve of production per manual worker rises again from 1959 at the same rate as hourly production, while, because of a continuing decrease in the proportion of manual workers among wage and salary earners, the curve of production per earner rises at a lower pace. The break in the trend, from the standpoint of labor productivity, occurs therefore between 1955 and 1956. Nineteen fifty-six is the first year when a fall in the growth rate of productivity per worker follows a decrease in working hours. It is only in construction that the rate of growth of the hourly wage changes in the same period, but as the result of an exceptional increase in the previous year. It remains stable or increases in most other industries. From the standpoint of hourly wages, an inflection point (fall in the growth rate) appears from 1957 to 1958 in steel, construction, metal processing, and clothing. (Yet, the year 1958 offers no real peculiarity, except for the stop in growth of employment and the temporary increase of male unemployment, 10.5 per cent.)

The fall in the growth rate of wages does not affect the average wage index of the whole industrial sector until 1959.

Another inflection point of the wage curves is supplied by the transition from 1954 to 1955. Everywhere the growth rate increases, while it often had decreased until then, particularly for average male wages. Again, 1955 is revealed as the pivot year; it is the year of maximum growth of the employment rate and of massive decrease in unemployment. The two downward inflection points for wages (1952–53 and 1957–58) appear therefore to have been generated by a shift in the labor market that was unfavorable to wage and salary earners. The two upward inflection points of 1954–55 and 1959–60 are characterized on the contrary by two massive reductions in unemployment (—30 per cent in the first and —50 per cent in the second case, for men).

On the other hand, the movement of productivity per man-hour for the whole industrial sector seems unrelated to the movement of wages.

The movement of wages and of productivity by industry. From 1950 to 1958, and for the following three years, the movement of average gross hourly wages (men and women) and of productivity for the major sectors of activity is shown in Table 71.

Table 71. Gross hourly wages (male and female) and production per worker/hour in different industrial sectors in Germany, 1958.
(1950 = 100)

Sector	Productivity	Hourly wages
Mining	150	189
Raw materials	164	182
Equipment	162	180
Consumer goods	146	181
Food	168	186
Total	158	182

There is no correlation between the productivity increase of a particular sector or industry and the increase of wages. Even from the standpoint of an ordering by magnitude of increase of both productivity and wages, no parallel is noticeable, either for 1956 or for 1958.

Table 72. Ordering by magnitude of increase in Germany, 1956 and 1958.

Sector	Productivity wages			
	1956		1958	
Mining	1	1	4	1
Raw materials	3	2	2	3
Equipment	1	3	3	5
Consumer goods	5	5	5	4
Food	2	4	1	2

An examination of the relationship between productivity and wages by sector would thus confirm the observation made when studying the relation between wages and the average movement of productivity; that is, the labor market of the sector has more influence on wages than variations in productivity.

The Aggregate Productivity of the Economy and the Movement of Wages

The aggregate productivity of the economy results from the productivity of the various sectors and from the share of each in the total. The sectors listed in the German social accounts for the domestic gross product are: (1) agriculture, forestry, fisheries; (2) production of goods; (3) trade and transportation; (4) production of services. Sector 2 is by far the most important and has had the highest rate of growth in volume as well as in value. Sector 3 has increased like the domestic gross product in volume and in value but less than 2. The same holds approximately for sector 4, although its rate of growth in volume has been below that of the domestic gross product. This is due to the particular impact of wage increases of this sector. Sector 1 has had the weakest growth in volume and in value, and the per cent rise in prices it experienced is almost as large as in 4.

There has thus been no growth beyond measure of the third sector in Germany—3 + 4. This sector has grown on the whole like the aggregate of the domestic gross product, and the latter has been essentially influenced by the movement of industrial production. A comparison of the curves showing the movement of value produced in the various sectors and of the curve of money wages shows an almost perfect parallel between the latter and the curve of agricultural production.

The sharp growth of aggregate productivity seems partly explained by the relatively slow growth of the low productivity third sector, and by the importance of employment increases in the second sector. The reserves of manpower, freed from the first sector or gained through immigration, have made possible a lessening of tensions in the labor market, except in certain industries (coal, extraction). However, because of the low weight of these industries in the labor market, the exceptional raises which they produced had no repercussions on other industries.

Conclusions

Growing productivity and employment in a relatively loose labor market led to:

(1) Downgrading in the professional structure (increasing percentage of semi-skilled and of unskilled women)

(2) Increasing differentials in geographic structure

(3) Decreasing differentials, on the average, between skill categories and industries

If one excludes the increase of differential between skill classes of women, only geographic differentials definitely increased, perhaps as a consequence of weak incentive for mobility in a loose labor market. On the contrary, increase of wages were more favorable to workers in lower wage industries and skills, perhaps as a consequence of weak competition between workers for higher wages, on the one hand, and between employers for scarce labor, on the other.

France

In France from 1954 to 1959, the purchasing power of the average hourly earning increased by 60.5 per cent. The gross national product per man hour (all activities) increased by 64.5 per cent. The aggregate productivity of factors with weighted man hours increased by 47.5 per cent.[2] The net productivity of labor[3] with weighted man hours increased by 65.5 per cent. The purchasing power of wage and salary earners has thus increased more than the aggregate productivity (which is due in large part to the elimination of the deficit in the balance of payments), but less than the net productivity of labor or than the gross national product per hour.

Table 73. Geographic differentials in all categories in France, 1956–1960.

Legal abatements[a] applicable to the SMIG[b]	1/1/56	1/1/57	1/1/58	1/1/59	1/1/60
2.22	12.9	13.6	16.2	16.8	16.4
4.44	16.4	18.4	19.1	19.2	19.1
6.67	20.5	22.4	23.3	23.3	22.8
8	22.6	24.3	24.9	24.9	24.6

a. Starting with April 1, 1956.
b. Legal minimum earnings.

2. The aggregate productivity factor according to L. A. Vincent, *Etudes et Conjuncture: Revue Mensuelle,* May 1961, pp. 393–402, is the ratio of the growth of gross production index (consumption plus gross capital formation plus exports) to the growth of production factors index (labor in the three sectors, including civil government, plus amortization and imports).
3. The net productivity of labor, according to Vincent's definition, is the ratio of the growth of net production index (gross production minus amortization and imports) to the growth of labor index in the three sectors (including civil government).

This fact must be attributed mostly to the importance assumed by the tertiary sector in the economy at large.

Geographic disparity of average hourly wage rates and professional structure. The geographic differentials (base 100 in 1949) are stable for a given skill class. However, the average differentials (all categories) between "provincial" wages and wages in Paris have not ceased to grow since 1956 in all the wage zones. In the period 1949–56, the average rise of wages was already a little stronger in Paris than in the provinces.

This paradox of a stability of geographic differentials for each skill category and of their widening in the aggregate can be explained by a change in the structure of the labor force.

If one observes the movement of wage rates in industries where the proportion of semi-skilled workers is largest—mechanical and electrical industries (44 per cent) on the one hand, textile industries (45 per cent) on the other—it appears that geographic disparities have greatly increased for semi-skilled workers, while remaining stable for unskilled and skilled workers. The mechanical and electrical industries in 1954 employed more than half the semi-skilled workers of the secondary sector, according to statistics of the labor ministry (564,000 out of 1,086,400), and more than one sixth of all workers of this sector, according to the same sources.[4] Employment decreased in the textile industry; the activity index (hours worked times number employed) fell by almost 20 per cent between 1950 and 1960. But it increased by about 15 per cent in metal processing, the total employment of which is thrice that of the textile industry.

The increase in geographic differentials for the semi-skilled category, in industries which employ the largest number in this grouping and whose total personnel (for mechanical-electrical industries) has increased most, can explain the growth of average geographic differentials (all categories) for the whole industrial sector, even though the geographic differentials *for each skill category in the whole industrial sector* did remain stable.

It seems therefore that the distribution of labor by skill class in France, between 1950 and 1960, has moved toward a relative increase of the number of semi-skilled workers, as it has in Germany. However, while in Germany the wages of the semi-skilled have fallen relative to the rest, the opposite seems to have happened in France, though in a mild way and in the Paris region only. This can be attributed to the relative tightness of labor markets in France.

4. J. Marchal, J. Lecaillon, L. Gualielmi, F. Sellier, A. Touraine, P. Vignaux, *Les Qualifications et le Comportement des Salariés* (Paris, 1957), p. 164.

Wage disparity by industry. During the period, the stability of differentials by skill level is accompanied by a widening of geographic differentials. What of the differentials between industries and activities?

From 1949 to 1956 (January 1, 1957), average indexes of the wage rate observed in the various sectors by the labor ministry have moved in very similar ways, since the coefficients of increase varied from a low of 2.08 (metals) to a high of 2.28 (paper-cardboard). From 1956 to 1960, the average of all activities in the census (including trade and health) increased to 144.3 (base 100 in 1956). The industries in best position are printing (159.3), road transportation (149.5), and chemicals (148.7), all of which have a dominantly male labor force. The activities in lowest position are health (138.9), textiles (139.9), and clothing (140.7), all of which have a chiefly female labor force and are mostly located in the provinces.

It can thus be said that variations in inter-industry differentials are only the reflection of differentials observed between regions and between sexes, account being taken of probable variations in the skill distribution.

As a conclusion bearing on the structure of wages during the period, one may say that technical factors (skill level, production sector) have played a *stabilizing* role in maintaining differentials, while sociological and geographical factors (sex and region) have contributed to *increasing differences.*

The same situation is more or less observed in Germany. But the main difference lies in the fact of relative increase for semi-skilled wages in France, and relative decrease in Germany, whereas in both countries numbers in this class seem to have grown.

Labor Productivity in the Industrial Sector and the Movement of Wages

Average wages and industrial production. The movement of average money wages has been largely influenced in France by the strong and irregular variations of the cost of living, especially from 1949 to 1952 and from 1955 to 1957. It is thus necessary to examine the relations between wages and productivity—that is, to observe real wages.

While industrial production has increased by 52 per cent in 1959 (including construction) and by 58 per cent (excluding construction), production per man-hour has increased by 44.6 per cent between 1952 and 1959 (without construction). Differences in the bases of calculation used for industrial production and for wages prevent, however, an exact comparison of the two series. Still, it can be estimated that from 1949 to 1959 industrial production per man-hour has increased by about 50 per cent. In the same period, the index of purchasing power of average hourly earnings has increased by 60.5 per cent.[5]

A comparison of annual variations in average real earnings and of annual variations in industrial production shows a certain coincidence in the direction of variations in Table 74.

Table 74. Comparison of annual variations in average real earnings and industrial production in France, 1951–1959.

Years	Earnings	Industrial production	
1951–52	decrease	decrease	=
1952–53	increase	stability	=
1953–54	increase	increase	=
1954–55	decrease	decrease	=
1955–56	increase	increase	=
1956–57	decrease	decrease	=
1957–58	decrease	decrease	=
1958–59	increase	decrease	+

Except from 1952 to 1953 and from 1958 to 1959, the movements of the two series are in the same direction. The 1952–53 contradiction is explained by the quasi-general strike of August 1953, which led to wage increases in the second semester of that year. The 1958–59 contradiction is the result of the sharp fall in purchasing power following measures taken by the government in 1958, a fall which employers attempted to compensate in part in 1959 to avoid trouble.

However, while the direction of variations in growth rates is comparable, the amplitude of these variations is definitely not. At one time, variations in the growth of earnings are sharper than in production; at another time, the reverse is true. Except from 1957 to 1958, however, the amplitude of variations in earnings is less than in production. A valid conclusion is that in France, except in years when social (1953) or political (1958) unrest led to special constraints in wage adjustment, the movement of wages has been in the same direction as the movements of production and productivity. The stability of behavior can be explained by the constantly tight situation of the labor market, the variations of which have not, as in Germany, introduced an independent factor in the movement of wages.

5. Vincent, *Etudes et Conjoncture*, May 1961, p. 402.

Table 75. Annual variations in production and average
real hourly earnings in France, 1950–1959.

Year	Annual variations of production	Annual variations of average real hourly earnings[a]
1950		+1.5
1951	+12.5	+1.3
1952	+ 1	+3.6
1953	+ 1	+4.3
1954	+ 8.9	+7.9
1955	+ 8.1	+5.8
1956	+ 9.2	+8.8
1957	+ 8.5	+4.7
1958	4.2	−2.6
1959	3.4	+1

a. L. A. Vincent, *Etudes et Conjuncture: Revue Mensuelle*,
May 1961, p. 402, Table 6.

Wages and productivity by industry. Here we are concerned with real wages. An analysis of the relationship between wage movements and labor productivity will be limited to the mechanical and electrical industries on the one hand, and the textile industry on the other. In both cases, we shall study the behavior of the most sensitive wage—the wage of semi-skilled workers.

In the mechanical and electrical industries, we have noted the very peculiar pattern of the semi-skilled wage—its variation when paid in Paris or in the other regions, or to men rather than to women. The wage of the unskilled or skilled worker moves approximately like the wage of the semi-skilled worker, and the series are confounded until 1954–1955. After that time, the semi-skilled wage in the Paris region increases faster. As it happens, it is in this period that the growth rate of production and productivity per wage and salary earner increases most. It is also in this period that the growth of employment in the industrial sector increases significantly. The conjunction of demand for labor and demand for the product leads therefore to an increase in the wages of workers whose productivity is the major determinant of wages—the semi-skilled. However, the movement of wages other than the semi-skilled coincides almost exactly, since 1952, with the movement of productivity per earner. It can thus be said that the general productivity of labor in the industrial sector has determined real wages, but that a *productivity rent* has been paid to the male semi-skilled of the highest wage areas, in periods of labor market tightness and production increase.

In the textile industries the situation has been quite different. Employment has decreased since 1951, and productivity has increased more than production. In this industry, sex disparities are stable, but we have again for the semi-skilled worker a widening of disparities between regions. The movement of semi-skilled wages in various areas traces the upper and lower limits of the general movement of wages. We shall thus take this movement as a basis of comparison. Here, the wage of the lower-zone semi-skilled has moved like productivity per wage and salary earner in industry, except from 1953 to 1954, following a government raise of the minimum wage whose effects were particularly felt in low-wage industries. However, the wage of the upper-zone semi-skilled worker has risen faster than productivity. Yet, this wage was very sensitive in 1957–58 to the fall in productivity, and production suffered in the industrial sector, while the wage of the lower-zone semi-skilled did not react. It is thus obvious that the movement of labor productivity has determined the real wage, the highest wages being more sensitive to falls in productivity (and production) than the lowest wages.

Aggregate Productivity of the Economy and Movement of Real Wages

The gross national product per man-hour (for the whole economy) and the purchasing power of average hourly earnings have moved in the following manner between 1954 and 1959.

Table 76. Aggregate productivity of the economy and movement of real wages in France, 1954–1959.

Years	Earnings	GNP M/H[a]	
1950–51	Increase	Decrease	
1951–52	Decrease	Decrease	=
1952–53	Decrease	Increase	=
1953–54	Increase	Increase/st	=
1954–55	Decrease	Increase	+
1955–56	Increase	Decrease	+
1956–57	Decrease	Increase	+
1957–58	Decrease	Decrease	=
1958–59	Increase	Increase	=

[a] Gross national product per man-hour.

Note that the movements of rates of variation in earnings and in aggregate labor productivity (GNPM/H) are much more independent of one another than was the case for earnings and production in the industrial sector. If cases where one of the elements is stable are counted as positive correlations, it can thus be said that variations in industrial production have more influence on wages (and industrial wages in particular) than variations in aggregate productivity per man-hour. Out of eight cases (from 1951 to 1959) there are five cases of co-variation and three cases of independence, while previously we had seven cases of co-variation and one case of independence.

Over the whole period, variations are more or less comparable to real earnings according to whether we take:

Real earnings	153.5
Aggregate factor productivity	140.5
Net labor productivity	157.5
Gross national product per man-hour	156.5
Gross national product per active person	155

(1949 = 100, 1956 weights, 1949–1959)

It is the figure of gross national product per active person which is closest to real earnings; this would indicate a relative equality in the sharing of earnings between wage and salary earners and other economic agents.

Conclusion

This comparison of French and German evolution in the field of wages and productivity shows that, in both countries, wages moved more in relation with production or labor market conditions than with productivity conditions *stricto sensu*.

Production variations were important in France, where the labor market was tight; labor market conditions were important in Germany, where the labor market was loose.

The relation between wages movement and productivity, if clear in the long run, is rather obscure in the short run. It is especially obscured by changes in industrial and professional structure. Hence, any institutional link between productivity and wages in the short run does not seem to be workable.

PART IV

Technical, Managerial, and Organizational Factors Affecting Productivity

CHAPTER 23

Planning and Organizing the Increase of Labor Productivity in the German Democratic Republic

GERHARD RICHTER

Karl Marx University

When Fourastié stated in his work *The Great Hope of the Twentieth Century* that Soviet economists had recognized from the very beginning the essential role of labor productivity and that they had made the increase of labor productivity the main goal of their plans, he was certainly right. It seems to me, however, that this estimation of labor productivity is not a question of subjective thinking on the part of Soviet economists, but that the target of economic policy as a whole, the purpose of which is to satisfy to the fullest possible extent the needs of all members of society, clearly points to this central problem.

In accordance with the very nature of a planned economy, increase in labor productivity also involves a definite task, as a result of adapting (and with the object of harmonizing) the possibilities in the factories to the requirements of national economy. All economists share the opinion that labor productivity is theoretically and practically one of the most difficult coefficients to comprehend. It is not necessary, therefore, to explain at length why the planning of a systematic increase in labor productivity gives rise to further problems. It is well known that the uniform direction of means and effort towards a maximum increase in labor productivity will secure for the national economy more stable results than the spontaneous and uncoordinated sum of individual developments. But, on the other hand, experience and constant methodological improvements are necessary to achieve a comprehensive realization of the superior possibilities existing in the economic system. The questions connected with the increase in labor productivity, as well as its planning and measurement, are thus most important in economic research in all socialist countries and, in my opinion, will be more so in the future.

In this study, I shall confine myself to the practical questions of planning and organizing the increase in labor productivity. I shall not touch on such questions as general standardization, socialist reconstruction as the systematic long-term establishment of the structure of social division of labor, manufacturing methods with the aim of increasing labor productivity and facilitating work, or the movement of innovators and rationalizers. My main concern will be questions of method, of how economic tasks, with regard to the increase in labor productivity, are planned and fulfilled. I shall make broad use of documents from the State Planning Commission of the German Democratic Republic, as well as of papers worked out by the central labor productivity research group attached to the German Academy of Sciences of Berlin.

Planning the Development of Labor Productivity in Industry Down to the Factory Level

Although we distinguish the planning of labor productivity down to the factory level from the planning of labor productivity inside the factory, it is an established fact that we are dealing with a *single* planning process —that is, the adaption of the possibilities of the factory to the requirements of the national economy. It is only the difference in methods (breaking down of concentration within national economy on the one hand, and the tapping of all existing possibilities of increasing labor productivity in the factory for the new plan proposal on the other) that makes a separate treatment of the problem seem appropriate.

During the first few years of this practice, the development in planning and summing up actual labor productivity was put on an equal footing with the development of per capita output of production workers. Because of the well-known phenomena of changes in the assortment of products with different portions of material labor as well as changes in cooperation, alterations in per capita output do not correctly reflect changes in labor productivity. This is true in the first line for smaller units—that is, first and foremost for the factory. With the increasing degree of concentration, a compensation of the deviations in the different factories takes place, as the controlling calculations undertaken by the Central State Administration of Statistics demonstrate. These possibilities of influencing per capita output favor the manufacture of products which have a high input share of materials and require little human labor, as well as cooperation even under economically unfavorable conditions.

At least as unsatisfactory is the fact that the per capita output gives no sufficient indication of the factors influencing the development of labor productivity and does not permit the breaking down of the plan for increasing labor productivity to the various divisions and manufacturing departments of the factory. Thus, economic theory and economic practice were persistently concerned with the possibilities of exactly grasping labor productivity from the point of view of measurement and analysis, but the principle of uniformity of planning and accounting naturally makes for an improvement in the methods of fixing and raising labor productivity.

At present we can report the following: the centrally administered, nationally owned industrial enterprises based their plan proposals for the development of labor productivity in 1962 on the time-sum method. In compliance with this, preparatory work had been underway for some time. The application of the time-sum method in basic industries goes back to 1957, and since 1958 the machine industry has also been planning the development of labor productivity by this method. As a result of an analysis of these experiences, a central working group attached to the Academy of Sciences, in conjunction with representatives of the State Planning Commission, the Central State Administration of Statistics, and the factories, worked out a *draft of guiding principles for the planning and measurement of labor productivity according to factors on the basis of the time-sum method*. In accordance with directions issued by the State Planning Commission, the branches of industry work out specialized guiding principles, which take into consideration the peculiarities of the branch concerned and the resulting variants of the time-sum method, and guarantee a uniform planning and accounting for the branch of industry as a whole.

In establishing time-sum methods, the *obligatory* form of planning and judging results of labor productivity in the factories, we looked for the following requirements: (1) Opening to a maximum the reserves for an increase in labor productivity; (2) Pointing out the most important factors for developing labor productivity; (3) Breaking down the coefficients of rising labor productivity to master divisions, brigades, and working places;

(4) Developing an economically founded relationship between labor productivity and wages.

The draft of guiding principles briefly describes the economic content of the time-sum method and makes clear that national accounting cannot dispense with the gross-production method (plan-price method and time-sum method). Rules for the following fields are laid down in the individual sections.

The program of coefficients for measuring and planning includes increase of labor productivity in relation to the actually expended labor time and such outage time as can be influenced (in per cent): (*a*) with regard to basic production workers; (*b*) with regard to basic production workers (taking into consideration the rejected scrap); (*c*) with regard to output, including scrap; (*d*) with regard to output, including scrap and such outage time as can be influenced; (*e*) with regard to the work performed by employees in industry, including scrap and such outage time as can be influenced, and increase of labor productivity in relation to the nominal labor time (in per cent); (*f*) with regard to employees in industry.

Relative changes in the consumption of human labor (in hours and workers) affect the draft of guiding principles. The State Planning Commission demands that the growth of labor productivity be determined according to the following major factor groups: (*a*) introduction of new techniques, especially measures toward mechanization and automation as well as technical-organizational measures; (*b*) decrease of labor input for salvaging damaged goods and for guarantee work; (*c*) improved use of disposable labor time. (Main stress should be laid on the first factor.)

These changes, which are derived from the definite measures concerning ways and means as well as time limits, to include all employees from basic production workers up to industrial personnel, indicate the demand for manpower for the needed output in the plan year.

The draft of guiding principles would be incomplete if it did not at the same time contain directions for working out the guiding principles for separate branches of industry. An appendix therefore refers to such questions as uniformity of planning and measuring of labor productivity, the treatment of such labor time which can only be calculated indirectly, the periodicity of coefficients, the statements on the level of labor productivity with the help of the time-sum method, the inclusion of new products in the production program, the comparison of the plan with actual performance as well as references to working out valid regulations for separate branches of industry. The separate branches of industry have included very

useful ideas in their guiding principles and have brought the problems close
to the people through broad discussions.

The fact that, on the national economy level, calculations are based on
the per capita output, while the factories are obliged to plan and account
on the basis of the time-sum method, shows that somewhere in the economy
a transformation of per capita output to time-sum method must take place
to bring both into accord. This happens in the Associations of Nationally
Owned Enterprises (VVB). They, of course, receive their plan of labor
productivity growth already adapted as an index on the basis of the gross-
production method—that is:

$$\frac{\text{Index of gross production in fixed plan prices}}{\text{Index of the average number of production workers}}$$

These plan values are now broken down to the factories which build up
their planning method according to the time-sum method, taking into consideration in this context the effects of carrying through the plan of new
technique. The influence of these measures on the volume of auxiliary production should also be noted.

Results show that the factories have studied the reality of the plan task
which they received on the basis of the gross-production method with the
help of the time-sum method. In the joint stipulation of the tasks through
factory and VVB which now follows, three variants are possible:

(1) The development of gross production (assortment and volume) as
    well as the development of the average number of production
    workers and total industrial employees can be planned in accord-
    ance with the plan directive.

(2) Time studies have proved that the number of production workers
    and industrial employees is not fully required in order to fulfill the
    plan of gross production (assortment and volume). In this case, it
    has to be decided whether (a) output should be extended, (b) man-
    power dismissed, or (c) investments curtailed.

(3) Time studies have proved that the number of production workers
    and industrial employees is not sufficient to fulfill the plan of gross
    production (assortment and volume). In this case it has to be
    decided whether (a) output should be reduced, (b) additional man-
    power employed, or (c) investments increased.

As a rule, the first variant should be obligatory in a plan for the development of labor productivity. In the case of the variants 2 and 3, (*a*) and (*c*) are, of course, interrelated, and it is quite possible that the original tasks set with regard to the volume of production, the number of workers, and the volume of investments may be changed.

In order to guarantee the reality of the plans and to make possible a detailed control of their fulfillment, it is, of course, not sufficient just to stipulate the figures regarding production and manpower. Hence, the founding of the plan for the growth of labor productivity in 1962 comprehends the following sections:

(1) Plan proposal for the development of gross production (in fixed plan prices) and the volume of production of the factory (in labor time units) as well as for the labor time, in respect to manpower requirements.

(2) Plan proposal for the development of labor productivity following the plan-price and the time-sum method.

(3) Proof for the planned smaller or greater labor time and manpower requirements.

(4) The main motives for the planned development of labor productivity and for the smaller or greater labor time requirements.

(5) Proof of the major factors affecting productivity and their influence on the smaller or greater labor time requirements.

Through the uniformity of methods, the VVB is in a position to summarize the savings in labor time and manpower achieved within its sphere of responsibility according to major factor groups, to calculate an average index of the growth of labor productivity for the VVB, and to compare this with the result attained on the basis of the gross-production method (plan-price method).

Of course, the changes in planning for labor productivity depicted above cannot be successfully carried through on a short-term basis or through administrative methods. That is why intensive preparations on a broad level have been carried out in the nationally owned factories since the middle of 1961. It is intended to create prerequisites so that, starting from 1962, with regard to the main share of production, the time-sum method may be used to plan and judge the results of the development of labor productivity.

The development of labor productivity in the factories. Planning the development of labor productivity in the factories is the most important link in the chain of rapidly increasing labor productivity in the national economy as a whole. For here measures to produce the planned coefficients are debated and studied, and, in the last analysis, it is here that the actual growth of labor productivity in the day-to-day work process is determined. The last step is taken by workers in the factories, and they must therefore receive highly efficient guidance. It was often surprising to note how very able the workers are, how well they recognized the essential facts when solving the problems connected with the introduction of the time-sum method.

Since, in the discussions concerning the introduction of the time-sum method, one often hears the view that this method will meet with extraordinary difficulties in plants with single-part or small-lot production, we shall choose such a factory to explain our point and indicate possible solutions. The factory concerned is one producing tobacco-processing machinery. Annually about fifty types, of each type up to about 20 units, are produced. Only in the case of two types does the number of units amount to about 100. Every machine has from 200 to 3000 component parts, not counting the standard parts, involving up to 26 passes of operation. Production is characterized by a high proportion of human labor input. Work per machine amounts to from 300 to 7000 hours. The factory is organized in 36 production divisions, which are concentrated to 16 divisions in the accounting sector. Through this concentration, short-term accounting has been simplified, but the control of the various divisions cannot be dispensed with and thus makes for additional effort.

The main problem in connection with the application of the time-sum method, which has to be stressed again and again, is to prove the percentage of labor time to be saved, the laying down of measures necessary to achieve this end, and their control. This is possible on the basis of the plan of technical and organizational measures (TOM-Plan), the most important section of the plan of new technique. The latter also includes the steps to be taken towards further mechanization and automation, which play an important role in cutting down labor costs per unit. In order to give a plastic impression of the numerous measures contained in the TOM-Plan, we shall present a number of examples:

Fitting out lathes with clamping chucks: expected benefit 300 hours, 1800 D.M.
Centralized manufacture of bearing bushings: expected benefit 150 hours, 1800 D.M.

Setting up an improved assembling technology for machines: expected benefit 17,650 hours, 106,000 D.M.

Introduction of sorting for cash accounting: expected benefit 130 hours, 260 D.M.

The plan contains about 120 such items. In each case the department, where the measure in question is to be used, is identified, the person in charge is named, and the time limit for its introduction is calculated.

Setting up such a plan requires a great deal of work, and no one man could manage it. However, since it contains the ideas of the whole working collective, the efforts demanded of the individual are small, and the plan itself is the concentration of numerous useful suggestions stemming from the experiences of daily work.

Of great moment for systematic growth in labor productivity in the factory is the final check on whether the measures really produce the expected benefit. When the measures have been introduced, it is not satisfactory merely to estimate the probable total benefit for the rest of the year. The actual saving of labor time in a factory is expressed by the pay slips. If the standard time is changed, the TOM register number and the new standard time are written on the pay slip, which receives a special mark in the form of a TOM stamp. If the proofs are already in the workshop, the standard time on the pay slip is changed. In case measures are carried out before a pay slip has been issued, the new standard time and the TOM register number are imprinted. The savings are determined centrally by the expert responsible for the TOM. To this end, he receives from the accounting sector the pay slips with the TOM stamp. The working time actually saved is written down on special sheets (one for each individual measure), and at the end of the month the savings of the individual production divisions, subdivided according to measures, are extracted from these sheets and made evident in total. Beside these monthly savings, accounts are settled on a cumulative basis, and the percentage fulfillment established.

Difficulties arise in connection with operations that have been fully eliminated. In the factory in question, this problem has been solved as follows:

If alterations in design are being carried out, the design office announces which operations are to be eliminated, which are to be altered, or which new operations are to be included. The technological document is altered, and the new time, as well as the time to be eliminated, are written down on a separate sheet. This is carried out individually for production divisions and single operations. Thus the TOM expert is in possession of the document, which enables him to concentrate the savings, in respect to the additional requirements of the division. It is, however, not yet possible to establish the number of units for which the savings have been made. All that is known is when the change is to take place. The department for production preparation therefore bases itself on the obligatory output plan which indicates in which month a given product is to be produced. It is thus guaranteed that savings will be made evident only for the actually delivered products.

At the same time, the measures laid down for growth in labor productivity show which groups of industrial personnel are affected, so that it is possible to construct the index of basic production workers to auxiliary production workers, and from here to the industrial personnel, as envisaged in the draft of guiding principles. A difficulty arises because the wage office makes no difference between basic work, auxiliary work, and scrap. Such a differentiation first takes place in cost accounting. Since the latter is carried out on a money basis, the number of hours has to be ascertained by conversion. To this end, the basic wage allowed for the performers in question in the production divisions is divided by the average standard hour rate. Checks have proved that this calculation is sufficiently exact.

I should like to abstain from touching on the numerous technical problems of planning and accounting which arise in this context. I simply wanted to submit an example in the field of single-part and small-lot production to demonstrate that planning an increase in labor productivity as well as dependable control and, thus, the proof of the actual effectiveness of the factors, are possible on the basis of a justifiable expense of working time.

The working group attached to the academy has produced a number of examples in factories. These experiences can be used in the course of the general planning of labor productivity, and, at the same time, they are useful for the factories in respective branches of industry. We are convinced that the efforts which have been made and which are still being made to introduce this method are not in vain, because in this way all managerial activity in the factories and in the associations of nationally owned factories will be economically more securely founded. Time control now takes its place next to the hitherto dominating financial control of economic processes. As Marx said: "In the final analysis, all economy is reduced to time."

CHAPTER 24

High-Level Manpower, Productivity, and Economic Progress

FREDERICK HARBISON

Princeton University

Introduction

The productivity of modern industrial societies is dependent upon many factors. Among the more obvious are the availability of natural resources, the levels of technology employed in production, and the nature and quantity of investment in plant, machinery, and equipment of all kinds. In his paper, Professor Myers has suggested that the structure and philosophy of management may be one of the most important determinants of enterprise efficiency. I shall stress "brainpower"—or high-level manpower—as a strategic determinant of both enterprise efficiency and the over-all productivity of an economy. I shall argue that the wealth of a nation may be measured in significant degree by the levels of education and the kinds of skills possessed by its people. I shall also make the assertion that *investment in man* is equally as important as investment in material things, and that a country's rate of growth is dependent as much upon the development of human resources and the rate of human capital formation as upon its rate of physical capital formation.

This presentation is divided into four parts. The first defines the terms and concepts which are used; the second deals with some general statistics relating to the ever-increasing use of brainpower in the United States; the third summarizes the findings of some case studies of the use of manpower in business enterprises in the United States since World War II; and the fourth draws some speculative inferences from the available evidence.

Some Definitions of Concepts

Human resource development is a broad term which refers to the recruitment, placement, commitment, training, and education of a country's labor force. The word development implies that members of the labor force are "upgraded" as they acquire greater skill and know-how through education, training, or experience. Thus human resource development is associated with growth and progress—with improving the creative and productive capacities of man.

High-level manpower is a term used to designate the most critical or strategic human resources in a country. Obviously, it is difficult to say precisely what persons or occupations fall into this category, and there may be significant differences in classification in various countries. High-level manpower may be delineated in two ways: a) on the basis of occupational categories, and b) on the basis of normal or common minimum educational requirements. Tentatively, I would suggest inclusion of the following in the high-level manpower category:

(a) *Occupational classification*

Senior category:

Administrators, executives, managers and principals of sizable establishments in government, industry, commerce, transportation, education, and so forth.

Professional personnel including scientists, doctors, engineers, architects, agricultural officers, lawyers, university professors, and so forth.

Political leaders, officers of police and armed forces, judges, senior union leaders, and so forth.

Intermediate category:

Sub-professional personnel (technicians) in agriculture, engineering, and the like—also nurses, higher supervisory personnel, chief clerks, laboratory assistants, and so forth.

Teachers (qualified but not university graduates) in secondary schools, technical schools, teacher-training institutions, and (in some cases) primary schools.

(b) *Educational classification*

Senior category:

University graduates, "college" graduates (four years beyond equivalent of high-school in United States or secondary school certificate in British system).

Intermediate category:

Persons with one-three years specialized education beyond high school equivalent in college, technical institutions, teacher-training college, and so forth.

Skilled manpower, according to my definition, would include such groups as highly skilled manual workers and craftsmen, lower-level supervisory personnel, and clerical workers. The required education for this group would normally vary from two to four years beyond the primary level, and in most cases would include some training in vocational, trade, or technical schools.

Unskilled and semi-skilled manpower would include all those in the working force not classified as high-level or skilled. The required education may vary from none at all to completion of eight years of primary school.

Human capital formation, as used in this paper, is the process of acquiring and increasing the numbers of persons who have the skills, education, and experience which are strategic for the economic and political development of a country. It is associated with investment in man and his development as a creative and productive resource. It includes investment by society in education, investment by employers in training, as well as investment by individuals in time, money, and foregone earnings in their own development. Such investments have both qualitative and quantitative dimensions—that is, human capital formation includes not only expenditures for education and training but also the development of attitudes toward productive activity. The development of high-level manpower obviously requires greater investment than the development of skilled manpower, whereas relatively little investment may be required to develop unskilled and semi-skilled manpower. Thus, *human capital formation* is largely, though not entirely, associated with development of high-level manpower.

High-level manpower may be accumulated by a country in several ways:

(1) It may be *imported from abroad* through a variety of means such as technical assistance, expatriate enterprises, hiring of consultants, immigration, and so forth.

(2) It may be *developed in employment* through on-the-job training, in-service programs of training, management development programs, part-time adult education classes, and many other means. It is also developed in employment through such measures as better organization of work, creation of appropriate incentives and attitudes, and better management of people.

(3) It may be developed through *training and education of new generations of manpower* (through formal education in schools, technical training centers, colleges, universities and other institutions of higher learning).

The Trend of High-Level Manpower Growth in the United States

The trend toward greater use of high-level manpower in the United States is reflected in practically every statistical indicator that can be found. Unfortunately, there are no statistics for "high-level manpower" as defined in this paper, but there are figures for a few occupational groups within the high-level manpower category, and these may be used as indicators of the probable trend for the category as a whole. Table 77 gives some of the more important indicators for the forty-year period prior to 1950.

From these indicators we can make several generalizations. The percentage increase of persons in all the high-level manpower occupations (including managers and professional personnel) has been much greater than the percentage increase in the labor force as a whole. The same is true of clerical workers. The increase in manual and service workers barely kept pace with the increase in the labor force. The great decline has been in the farm worker category. The occupations showing the sharpest rise are scientists, engineers, and teachers in higher education. In these occupations the rate of increase is significantly greater than that of real gross national product. The high rate of increase in teachers in higher education reflects a great expansion in enrollment in colleges and other institutions of higher learning. In 1910, for example, the percentage enrollment of the population eighteen–twenty-one years old in the institutions of higher learning was only 5 per cent; by 1950, it had increased to nearly 30 per cent. This sixfold increase in the percentage of persons pursuing higher education is in itself an indicator of the rate of growth of high-level manpower relative to both the growth of the labor force and real gross national product. There was no equivalent percentage expansion in primary and secondary school teachers simply because by 1910 the United States already had for practical purposes

Table 77. Growth indicators: population, manpower, and gross national product in the United States, 1910 and 1950.

	1910	1950	Percentage increase 1950/1910
Population[a]	91,972,000	151,179,000	64.4
Total labor force[b]	37,291,000	58,999,000	58.2
Total professional, technical, and kindred workers[b]	1,758,000	5,081,000	189.0
Scientists[c]	2,000	39,000	1850.0
Engineers[c]	84,000	534,000	535.7
Teachers (higher education)[d]	36,480	246,722	576.3
Teachers (elementary and secondary education)[e]	523,210	962,174	83.9
Managers, officials, and proprietors, except farm[f]	2,462,000	5,155,000	109.4
Clerical and kindred workers[f]	1,987,000	7,232,000	264.0
Manual and service workers[f]	17,797,000	30,445,000	71.1
Farm workers[f]	11,533,000	6,953,000	39.7
Real gross national product[g]	36.3	110.6	204.7

a. National Science Foundation, *Scientific Personnel Resources*, NSF, 1955, p. 9, Table A-4.

b. U.S. Bureau of the Census, *Historical Statistics of the United States, Colonial Times to 1957* (Washington, 1960), Series D-72-122, p. 74.

c. National Science Foundation, *loc. cit.*, Table A-5. Includes those Ph.D.s in the physical, biological, and earth sciences as well as those in engineering, medicine, nutrition, and pharmacy. It excludes anthropology and psychology, for example.

d. U.S. Bureau of the Census, *op. cit.* Series H 262-315, pp. 210-211.

e. *Ibid.*, Series H 234-245, p. 208.

f. *Ibid.*, Series D 72-122, p. 74.

g. U.S. Congress, Joint Economic Committee, *Productivity, Prices, and Incomes.* 85th Cong., 1st Sess., 1957, Index of real gross national product in 1947 dollars.

a system of universal primary education and was well along in the development of secondary education.

The occupational group "managers, officials and proprietors" is largely composed of shopkeepers and proprietors of very small enterprises, and most of these really should not be considered in the high-level manpower category. If managers and officials in sizable enterprises could be broken out, their percentage increase would undoubtedly be several times greater than that for the group as a whole. The difficulty in all long-range comparisons of this kind, of course, is the lack of really reliable historical data.

Within the last two decades the rate of increase in many critical high-level manpower occupations has been maintained, if not accelerated. For example, the number of employed scientists and engineers increased from 261,000 in 1938 to over a million in 1960, and it is reasonable to expect that this number will double by 1970. This reflects in part the tremendous increase in expenditures for scientific research and development (a rise of 900 per cent in the period 1947–1961). The Princeton case studies of industry, which are summarized in the next section, indicate that there has been also a sharp rise in managerial and administrative personnel in medium and large-scale industry. These trends, as we shall argue later, are probably related to scientific and managerial innovations. At the same time, employment of production workers in industry has increased hardly at all, and the future trend is likely to be one of absolute decline. But, nonproduction workers of all kinds, and particularly those in the high-level manpower category, are increasing at a rapid rate. Indeed, over 90 per cent of the total increase in manufacturing employment in the decade 1947–1957 was accounted for by nonproductive workers.[1]

Case Studies of Manpower Use in U.S. Business Enterprises

The nature of the changes taking place in the employment structure of American industry and particularly the reasons for the increasing proportion of required high-level manpower are suggested in a study of trends in 50 companies which we made at Princeton University several years ago.[2] As one might expect, we found that in the decade following World War II the proportion of high-level manpower rose sharply in a few companies, increased gradually in most, and decreased in relatively few. A statistical summary of the shifts in the occupational structure within the firms studied is contained in the Princeton study. However, *the explanations given by the companies* for the increased use of managerial, administrative, professional and technical personnel are much more significant than the figures themselves.

1. Murray Wernick, paper delivered before the Business Statistics Section of the Cleveland Chapter, American Statistical Association, March 4, 1958, Table 1 A.
2. Samuel E. Hill and Frederick Harbison, *Manpower and Innovation in American Industry* (Princeton, 1959).

Very early in our study we became aware of a number of possible explanations for increased use of high-level manpower in American industry. According to some who have written on this subject, the multiplication of managers, and professional personnel could be a consequence of "empire building," pure and simple. Others have suggested that the proliferation of reports required by government agencies was a major factor. Still others have attributed the changes to automation, increased investment in research and development, and the quickened pace of process and product innovation. Company reorganizations, new fads in administration, and high tax rates on profits have also been advanced as possible explanations. Our task in undertaking the study was to try to determine what the truth was. The following are the major conclusions of the study:

(1) The increase in high-level manpower as a percentage of total employment in the companies studied was primarily the result of *innovation*. Both technological innovation, which was associated with the introduction of new products or processes, and organizational innovation, which created new administrative units and new systems of management, required increases in executive, administrative, professional, and technical staff. Technological innovation also changed the composition of employment by decreasing the employment of production workers. Automation usually resulted in greater use of highly trained specialists at the same time that it made possible substantial savings in manual or clerical working forces. In other words, automation nearly always led to substitution of both high-level manpower and capital for unskilled and semi-skilled personnel.

(2) In a very general sense, it appeared that the rate of innovation in enterprises governed the rate of increase in use of high-level manpower of all kinds. In other words, the companies showing the greatest increases in nonproduction workers as a proportion of total employment were invariably those which had made the most spectacular or far-reaching changes in products, processes, and organization. Those which experienced little or no increase in nonproduction workers were invariably the companies which had made the fewest changes in technology or organization.

(3) The companies which themselves developed new products or designed new processes or systems of administration showed a much sharper increase in employment of high-level manpower than those which relied primarily on outside consultants or machinery suppliers. For example, a computer manufacturer requires vastly more high-level manpower than the firms which use the computers. Our evidence indicated, in other words, that the companies which originated new processes, products, or administrative

methods invariably used a greater proportion of high-level manpower than the companies that merely adopted the innovations which others had developed.

(4) The development of innovations has apparently affected the occupational structure of entire industries. For example, between 1947 and 1955 the ratio of high-level manpower increased sharply in aircraft, electronics, chemicals, ordnance, and petroleum. Each of these industries developed innovations for its own use, or for use by others. The proportion of high-level manpower increased less rapidly in the textile, apparel, lumber, railroad, and utility industries, which adopted, for the most part, innovations developed by others.

(5) Our evidence indicated that innovation is likely to spawn more innovation. For example, product and process innovation by one firm in an industry tended to cause innovation in competing firms. The growth of research and development was one indication of this tendency.

(6) Bureaucratic expansion, more popularly referred to as "empire building," was probably a factor in some of the companies studied, particularly during periods of high prosperity and high profits. Nevertheless, we found that, in comparison with other factors, it was a very minor cause of expansion in the proportion of high-level manpower in company work forces.

(7) The increasing size of companies and the alleged increase in the number of reports required by government agencies were found to be erroneous explanations for shifts in occupational structure. Companies that grew in size but did not innovate tended to employ a constant or declining percentage of their work forces in executive, professional, and related occupations. Reports required by government agencies were mentioned as a source of change in employment structure only by public utilities and railroads—in other words, only by companies subject to direct government regulation. Companies in other industries indicated that most of the information required by government agencies was also required for effective management of their affairs.

(8) The greater use of professional and managerial manpower resulted in an increase in fixed and overhead costs. Almost all the companies we studied were concerned with the problem of mounting overhead expenses. In some industrial companies the total payments to salaried workers were already greater than the total wage bill for hourly rated or pieceworkers. In a few cases, the total compensation of managers and professional personnel was nearly equal to that of production personnel. The trend here was clear. The total payments to wage earners were decreasing, whereas the total pay-

ments to salaried workers were increasing, and in most companies the sharpest increases in total labor costs were those represented by managerial and professional personnel. The increase in employment of professional, managerial, and other groups of salaried employees in manufacturing between 1947 and 1957 resulted in total salaries rising from one fourth of manufacturing labor costs in 1947 to about one third in 1957.

(9) In general, the shift to greater use of high-level manpower in the companies studied was associated primarily with dynamism and progress rather than with expansion of bureaucracies or unwarranted increases in overhead costs. Although we were not able to measure the impact of greater use of such personnel on total payroll cost, our interviews indicated that innovation, and the increases in employment of high-level manpower which it required, bore fruit either in decreasing total costs, or improving the quality of the products or services supplied or both.

Inferences Drawn

The evidence presented in the previous sections, though admittedly spotty, clearly shows that in the United States the proportion of high-level manpower in the labor force has been increasing steadily during the last fifty years. There is some reason to believe that this increase has been more rapid during the post-World War II era, and that it is related not only to increases in productivity but also to the process of technological and managerial innovation which in turn are related to productivity. Furthermore, the available information from several other countries seems to indicate that the proportion of high-level manpower is also rising in all nations which are making significant progress in economic and political development.

On the basis of such facts, I should like to propose for consideration a number of propositions regarding the possible relationships between high-level manpower and economic growth in modern societies. They are presented frankly as plausible hypotheses rather than as conclusions from definitive evidence.

First, the proportion of high-level manpower to the total labor force (or to the total population) of a country is a reasonably good measure of that country's stage of economic advancement. And the rate of increase in the stock of high-level manpower is closely associated with a country's rate of economic growth. In other words, the wealth of a nation depends upon its human capital as well as its material capital, and its rate of growth depends as much upon its rate of human capital formation as upon its rate of material capital formation. It is a well-known fact that the proportion of people in the high-level manpower category in an advanced country is much greater than that in an underdeveloped society. For example, in Nigeria the total number of persons in the high-level category is less than one tenth of 1 per cent of the population. In somewhat more advanced societies such as Egypt and India, it may be as high as five tenths of 1 per cent. In the advanced societies of Western Europe and in the United States, it may be as high as 3 to 5 per cent. Thus, the United States may have fifty times the proportion of high-level manpower in Nigeria.

But, why do advanced countries have a greater density of high-level manpower than less developed ones? Let us digress briefly to examine this question. One answer may be that they have a higher *per capita national income*. It could be argued that a rich country will always have more highly educated people than a poor one. But there are obvious flaws in this argument. Kuwait, for example, has a higher national income per head than the United States, but the proportion of high-level manpower in its population is much lower. Venezuela is much richer than Argentina, but its relative proportion of high-level manpower is much lower. Ghana has a smaller proportion of high-level manpower than Egypt, yet its national income per head is several times greater. Obviously, natural resources, whether they be petroleum (as in Kuwait and Venezuela) or favorable conditions for growing crops with high export value (as in Ghana) may offer a better explanation for wealth than the proportion of highly educated people. If one allows for such exceptions, however, there may be a fairly good correlation between income per capita and the density of high-level manpower.

One could also argue that the proportion of high-level manpower is associated with a country's *total investment measured in per capita terms*. This is plausible since capital-intensive activities are usually intensive in their use of high-level manpower. Thus, conceivably if a country were to double its investment per capita over a specified period of time, its proportion of high-level manpower might be expected to increase in a certain ratio. This relationship, however, suffers from the same shortcomings as that based upon national income—that is, it may be distorted by great differences in natural resources.

A much more plausible hypothesis, yet one which is difficult to test precisely, is that the accumulation of high-level manpower is related to *change and innovation* in economic, social and political activity, that is, to the progressive introduction over time of new ways of producing goods and services and new patterns of social and political life. According to this hypothesis, human capital formation is associated with both economic, social and political development. In a static, traditional society one would expect that the proportion of persons in the high-level category would be relatively constant. But, as the traditional society begins to modernize, it must accumulate high-level manpower to staff a new and expanding government service, to introduce new systems of land use and new methods in agriculture, to develop new means of communication, to carry forward industrialization, and to build a system of education. Changes in all these fields require persons with professional and technical skills and organizing ability. In India, for example, large numbers of trained people are required in community development programs and agricultural research and extension. The objective of these programs is to increase agricultural production and to press forward a modernization of rural life. High-level manpower is needed to organize and direct the necessary changes.

High-level manpower is also required in ever-increasing numbers as a country develops new systems of transportation, new means of communication, new factories, new commercial establishments, and new banking institutions. And, in the advanced countries, new products and new processes may be introduced continually, all of which require substantial "inputs" of high-level manpower. For example, the very high demand for scientific and professional personnel in the United States today is associated with the rapid expansion of industrial research and development laboratories and the investment by government in a wide variety of basic and applied research projects—all manifestations of change. A dynamic economy is likely to be one in which the pace of innovation is sustained and rapid, calling for a cumulative process of human capital formation.

Education is an activity requiring very intensive use of high-level manpower, particularly at the secondary school level and above. Thus, a country which decides to expand its system of education is committing itself to changes which will require relatively large numbers of teachers with substantial training.

Finally, the replacement of colonial and traditional ruling institutions by new forms of local, regional and national government calls for new kinds of administrative and professional personnel in the high-level manpower category. And as government grows, it takes on new activities, all of which are potential consumers of high-level manpower.

The logic of the relationship between progressive innovation and requirements for high-level manpower is quite obvious, and it appears to be consistent with the scattered empirical evidence which one finds in all modern, developing societies. It suggests that the countries which are making the most rapid and spectacular innovations are those which are under the greatest pressure to accumulate human capital at a fast rate.

A theoretical framework relating manpower use to the rate and type of innovation may also provide insights into the problems of unemployment and under-employment of particular kinds of manpower. Innovation renders some skills obsolete by creating new ones; it shifts employment opportunities from one area to another; and it usually diminishes the long-run requirements for less-skilled and unskilled human resources.

Admittedly, there are difficulties in properly defining the categories of people included in high-level manpower, and the comparison of occupations between different countries presents thorny problems. Yet, I would argue that the stock of high-level manpower, or some other appropriate measure of human capital, may be more meaningful for comparison of the stage of development between countries than a measure based on national income per capita, which often involves quite unrealistic assumptions concerning the value of money in different countries.

Second, in all developing economies the rate of accumulation of high-level manpower exceeds the rate of increase of the total labor force. In the United States, for example, the increase in high-level manpower during the past fifty years is certainly more than twice as great as the increase in the nation's labor force. I would think that this has been true also of the Soviet Union. And I would suggest that most newly developing countries in their early stages of growth may have to increase high-level manpower at least three times as rapidly as the increase in their labor forces, if they are to achieve a rise in per capita income of 2 per cent or more a year. Within the high-level manpower category, of course, certain critical occupational groups, such as engineers, technicians, agricultural experts and secondary school teachers, may need to increase at a much more rapid rate, whereas lawyers and arts graduates should probably increase at a more moderate pace.

Third, in most countries, the rate of increase of high-level manpower (or the rate of human capital formation) will also exceed the rate of economic growth. In newly developing countries which already have critical shortages of highly skilled persons, the ratio of the annual increase in high-level manpower to the annual increase in national income may need to be as high as three to one, or even higher in those cases where expatriates are to be replaced by the citizens of the developing country. In more advanced societies, which already have a sizable stock of high-level manpower, this ratio may be considerably lower. Here again the ratios of increases of particular occupational groups within the high-level manpower category are even more significant than the ratio for the high-level manpower group in the aggregate.

This hypothesis suggests that, on the basis of comparative research in a number of countries at different stages of growth and with different patterns of development, it might be possible to devise "multipliers" to estimate future requirements of strategic occupational groups in relation to projected growth patterns and growth rates for an economy. Such "multipliers," of course, would be particularly useful in planning investments in various kinds of education. In this way, the programming of investments in human resource development could be integrated effectively with planning for general economic growth.

Admittedly, much empirical evidence would need to be accumulated to build reliable "multipliers" of this kind. And, if such "multipliers" are to be useful for policy planners, one would need to construct them for various categories of critical occupations. From a theoretical standpoint, however, the concept of "high-level manpower to growth ratios" is a useful tool of analysis, parallel in many respects to the marginal capital to output ratio in economic analysis.

Fourth, equally important as the rate of high-level manpower accumulation is the efficiency with which it is employed. In the newly developing countries in particular, high-level manpower may be poorly used because of a poor balance of skills in relation to needs. There may be too many lawyers, and too few engineers and technical foremen. Doctors may not be used effectively because of a shortage of nurses or medical technicians. In many countries, fewer highly trained engineers would be needed if there was a more adequate supply of engineering technicians. In nearly all newly developing countries, highly trained people may be employed on jobs beneath their skill merely because there is a more critical shortage of persons with lesser intermediate skills. Thus, as in the case of capital funds, the proper use or "investment" of high-level manpower may be as important as its rate of accumulation. Here the patterns of incentives which education generates, the type of persons produced, and the manner in which they become allocated to strategic activities are of supreme importance.

A Final Suggestion

The propositions set forth above may be useful in building a conceptual framework for a research program of human resource development in relation to economic and political growth. If persons in a number of countries could make manpower and education studies using some common framework of this kind, they could contribute to the building of a general theory of human resource development in the modern world. This would be of great value, not only to the advanced nations, but also to all of the newly developing countries. Already, there is collaboration on research of this kind among some countries. The exchange of ideas in this field and particularly the broadening of collaborative effort between economists from many lands offers exciting and challenging opportunities for the future. A decision to undertake a comparative research project in collaboration would indeed be a great step forward in broadening the horizons of understanding in our common field of professional interest.

CHAPTER 25

Management and Enterprise Efficiency
(The American Experience)

CHARLES A. MYERS

Massachusetts Institute of Technology

The central proposition of this paper is that the structure and philosophy of management in an enterprise are important determinants, perhaps *the* determinants, of enterprise efficiency and hence of labor productivity. The level of technology is, of course, a critical factor in enterprise efficiency, and I do not mean to ignore it. But technological innovation and implementation in any enterprise are successful only if the people in it are technically competent and cooperate in the implementation process. Technical decisions, as well as other managerial decisions, involve the classic managerial functions of planning, organization, direction, coordination and control, and all these are accomplished through the combined efforts of the hierarchy which constitutes the enterprise or the larger organization of which it is a part. Thus, we return to the central theme of the structure and philosophy of management, particularly the top management.[1]

1. Discussion of management techniques, particularly those associated with the concept of "scientific management" (time and motion study, establishment of output norms, wage incentives, and so forth) has been omitted from this paper. I do not deliberately minimize their importance, but there is a full literature dealing with "scientific management," and too often there is insufficient attention to organizational structures and management philosophies in relation to enterprise efficiency. This paper, however, cannot claim to present a review of the growing literature on organization theory; it is only a sampling of what seems most important.

The structure and philosophy of management constitute an authority system. In an earlier study of the managerial function in a number of countries, Frederick Harbison and I concluded: "The efficiency of management as a resource is related not only to the individuals within the hierarchy, but also to the system of authority which binds them together. The methods of leadership, the structure of the organization, the art of delegation of authority are crucial to successful industrial development."[2] The system of authority which exists in a small family-type enterprise found predominantly in the earlier stages of economic development in many countries is vastly different from that in the modern large-scale enterprise. Direct interpersonal relations between the manager and the managed are usually possible in the small firm; there is little need for organization charts, delegation of managerial functions to line and staff executives, control procedures, and the like. But as enterprises grow, beyond, say, one hundred employees, there is need for subdivision and coordination of managerial functions; over five hundred, the problem of delegation and decentralization becomes more urgent; and over one thousand, it becomes critical.[3] The larger an organization grows, the more attention it must devote to problems of structure and to the generation of its own managerial resources,[4] which are a limiting factor on its own efficiency and growth. This is obvious in the very large organizations and enterprises, but it is less important in degree for those above five hundred or one thousand employees.[5]

Brech's definition of organizational structure is a useful and inclusive one: "The structure of organization of an enterprise is the framework for carrying out the responsibilities of management, for delegation of such responsibilities, for the co-ordination of activities or operations, and for the

2. Frederick Harbison and Charles A. Myers, *Management in the Industrial World: An International Analysis* (New York, 1959). See also Chapter 6, "Managers of Enterprises: Their Power, Position, and Policies," in Clark Kerr, John T. Dunlop, Frederick H. Harbison and Charles A. Myers, *Industrialism and Industrial Man: The Problems of Labor and Management in Economic Growth* (Cambridge, Mass., 1960). Both studies were part of the Inter-University Study of Labor Problems in Economic Development, financed by a grant from the Ford Foundation.
3. For a stage analysis of this type, see Ernest Dale, *Planning and Developing the Company Organization Structure,* Research Report No. 20 (New York, 1952).
4. "The supply of internally experienced managerial services is one of the strongest, if not the strongest, limiting factor on the growth of business organizations." Edith Penrose, "Limits to the Growth and Size of Firms," *American Economic Review,* vol. 45, no. 2 (May 1955), pp. 531–543.
5. According to *Fortune* magazine, among the largest non-governmental organizations in Western Europe and the United States, 4 employ more than 250,000 people; 14 employ 100,000 or more; and 16, 75,000 or more. *Fortune,* July 1959, pp. 125–144.

motivation of members." [6] This does not tell us anything about the appriate organizational structure, for it will depend on the circumstances and, indeed, on the philosophy of the particular management. There is no ideal degree of delegation and decentralization, for, as Simon has observed, "Hiararchy always implied intrinsically some measure of decentralization. It always involves a balancing of the cost savings through direct local action against the losses through ignoring indirect consequences for the whole organization." [7] This balance will vary with the capacity of subordinates to make decisions within the framework of delegated authority and central controls, and this capacity will reflect the philosophy and behavior of the top management. Thus, a discussion of the structure of management in relation to enterprise efficiency also involves a consideration of the philosophy and behavior of management.

With these introductory comments in mind, my observations will be centered on the following areas: (1) the evolution of organizational structure in American industrial enterprises; (2) organizational planning and management development as growing managerial responsibilities; (3) alternative theories or philosophies of management and their impact on organizational structure and enterprise efficiency; and (4) implications of trends in industrial societies for efficient management structure and philosophy.

Evolution of Organizational Structure in American Industry

Until about World War II, many of the largest American industrial enterprises were highly centralized, with large functional departments, such as manufacturing, sales, engineering, finance, and so forth. This was especially true when the enterprise produced a single line of products, such as in steel, farm machinery, petroleum, and some of the rubber and automobile firms. But in these industries, as in a chemical firm and an automobile manufacturing company earlier, innovation and product diversification in more than one industry broke down excessive centralization and brought decentralization into product divisions coordinated through headquarters

---

6. E. L. Brech, *Organization—The Framework of Management* (London, 1957), p. 10. For a more inclusive definition and analysis, see E. Wight Bakke, *Bonds of Organization* (New York, 1950).
7. Herbert A. Simon, *The New Science of Management Decision* (New York, 1960), p. 44.

staff divisions. This evolution is important enough to warrant a brief survey.[8] The role of the "organization builder" was decisive.

One of the first large American companies to develop a decentralized organizational structure was E. I. duPont de Nemours and Company, the largest chemical company. Before World War I, the company was still manufacturing and primarily selling one product (high explosives), and its organizational structure was highly centralized through functional departments in manufacturing, sales, development, and finance. During the war, it began to manufacture artificial leather, paints and varnishes, dyestuffs, organic chemicals, and started experimental work on artificial silk. The existing centralized, functionalized organizational structure had difficulties in handling this product diversification, and by 1921 the company had placed each of its five principal product groups—explosives, cellulose products, plastics, paint, and dyestuffs, in the charge of a general manager. The functional departments "became advisory or service departments whose staff officers audited, advised, and helped to coordinate the work of the operating departments; and they also assisted the new general office." [9] With this new decentralized organization, the duPont Company continued to diversify, and new products were developed by its research laboratories and product divisions. The basic organizational structure has changed little since 1921, although it has been widely copied, as we shall see. The company is outstandingly efficient, has continued to grow, and some of its products with trade names "nylon," "orlon," "dacron" (all synthetic fibers) have almost revolutionized the clothing and apparel industries and the habits of consumers.

8. Much of this section is based on the historical work by my M.I.T. colleague, Professor Alfred D. Chandler, Jr. This is reported, with some duplication, in three articles: "The Beginnings of Big Business in American Industry," *Business History Review,* Spring 1959, pp. 1–31; "Management Decentralization: An Historical Analysis," *Business History Review,* June 1956, pp. 111–174; and "Development, Diversification and Decentralization," in Ralph E. Freeman, ed., *Postwar Economic Trends in the United States* (New York, 1960), pp. 237–288. I have also drawn on Ernest Dale, *The Great Organizers* (New York, 1960). The latter is a study of some of the outstanding personalities, such as Pierre, Irenee and Lamont duPont; Alfred P. Sloan, Jr.; E. T. Weir; and A. W. Robertson, all of whom had a profound impact on the organization of their companies. Chandler's studies, on the other hand, cover fifty of the largest American industrial concerns, which are analyzed in three groups: Metals and Agricultural Processing; Assembling; and Process industries. The subgroups within these three broad groups include steel, non-ferrous metals, agricultural processing (tobacco, meat packing, distilling, dairy products, and soap), electrical manufacturing, power machinery, automobiles, rubber, oil, and chemicals.

9. Chandler, "Development, Diversification, and Decentralization," p. 273.

About the same time that duPont was changing its organizational structure for greater efficiency under product diversification, a similar change was taking place in the General Motors Corporation, formed in 1908 by William C. Durant, who combined some of the leading automobile producers of that day. Durant's methods involved expansion through purchase of existing production facilities, rather than through careful organization and rationalization of production. Postwar difficulties in the industry forced Durant out and brought in a new team through duPont financing. The key organization builder was Alfred P. Sloan, Jr., who brought some unity into what had been a loose, almost completely decentralized set of companies under Durant. Sloan established a central office to make plans for the corporation as a whole and coordinate the separate units. The operating divisions were divided into four groups—motor car, parts, accessories, and miscellany. This organizational structure was developed in its central outlines by 1921, and it subsequently enabled the company to expand more quickly than the highly centralized Ford Motor Company under the direction of Henry Ford. In 1925, Chandler reports, General Motors had less than 20 per cent of the market and Ford more than 50 per cent. By 1940 their positions were almost reversed, and General Motors is still the dominant company in the industry.

Strikingly enough, its outdistanced rival, Ford, later emulated its organizational structure after World War II. Under the founder's grandson, Henry Ford II, the Ford Motor Company adopted the General Motors pattern of autonomous operating divisions, group vice-presidents, and central advisory and service staffs. According to *Fortune,* the former General Motors executive hired by Ford as executive vice-president began "by clapping the GM organizational garment onto the Ford manufacturing frame, trimming the garment here and pulling out the frame there. Nobody around Ford makes any bones about this, and indeed one of (his) first acts was to send around copies of a semi-official GM text on decentralization." [10] The resulting rejuvenation of the Ford Motor Company as an efficient producer is well known in American industry.

The petroleum companies followed a similar pattern as product diversification forced them out of the organizational mold of highly centralized, vertically integrated companies producing and marketing a single line of products: gasoline and lubricating oils and greases. Research and development turned out petro-chemicals, especially during World War II when synthetic rubber production grew out of military necessity. The establishment of chemical product divisions, or even subsidiaries, accompanied ex-

10. *Fortune,* vol. 35, May 1947, p. 88.

tensive reorganizations of the management structure. A parallel development occurred in at least two of the Big Four rubber companies, which originally concentrated on the manufacture of automobile and truck tires but added new and different product lines through research. Product diversification brought management decentralization; while management in those companies which remained largely tire producers remained relatively centralized.[11]

The electrical manufacturing firms—General Electric and Westinghouse —have experienced similar changes in organizational structure as a consequence of product diversification resulting from research and development. General Electric's research laboratory, for example, was established as early as 1900. But power machinery, lamps and electrical appliances for consumers did not in themselves bring decentralization of management; the General Electric organizational structure up through World War II was complex. It was a mixture of functional and product divisions; partly centralized and partly decentralized. With the accession of Ralph J. Cordiner to the presidency in 1946, there was a major reorganization along product lines: apparatus, lamp, appliances, air conditioning, electronics, and chemical—each headed by a senior executive responsible for the financial performance of products in his department. The former functional departments were transformed into central staff advisory and coordinating departments at headquarters. Later organizational modifications led to subdivision of the product departments into more than seventy units headed by managers whose responsibilities matched those of the former product department executives, although general division managers supervised several units or smaller departments. Four new group vice-presidents at headquarters appraised the performance of the departments and divisions under their guidance, and, together with the president, the chairman, and the head of the central staff departments, they comprised the group responsible for over-all company policies.[12] Westinghouse, under a new president with a management consulting firm background, went through a similar managerial reorganization

---

11. "Concentration on low-priced, mass-volume product (tires) led to a highly integrated, centralized management organization; and this organization was, in turn, ill-equipped to manufacture and sell a variety of products based on rubber chemistry. Only a series of drastic events brought change." Chandler, "Development, Diversification, and Decentralization," p. 265.

12. For further discussion of Mr. Cordiner's organizational philosophy, see his McKinsey Foundation Lectures given at the Graduate School of Business, Columbia University, and published as *New Frontiers for Professional Managers* (New York, 1956).

after 1950, although initial decentralization began in 1934. Both changes were responses to the product diversification and technological complexity which has characterized the electrical manufacturing industry in the United States over the last two decades.

This review of the evolution of organizational structure in American industry indicates a "natural history" of organizational changes within enterprises:

(1) As an enterprise grows and acquires operations which permit vertical integration in the production and distribution of a single line of products, a highly centralized organizational structure first develops to control the complex of operations. There are large functional departments, usually manufacturing, sales, engineering, and finance, directed from a central headquarters.

(2) In industries where research and development activities—as well as mergers and corporate acquisitions—bring product diversification and thus more complex and expanding operations, the centralized organizational structure becomes top-heavy and inefficient. More decisions have to be made down the line, and the large functional departments are replaced by product divisions and subdivisions. Managers of these units become responsible for over-all performance of their operations, subject to central budget controls and staff assistance. The need for accurate data in operations of decentralized units is essential, but there is danger that this may lead to controls which vitiate its whole concept of delegation and decentralization.

(3) In most cases, organizational decentralization comes only with a change in top management. "The older executives usually had neither the awareness of the organizational needs caused by diversification nor a specific interest in defining organizational relationships." [13] Decentralization requires more capable managers, and the lack of these is a limiting factor.

(4) Decentralization in a growing number of enterprises meets the test of "success" as measured by increased efficiency, enterprise growth, and profit margins (excess of income over outgo) which make further investment and growth possible. The contrast between General Motors and Ford (prior to 1947) is a classic illustration.

(5) These changes—research and development, product diversification, and organizational decentralization—all reflect more complex technology, wider national and international markets, growing size of enterprises, and other characteristics of an advanced industrial society. Organizational structures that are appropriate for a less advanced industrial society give way to

13. Chandler, "Development, Diversification, and Decentralization," p. 280.

the inevitable pressures of industrial growth and efficiency which decentralization makes possible.

Organization Planning and Management Development

Since decentralization requires careful attention to planning and executing organizational changes, as well as to developing greater numbers of more capable managers at all levels, it has brought changes in the hierarchy of managerial responsibilities. Several decades ago, or even less, few top managements in American enterprises paid much attention to planning organizational changes, and few had staff departments devoted to this planning. Fewer still had much interest in formal programs of management development, preferring to depend on the time-honored method of "training on the job."

Since World War II especially, there has been an upsurge of interest in organization planning and management development programs, and few management conferences lack papers or discussions on these subjects. Organization planning is a top managerial responsibility, as the historical survey has shown, although in the process of planning organizational changes, top management may have the assistance of a staff department, of a managerial committee, or of outside consultants, or even of all three. But "the *process* of organization planning is crucial rather than the formal organization you come out with. In the process, resistance and fear must be converted into support and understanding; human energy and initiative must be released—not controlled." [14]

Organizational planners in American industry deal with such problems as span of control (the number of people reporting to a superior), degree of verticalness or flatness in the organizational structure (number of layers between the top management and the work force),[15] organization charts, methods of delegation of authority, control procedures, and so forth. They have also been concerned with the procedures of management development: management inventories, replacement tables (showing actual or potential replacements for each existing managerial position), planned rotation in man-

14. Charles R. Hook, Jr., *Organization Planning: Its Challenges and Limitations,* American Management Association, Personnel Series, no. 141 (New York, 1951), p. 21.
15. For a provocative discussion of vertical (tall) and flat organizational structures, see Herbert E. Krugman, "Organization Structure and the Organization Man," *Personnel* (American Management Association), vol. 38, no. 2 (March–April 1961), pp. 18–23.

agerial positions, inside and outside training programs, and so forth. In the latter, American universities, particularly schools of business and management, have played increasing roles since the war. Executive training programs for men nominated and financed by their companies have become a major educational effort of graduate schools of business administration and industrial management at these universities.[16] They are most effective, however, when they supplement a planned program *within* the enterprise for development of managerial talent.

It is increasingly recognized, moreover, that management development toward greater enterprise efficiency takes place best in an atmosphere of organizational climate conducive to *self-development*.[17] In a viable and effective organization, members of the managerial hierarchy are "developed" by their superiors only in the sense that they are given increased responsibilities and challenges to develop their capacities as more effective managers. In the highly centralized vertical type of organizational structure, dominated by a chief executive who holds the reins tightly and makes many detailed decisions himself, subordinate managers carry out orders but seldom initiate action themselves. On the other hand, in the more decentralized, flatter type of organizational structure, subordinate managers are held responsible for *results* (as measured by excess of income over outgo, reduction in costs, or other objectives covering specified time periods), but they must make the operating decisions themselves. The challenge of this greater responsibility, and the relative freedom to manage his own organization to achieve the established targets, give the subordinate manager an opportunity to grow on the job—or fall by the wayside. Thus the philosophy and behavior of top management toward its subordinates is a critical factor in the development of better management, and this philosophy permeates the whole organization. We need to consider this further in connection with enterprise efficiency and labor productivity.

16. For a recent extensive survey of experience with these programs, see Kenneth R. Andrews, "Reaction to University Development Programs," *Harvard Business Review*, vol. 39, no. 3 (May–June, 1961), pp. 116–134. Professor Andrews bases his findings on replies from 6074 participants in 39 university programs between 1949 and 1958. The principal conclusion is that these programs broadened the business executive who had been restricted functionally, organizationally, or intellectually, and needed something more to assume higher managerial responsibilities.

17. For a more extended summary of this approach and references to the literature, see "Organization Planning and Management Development," Chapter 7, in Paul Pigors and Charles A. Myers, *Personnel Administration* (4th ed.: New York, 1961), pp. 131–150.

Alternative Theories or Philosophies of Management

In evaluating the impact of managerial philosophies on enterprise efficiency, it is useful to distinguish between the conventional theory of management and the newer theory growing out of social science research. The conventional theory has a long history, beginning with the authoritarian concepts of the military organization, the church, and other organizations in which subordinates at all levels (including manual workers) must do what they are ordered, under threat of punishment. Rewards are also involved, so there is a "carrot and stick approach." Frederick Taylor, the father of "scientific management," had a more sophisticated but no less authoritarian approach. His philosophy toward management and workers is clear in the following statement:

Now one of the very first requirements for a man who is fit to handle pig iron . . . is that he shall be so stupid and so phlegmatic that he more nearly resembles . . . the ox than any other type. . . . he must consequently be trained by a man more intelligent than himself.[18]

In this concept of management, the organizational and planning functions are given to specialists—often the industrial engineers—and subordinates are to carry out the more routine duties. There must be subdivision of jobs, establishment of work standards, training in specific duties, rewards for exceeding the norms, and penalties for not achieving them. "With respect to people, this is a process of directing their efforts, motivating them, controlling their actions, modifying their behavior to fit the needs of the organization." There is the further assumption that "without this active intervention by management, people would be passive—even resistant to organizational needs. They must therefore be persuaded, rewarded, punished, controlled—their activities must be directed. This is management's task—in managing subordinate managers or workers." This conventional theory of management has been called "Theory X" to distinguish it from "Theory Y" based on concepts growing out of social science research.[19]

This research, beginning with the extended studies in the Hawthorne works of the Western Electric Company in Chicago by a team of Harvard

18. Frederick W. Taylor, *Scientific Management* (New York, 1911), p. 59.
19. Douglas McGregor, *The Human Side of Enterprise* (New York, 1960). The quotations are from an earlier article by McGregor of the same title; the concepts are developed more fully in Chapters 3 and 4 of this book.

Business School professors,[20] developed the relationship between the socio-psychological aspects of human behavior and worker productivity. The human relations approach to management has also come under attack, largely because of its misuse by managers who saw it as a way of manipulating subordinates. The manager does not abdicate under the alternative theory of management, Theory Y. He is still responsible for organizing the elements of the productive enterprise, but his assumptions about people are different—and if he merely gives lip service to these assumptions and does not really believe in them, manipulation is possible. These assumptions are:

(1) "People are *not* by nature passive or resistant to organizational needs. They have become so as a result of experience in organizations."

(2) "The motivation, the potential for development, the capacity for assuming responsibility, the readiness to direct behavior toward organizational goals are all present in people. Management does not put them there. It is a responsibility of management to make it possible for people to recognize and develop these human characteristics for themselves."

(3) "The essential task of management is to arrange organizational conditions and methods of operation so that people can achieve their own goals *best* by directing *their own* efforts toward organizational objectives. This is a process primarily of creating opportunities, releasing potential, removing obstacles, encouraging growth, providing guidance. It is . . . 'management by objectives' in contrast to 'management by control.' "[21]

Some recent research on the differences between supervision in high and low productivity sections (alike in other respects) and in hierarchically controlled and participative work groups gives strong support to this Theory Y approach,[22] which also squares with the practical experience of an increasing number of successful supervisors and managers in American industry.

Authoritarian order-giving may increase output in the short run, but the question is: what are the consequences on the long-run efficiency of the or-

20. F. J. Roethlisberger and W. J. Dickson, *Management and the Worker* (Cambridge, Mass., 1939).

21. McGregor.

22. As an example, see the reports of research by the Institute of Social Research, University of Michigan, as summarized by the Director, Rensis Likert, in "Motivation: The Core of Management," Personnel Series No. 155 (New York, 1953); and "Measuring Organizational Performance," *Harvard Business Review*, vol. 36, no. 2 (March–April 1958), pp. 41–50. (Both are reprinted in Paul Pigors, Charles A. Myers and F. T. Malm, *Readings in Personnel Administration* (2nd ed.: New York, 1959), along with McGregor's paper, "The Human Side of Enterprise."

ganization, which, after all, is composed of a hierarchy of people who must be motivated to give their best efforts to the achievement of the organizational objectives? Admittedly, the high-morale organization is not necessarily or always the most productive because people in work groups may be so "happy" that they are satisfied with low productivity. The relationship of managerial philosophy, employee morale, and productivity of the work group is, therefore, not simple. But, in the words of the director of a major social science research project on management and productivity: "These (research) results demonstrate that, on the average, *pressure-oriented, threatening, punitive management yields lower productivity, higher costs, increased absence, and less employee satisfaction than supportive, employee-centered management which uses group methods of supervision coupled with high-performance expectations."* [23]

These studies, it should be noted, refer to the response of subordinates who are not part of the management group to different managerial philosophies and behavior. In this paper, however, we have been considering *primarily* the organizational structure and philosophy of *management*. But do workers respond to the same types of organizational structures and managerial philosophies which seem to bring greater productivity and efficiency within the management group? The research results, as interpreted by students of organizational behavior, do not all point one way on this question. For example, some people may actually like direction and minute supervision, prefer repetitive jobs with little responsibility, or lack the temperament or capacity for contributing ideas and enthusiasm to the accomplishment of changing tasks. Perhaps the assembly-line type of operation is necessarily one in which workers must be expected to perform minute, specified tasks, in a sequence and at a pace established by management.

But these assumptions about human behavior and human responses may not be valid even in these cases, if organizational conditions, the nature of jobs, and managerial practices were different. There are enterprises, operating under a different managerial philosophy and a different organizational structure, in which the ideas of workers about increasing productivity, reducing costs, eliminating wastes, and so forth, are encouraged by specific methods. I refer here to the example of firms and labor unions in the United States which have adopted a form of labor-management cooperation on production problems known as "The Scanlon Plan." The details of this ap-

23. Likert, "Measuring Organizational Performance," p. 211. (Emphasis is in the original source.)

proach and the experience under it are available elsewhere,[24] and there are similar experiences in a number of other countries.[25] These cast doubt on assumptions that if the management group itself is efficient, there is no need to tap the ideas and enthusiasm of the work group. The Theory Y management approach assumes that *all* people in an organization will respond to "management by objectives."

Implications of Trends in Industrial Societies for Efficient Management Structure and Philosophy

Earlier, in pointing out the "natural history" or organizational changes within American industrial enterprises, I suggested certain forces which brought decentralization. In the preceding discussion of managerial philosophy, the adequacy of the traditional theory of managerial authority in a modern industrial society was questioned. Are these two developments related?

I believe that both are the results of the process of industrialization, viewed in terms of its social as well as economic impacts. Elsewhere, my colleagues and I in the Inter-University Study of Labor Problems in Economic Development have suggested that in advanced industrializing societies such as the United States, Great Britain, Sweden, and Germany, "managers are forced increasingly to abandon many of their authoritarian and paternalistic practices" in the direction of "constitutional management" and even participative management.[26] A number of pressures force management in this direction: social values, labor shortages, worker resistance, government

24. For details, see Frederick G. Lesieur, ed., *The Scanlon Plan: A Frontier in Labor-Management Cooperation* (New York, 1958). Productivity increases in ten companies averaged 23.1 per cent in the first two years (p. 113). For another analysis in a broader context, see Sumner H. Slichter, James J. Healy and E. Robert Livernash, *The Impact of Collective Bargaining on Management* (Washington, 1961), Chapter 28.

25. The experience with "enterprise councils" in Sweden, with "joint consultation" in Great Britain, and with "co-determination" in the German coal and steel industries, are examples, although the evidence is not always favorable for higher productivity. Somewhat more success seems to have been achieved by the "workers councils" in Yugoslavia, as reported in John T. Dunlop, *Industrial Relations Systems* (New York, 1958).

26. Kerr, Dunlop, Harbison and Myers, *Industrialism and Industrial Man,* Chapter 6. The same tendencies seem to be found in Russian management, although the evidence is largely second-hand. See Ralph C. James, "Management in the Soviet Union," Chapter 17 in Harbison and Myers, *Management in the Industrial World,* 1959. See also David Gronick, *The Red Executive: A Study of the Organization Man in Russian Industry* (New York, 1961).

legislation, rise of labor unions, examples of other managements, pressure of competition, and pace of economic development. The exercise of pure authority over subordinates is increasingly inadequate to achieve organizational objectives, when subordinates have alternatives (such as freedom to leave a job or withhold effort individually or through organized means), or can adopt countermeasures to limit or control managerial authority. Thus, in the modern industrial society, managers must increasingly earn and win the enthusiastic support of their subordinates. Managers and the managed are *interdependent*.

These same pressures, plus the growing complexity of enterprises and increasing technology, compel management to re-structure its organization and to *share* decision-making and responsibility further down in the management hiararchy—and even still further down to the work group. There is bound to be some differentiation in tasks and responsibility, depending upon the nature of the work to be done and the capacity of the people to do it with competence and enthusiasm. But these are not static forces or "givens," they are subject to change also—with increased education of the labor force, with changing social values and objectives, and with the philosophy and behavior of managers in dealing with people in organizations. The more advanced the industrial society, the more cumulative are these pressures for change.

Greater efficiency and higher productivity in the industrial society, therefore, require greater attention to organizational structure, to the development and replacement of managerial resources, and to the kinds of managerial philosophy and behavior which will tap to the fullest the capacities, the energies, and the enthusiasms of the human resources in the enterprise or organization. This is the opposite of the engineering concept of productivity, for without the cooperation of people, technical measures to increase productivity will fall short of their objectives.

CHAPTER 26

Organizational Factors in Productivity

E. WIGHT BAKKE

Yale University

Research on productivity is very properly concerned first of all with the questions: "What is it?" and "How can we measure it?" If those questions cannot be answered satisfactorily there is little sense in trying to account for it. But the question, "Why the variations?" is an equally persistent and important one both for theorists and those concerned with the practical problem of maintaining and improving productivity.

Economists very naturally turn first to explanations in terms of the quantity, quality, and proportions of basic resources being used, both material and human. But even if productivity is defined as a ratio between resource inputs and product outputs, the measurement of both, however accurate and precise, is unlikely to suggest the full range of intervening variables which account for the observed ratio.

This paper is concerned with a relatively neglected area of intervening variables, those associated with the *structure* of patterns of organizational activities by which inputs are transformed into outputs. It sets forth a research design suggested by a re-study of the data gathered in several studies of organizations conducted at the Yale Labor and Management Center and the Yale Technology Project since 1944. The organizations studied which are particularly relevant to this problem include one of the Bell Telephone

Systems, a government agency, three steel plants, an automobile plant, a business machines plant, and a bank.[1]

The research design envisaged here assumes, of course, that there are two organizations available for comparison whose quantity, quality, and proportions of resource inputs are basically similar, but whose output varies. This could be the same organization at two points in time. It also assumes that there exists in both cases a similar and consistent measure of productivity. These are large assumptions, and, together with problems of observation, measurement, and analysis of the variables to which we are giving attention, present major obstacles to definitive results from such research. But the construction of a research design is the best way of presenting systematically the intervening variables involved in answering the question: "Why variations in productivity?"

Concept of Organizational Structure

If we are to study the impact of organizational structure on productivity, we must first be clear about what we mean by that term. What is our concept of social organization? The concept we shall use has been reported in detail in another publication[2] and, therefore, may be briefly summarized here. It defines the structure of the organization as the steady state or pattern of *all* activities (directed both internally and externally) essential to the operation of the organization and to the maintenance of its stability, viability, and power.

These activities are grouped into five major processes or "bonds"[3] of organization each with a distinctive function to perform.

The basic and central process to which all others are essentially "helper"

---

1. These studies have been reported in E. Wight Bakke, *Bonds of Organization* (New York, 1950); C. R. Walker, *Steeltown* (New York, 1950); F. L. W. Richardson, Jr. and C. R. Walker, *Human Relations in An Expanding Company* (New Haven, 1948); C. R. Walker and R. H. Guest, *The Man on the Assembly Line* (Cambridge, Massachusetts, 1952); Neil W. Chamberlain, *Management in Motion* (New Haven, 1950); Chris Argyris, *Organization of a Bank* (New Haven, 1954); and an unpublished analysis of the operation of the Depford (England) employment exchange.
2. E. Wight Bakke, "Concept of Social Organization," Chapter 2 in *Modern Organization Theory,* by Mason Haire and others (New York, 1959). Also in *General Systems Yearbook,* reprints of which are available upon application to the author.
3. The concept of *bonds* of organization is a way of indicating the interaction and integration of a particular process with the other elements in the organization, namely, the Organizational Charter, the basic resources used as instruments in the process, and the activity contributions of the other processes to the functioning of the one upon which primary attention is being focused. See Bakke, *Ibid.*

processes is the *Workflow,* or the production and distribution process. It is operationally defined as the series of tasks directly functioning to create or produce and distribute an output. Productivity is frequently defined as the ratio between inputs and outputs of this process.

The Workflow tasks are directly assisted by tasks in at least two other processes.[4] The first of these can be called the *Perpetuation* processes, which supply, maintain, and develop the quantity and quality of basic resources used by the organization. They are labeled in accordance with the particular resource which they supply and maintain: Finance (money), Services (materials and equipment), Personnel (people), Thoughtways (ideas),[5] Cultivation (factor and product markets), Conversation (nature), and Scheduling (time).

The other type of "helper" processes are the *Control* processes, which direct, coordinate, regulate, stimulate, appraise, and clarify all the differentiated activities (including of course the Workflow activities) so that the function of the organization will be accomplished effectively and efficiently, in line with organizational objectives. Accordingly they are labeled the processes of Direction, Motivation, Evaluation, and Communication.

The Workflow, Perpetuation, and Control processes include those tasks normally encountered in the descriptions of organizations written by those whose primary interest is in the organization as a means-ends system, where those ends are considered to be intended consequences chiefly related to its effectiveness and efficiency in the production and distribution of a specific product or service. But every organization is from the beginning, and increasingly becomes, more than such a means-ends system. It comes to have a unique wholeness, a particular image, and character charged with value to participants and non-participants; and both groups, and particularly the participants, have an interest in the functional stability and viability of that unique wholeness.

Activities related to the achievement and preservation of this unique

4. Actually each process is a "helper" to *all* the others. But since the Workflow is that process whose activities lead directly to results involved in calculating productivity, the indicated relationship will be emphasized in this paper. Ideas include plans, rosters of strategies, organized bodies of data and knowledge, concepts of objectives, values, relationships, and many others which give structure and meaning to the world of work, and so forth (the premises on the basis of which work and working relationships are carried on).

5. Incorporated in this concept of Direction are traditionally referred to activities by which the directing of operations toward organizational goals is accomplished, such as goal determination, organization, command, coordination, supervision, and so forth.

wholeness can be observed in organizations. Such activities can be grouped into two additional essential processes, labeled *Identification* and *Homeostatic* processes. They may be briefly described as follows:

The *Identification* process has as its function to define, make clear, and symbolize the unique wholeness of the organization by establishing and maintaining, for example, to its central goals, and functions, its standing, its major policies, its basic values, and so forth.

The *Homeostatic* processes have as their function to meet the major threats to the functional stability and viability of this unique wholeness. They marshal the other more elementary processes in the face of such threats. Four Homeostatic processes are indicated here:

(1) The *Legitimization* process attempts to meet the threats to the right of the organization to exist and to operate and to obtain consent and cooperation toward this end.

(2) The *Fusion* process attempts to meet the threat of non-compatibility and non-integration among the interests and functions of people and groups related to it. Its positive function is to make consistent and compatible, and to integrate, such interests and functions advantageously to the stability and viability of the organization.

(3) The *Problem Solving* process attempts to meet the threat (as well as the promise) of non-routine difficulties and of unexploited non-routine opportunities the dealing with which is not adequately provided for in the patterns of activity developed for handling recurrent and routine matters.

(4) The *Leadership* process attempts to provide the vision, foresight, innovation, and guidance essential to meeting the threat to stability and viability present in non-adaptation to a changing world.

The relationship among these essential processes is represented in Figure 3.

In suggesting that research is possible the objective of which is to indicate the way in which and the extent to which factors of organizational structure affect productivity, this is the model of organizational structure I have in mind. *Structure is the steady state or pattern of the activities classified as the Workflow, Perpetuation, Control, Identification, and Homeostatic processes.*

The impact of organizational structure factors upon the productivity of the Workflow can be analyzed then as the degree to which, in organizations

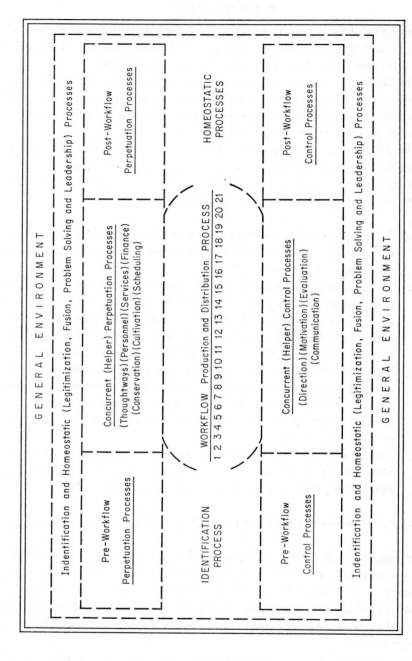

Fig. 3. Model of relationships among organizational processes.

with essentially the same available resources, the variations in the pattern of the Workflow, Perpetuation, Control, Identification, and Homeostatic activities are associated with variations in the input-output ratio of the Workflow.

Model of Dynamic Relationships

In summary, then, our model of dynamic interrelationships with respect to productivity attainment is:

(1) Dependent variable: degree of productivity defined as a ratio between quantity, quality, and value of inputs; and quantity, quality, and value of outputs.

(2) Primary independent variables: the nature, qualities, and proportions of basic resource inputs used in the Workflow.

(3) Primary intervening variables: the nature, qualities and structure of the Workflow tasks and of that process as a whole.

(4) Secondary intervening variables: the nature, qualities, and structure of the Perpetuation, Control, Identification, and Homeostatic processes *as they impinge upon the Workflow tasks and the Workflow process as a whole.*

It should be noted that, while reference in this paper is to the operations of the individual firm, industries and national economies are also organizational systems which can be described in terms of the same concept of organization.

The Research Design

The problem of research design, then, at the point where organizational structure factors come into play, is to indicate a way in which factors with respect to the nature, qualities, and structure of these "helper" processes can be related causally to the nature, qualities, and structure of activities in the Workflow and hence to the productivity results of those activities.

Data Required

Three kinds of data will be required in addition to the comparative productivity measurements:

(1) A description of the nature of, and a serial charting of, the tasks in the Workflow. Included in the description of each task or grouping of tasks will be (a) the objective, (b) basic resources and type of energy used, (c) nature of the contributions made and constraints exercised from people or other resources associated with the performance of tasks in the other processes.

(2) A description of these latter "helper" tasks related to the Perpetuation, Control, Identification, and Homeostatic processes including an indication of the points at which they affect the flow of work.

(3) A measurement of the reported effectiveness of these "helper" tasks (and the immediately preceding Workflow tasks) in making possible the effective performance of each Workflow task or grouping of tasks. The evidence will come in the first instance from the Workflow task performers. The dimensions and qualities associated with "effectiveness" in our research have been (a) timeliness, (b) adequacy, (c) authoritativeness, (d) dependability, (e) clarity of purpose, (f) consistency and congruity with the task or tasks affected, and (g) acceptability by the performers of the latter tasks.

The operational definition of and the construction of a scale for measuring these latter dimensions or qualities is difficult. That difficulty is one reason so little progress has been made in relating organizational structural factors to productivity results except in the most general terms. One major difficulty is that the definition and measurement must take account of the specific production and distribution process being studied. Timeliness for example is not defined in the same way operationally in a coal mine, a job lot factory, an assembly line factory, a telephone company, and a bank. Another difficulty is that, if reliance is placed on induction from empirical evidence provided by participants, the qualities and capacities of the respondent giving the evidence will inevitably affect the way these dimensions are perceived, interpreted, and reported to the researcher, and indeed will affect the kind of "helper" performance needed for performance of the Workflow task *by that respondent*. But evidence from such reports in a number of studies will provide content from which increasingly realistic operational definitions of the dimensions can be constructed.

Nevertheless these difficulties among others must be surmounted by each researcher unless we are satisfied to let our results be deductions from our models and assumptions rather than inductions from the observation of actual behavior producing whatever observed productivity results we are trying to explain.

Analysis

With the completion of these three steps in data collection, and assuming that we have a productivity measure, we are now in a position to (*a*) characterize the organizational structural features of the several processes, (*b*) note the degree of consistency and congruity between the organizational structural features of the Workflow and the other processes, (*c*) hypothesize the impact of this relationship on reported effectiveness and on the measured productivity of the Workflow, and (*d*) test the hypotheses.

Analysis: Character of the Structural Feature

It will be recalled that *structure* in our terms is taken to be the steady state or pattern of activities related to the several essential processes of organization. It does not include the qualities and characteristics of the basic resources whether these be personal or impersonal. These latter variables were included in our model as primary independent variables. Here we focus attention upon organization structural features as intervening variables. In order to indicate what is meant by such features I shall list, as examples, from our research, features only from the Workflow and the several Control processes.[6]

Relevant to *Workflow Process* specifically:

(1) Number of virtually autonomous Workflows.
(2) *With* or *without* tributary, feedback, and parallel subsidiary Workflows.
(3) Single or multiple departmental responsibility for operation of main, tributary, feedback, and parallel lines.
(4) Similarity or variety in hierarchical positions of performers in the series of tasks whether they be in the main or subsidiary Workflows.
(5) Constant or only periodic interaction with respect to tasks from "helper" processes.

Relevant to *All Processes* (including Workflow):

(1) *Constraints*

6. In case more than four features are given for each of the main or sub-categories, the first four listed are those which appear likely to be most significantly related to productivity.

(*a*) Extent of formalized procedural rules and regulations for performance.

(*b*) Types and proportion of constraints upon or regulation of performance imposed by the nature and qualities of the several basic resources (money, materials, ideas, people, nature, markets, and time).

(*c*) Mechanical or personal determination of method and pace of work.[7]

(*d*) Nature of the output of the process (objects or services).

(2) *Interdependency*

(*a*) Degree of autonomy or dependency upon other processes of the process as a whole.

(*b*) Single or multiple departmental affiliation of tasks in any sequence of tasks.

(3) *Flexibility*

(*a*) Degree of tolerance for adjustment, modification, and invention of procedures.

(*b*) Degree of definiteness in boundaries of departmental jurisdictions.

(*c*) Extent of decision making discretion at point of interaction in respect to tasks related to other processes.

(*d*) Unilateral or participative determination of goals and procedures.

(4) *Task characteristics*

(*a*) Degree of generality of tasks assigned to particular stations.

(*b*) Routine or adaptive character of tasks.

(*c*) Proportions of physical, intellectual, and mechanical energy requirements for task performance.

(*d*) Distribution of initiating tasks.

(*e*) Repetitiveness or variation in tasks.

(5) *Assignments*

(*a*) Manning of tasks to individuals or teams.

(*b*) Permanency or rotation in manpower assignments.

Relevant to *Control Processes*

(1) *Generally relevant to all Control Processes*

(*a*) Proportion of reference to productivity, stability, and viability

---

7. Note that with the extension of office automation this feature, traditionally assumed to apply chiefly to the production process becomes increasingly relevant to Control and Perpetuation processes as well.

requirements for the total organization or for sub-units as an integrating control objective.

(*b*) Unity or multiplicity of sources of direction, and accountability, administration of evaluations, rewards and penalties, and of communications.

(*c*) Degree of centralized or decentralized determination of performance and performance requirements, and of appraisal.

(*d*) Extent of countervailing control functions exercised by those who are formally intended to be controlled.

(*e*) Balance of help and guidance in relation to influence and power in objectives of control processes.

(2) Relevant specifically to *Direction Process*

(*a*) Balance between authority based on delegation and on acceptance.

(*b*) Route, length, and number of "clearance" procedures needed for authority or permission to act.

(*c*) Command primarily by, or merely reenforced by, power inherent in rank.

(*d*) Nature of bases of power to direct downward, upward, horizontally, and diagonally.

(*e*) Adjudication of differences by reference to stabilized and customary or by reference to situational rights and obligations.

(*f*) Conflict and tension management by fiat or by cooperative or by competitive adjustment mechanisms.

(*g*) See also items in 1 above.

(3) Relevant specifically to *Motivation Process*

(*a*) Balance of reliance on reward or penalty.

(*b*) Degree of sole reliance on hierarchically administered rewards and penalties.

(*c*) Types of, and proportioning among, economic and non-economic rewards and penalties.

(*d*) Geared to elicitation of, or compliance in, specified performance.

(*e*) Rigidity or flexibility of criteria for achievement of rank and status.

(*f*) See also items in 1 above.

(4) Relevant specifically to *Evaluation Process*

(*a*) Character of criteria for evaluation of performance (time per unit, economizing of resources, costs, quality, volume of output, quota meeting, consistency with certain value premises, and so forth).

(b) Single criterion or multiple criteria for performance evaluation.

(c) Procedure observance or results as criteria for performance.

(d) Managerial or professional referrants for standards of performance.

(e) Proportion of internal and external (to the organization) determination of standards of acceptability for the "product" of the process.

(f) See also items in 1 above.

(5) Relevant specifically to *Communication Process*

(a) Source, direction, and stations of information flows.

(b) Degree of rigidity and flexibility in routing of communications.

(c) Timing, including frequency and speed.

(d) Nature and extent of feedback mechanisms.

(e) Attention to and mechanisms for authentication.

(f) Individually or conference oriented.

(g) Proportion of content of reports relevant to determination of "what?" and "why?".

(h) See also items in 1 above.

Analysis: Degree of Consistency and Congruity among Structural Features

With these generalizations about the organizational structural features in hand, we are now ready to take the second and critical step in analysis. The objective of that step is to note the degree of consistency and congruity among the structural features of the Workflow and the other process. This step is critical because we shall hypothesize that both reported effectiveness and productivity vary directly with the degree of consistency and congruity among these structural features.

The nature of generalizations resulting from this step may be illustrated by reference to certain of the incongruities and inconsistencies which we have observed in our research findings:[8] Incongruities have been found to

---

8. Types of relationships, potentially damaging to productivity, have also, of course, been observed in relations between the Workflow process and the Perpetuation, Identification and Homeostatic processes as well as the Control processes which are referred to in this paper.

exist in the *direction and route* of the Workflow on the one hand and of the direction and route of communications or of clearances for authority to direct on the other. The Workflow frequently moves horizontally, while communications and clearances essential to it move vertically up and down the hierarchy of management. Such an incongruity can and does frequently result in a slowing down, confusion, jamming, or misdirection in the Workflow process due to lack of constant and timely integration with the "helper" processes.

Inconsistencies have been noted in the *objectives and emphases with respect to productivity* between the Workflow and certain of the Control processes. *Standards of evaluation of performance* inconsistent with, irrelevant to, or in conflict with the achievement of productivity, have been found. *Multiple sources of direction* of the Workflow whose objectives and procedures are in conflict are not infrequent. *Direction* has been observed to operate through power whose base is *rank* in a Workflow whose complicated procedures require direction through power whose base must necessarily be *knowledge*. Workflows involving considerable unpredictability and need for continuous adjustment in the course of the process have been routinized and regulated to an extent that makes procedure observance rather than result achievement a necessary focus of attention for performers. The *rewards and penalties* administered are on occasion found to be for achievements or failures *irrelevant to or inhibitory to productivity* from the type of Workflow existing. *Incentives* to production based on the assumption of personal discretion in determining method and pace of work have been administered in a Workflow whose method and pace are largely mechanically controlled.

Such evidences of the degree of consistency and congruity in patterns of relationship in organizational structure are to be noted, and hypothesized as having a positive or negative effect upon (*a*) the experienced effectiveness of the processes reported below in the next stage and upon (*b*) the observed degree of productivity.

Analysis: Effectiveness of Helper Processes

The next step in analysis is to summarize the reports from performers of Workflow tasks as to the degree of effectiveness of contributions and constraints from the "helper" processes in doing their work. As indicated above this step leads to generalizations as to the degree of (*a*) timeliness, (*b*) adequacy, (*c*) authoritativeness, (*d*) dependability, (*e*) clarity of structure and purpose, (*f*) perceived consistency and congruity with the task or tasks affected, and (*g*) acceptability by the performers of the latter tasks. The most obvious examples from our research have to do with the timeliness or untimeliness of the performance of a preceding or helper task. A frequent typical finding is the lack of feed-in of information from the Communication process at the point of a task in the Workflow obviously requiring such information. Likewise a feed-in from the Direction or the Evaluation processes is not always provided at a point where there is a dependency of the task on such feed-in. Such situations can and do frequently result in a lack of "help" from these processes at the time and place needed in the Workflow and in jurisdictional conflicts which disturb the smooth flow of work. At best then there is a slowing down or interruption in the Workflow. The illustrations need not be extended, for the criteria for effectiveness set forth in the preceding paragraph suggest adequately the dimensions of help and support which are involved.

These summaries of reports of degree of effectiveness can be used to verify, modify, or negate the hypotheses developed in the preceding stage of the analysis. They may also be used, where the rating of a large proportion of the tasks in a particular process is high, to hypothesize that that structuring of the process, given the instant Workflow structuring, will have a positive effect upon the measured degree of productivity, and, where it is low, will have the opposite effect.

Testing of Hypotheses

We now have three sets of hypotheses with respect to the impact of organizational structure features on productivity which may be tested as indicated below.

(*a*) Hypotheses indicating that the degree of consistency and congruity of tasks in the helper processes with those in the Workflow process (observed by the researcher) varies directly with the perceived degree of effectiveness reported by the performers of Workflow tasks. These may be tested by reference to the summary of these performers' reports.

(*b*) Hypotheses indicating that the degree of consistency and congruity of tasks in the helper processes with those in the Workflow process (observed by the researcher and verified by performer reports) varies directly with the degree of measured productivity. These may be tested by reference to the productivity measurement.

(c) Hypotheses indicating that the degree of perceived and reported effectiveness varies directly with the degree of measured productivity. These may be tested by reference to the productivity measurement.

CHAPTER 27

New Techniques and Labor Productivity

ZOFIA MORECKA

University of Warsaw

There are many concepts and measures of labor productivity in our economic literature. In these papers we apply the Marxist concept: labor productivity is understood to be the number of products and material services produced by living labor in a unit of time. Non-material services are excluded from this account, and labor used in producing them is treated as unproductive. The great importance of saving labor in all cases, even in its unproductive functions, can be best expressed by a separate analysis of the effectiveness of unproductive labor. There also exists a theory which indirectly includes this statement, namely, social labor productivity. It discloses "productive" results for the whole economy and is measured by the national product or national income per person employed or per head of population. The principal analysis in these papers deals with labor productivity in the Marxist concept *stricto sensu,* but from time to time we also endeavor to answer the questions: What is the influence of technique on the final effect of labor in one economy? What is its influence on the social productivity of labor?

Labor productivity can be measured in every workplace as an individual quantity. Its level is the most important element in the account of productivity on every level. But these levels are differentiated by persons, professions, enterprises, and industries, and the general average level is related not only to individual quantities but also to these differences—to the structure. This elementary truth about all aggregates is relevant in the analysis of our subject, because of the possibility of changing the average national or industrial level of productivity through changes in structure, that is, imputing the technique but without technical progress (innovation). Different levels of aggregation are expressed of the quantitative and also of the qualitative nature. The importance of the structure of employment increases steadily since, as we move away from particular jobs, it begins to comprise types of employment which more and more indirectly affect the amount of goods produced, and social labor productivity comprises both productive and unproductive types of employment. For this reason an increase in labor productivity achieved in certain occupations because of improved technique may be offset by changes in the structure of employment. Thus, a distinct divergence in the dynamics of productivity in particular sectors and in the whole economy will appear. This divergence may also have the opposite effect, that is, structural changes in production may increase. Average labor productivity in industry of the whole economy may increase without a parallel increase in certain occupations.

General Problems of New Techniques on Labor Productivity

The decisive influence of technique on labor productivity is recognized both by technicians and by economists. A correlation can be found between the input of technique and the dynamics of labor productivity. In particular, the growth of capital intensity (the amount of means of production per worker employed in the national economy or in one of its sectors) leads to an increase in labor productivity. It can be analyzed statistically and explained theoretically. From these efforts one can easily draw the conclusion that the relation may be very complicated, and that concrete terms play an important role in analyzing influence and that they condition its quantitative results.

In this paper we are attempting to systematize the relationships between technique and labor productivity with some reference to the actual conditions which exist in a period of industrialization and during the transition from capitalism to socialism now taking place in Poland.

Because the growth of capital intensity per worker leads to the saving of living labor per unit of production, the influence of technique on individual labor productivity[1] should be related, from the theoretical point of view, to the problems of inter-factor and intra-factor substitution.[2]

Inter-factor substitution consists in a full or partial substitution of technique for "living" labor. Full substitution means that the functions previously performed by a worker have been fully mechanized. A typical example is the introduction of automatic equipment for controlling production. A partial inter-factor substitution consists in increased capital intensity which replaces a worker in the performance of certain functions and reduces the intensity of his physical efforts and skill requirements. In inter-factor substitution changes occur in the technical composition of capital (in the Marxian concept as measured by the amount of equipment and other forms of "stored up" labor per employee). Changes in technical composition tend to release labor power. In contrast, intra-factor substitution (taking place with "living" labor under the influence of technique) is not accompanied by changes in technical composition. The number of employees remains the same, but the qualification structure changes, as well as the occupational structure and the ratio of male and female employees. Thus technique causing this type of substitution does not influence the level of labor productivity through employment. In practice both types of substitution usually appear simultaneously and lead to changes in the technical composition of capital and in the occupation and qualification structure of the employees.[3] The problem of the substitution of "living" and "stored up" labor is of great methodological importance. The equal treatment of "living" and "stored up" labor as factors of production creating national income constitutes a starting point for different concepts of the distribution of the national product. The Marxian method, accepting the second solution, sometimes appears to be at odds with obvious facts of increased productivity due to technique without any noticeable changes in "living" labor. This apparent contradiction comes from the lack of insight in the analysis of the factors affecting labor productivity related to its very nature.

Labor productivity understood as the amount of the product per unit of working time depends on two characteristics: labor's intensity and its productive power. The intensity of labor is the amount of work performed within a unit of time. The productive power of labor is the ability of achiev-

1. That is, excluding the influence of changing the structure of employment.
2. K. Wandelt, *The Essence and Types of Technical Progress* (Poznan, 1960).
3. These processes were very well described by Marx as a characteristic feature of capital during the period of mechanization. Even today his description occupies the foremost position in the theory of employment and wages.

ing a defined material effect per unit of labor. We can say that it is a potential amount of production per unit of concrete labor. Thus the effective
labor productivity is the product of the intensity and productive power.
"The productive power of labor is determined by different circumstances,
such as the average level of skill of the worker, the level of science and its
technological application, the social organization of the production process,
the amount and the effectiveness of the means of production and the natural
conditions." [4] Almost the same can be said about labor intensity, replacing
the worker's skill and natural conditions by his psycho-physiological efficiency. Among the factors mentioned the most changeable perhaps is
technique. Consequently, it plays an important part in developing the
characteristics of "living" labor, thus influencing the final production effect
and labor productivity.

Technique influences the intensity of labor in two directions, reducing
and increasing it simultaneously. A decrease in the labor intensity is connected with the process of taking over a physical effort by a machine; it
is particularly noticeable in the mechanization of strenuous processes. An
increase in intensity results from the pace and rhythm of work imposed
upon the worker by the machine, from "increased density" of the working
day which is equivalent to a more uniform intensity of effort. Decreased
intensity as a result of making work easier by using new techniques does
not manifest itself directly and so does not produce direct productivity
effects. Increased density of the working day, however, means increased
labor inputs producing a greater number of products per unit of time, and
thus resulting in an increase of productivity. If the intensity of labor were
treated as an index of social costs,[5] we would have to say that in the first case
we deal with a saving in "living" labor which cannot be directly measured,
and in the second case with invisibly increased labor inputs reflected in
increased productivity.[6]

With regard to the other characteristic determining productivity—the
productive power of labor—the determination of the influence of technique
is more complicated. The productive power of labor depends not only on
the means of production that it operates but also on its technical efficiency.
The latter cannot be directly reduced to "living" labor since it combines
productive labor, conceptual labor of the designers, and the use of the

4. J. Zieleniewski, *Labor Productivity* (Poznan, 1960).
5. J. Zieleniewski, *Labor Productivity* (Poznan, 1960).
6. It is a different matter that scientific methods so far do not allow us to separate
   satisfactorily the influence of the intensity of labor on productivity from other determining factors.

power of nature. Without denying this diversity, we have to remember that efficiency is only potential as long as it is put in motion by "living" labor. The specific use of particular organs—muscles, nerves, brains—and the specific level of qualifications and psycho-physiological qualities of the worker required for a given technique confirm the known Marxian thesis: technique is dead without "living" labor and cannot, by itself, constitute a source for creating a product. For this reason the phrase, "the substitution of 'living' and 'stored up' labor" should be treated as an abbreviated term. After closer analysis it turns out that it is an intra-factor substitution—the substitution of the productive power of labor (quality) or its quantity conditioned by technique, but dependent upon adaptation processes taking place in the *nature* of "living" labor.

The problem of inter-factor substitution, as mentioned above, gives a qualitative analysis of relationships between technique and labor productivity.

The quantitative relation requires the measurement of the technique used and of the changes in labor productivity. Before we start considering these relationships, we shall stress the point that in the most general terms the impact of technique on labor productivity, its quantitative effect, depends upon: (1) the nature of technique used; (2) the importance of the sector of the economy to which it has been applied; (3) the role and the character of certain occupations which this technique serves or replaces; and (4) the degree of the use of the productive power of technique applied.

Labor Productivity and the Nature of New Techniques

Under a technnical expansion one accepts as a fact the application of innovation—technical progress. But it is not always true. Often the expansion of technique is realized in cases where an expansion of production, not accompanied by changes in the intensity of capital and without changes in the methods of production, takes place. Only the means of production are being added on the same or on a very similar technical level as before. This type of expansion will be called applying extensive technique contrary to the intensive method (which revolutionizes the methods of production).[7]

The extensive technique does not lead to changes in individual labor productivity related to one occupation or product. It essentially affects the average level of productivity in enterprises, industry, or the whole economy indirectly through the structural changes mentioned above.

7. K. Secomski, *Studies in the Effectiveness of Investment* (Warsaw, 1957), p. 69.

The concentration of production based on given technique results in the increased importance of its corresponding level of productivity at the aggregate level. Moreover, this concentration puts in motion other factors which increase productivity (organization, for example). This problem is of particular importance in countries possessing substantial reserves of free labor power, limited capital resources, and unsatisfied demand. Under these circumstances the use of cheaper techniques[8] result in a more rapid growth of production with a simultaneous solution of the employment problem. This process is accompanied by an increase in the social productivity of labor.

An intensive use of new techniques is characterized by an increase in capital intensity and changes in production methods. It almost always leads to an increase in labor productivity where it is applied. It always reduces the labor required per unit of production and therefore makes possible the reduction of the labor force in occupations where new techniques were applied or it increases the volume of production. In some cases it makes it possible to achieve both these effects simultaneously. From a social point of view each of these alternatives produces somewhat different results. An increase in the amount of the product because of intensive use of new techniques at the same level of employment as before means an increase in individual, aggregated, and social labor productivity. The greater the importance of a given sector in total production, the greater is this increase. Thus we deal here with a certain parallelism of the dynamics of labor productivity in a sector and in the whole economy resulting from the application of new techniques which revolutionize production methods. The degree of the parallelism of these changes may undergo substantial modifications in cases of diminished employment in a sector where new techniques are used. Labor power released in this way increases labor resources in the national economy. This offers for an economy where the demand for labor exceeds its supply the possibility of additional employment in other sectors and the possibility of expansion of production on the old or on the new level of technique. This leads to changes in the general level of productivity (predominantly an increase). But it can also happen that the released worker (always less qualified compared with the one who remains employed) finds employment in a lower level of productivity or simply stays unemployed.[9]

8. The problem of the lower cost of applying extensive technique in comparison with intensive technique is debatable. J. Pojestka, "Economiczna efektywnosc wprowadzania postepu technicznego" (Economic Effectiveness of Technical Progress), *Nowe Drogi,* no. 2, 1960.
9. Karl Marx, *Das Kapital* (Berlin, 1949), vol. I, chap. 23.

That will naturally decrease the level of general and social labor productivity. Which of these alternatives is more likely to materialize depends upon the factors outside technique—such as the level of development of productive resources seen in the supply of means of labor and demand for labor, the social conditions of production determined by the social system, and, finally, the state of the economy. An insufficient supply of capital goods, related to the actually achieved level of development of productive resources, may act as an essential deterrent on the road to employment. One of the basic remedies for such an insufficient supply is a rapid increase in labor productivity which increases the possibility of accumulation. Thus we have a kind of closed circle: on lower levels of economic development a danger of conflict may arise between labor productivity and full employment, leading to a divergence between labor productivity on industrial and on national levels. A planned socialist economy, from its very nature, has greater possibilities of solving this conflict than an uncontrolled economy based on the private ownership of the means of production. These possibilities are created both by the centralization of accumulation funds and by applying to their distribution criteria other than those imposed by the profit motive.[10]

Intensive use of new techniques is always hand in hand with progress. But three types of progress can be distinguished, and each of them furnishes another relationship between the dynamics of labor productivity and the dynamices of use of technique measured by intensity of capital per worker.

This relationship can be expressed as follows:[11]

I = new investment

Zy = number of newly employed workers (employed in result of investments)

ΔDy = increase of income as effect of new investments

m = the coefficient of capital absorption of the new income (also called coefficient of capital absorption of investments)

We thus have:

$$\Delta Dy = \frac{I}{m} I$$

10. A considerable time was devoted to this problem at the Fourth and the Fifth Plenary Sessions of the Central Committee of the Polish United Workers Party in 1960. See an interesting discussion in the article by S. Kuzinski, "The Conditions of Technical Progress," *Nowe Drogi,* no. 2, 1960.

11. K. Laski, "Factors of Growth of National Income," *Ekonomista,* no. 2, 1960, pp. 245–248.

Dividing both sides by Zy, we obtain

$$\frac{\Delta Dy}{Zy} = \frac{I}{m} \cdot \frac{I}{Zy}$$

denoting:

$$\frac{I}{Zy} \text{ by } S$$

and:

$$\frac{\Delta W}{Zy} \text{ by } W$$

we finally obtain the relation

$$W = \frac{I}{m} \cdot S$$

where S denotes the degree of capital intensity per worker, that is, the amount of investment per newly employed worker, W equals labor productivity measured by an increase in national income per newly employed worker.

It appears from this relationship that the rate of growth in labor productivity is directly proportional to the degree of capital intensity and inversely proportional to the coefficient of capital intensity of investments. In a neutral type of technical progress (constant m), labor productivity will increase in the same proportion as the capital intensity. The capital-using type of technical progress (increasing m) is characterized by a reduced rate of growth in productivity in relation to the growth in capital intensity. Finally the capital-saving type of technical progress (decreasing m) is accompanied by an accelerated rate of growth in productivity in comparison with the rate of growth in capital intensity.

These considerations emphasize again, from a somewhat different angle, the difficulties in a period of industrialization. Capital-intensive type of technical progress usual in this period carries with it a reduced rate of growth in labor productivity in relation to social outlays on the application of technique, and consequently limited possibilities of accumulation. A general switch to a different, more effective, type of technical progress requires, however, a previous "industrialization leap," and a certain minimum of capital: consuming investments.

Interesting from this point of view is a comparison of data on the dynamics of the capital intensity of investments and on the capital intensity of labor and its productivity during the last ten years in People's Poland—the ten years devoted to industrialization. (See Table 78.)

Table 78. Costs of new investments according to their net production in Poland, 1950–1960
(In billion zlotys per 100,000 workers)

Particulars	1950	1951	1952	1953	1954	1955	1956	1957	1958	1959	1960
Coefficient of capital intensity of net production	5.03	5.05	5.09	4.93	5.01	4.92	4.94	4.92	5.23	5.32	5.18
Coefficient of capital intensity (new capital goods per newly employed)	4.1	4.8	6.1	6.6	8.1	9.5	10.2	10.9	12.6	13.6	15.0
Labor productivity (new production per newly employed)	5.38	5.20	6.18	6.34	7.45	8.28	8.24	8.28	9.00	9.30	10.1

Source: J. Pojestka, *Employment, Investments and Economic Growth* (Warsaw, 1961), pp. 123, 131, 135.

Table 78 shows a certain parallelism between an increase in labor productivity and in capital intensity, but the rate of change in productivity is obviously slower, particularly starting in 1955.

It can be said that we are dealing here with the characteristic capital-intensive type of technical progress (though the divergence between the dynamics of capital intensity of labor and labor productivity is the reason for incomplete use of applied technique).

Labor Productivity and Sectors Where New Techniques Are Applied

The influence of new techniques or the modernization of old techniques on labor productivity depends upon the sector of production where it is applied. Non-uniform labor intensity and capital intensity play important parts in certain branches of production.[12] Furthermore, the extent of the

12. Interbranch differences in these coefficients are tremendous in Poland. For example, the labor absorption of production measured by the number of employees per one million zlotys worth of net production fluctuates from 9.2 in the food industry to 80 per cent in transport and communication, 81 per cent in agriculture, 56 per cent in the building materials industry; the coefficient of capital absorption, measured by new capital goods per net production from 1.0 in the food industry, 1.3 in construction, 9.1 in the fuel industry, and 10.1 in the power industry (J. Pojestka, "Economiczna efektywnosc," pp. 115 and 123).

influence of changes in technique on productivity varies. Technique used in the last stages of production, or even in the stage that produces consumer goods, brings about effects in the same sector and influences the general level of labor productivity through changes in production structure. The influence of technique used in creating the means of production—is much more manysided. In addition to effects analogous to those appearing in the last stages of production, it induces secondary processes of growth in labor productivity.

New means of labor either serve as elements of new capital intensity for those already employed or create new jobs. In the first case, they raise labor productivity per worker in the sectors where they are used. In the second, they activate free labor reserves or attract workers from jobs in which labor productivity is lower, thus bringing about cumulative processes of growth in the general level of labor productivity. Finally, the third aspect is connected with the quality of the product. Experience has shown that an increase in labor productivity, particularly in creating the means of production, is usually accompanied by an improved product. This means an improved technical efficiency in the equipment produced and increased labor productivity in the following stages of production.

Therefore, it is easier to understand how an investment policy in a socialist state during the period of industrialization gives preference not only to a more extensive development of the means of production but also emphasizes increased labor productivity at this stage. The concentration of investment outlays, the highest degree of capital intensity and power intensity, the fastest rate of replacement of machinery, the most elaborate material incentives are the main elements characterizing this policy.

Labor Productivity and the Character of Labor Equipped with New Techniques

Analyzing the role of the nature of labor (served or replaced by technique) in determining the influence of new techniques on labor productivity, we have first to consider the division of labor into productive and unproductive sections and then into labor used directly in production (key jobs) and in auxiliary work.

Unproductive labor and auxiliary work influence labor productivity indirectly—through services for key workers which enable them to produce more. But when the productive power of the producing worker is fully used, and his job is indivisible in the given circumstances, the better services of auxiliary workers do not lead to an increase in production or the individual level of labor productivity.

The application of technique in the form of mechanization, or even automation, in relation to auxiliary productive labor or in relation to unproductive labor only indirectly affects the dynamics of labor productivity as interpreted in this paper. It may lead to a decrease in the effort of the auxiliary worker (mechanization of factory transport, for example), or to a change in the jobs of non-manual workers (the automation of control operations, for instance), without a change in employment. In this case it will affect labor productivity only by providing better services for the directly productive worker. It may also lead to reduced employment in a given type of work because of this greater effectiveness, thus bringing about a change in the average level of productivity in an enterprise or a division, without contributing, however, to an increase in the product. Hence, in rapidly developing countries, where the pressure of demand is great, and where it is thus imperative to increase productivity, it is of the utmost importance to apply technique to directly productive jobs. An increase in capital intensity in auxiliary jobs in production or in unproductive jobs is from this point of view of secondary importance and of lower priority.

This approach, however, is clearly at odds with the principle of making man's work easier in contrast to the principle of direct profit in making decisions concerning the application of technique. The majority of difficult and dangerous jobs that should be fully or partly replaced by technique are (especially in an economy in the middle level of development) not in the directly productive but in the auxiliary sector.[13]

When capital resources are limited, it is always necessary to choose between technique increasing production and productivity, and technique saving effort but not increasing productivity. In practice in a socialist econ-

13. In Poland the leading transportation and excavation works are particularly backward technically and based primarily on manual labor. For instance, only 22.6 per cent of bituminous coal is loaded mechanically in mines; in truck transport 3 per cent of the total is loaded mechanically; in construction 23 per cent of excavation work is performed manually; in extracting and sorting limestone—50 per cent; in extracting clay—20 per cent, and so forth. Also in industrial production the degree of mechanization is not sufficiently high (in the machinery industry the share of manually performed work is about 50 per cent; in metallurgy about 30 per cent of blast furnaces are not mechanized; in metal rolling only about 15 per cent of aggregates can be considered sufficiently mechanized). Also insufficient is the degree of automation as measured by the ratio of the value of automation equipment to the value of machinery and equipment: it amounts to a mere 0.5 per cent (from the records of the Fourth Plenum of the Central Committee of the Polish United Workers Party).

omy the resources are divided to meet both these investment requirements. It is reflected both in the investment plans for our economy and in appropriate resolutions by the party concerning technical progress. The targets for increased labor productivity and reduced physical effort of workers along with improvements in safety and work hygiene are treated as basic objectives of the investment policy.[14]

Labor Productivity and the Degree of Use of New Techniques

A consideration of the relationship between technique and its sphere of application, on one hand (in the sense of nature of work or division of economy) and labor productivity, on the other hand, may constitute the most general starting point for the choice of new techniques and the areas of application. However, the application of new techniques to particular sectors is only the first step in controlling labor productivity by creating technical possibilities for its growth. The transformation of possibility into reality depends upon the degree of use of existing productive capacity and equipment. The most efficient technique applied with the greatest social outlays may be wasted by improper or inefficient use.

In a planned socialist economy less than full use of productive capacity is primarily the result of bottlenecks in supplies and shortages of skilled personnel, and it is rarely the result of production restrictions caused by selling difficulties. Insufficient supplies, organization, and personnel difficulties are connected both with the actual level of the development of productive resources and with the rapid changes characteristic of a period of industrialization and radical socio-economic transformation.

Particularly worth improving is the difficult process of adapting labor power to new methods of production, since it is of great importance to the dynamics of labor productivity. These difficulties are mainly connected with mass migration of population from the country to the city, which requires a basic change in qualifications and way of life.[15] These circumstances, during the first stage of industrialization in Polish production, brought about increases from added employment without full use of technique. Only during the second stage was it possible to concentrate on labor

14. The Fourth Plenary Session of the Central Committee of the Polish United Workers Party, January 20–22, 1960; and the Fifth Plenary Session, June 21–22, 1960.
15. A very interesting discussion of this subject can be found in Walter Galenson and Harvey Liebenstein, "Investment Criteria, Productivity and Economic Development," QJE, August 1955.

productivity, which depends on raising the qualifications of new workers. The current five-year plan postulates the achievement of 80 per cent of the production increase through increased labor productivity.

The main forms in which less than full use of technique show up and limit its influence on social labor productivity are, first of all, the number of shifts and shutdowns. The swift turnover coefficient constituted a planned degree of use of technique, determined for long periods and with allowances made for the possibilities of supplies and personnel. Shutdowns, on the other hand, are short-lasting phenomena. They usually are a sign of poor organization (although equipment is also important) and considerably disorganize the production process.[16]

Summary

Summing up these short considerations we may state:

(1) Technique undoubtedly plays an important part in raising labor productivity, although it does not constitute its independent source, but is a factor determining the productive power of "living" labor.

(2) The application of new techniques may produce different productivity effects in the enterprise (the sector of application) and in the whole national economy; (a) with extensive technique the unchanged productivity of a sector may be accompanied by increased social productivity resulting from the concentration of technique with a defined efficiency; (b) an increase in the productivity of a sector when intensive technique is applied does not always lead to increased social labor productivity; an intermediate link here is change in employment in the sector where new technique was used and in other sectors.

(3) The degree of influence of technique on labor productivity depends upon the type of technical progress; a capital-consuming type of progress results in a weaker relationship, and a capital-saving type of progress results in a stronger relationship between capital intensity and labor productivity, as measured by a relative rate of growth of both of these quantities.

(4) The influence of technique on labor productivity of a sector depends upon the nature of labor served or replaced by technique; the further away

16. The degree of use of equipment in Polish industry should also be considerably improved. In the machinery industry, which is one of our bottlenecks, the shift coefficient is only 1.3 per cent. Equally unsatisfactory is the use of calendar time of the workers. In 1958 in "bottlenecks" in steel works it amounted to 84.2 per cent, in rolling mills—62.5 per cent, in cement furnaces—80.3 per cent, in the machinery industry—70 per cent to 80.

from the direct process of producing a commodity is the link undergoing mechanization or automation, the smaller is this influence.

(5) An important element reducing the influence of technique on labor productivity is the degree of its use limited during the process of industrialization by material supplies and the qualifications of the workers.

CHAPTER 28

Labor Productivity in Industry and the Economics of Energy

Gyorgy Cukor

Hungarian Academy of Sciences

There exists a manysided and complicated interrelation among the increase in labor productivity, volume of production and consumption of sources of energy, proportions of different sources of energy, efficiency of energy transformation as well as development of demand for energy in industrial production as a whole or in production of various branches or in single products.

As a result of mechanization and automation, labor productivity increases on the one hand, and the demand for energy per worker on the other—especially that for electric energy. Mechanization and the accompanying growth of demand for electric energy are important factors in the increase of labor productivity. We must not consider only the use of live labor, that is, labor applied in the given working process. Examining the development of labor productivity at the level of the national economy or at an all-industrial level, the changes in the use of stored-up labor must also be taken into account. An analysis of productivity which neglects the changes in the use of stored-up labor gives a distorted picture of the real changes. It is obvious, for example, that the electric energy consumed in the production process also includes labor, and thus if we neglect the increase in the consumption of electric energy and consider only the decrease in the use of live labor, we do not get an adequate picture of the effective change in productivity. Energy is just that factor of the total input necessary for production which—compared to other elements of stored-up labor—is liable to relatively quick changes. In some branches and in some cases, naturally, material consumption may also change quickly. The general tendency, however, is that material consumption, especially that of basic materials when compared to production, changes rather slowly.

In energy consumption we witness a two-way change. As already mentioned, the rise in labor productivity is accompanied by a growth in the consumption of electric energy per worker. In one sense, this phenomenon means substitution: mechanical work and the energy necessary for driving the machine take the place indirectly of human labor.

As to energy consumption, we also meet a change of another kind and of no less importance, especially in the last decade. The point is that total energy consumption of single countries, the demand for energy in industry as a whole (or in some branches) grows more slowly than the gross national product, the national income, or industrial production.

The decrease of specific energy consumption naturally means that a lesser amount of labor is needed to produce the same volume of use-values, that is, productivity is growing. Increasing labor productivity by a more rational use of energy is storing up considerable reserves, because the calorific efficiency of energy is still very low in many processes. Besides, there is a wide range of substitution possibilities; we can find a means to interchange certain sources of energy in such a way that it results in increasing labor productivity.

Because the demand for energy is increasing and because this increase may be considered an important factor in raising productivity and because there is a possiblity of reducing the specific consumption of energy and thus productivity measured at the level of the national economy, the interrelations of the economics of energy and of labor productivity need a thorough analysis. Here we are going to examine the interrelations somewhat more closely and try to quantify them.

Labor Productivity and the Consumption of Electric Energy

The connection between the use of energy and productivity is being treated in literature on the subject mostly from the point of view of the dynamics of labor productivity and the electric energy consumption per head. A more or less close connection is established between electric energy consumption per head (or per hour) and production per head (or per hour). For example, Stepankow states: "There is a nearly directly proportionate connection between the productivity of labor and its supply energy." [1] This connection is supported by several examples. Certain data on Hungarian industry also show similar relations. As compared to 1950, the index of electric energy consumption per worker in 1955 was 117 per cent, that of labor productivity was 118; in 1959 both indexes stood at 133 per cent. In 1958, the level of productivity in Czechoslovakia was higher by 60 per cent than in Hungarian industry when weighted with the pattern (labor input) of Czechoslovak industry and by 75 per cent when weighted with that of Hungarian industry. Electric energy consumption per industrial worker, however, was higher by 77 per cent—after eliminating the differences in the pattern of industry.[2]

It is obvious that here we have a most important connection. If the productivity and the electric energy consumption per head or per hour are really directly proportionate to each other, we can come to important conclusions from the point of view of economic analysis and of economic planning. The connections of production, number of workers, and energy consumption can be interpreted as follows:

$$\text{productivity} = \frac{T}{L} = \frac{E}{L} \cdot \frac{T}{E} \quad \text{or:} \frac{T}{L} = \frac{E/L}{E/T}$$

$T = $ production; $L = $ number of workers; $E = $ electric energy consumption; $E/T = $ "specific" demand for energy; $E/L = $ labor's supply of energy (energy consumption per worker). Productivity (T/L) and supply of energy (E/L) can change proportionately when and only when the specific demand of production for energy remains unchanged. In so far as such a relation really exists, it enables us, among other things, to anticipate industry's demand for electric energy, since the proportion of industry within the total electric energy consumption—established by empirical figures—is fairly constant. It also enables us to anticipate the entire demand for electric energy.

The above relation also makes possible an analysis of the connection between electric energy consumption and productivity by examining the indicator of specific electric energy consumption. If quotient T/E is increas-

1. "On the Rate of Development and the Organization of the Economics of Electric Energy," *Voprosy Ekonomiki,* no. 5, 1961, p. 21.
2. Zoltán Román, "A Comparison of the Productivity of the Czechoslovak and the Hungarian Industries," *Közgazdasági Szemle,* July-August 1961.

ing, it means that productivity (T/L) is rising faster than the supply of energy (E/I). With dynamic comparisons and comparisons of industries of different countries (or their branches), productivity and supply of energy are proportionate and have the same value only when the specific demand of production for energy remains unchanged.

In Hungarian industry and in some of its branches industrial electric energy consumption per unit of net production (E/T) and industrial electric energy consumption per worker (L/E) in 1955 and 1959 (1950 = 100) are shown in Table 79.

Table 79. Industrial electric energy consumption per unit of net production and per worker in Hungarian industry, 1955 and 1959.
(In per cent)

Industry	1955^a	1959^a	1955^b	1959^b
Mining	108	120	99	109
Metallurgy	123	129	135	152
Engineering	108	84	134	140
Building materials	122	118	145	181
Chemicals	85	83	108	136
Rubber and synthetic processing	70	89	88	118
Heavy industry total	109	100	124	137
Timber	98	118	135	170
Paper	92	88	119	128
Printing	98	105	151	184
Textiles	101	107	120	120
Leather and fur	119	138	122	125
Clothing	113	206	130	229
Light industry total	83	84	96	97
Foodstuffs, drinks, tobacco	80	124	98	162
State industry total	103	101	118	133

    a. Index of industrial electric energy consumption per net value in the years 1955 and 1959, in per cent (1950 = 100).
    b. Index of industrial electric energy consumption per head of workers for the years 1955 and 1959, in per cent (1950 = 100).

Table 79 shows that the development of the specific consumption of energy is rather different in various branches of industry. Neither do we find proportionate changes—at least in regard to branches of industry—between productivity and electric energy consumption in Czechoslovak industry. The data for 1958 are shown in Table 80 (1950 = 100).

Table 80 shows that specific electric energy consumption changes in the different branches of industry at differing rates and in divergent directions. The main tendency is an increase in specific electric energy consumption.

Table 80. Productivity and energy consumption in Czechoslovak industry, 1958.
(1950 = 100)

Industry	Per worker		Specific electric energy consumption index (T/E)
	Gross production index	Electric energy consumption index	
Electric energy	185	199[a]	93
Fuel	151	148	102
Ferrous metallurgy	183	203	90
Non-ferrous metallurgy	191	376	51
Engineering	218	125	174
Chemicals and rubber	216	121	178
Building materials	262	139	188
Timber	206	139	148
Paper	139	122	114
Glass and ceramics	182	168	108
Textiles	166	137	121
Clothing	182	200	91
Leather and shoes	181	153	118
Printing	159	150	106
Food	171	150	114

a. Including consumption of energy by the power plants.

Source: Statiscka Rocenka CSSR, 1959.

When, making international comparisons, we take in some branches of industry the ratios of labor productivity and of electric energy consumption per worker in Hungarian and Czechoslovak industries, concluding that besides those industrial branches where the two ratios are rather similar (electric energy production or the paper industry), there are also branches where these ratios differ considerably.

The specific consumption of electric energy in industry (E/T) as an average of the countries belonging to the OEEC and in some other countries according to OEEC, *Industrial Statistics,* 1900–1950 was as follows: Total OEEC energy consumption was 112.6. In England it was 121.7; the German Federal Republic, 102.4; Austria, 109.6; France, 111.1; and Italy, 82.4.

Thus, except for Italy, specific consumption of electric energy is increasing, that is, electric energy consumption per hour is rising faster than productivity. Accordingly, specific consumption of electric energy developed fairly differently by countries and by industrial branches. In the case of Hungary, the stability of the specific consumption of electric energy (T/E) for 1955 and 1959 is an average which took shape from the changes of different sizes and directions to be found in the various industrial branches.

If we consider how the increase of industrial electric energy consumption, on the one hand, and the increase in productivity, on the other, take place, it becomes clear that the processes are so complicated and manifold that we cannot expect a lasting and general direct proportion between productivity and electric energy consumption per head. It depends on the rate of mechanization and automation, on the development of energy consumption for technological purposes, and, in the case of industry as a whole, on the changes in the pattern of industry structure. The formation of a directly proportionate relationship should be regarded rather as an accident and not as some kind of pattern. The general tendency is that consumption of electric energy is increasing faster than industrial production and that there is thus no proportionality between productivity and electrical energy consumption per worker.

W. Nowak, in his article,[3] "The electric energy consumption of industry and the productivity of labour," comes to a similar conclusion. He establishes that the connection between productivity and electric energy consumption per worker shows there is a relation between the two quantities, but there is no close correlation.

The Effect of the Changes in the Use of Energy upon the Total Labor Input

One relation between labor productivity and consumption of energy is the one we have already mentioned—the increase in productivity and of electric energy consumption per head generally go together. If the efficiency in the production of sources of energy and in their transformation into electric energy remains unchanged, the increase in the consumption of electric energy causes the demand for labor to rise and thus works toward lowering productivity.

There is, however, another no less important relation between the use of energy and the total demand for labor in production. In recent years the relative decrease of total energy consumption calculated in calories—as compared to national income, to gross national product, or to industrial production—and the change in the structure of the sources of energy used have

3. *Gospodarka Planowa,* no. 2, 1961.

been characteristic manifestations of technological development. Beyond doubt, both the relative savings in calories and the changes in the pattern of sources of energy change the demand for stored-up labor in the form of energy consumption, and they generally reduce it to a large degree. This reduction, however, is not adequately characterized by the savings shown in the balances of energy as expressed in calories, because they neither show what savings in total labor input are effected by the reduction expressed in calories, or what the effect of the changes in the pattern of the balance of energy is.

The balance of inter-industry relations (input-output) renders the calculation of the so-called total input coefficients possible.[4] This balance and its inverse enable us to reduce energy inputs to primary inputs. With the use of an approaching method, imports and even amortization can be reduced to live labor. In such a way, energy inputs and structural and dynamic changes in the balance of energy can also be reduced to the changes in live labor inputs. Such a reduction is practical not only because it gives information about the changes in one element of stored-up labor, but also because the usual balance of energy is unable to yield entirely satisfactory information about the changes in the energy inputs. It is evident that in case of structural change the change expressed in calories or in tons of coal-equivalent does not show the real changes in the inputs at the level of the national economy; the calorific content of the various primary and secondary sources of energy is not proportionate to the production costs of the same. Nor does the measuring of energy consumption with prices give an adequate picture of the changes in the size of inputs from the point of view of the national economy. Such is the situation with socialist and capitalist countries alike. In socialist countries, the price proportions are often being purposefully diverted from the value proportions. This deviation can be made to an especially great extent with sources of energy, where in the interest of attaining certain goals of economic policy the price proportions of the single sources of energy are nearer sometimes to their use values and not to the proportions of their production costs. In capitalist countries, however, the price policy of all-powerful trusts interested in the production of sources of energy as well as certain measures of economic policy of government vigorously divert the price proportions of energy sources from their cost proportions. Therefore, working out the total input content (the reduction of inputs to labor), imports and amortization have a great significance in

4. Economic literature has introduced the method of the balance of inter-industry relations in detail. We have supposed, therefore, that the basic notions are known.

planning for the measurement of the effects of various measures of economic policy. This is because it enables us to estimate what labor input, what demand for import, and what other economic changes there are at the back of the changes in the volume and structure shown in calories (in a technical unit of measurement). In this paper, however, we intend to deal only with the connections of energy consumption and of labor productivity. The usual indexes of productivity neglect the changes in the consumption of stored-up labor within one branch. We shall attempt to prove through some calculations (of only approximate and illustrative character) that this neglect may be so large relating to the whole of industry and in cases of single branches of industry that the average index of productivity is inaccurate. The usual indexes are derived from the quotient of the production index and of an index of labor input (the number of workers or of working hours). The so-called net indexes of production, contrary to the indexes of gross production, show the development of net production correctly even when the proportions of the single industrial branches or those of a series of products constituting the single net indexes change, thus eliminating the distortions of structural changes. From this point of view these indexes approach net production correctly. If, however, the consumption of stored-up labor changes considerably, such an index is not quite correct, because it does not reflect the changes in net production in connection with the changes in the consumption of stored-up labor. In our introduction we have pointed out that the specific energy consumption of industry had significantly decreased in the past decade. Table 81 shows this decrease in the Hungarian state industry as a whole and in some important industrial branches.

Table 81. The decrease of specific energy[a] consumption in
Hungarian industry, 1955 and 1959.
(1950 = 100)

Industry	1955[b]	1959[b]	1955[c]	1959[c]
Mining	123	95	127	109
Metallurgy	113	121	116	131
Engineering	103	66	97	73
Building materials	86	74	87	76
Textiles	96	84	99	92
Food	67	60	68	64
State industry total	94	80	95	86

a. Various sources of energy converted into calories.
b. Electric energy consumption converted into basic sources of energy by means of the actual efficiency of the year in question.
c. By means of 1950 efficiency.

It may be seen from the figures that the decrease of the specific energy consumption in industry as a whole derives from changes of direction; specific energy consumption increased in metallurgy and decreased in the other branches. If, however, the specific consumption of energy which constitutes a considerable share of stored-up labor is decreasing in such a measure, it is doubtful whether the usual indexes properly show the development of productivity. We question whether, when we want to present the effect of energy economy on labor productivity, it is not justified to correct these indexes. We have briefly reviewed how the various inputs (including energy inputs) can be converted into labor inputs with the help of the balance of inter-industry relations. After conversion into labor input, the index of productivity may be also corrected.

In an earlier paper—for the purposes of studying the structure of industry by branches—we had worked out the full input coefficients of the different industrial branches with the help of the balance of inter-industry relations for 1957 (total labor input, total import content, and total amortization). We also worked out the key numbers for reducing import content and the amortization to labor input.[5] With the help of the calculations and indicators presented therein the total labor inputs of energy inputs can also be worked out. As we know, calculations of this kind contain many sources of error not to be treated here in detail. They presume, for example, that the different branches are homogeneous in regard to their products and the distribution of their products as well; they presume the homogeneity of exports and imports from the point of view of their countervalue in foreign exchange, and so forth. With the help of the total input coefficients published in the paper mentioned, we worked out the primary inputs per 10^9 calorie of the major sources of energy. Owing to the errors and distortions mentioned above, it is only of an illustrative character. Still, it properly demonstrates certain tendencies, as is seen in Table 82.

In Table 82 we have adopted some simplifications, which may also jeopardize the accuracy of the calculations. The table in question shows that the inputs of fuel oil and natural gas, calculated for the same amount of calories, are much lower than in the case of coal. (The exceptional circumstances of the year 1957 distort the figures disadvantageously for fuel oil and natural gas; in other years these would present a picture still more favorable.)

The total input coefficients employed may be used not only for analyzing

5. Gyorgy Cukor and Zoltán Román, "The Utilization of the Balance of Inter-Industry Relations for Analyzing and Planning the Structure of Industry."

the structure of the balance of energy but also for examining its changes over time. The total labor input of energy consumption could be arrived at if we carried out the same conversion for other years as was done for 1957. Since, however, the balance of inter-industry relations and its inverse are available only for the year 1957 [6] (the inversion of the balance for 1959 is now in process), this idea had to be abandoned. However, we have converted the energy consumption in the years 1950, 1957, and 1959 into their total labor content on the basis of the total input coefficients for 1957. The result obtained is not the total demand for labor, since the productivity (and

Table 82. Primary inputs per 10⁹ calorie of the major sources of energy in Hungarian industry, 1957.

Industry	Number of workers per year	Imports (in 1000 foreign exchange forints)	Amortization (1000 forints)	Number of workers incl. imports	Amortization converted into number of workers	Total[a] input converted into number of workers per year
Coal	1.85	2.94	8.45	2.20	0.47	2.67
Coke	—	50.93	—	6.04	—	6.04
Electric energy	2.35	13.78	25.79	3.98	1.44	5.42
Fuel oil	0.52	9.71	8.32	1.67	0.47	2.14
Petrol and gas oil	0.52	9.71	8.32	1.67	0.47	2.14
Natural gas	0.81	1.57	19.07	1.00	1.07	2.07

a. Total of the two preceding columns.

the coefficients of the balance of inter-industry relations) changed between 1950 and 1959. The results of the calculations, however, show how great the savings in labor input in industry achieved through the changes in energy consumption and in the structure of the balance of energy would have been if the input coefficients and the structural relations of the year 1957 had remained unchanged (apart from the changes which took place in the consumption of energy).

In the following calculations we have taken into account the electric energy consumption with an unchanged calorific content (with that in 1950), and thus we have disregarded the improvement in the transforming efficiency of electric energy production. This seemed expedient for examin-

6. Publications of the Institute of Economics of the Hungarian Academy of Sciences. No. 9 Publishing House for Economics and Law, 1960.

ing the savings achieved in the various branches of industry by themselves.

The savings achieved are partly a result of the decrease in the total consumption of energy and partly of the changes in the structure of energy consumption. In the case of the whole industry this is a quantity to be taken into account, though it would not essentially change the index of net production or that of productivity. The case is somewhat different if we make the same calculations for industrial branches. Here we may find that the change in energy consumption results in a change of total labor input to such a degree that the accuracy of the index of productivity is doubtful. In metallurgy, for instance, energy consumption in calories and when converted into total labor input had risen from 1950 to 1957 in a greater measure than production. The increase in manpower calculated in this manner is 1000 workers for 1955, nearly 19,000 for 1957, and 17,000 for 1959. Since

Table 83. Electric energy consumption (with an unchanged calorific content) in Hungary, 1950, 1957, 1959.

Savings	1950	1957	1959
Index of industrial production	100	181	228
Index of energy consumption in industry (converted into labor)	100	166	206
Relative savings in manpower	—	14,000	26,000
As percentage of the manpower in industry	—	1.8	3.0

the total number of workers in metallurgy was 59,600 in 1959, the effect of the increase in energy consumption amounted to 29 per cent of the manpower in metallurgy. Thus, it is very significant. Naturally, the increase in question cannot be entirely attributed to the increase in specific energy consumption of metallurgy; it is mainly an outcome of the changes in the pattern of products within metallurgy.

We may discover changes in the opposite direction in the building material industry where the decrease of specific energy consumption from 1950 to 1959 converted into total labor input, means more than 5000 people—10 per cent of the manpower in the building material industry in 1959. Here, therefore, the index for productivity should be corrected upwards. The situation is similar in the textile industry where we also find savings. The extent of the latter, however, is smaller: about 2 per cent of manpower in 1959. The increase in transforming efficiency of electric energy production can also be converted into total labor input. The saving in calories and in total use of manpower is seen in Table 84.

Table 84. The saving in calories and total use of manpower
in Hungary, 1951–1959.

Year	Savings in 10^9 of calories	Savings in labor input	Savings as percentage of manpower in industry
1951	641	2,551	0.5
1952	387	1,540	0.2
1953	444	1,767	0.3
1954	1,407	5,600	0.8
1955	2,076	8,262	1.2
1956	3,042	12,107	1.7
1957	4,197	16,704	2.3
1958	5,590	22,248	2.9
1959	7,481	29,774	3.1

From the above calculations, we can see that the changes in the volume and in the pattern of energy consumption may result in a considerable change in the future use of stored-up labor both in industry as a whole and various industrial branches. It is practical, therefore, to take the effects of energy economics into account when analyzing the productivity.

CHAPTER 29

Mechanization and Automation of Production: The Decisive Factors in Raising Labor Productivity

A. S. TOLKACHYOV

Research Economic Institute, Moscow

Steady growth of labor productivity is the most important source of economic advancement and social progress in the USSR. In the period 1961–1980 growth of labor productivity will bring about approximately 90 per cent of the expected increase in industrial output, in comparison with 69 per cent in the fourth five-year plan and 68 per cent in the fifth five-year plan. It will also bring over 90 per cent of the increase in the national income.

Labor productivity is expressed by the efficiency of live labor outlays, and it is the result of the effectiveness of live labor outlays.

At present, with mechanical production and especially under today's conditions, labor efficiency depends a great deal on the degree of mechanization, on the use and degree of mechanical means to equip industrial labor, and on the supply of resources.

Mechanization and automation are the main reasons for the reduction in both live and embodied labor outlays per production unit in the USSR. However, live labor outlays are being reduced relatively more than those of embodied labor. The influence of this factor in raising labor productivity is being analyzed through practical methods. Under socialist production it means determining the efficiency of expenditure on mechanization of labor to provide better working conditions.

In this report certain general questions of methods and approaches in defining the influence of mechanization and automation on raising labor productivity are being discussed as are economic incentives applied in the USSR in order to introduce mechanization and automation in mechanical production.

Initial Methodological Principles

Mechanization and automation of the production processes are collective concepts embracing the development of all implements used in material production. The program of the CPSU envisages the comprehensive mechanization of the national economy in the current decade, and within the twenty-year period, 1961–1980, automation of production will be effected on a large scale. In 1965 hard manual labor will be fully replaced by mechanized labor.

The seven-year plan of economic development in the USSR for 1959–1965 foresaw allocating over 7600 million rubles for the mechanization and automation of eleven key industries. According to the calculations of the Scientific-Research Economic Institute of the USSR State Economic Council the mean annual economy from the cost reduction will amount to 65 kopecks per ruble of outlay, ensuring their total compensation in less than a half year. Out of 56 per cent of the total labor productivity increase in the eleven key industries in this period, 27 per cent will be achieved by mechanization and automation alone. This will fulfill almost half the plan targets. A survey of the economic efficiency of mechanization and automation in 1236 establishments in the USSR was carried out in 1960. Data showed that labor productivity in the mechanized and automated enterprises increased on the average by 72 per cent.

The average labor productivity rise due to the introduction of mechanization and automation in various industries in 1960 is shown below (all figures are precentages):

All inspected enterprises	72.0
Iron and steel	7.57
Oil-working	15.7
Chemicals	17.2
Machine-building	31.0
Paper and wood-working	52.7
Building materials	35.3
Light industry	80.5
Food	108.3

Expenditure per worker is shown in Table 85.

Table 85. Expenditure per worker released because of automation
and mechanization in Soviet industry, 1960.

Industry	Mechanization	Automation
All inspected enterprises	100.0	100.0
Iron and steel	160.0	90.0
Oil-working	90.0	24.0
Chemicals	150.0	90.0
Machine building	248.0	164.0
Paper and wood-working	90.0	40.0
Building materials	335.0	106.0
Light industry	91.0	87.0
Food	37.0	44.0

Technical progress produces the most impressive economic effect when, along with mechanization and automation, new technology, better work organization, and improved worker qualifictions are introduced. It is the structure of production outlays that determines the nature of labor productivity as a social category. Social labor productivity growth is assumed in the USSR to be the major criterion for the economic efficiency of mechanization and automation.

The method of determining the efficiency of mechanization and automation for the national economy conforms with social labor productivity. The main point of this method is as follows: it is necessary to take into account both the effect of the introduction of mechanization and automation and the production outlays for their introduction not only in a particular enterprise but in enterprises of adjacent industries. With this in view, it is necessary to consider the so-called combined outlays for fixed and circulating funds used in connection with the introduction of mechanization and automation. The degree of this combination conforms with the amount of these additional investments. In many cases it may be limited to a combination of the first order. For example, the estimate of outlays for hydraulic coal mining includes the expenditures for constructing coal-drying installations. Calculations for the combined capital investments can be made on the basis of the accepted standards of the specific outlays. The capital investments saved by mechanization and automation in a particular enterprise of an adjacent industry are to be taken into account.

The method of national economic efficiency is also used to define a current outlay economy. For instance, the improvement in quality of the product because of automation in the enterprise producing semi-manufactured material for another enterprise reduces the outlays at the latter accordingly. Therefore, the first enterprise, while assessing the efficiency of automation, takes this reduction into account. Because of the national economy's approach to the definition of economic efficiency, profit is no longer the main criterion in the efficiency of mechanization and automation, not only because it reflects distributive relations but because it also includes extra working time. A socialist society is interested in effective use of live labor as a whole.

The continuity principle established in the national economy planning

Table 86. Normative gradients of the economic estimate of the efficiency of automation and mechanization in Soviet industry.

Degree	Maximum terms of justification of the expenses T (per year)	Minimum rate of efficiency $E = \frac{1}{T} 100$ (per cent)
Partial mechanization and automation of new types of equipment; installation of new apparatus and devices for the units in operation	1–1.5	100–65
Mechanization and automation of some processes and operations; modernization and partial replacement of the equipment	2–3	50–95
Introduction of comprehensively mechanized and automated processes; establishing of automatic production lines and shops (without revising the flow-sheet)	4–5	25–20
Comprehensive mechanization and automation of production in shops and at the enterprises; full reequipment and revision of technology	6	16–17

of the USSR conforms with the most precise estimate of the influence of mechanization and automation on raising social labor productivity.

One of the most important peculiarities of this method is that annually the main tasks of the perspective plan are being amended on the basis of the additional resources of production revealed by the introduction of new techniques. Finally, while selecting the most effective means of mechanization and automation, besides the indexes of the output growth, the following factors including outlays of past labor are being taken into account: reduction of production costs; necessary capital investments; justification in terms of the expenses and the corresponding rates of efficiency of these investments.

The last of the factors expresses the efficiency of the above-mentioned outlays both current and past.

In the USSR the normative gradients of the economic estimate of the efficiency of mechanization and automation are differentiated according to the type of work or to branches of industry.

As to the types of work these normatives as a rule do not exceed the figures in Table 86.

The estimates of mechanization and automation reveal the aggregate effect of both live and embodied labor, providing thorough evaluation of the new techniques from the view of social labor productivity. At the same time they are in full conformity with the economic and technical principles executed in the national economic planning of the USSR. On the basis of this principle the leading figures of the state plan are worked out: the volume of production output; production outlays; labor productivity; the efficiency of capital investments. The plan for introducing new techniques worked out in an enterprise and brought to the State Planning Committee is to be taken into account.

Methods of Gauging the Effect of Mechanization and Automation

Analysis of labor productivity to determine the influence of certain factors on the change in labor productivity is being carried out at different stages of planning and calculation both in the enterprises and in central planning bodies. For this purpose two methods are used in the USSR: production-analytical and economic-statistical. The first is used to study and plan labor productivity at different stages of the production process—preparatory, processing, assembly, and so forth. Classification of the influencing factors is made in accordance with the specific type of each branch of industry. For instance, in machine-building enterprises the analysis is based on: the introduction of new techniques, advanced technology, the change in the specific weight of specialized production, enlarging the volume of machine components, standardization and normalization, mastering the design of articles in production, improvement of labor conditions, advancement of work skills and qualifications, improvement of management organization, bettering quality of labor products, and better use of working time. These factors are compiled in the next stage of planning and analyzing. All these factors or the majority of them simultaneously influence the growth of labor productivity and in many cases are interacting. Thus it is difficult to gauge precisely the influence of each of them separately. However, a certain conventionality is possible. The target indexes of labor productivity growth are based on them. The influence of mechanization and automation on labor productivity is estimated at every stage of work: projecting, working out design, as well as in drawing up the general plan for the national economy. For this purpose the method of direct calculation for every introduced measure is applied. The total data of these calculations is reflected in the state plan for introduction of new equipment and in the plan for labor. This method of direct calculation affords the opportunity of obtaining the most exact data for every arrangement which provides the possibility of comparing and obtaining exact summary data if the same methods of analysis are applied. At the planning stage for gauging labor productivity growth, the calculations are made on the basis of the most efficient machines, apparatuses and devices both of the USSR and other countries. At the production stage comparison between the old and new machines is made by determining the time required per production item of the same program before and after the innovations. An evaluation of the saving in working time at the enterprises because of mechanization and automation is effected in the following way:

First, the number of machines and their terms of introduction are fixed; the efficiency of the new equipment is determined by comparing it with that now in operation; thus the expected reduction of the amount of labor consumed for producing the unit of output in norm-hours and the mean growth of labor productivity (in per cent) are revealed at the sector of production where mechanization and automation are introduced—according to the formula:

$$\pi_{2av} = \frac{\Sigma\ \pi_2 P_2}{\Sigma\ P_2}$$

where: $\pi_2 =$ the growth of labor productivity; $P_2 =$ the number of workers engaged. The mean growth of labor productivity π average for all the introduced machinery can be found according to the formula:

$$\pi_{av} = \frac{\pi_{2av} - \pi_{1av}}{\pi_{1av}} \times 100$$

where:

$\pi_{1av} = $ *productivity* (with old equipment);
$\pi_{2av} = $ average productivity (with new equipment).

The stock of working time required to fulfill the predetermined program is found by the rate of labor productivity growth with introduction of new equipment.

The saving in working time during official working hours is bound to be the difference between the working time needed in programs with old and new equipment. Taking the percentage of the fulfillment of the planned rate of output (or actual rate in the current period) as well as the annual budget of working time we can determine relative reduction in the number of workers.

The change in the number of other categories of workers after mechanization and automation have been brought about can be established by the quota of service outlays and other factors. The number of factory and office workers liable to transfer to other sectors of production because of mechanization and automation is the total reduction in all categories of industrial-production personnel.

The ratio of the above gradient to the total number of industrial-production personnel in an enterprise, fixed for the goals of the plan period with the labor productivity level of the base period, reveals the reduction in the number of workers (in per cent) caused by mechanization and automation.

These indexes of labor productivity growth obtained as the result of mechanization and automation under new production conditions are being corrected when the conditions do not depend on the introduction of mechanization and automation. In this case the following factors are to be taken into account: when change in the structure of the products, influencing the monetary value of the production, do not conform with the labor outlays; change in volume of products and semi-manufactured goods brought about by cooperation; increase (or reduction) in a production program which determines the changes in the number of certain categories of workers (whose number is directly related to the output volume).

After the figures (obtained by direct calculation) on labor productivity growth brought about by mechanization and automation have been corrected, we may determine the influence of this factor on the total index of labor productivity according to the following formula (in per cent):

$$\pi_H = \pi_{av} \cdot \frac{\pi_m}{\pi}$$

π_{av} = mean growth of labor productivity for all arrangements;
π_m = the number of workers in mechanized and automated sectors;
π = the total number of workers in an enterprise.

In the preparatory stages of plan calculations for growth of labor productivity, the economo-statistic method is used. This method also finds application while working out the hypothesis for the lengthy perspective since it is rather complicated to foresee all the changes in the development of technique and production technology that may take place within this period.

In this case, in addition to the above mentioned method of estimating labor productivity growth, the following data are used: the coefficients of correlation ratio of labor productivity to labor mechanization as well as the ratio of labor productivity growth to the level of power and electrical equipment of labor.

Thus according to the estimates made by the Scientific-Research Economic Institute of the USSR State Economic Council, over the period, 1951–1955, the mean annual growth of labor productivity was 1.055 per cent and 1.1 per cent in the 1955–1960 period per 1 per cent increase in fund equipment of labor.

The establishment of the dependence between the amount of new equipment installed, power equipment of labor, and the growth of labor productivity conforms even more with our task.

The estimates have shown that over the period, 1951–1959, the index ratio of labor productivity growth to the amount of equipment installed amounted to 0.88. The estimates of the index ratio of labor productivity and the power equipment of labor for the period, 1940–1959, revealed the steady quantitative ratio equal to 0.84–0.85.

The comparison of labor productivity growth with the growth of all major production funds and the installation of new equipment and the power equipment of labor for a number of years enable us to determine the quantitative relationship between them.

At the preliminary stages of the seven-year plan, this regular correlative ratio is used to find out the possible rate of labor productivity growth in the planned period. When the plan is drafted in detail these figures are replaced by technical-economic estimates.

Economic Stimulation of Mechanization and Automation

To raise the rates of labor productivity growth and to promote technical progress in the USSR, economic incentives for the introduction of mechanization and automation in production are being widely used.

Economic stimulation for technical progress include: prices for new techniques, the possibilities of justifying the expenses for new technique through the centralized fund of economic councils; enterprise fund, crediting, rewarding by a bonus plan, and others. It is well known that the working out of projects and the process of mastering the new techniques require additional outlays of money.

At present, the economic councils have a centralized fund to cover the related expenses and to ensure the most progressive development in different branches of industry and production. This fund relies on extra charges in price of production in all enterprises of the economic councils.

The establishment of the centralized fund gave us the opportunity to solve the problem of forming the base for the prices on new items of production. The prices quoted for the new techniques are beneficial for both the producer and the consumer. For this purpose the outlays for similar products corresponding to the period of their serial production plus rated profit are taken for the base to quote new prices. These prices as a rule are lower than the prime cost in the experimental period. For more effective techniques prices are quoted on a correspondingly higher level which stipulates both the production and the application of this technique.

Special credit extended by the USSR State Bank for mastering new techniques and for the mechanization of production has considerably accelerated technical progress. The bank credit encourages greater initiative on the part of the enterprises. The enterprise fund is also a stimulating factor.

In the USSR every enterprise allocates 40 per cent of its fund money for the development of new techniques. This sum is deducted from the plan and over plan profits and is transferred to the enterprise fund. Uusually this figure is limited by 5.5 per cent of the wages fund of the enterprise and reaches 7 per cent at the machine-building and metal-working plants.

Of great significance in expediting technical progress is the rewarding of workers and scientific personnel with bonuses for new designs and competence in the use of new techniques. Finally, the introduction of mechanization and automation in the USSR national economy is stimulated by the rapid growth of the volume of production output. Any workers released from a sector of production are immediately transferred to other jobs at the same enterprise or any other factories of the economic councils.

In the entire national economy of the USSR the comprehension of mechanization and automation is being determined, along with the optimum scale of economy in social labor and the proportionate development of the national economy.

The main criterion for the introduction of mechanization and automation in each separate branch of industry is the saving economy obtained from cutting costs and reducing capital investments, which includes the reduction in the outlays of social labor. This should not be confused with a profit motive. When production is of a social nature, society is interested not only in the profits from one part of outlays of live labor but in all the outlays and the income determined by them. At the same time mechanization and automation are introduced when they are not of high economic value but when they help toward improving the working conditions of the people.

CHAPTER 30

Reserves of the Growth of Labor Productivity and Methods for Revealing and Exploiting Them

FRANTISEK KUTTA

Czechoslovak Academy of Sciences

The Objective Laws of the Development of Labor and Production Operations

All labor or production processes consist of parts, phases, and operations which constantly recur in cycles. If we examine one of these cyclical processes in its dynamics and development, we find that in every part, on the basis of certain factors, new elements originate, which in relation to the other parts represent a step forward in development. As the complex of lower cyclical processes always relates to the higher processes, this "over-taking" takes place within the homogeneous processes as well as between the diverse processes of social production.[1] Conflicts arise constantly among the individual parts of the processes as well as between the cyclical processes as a whole in their stages of development because some develop more rapidly than others. Thus every cyclical process represents at every moment of its development a summary of parts, which are under the influence of certain factors at different stages of development—from the "most progressive" parts

1. Thus for instance the improvement of certain parts of technological processes is attained as new, highly effective technological procedures are discovered, and as the various workshops, guilds, and entire plants surpass other workshops, guilds, or plants.

inciting the entire move forward to the "most reactionary" parts hampering the general development.

This process is a complex development whole, the parts of which are in a certain mutual ratio. This corresponds with the complex nature of the effects of the development factors on this process. The constant disruption of this proportionality of the entire unit by the unequal development of its parts is accompanied by a tendency to renew it. The resumption of the disrupted proportionality is brought about in such a way that a part of the elements of the cyclical processes is attracted to the level of the most advanced, most progressive elements, and a part of the most backward elements ceases to exist, being liquidated in the interests of the further development of the whole.

This constant renewal of the proportionality of cyclical units is based on the principle of effectiveness, which is expressed by the effort to attain the highest results at the lowest costs.[2]

The unequal development, the mutual efforts of "overtaking" on the parts of the cyclically developing units, and the solving of conflicts between these, make up one of the fundamental laws of development. Every backwardness of a certain part of the whole in relation to the other parts of the same whole is a concealed reserve of development, the use of which influences the increase of effectiveness of the entire process. These general objective laws are also the bases of the development of social production, and the effectiveness of human labor productivity develops on these bases.

Reserves of the growth of labor productivity. The dynamics of the increase in labor productivity depends on the improvement of a large number of factors. According to these factors, we can classify the unused potential of labor productivity as the reserves of its growth. The reserves of the growth of labor productivity are the maximum realistic, unexploited possibilities of the qualitative development of production.[3]

2. The principle of effectiveness is not only a principle of the social forms of motion of matter, it is an analogically modified principle on the basis of which any five organism acting cyclically develops. This organism at each of its development cycles endeavors to choose from the many possibilities the one variant which is the most advantageous and most effective for its existence and further development.

3. Social production can increase either by the growth of the number of workers or by the increase in labor productivity. The increase in the number of workers cannot in itself be the foundation of growth of socialist production, the aim of which is a rise in the living standard of all working people, which necessitates the incessant increase in the per capita production and the constant increase of the effectivity of social labor. Extended socialist reproduction is being realized primarily by the qualitative changes in its method, on the basis of perfecting its technique, organiza-

The extent to which these reserves are exploited depends on the complexity of the action and improvement of all factors in the labor productivity increase in all phases of the process of extended reproduction in all stages of the production administration.

Let us follow the process of the origin, disclosure, and exploitation of the reserves of the growth of labor productivity in its micro-elementary form by looking at an example of one innovation in the building industry: Stakhonovite Fedose T. Shabliugin noticed in his normal two-men bricklaying team, which laid 3000 bricks in one shift, that the various operations hampered the work process. He therefore combined two bricklaying couples and took on one additional worker. In this five-member team, he used innovations made in the machine industry, and he separated qualified labor from unqualified labor. Two workers laid bricks, two helpers passed the bricks and mortar, and the third filled up the masonry. Labor productivity increased two and even three times by exploiting the reserves in the organization.

Further development of this method was brought to Czechoslovakia from the Soviet Union. Shabliugin's method was based on manual labor with unexploited possibilities of technical improvement. J. Tencer, a Czechoslovak innovator, used a highly productive technical device for bricklaying, the so-called "Tencer Frame," thus eliminating a number of formerly necessary operations. With a three-member work group, one bricklayer and two helpers, he increased the output by 50–60 per cent while saving two qualified bricklayers.

By combining Shabliugin's method and the former Tencer method, a new Tencer method originated: One helper spreads mortar, the second smooths it, the third passes the bricks, one mason lays the bricks, one helper fills out the walling and with the "mortar distributor" lifts the Tencer Frame. The average output with this method was 10 cubic meters of masonry per man and shift.

Improvement however did not stop here. While realizing the new method, Tencer himself pointed out that the progress of frame-bricklaying was slowed down because of insufficient supplies of material during the work process and because of unsatisfactory technical equipment. Extensive technical reserves of the growth of labor productivity were discovered in this method. For further progress, it was necessary to combine it with the

---

tion, and management and the raising of the cultural and technical standards of all workers on the basis of the growth of social labor productivity.

mechanization of all work operations in general and particularly of the supplying of material. This again was realized in the Soviet Union by the master stucco worker, Ivan Kutenkov, who in addition to dividing the work into individual operations and introducing nonstop production also brought in complex mechanization in 80 per cent of the operations thus increasing labor productivity 2.5 times while economizing on manpower and materials.

We see that new forms of work do not remain new for very long. More advanced forms spring from the old ones, keeping the most progressive elements and eliminating the obsolete ones. In every work method there is always something in the developing process and something slowing down and dying away. Progressive labor elements "transmigrate" from one method to another, not respecting the limits of factories, branches of industry, or countries.

There is a necessary dependence among the various types of reserves in the growth of labor productivity. By exploiting one reserve a new reserve is being created. The process of creating, revealing, and exploiting the reserves is unending.

Within the individual work method the perfection of one factor in the increase of labor productivity creates discord between the high level of the improved factor and the low level of the remaining factors. This is also true on a larger scale. For instance, the installing of a new machine in a workshop calls for changes in the organization and qualification of workers, while in a national economy, changes in one branch of production also call for changes in the other branches. The maximum exploitation of reserves of labor productivity necessitates a common level of combined labor, a proportionality between labor and production units, and also a level of the individual factors in the growth of labor productivity. It is to this complex action of factors in the growth of labor productivity that the systematic method of the uncovering and exploitation of reserves on all levels of administration, beginning with the work site and ending with the administration of national economy, must be subordinated.

The Exploitation of Reserves in the Growth of Labor Productivity in Socialist Production

Present-day planning and the administration of the development of socialist economics are based on the knowledge that because of the technical revolution the techical factor has come into the forefront as one of the principal reasons for labor productivity growth.[4]

The progress of technique however depends on the complex progress of all other factors in the increase of productivity—especially on the organizational, administrative, and on qualification factors.

Socialist relations of production based on a planned national economy made it possible to proceed with new technical and economic policies based on the principle of effectivity of capital investments. Large capital investments which are needed for technical progress should not be dispersed over the entire production front but should be concentrated on those leading sectors which would ensure collective and more effective development of new techniques. Since the extent of pure capital investments is always limited by the extent of accumulation, it is also necessary to uncover and exploit the internal reserves of production and to modernize and reconstruct the existing capacities. There is conspicuous intensifying of the significance of centralized long-term planning, concentrating on long-term concepts of the development of the national economy and at the same time strengthening the role of operative planning and administration on the basis of the increased competence of the individual production and economic units.

The state plan of national economy as a uniform, purposeful, mobilizing task unites the activities and concentrates the efforts of millions of workers on one goal. If, however, improved reserves in labor productivity are being introduced continuously while workers are striving to fulfill the plan, the given plan will not be able to withstand the diverse possibilities of increasing labor productivity. Therefore every operative plan itself is continually being improved and made more accurate because of unveiled possibilities in increasing labor productivity in the workshops and factories every day. The cooperation of the largest possible collective of workers is effected on the

4. In the Czechoslovak Socialist Republic, for instance, the increase in production is more and more being ensured by labor productivity and particularly by technical progress. Our industrial production has increased four times in comparison with prewar results. If in the years of the fourth and fifth five-year plans we would maintain the tempo of the third five-year plan at least to 56 per cent, we would in 1975 attain a production of about three times the production of 1960. This is possible even if the number of inhabitants of a productive age would increase in the years 1961–1975 only by 7 per cent. In those years there will be a basic shortening of work hours and a marked increase of time devoted to the education of the working people. The increase in production therefore must be based solely on the increase in labor productivity. The share of technical progress in the increase of labor productivity was in the first five-year plan estimated to be one third and in recent years one half, while in the third five-year plan technical progress will constitute at least two thirds of the productivity increase.

basis of the organization of socialist emulation and the innovation movement, the formation of permanent brigades of socialist and communist labor,
and complex brigades of leading workers, foremen, and technicians. The
aim of these brigades is to solve the most important technological and organizational problems of production, to organize construction, to develop
technological, and material controls, and to hold production conferences,
and so forth. The results of all these sectional analyses which help to reveal
the reserves in all sections of production are embodied in the plan of technical and organizational development and in all following plans.

On this basis, and by exploiting the great initiative of the workers, considerable results are being achieved in the sphere of modernizing factories
and in introducing the most advanced technique into production.

Technical progress effected by the production centers themselves releases
large amounts for central activities, subordinated to the principle of introducing the most progressive technique by the method of "principal
sector." Principal sectors in national economy are those branches of industry
which develop conditions for the rapid progress of technical revolution.
They are the power and chemical industries, together with mining, metallurgy, and agriculture, which form the power and raw-material bases, and
the machine industry which forms the technical basis.

Within the individual branches, with the exception of current building
investments, the rest of capital investment is concentrated in model produc-
tion-technical units, set up according to the highest level of all the factors
contributing to the development of labor productivity.[5]

In the Czechoslovak Socialist Republic during the third five-year plan
more than fifty model and experimental factories in all the principal
branches of industry were constructed. Among them automation was seven
times greater and the costs of production 60 per cent lower. There is a complex model automated dairy in which the labor productivity per worker per

---

5. The principle of the use of production units had already been tried before the war
in the Soviet Union. Thus in 1928, according to the project of engineer Marsak, an
experimental mechanized bakery was set up. The experiences from its operation
formed the basis of setting up the first "bread plants" which in 1931 had a production of 240 tons in a 24-hour cycle; in 1933 a capacity of 300 tons, which surpassed
the capacity of the largest bakery in the world by 120 tons (which was at that time
the Ward Baking Co., USA). At present there are many similar automatic bakeries
of the Marsak spiral type in the USSR. In 1950 the first automatic factory for the
production of pistons went into operation in the USSR. This plan produces automatically an automobile piston every nine seconds. Two years later an automated
guild went into operation in the First National producing bearings in Moscow
which produced 900,000 ball bearings and 600,000 rolling bearings annually.

year is to be increased from 241 tons to 608 tons, the quality improved from 92 per cent to 99 per cent, and the hygiene of production improved. There are also a number of automated machine works, and the like, under construction.

The results achieved by the model and experimental factories will be introduced into the largest possible number of factories in particular branches of production.

For instance, in black metallurgy it is expected that the experiences of the five model factories will be repeated in further factories producing 80 per cent of the production of this entire industrial branch.

The importance of model production technical units exceeds mere interest in increasing production. These units are the practical and most progressive examples of the best use of the factors contributing to the increase in labor productivity in their most effective operation. The difference between the level of analogous production and technical units and these units presents a general idea of the extent of reserves of labor productivity in whole industrial sectors, assuming that they will be built up to meet the highest technical standards in the world.

Socialist science and production practice have mastered the most progressive technical and technological elements; they have tested the practical functions of their mutual operations and thus prepared the present wide-scale introduction of perfect automatic lines and well-developed technological methods in production. If during the past years, the exemplary production and technical units were used only to a limited extent, at the present time experimental and model plants in the Czechoslovak Socialist Republic and complex mechanized plants with automation in the USSR are being built on a large scale. These model plants and enterprises are part of the preparations for a further upsurge of socialist technique on a mass scale. Technical problems of complex automation, connected with the progress of all forms of automatic regulation and control, appear in the spheres of ballistics and astronomy. That is why particular attention is being given to the advance of this research and to the application of its results in industrial practice of socialist construction. The technical factor of the increase in labor productivity is related to the development of power and raw material resources. The development of the power resources takes place along two principal roads: by the full exploitation of reserves in the existing sources; and by the development of new sources. Aiming to overtake the most advanced countries makes it preferable to build thermal power plants which use inferior grades of fuel.[6] Much attention is devoted to the possibility of increasing the capacities of electric works and to the possibility of setting up entire power systems handled by remote-control and the application of kibernetics.[7] The development of the chemical industry, and on its basis the exploitation of artificial materials, is coming to the forefront.[8] The transition from classical raw materials to artificial materials represents great savings and the possibility of transition to new highly effective continuous technologies which are the bases for the further development of automation.

Presently the machine production basis is being developed because of the rapid progress of the machine industry and especially its new branches of industrial automation. Here too the progress in production is connected with the discovery and exploitation of reserves of labor productivity. During the third five-year plan in the Czechoslovak Socialist Republic, for instance, it is planned to increase basic funds by 44 per cent which increased only 38 per cent during the years 1948–1951. With the exploitation of great reserves, there is the possibility of increasing relays.[9]

A general process of modernization and reconstruction on the basis of concentration and collectivization of production is being effected and ensured by planning in the whole social production.[10]

6. The initial capital investments of thermal power plants are 3 to 4 times lower than those of hydro-electric power plants, which are noted for their minimum costs of operation, but which require a disproportional length of time for their construction.
7. If at the end of the third five-year plan the Czechoslovak Socialist Republic will have used 6 blocs of 200 MW each instead of 12 power blocs of 110–100 MW it will mean a saving of at least 30 million Kčs in the cost of production, and with the increase in the capacities of the blocs it can mean as much as a saving of 100 million Kčs. That is Czechoslovakian production and development tends to concentrate on 200 or 400 MW blocs instead of the less effective 50 MW blocs used until now. Among the new sources, nuclear energy and helio energy are being developed.
8. The production of plastic materials in the CSR is to increase 4 times within the third five-year plan. If we compare the volume of production of plastic materials to the production of steel, the ratio in 1960 was about 1:24; in 1965 it will amount to 1:10; and in 1975 despite the rapid increase in the production of steel (in 1965 its production will amount to 740 kg per inhabitant), this ratio will change to 1:5.
9. In the machine industry of the Czechoslovak Socialist Republic, for instance, the coefficient of relays is 1.1–1.5, the main relay being occupied the most in relation to the number of working sites which can be utilized. For this reason also the number of certain machines is nearly doubled in relation to the number of workers. When the machine capacities will be fully utilized it will be possible to release as much as 40,000 different machines on a production area of 600,000 sq. meters.
10. The consistent concentration of production of sliding bearings in the CSR will, for example, decrease the cost of production about 5 times; the saving of metals will amount to about 3000 tons with a saving of 1500 workmen. Savings in manpower

The technical progress factor is inseparably related to the factor of raising the qualification of the cadres and to the progress of science on whose standards the economical power of a country is always more or less dependent.

Automation of production outlines the perspectives of revolutionary changes in the number and qualification structure of the cadres. A number of manual trades disappear; the laborer turns into a control worker or a highly qualified engineer; the focal point of production is changing from physical to brain work, to the organization of production where a number of new professions are originating—automation or production schedule workers. The need for mathematicians, economists, and engineers with wide theoretical knowledge is increasing.

This is also the reason for the extensive reform of the school system in socialist countries. Theoretical instruction is being combined with practical work. Studies are changing to preparation for a complete, practical life. Several new systems of study have been devised to complete the education of the working people—courses completing university and technical school training, and studies in all subjects. It is a known fact, for instance, that the number of graduates of universities and higher technical colleges in the USSR exceeds that of any other major power. At the same time a whole system of research is being developed beginning with the academies of sciences under the auspices of universities or technical colleges, and various research departments are being instituted under the auspices of ministries or factories. Nationwide research work is planned and administered uniformly to deal with the solution of key scientific problems. By uniformity in planning and directing the nationwide research, vast reserves can be used which could not be fully exploited before because they were dispersed and because cooperation among the various research centers was rather unsatisfactory.

The complex revelation and exploitation of reserves of labor productivity depends largely on the standard of organization and administration on all levels. The present-day progress in production is accompanied by a wide new division of labor. Specialization and cooperation are expanding in quantity and quality in all spheres and in all stages of social production. They are surpassing the scope of the individual production-economical units, production branches, and entire countries. The complex automated

---

due to the increase of durability of the automatically produced bearings is estimated at 5000 workmen. The total yearly savings in production are estimated to amount to 400 million Kčs. The period for the return of costs of building up the most modern units of this centralized production is only 9 months.

production of the future foretells further uniformity of production, a concentration into a single, precise, sensitive and highly productive "mechanism" to which the high standard of management must also be adjusted. That is why the improvement of planning and management in the national economy is also becoming a social necessity.

The further growth of planning in the socialist national economy is based on effectiveness and the creation of long-term concepts of the development of national economy and international scientific and economic cooperation.

If technical progress is dependent on the development and progress of management, then, on the other hand, the highest degree of automation expands the possibilities of society to direct the advance of production.

The rational exploitation of all abundant and versatile sources, the achievement of goals by the shortest and most effective means, the attainment of a complex combination of the effects of the factors contributing to the increase of labor productivity—both in individual production units and in the national economy—calls for the improvement of the system of continual circulation and elaboration of information. The socialist system is being faced by a new task: the use of automation in the administration of national economy together with the exact methods in economic sciences, the application of scientific methods in organizing management with the development of special automatic computing machines and the setting up of a centralized network as the technical basis of management.

The more perfect this system of planning and administration, the greater will be the initiative and creative activity of the working people, the closer will be the complex revelation and exploitation of the reserves in the increase of labor productivity to its theoretically most effective variant, and the more powerful will be the force of labor.